UNITED JERUSALEM
The Municipal Boundary since June 28, 1967

DOWTY

N →

TO JERICHO

ABU DIS

AL-AZARIYAH

HEBREW
UNIVERSITY

MOUNT SCOPUS

MOUNT OF OLIVES

SILWAN

GOVERNMENT
HILL

EAST TALPIOT

SUR BAHIR

SHEIKH
JARAH

THE OLD CITY

ABU TOR

UMM TUBA

RAMAT RAHEL

TO BETHLEHEM

BEIT SAFAFA

SHARAFAT

GILO

KIRYAT YOVEL

GIVAT SHAUL B

EIN KAREM

BEIT ZAYIT

MOTZA

HADASSAH
HOSPITAL

D1116512

BOUNDARY

...RHOODS

...NEIGHBORHOODS

JEWISH NEIGHBORHOODS IN
ANNEXED AREA

KM. 0   1   2

CARTA. JERUSALEM

JERUSALEM: The Torn City

JERUSALEM

THE TORN CITY

M<small>ERON</small> B<small>ENVENISTI</small>

THE UNIVERSITY OF MINNESOTA PRESS
Minneapolis

 ISRATYPESET LTD.
Jerusalem

The publishers wish to acknowledge their thanks to Mr. Peretz Kidron for translating the original manuscript from Hebrew, to Ms. Ina Friedman for editing the original manuscript, and to Mr. Julian J. Landau for editing the revised and up-dated manuscript and for seeing it through the press.

Published in the United States of America and Japan by the University of Minnesota Press, Minneapolis, Minnesota, and in Canada by Burns and Mac Eachern, Limited, Don Mills, Ontario

Library of Congress Catalog Card Number 76-12226
ISBN 0-8166-0795-8

This book has been designed, set and printed by Isratypeset Ltd. Jerusalem, Israel

CONTENTS

PREFACE

Jerusalem has been besieged and conquered 37 times in the 4,000 years of its history. In the last generation, however, it has not been foreign conquerors who have fought over the City of Peace, for the sake of distant empires or bands of believers. Today the struggle is being waged between people for whom this is their homeland. It is being fought by a people for whom Jerusalem is their Holy City, who remembered it during thousands of years of exile and yearned for its deliverance, who returned to it and became a majority of its population; and by a second people, who were born here and who love the place as a man loves his home.

I have tried, in the following pages, to trace the elements of this struggle and its development. Most of the book is devoted to the period since the unification of Jerusalem. But this period cannot be properly understood without examining the events which took place in the city on the eve of its division and the effects of that division which lasted for the following 19 years. These events, therefore, are dealt with in the first half of the book. The description is mainly based on written sources, both first- and second-hand accounts. I have avoided using personal interviews precisely because the people who took — and are still taking — an active part in the course of events under discussion, are inclined to describe them as they would have wished them to happen and not as they actually happened.

Many sources and documents of the period under study are still privileged information. Although I have had access to some of these documents during the course of my work, I have chosen not to publish classified material, and the reader will not find in this book any journalistic sensationalism concerning incidents behind the scenes. I have tried to describe and shed light on only those events and processes which seemed to me to be important for an understanding of the developments. I have no doubt that many matters, amongst them important ones, have not been mentioned; I did not intend to write a chronological history, but rather to try and clarify — out of the very large number — those matters which seemed to me to be essential.

When, on June 28, 1967, the Mayor of Jerusalem, Teddy Kollek, appointed me to the post of administrator for "the eastern sector" — as the area annexed by Israel was called in those days — I did not think that I was qualified for such a job. Although I was born in Jerusalem, had lived there all my life and had studied the city, my knowledge of "the Arabs" derived from my studies, and came to an end in 1291, the date of the final destruction of the Crusader Kingdom in Palestine. It was only after I had begun working at the job that I realized that this was actually an advantage. I certainly learned through experience — possibly, not in enough depth — but I was free of certain stereotyped images which are the legacy of some professional "Arabists." From my experience, I learned that the most appropriate approach did not necessitate extensive knowledge of Arab customs and of what is called "the Arab mentality." I found that sincerity, respect and a relationship between equals were far more important. Improvization and a refusal to rely on the conclusions drawn from "experience in dealing with Israel's Arabs," also proved to be useful.

At first, I was involved in everything: I took part in the first attempts at restoring order at the Western Wall; I chaired the committee which dealt with the voluntary evacuation of Arab residents from the Jewish Quarter and the remains of the Mugrabi Quarter; I participated in the discussions on the first land expropriations; I sat on the steering committee which formulated the plan for the restoration of the cemetery on the Mount of Olives. However, as, little by little, various bodies and companies were set up and people and committees were appointed, and the treatment of these matters and others became institutionalized, I found that I was devoting most of my time to the Arab population, whose political institutions had ceased to exist.

The small team which dealt with this population was as variegated as the population of Jerusalem itself: two Jews, a Druze, an Israeli Arab, a Jerusalem Arab, and a Jerusalem Armenian. This team was in daily contact with 44 *mukhtars* who represented the city's neighborhoods and its ethnic groups. As varied as the make-up of the team, were the matters we dealt with: we concerned ourselves with the restoration of the Muslim Quarter, which was damaged during the war; we located the evacuees of the Mugrabi Quarter and compensated them for the loss of their dwellings and property; we dealt with the repair of the Old City walls and of the Citadel; we managed a loan fund for businesses and mortgages; we put numbers on the houses in the Old City; we prepared a development plan for the municipal infrastructure and supervised its implementation; we ensured the supply of electricity to every neighborhood in the city; we prepared playgrounds for children; we made sure that gunpowder was available for the cannon that signalled the beginning and the end of each fast day during Ramadan; we fixed quotas for the agricultural produce which was brought from Judea and Samaria; we ensured the payment of bills owed by the Jordanian Municipality; we determined who was entitled to have water supplied free of charge; we mediated between quarreling familes; we found housing for families which had been evicted from their homes by the army.

We never established principles or set limits to our work, but, on looking back, it seems to me that a clear line eventually crystallized: in the absence of an Arab body that would deal with the population of East Jerusalem, we served to fill that function. We had no purpose other than to work for the well-being of the residents, the alleviation of their suffering, and the solving of their problems. We fought for a gradual, rather than a sudden, increase in municipal taxes; we negotiated for the designation of low tax areas wherever possible; we demanded identity cards for those residents who had not received them, and extensions for the imposition of Israeli sanitation regulations on Arab businesses; we fought for an increase in the number of Arab taxis. The responsibilities we took on ourselves brought us into dispute and even into conflict with various groups. We protested against what we heatedly referred to as "the lack of flexibility of the Israeli administration." We fought against people who tried to exploit the situation for selfish purposes; we quarreled with Muslim institutions which tried, for political reasons, to interfere with our work for the good of the population. When we requested that a school be completed on land which belonged to the *waqf* but had been leased to the Jordanian Municipality, a bitter campaign was waged against us; when we tried to contribute toys to the children's ward of a Muslim hospital which was poorly equipped, we were rudely refused.

At the same time that I engaged in these activities, I was a member of a body which was responsible for Jerusalem's security. I participated in decisions on the demolition and confiscation of houses, on the arrest and banishment of inciters, and on steps against resistance and terrorism I saw no contradiction between my taking part in a decision to demolish a house which contained arms, and, after this was done, in concerning myself with taking care of the evacuated family.

Whilst in close contact with the Arab population, I began to understand its general mood and its political position. After unsuccessful attempts to find a political denominator, I reached the conclusion that political arguments are not only meaningless but are even harmful, since they increase opposition and the great gulfs dividing us. Nevertheless, I felt that some of the political demands of the Arab population could be satisfied without violating the principle of Israeli sovereignty, and the objection of various Israeli bodies to these demands seemed to me to be motivated by outdated or unjustifiable ideas. My actions were based on the assumption that an agreement on the political future of Jerusalem would not be quickly reached, and I therefore asked myself what could be done in the absence of such an agreement. I dealt with the memorials to the Arab war dead, the secondary school curriculum, and the safeguarding of the rights of the East Jerusalem Electric Company. These, and other matters, brought down on me the wrath of various Israeli circles.

Fundamentally, it was an argument between two basically different schools of thought: the first maintains that, as individuals, the rights of East Jerusalem Arabs should be equal to those of Jews, but, as a group, they have no right to equality and no right to even demand it. The second school maintains that no differentiation should be made between individual and group equality, and that Jewish—Arab relations must be based on full equality.

I belong to the second school of thought. This is because of my deep belief in the equality of man and in the possibility of attaining social justice, and also because I see in the unification of Jerusalem not only the physical joining of two quarters but also an attempt to create a pattern of life based on co-existence. Jews and Arabs are divided on the question of the political future of Jerusalem but are agreed that it should never again be divided. Thus, since we must live together, we must begin to build real unification, for if we do not, it will never be achieved. The dispute concerning the political future of Jerusalem will not be settled quickly; despite this, the two sides must make an effort to co-exist, even under present circumstances. But because they refuse to recognize the unification of the city, the Arabs are also unwilling to make the effort required for co-existence, lest it be interpreted as coming to terms with the existing situation. If, however, co-existence is really important to both sides, and if it can be established only on the basis of equality, then the party with greater freedom of action, under the present political conditions, must accept the sole responsibility for the effort. Such responsibility may lead that party to "represent" the position of the other side — not necessarily because he identifies with it, but rather because if these positions and outlook are not heard, or taken into account, then confrontation results, and the effort to safeguard balance and equality is undermined.

I have found myself, on several occasions, in the position of a "representative," not elected but rather appointed and even self-appointed. This was, of course, an impossible situation, and I was finally accused, by many, of "pro-Arabism," and, by a few fanatics, of "treason." One honorable Member of Knesset even went so far as to demand, from the Knesset podium, that I be brought to trial.

Despite this, I did not cease in my search for a political solution. I participated in several "working groups" which were appointed to draft proposals for comprehensive political solutions and the solution of specific political disputes.

One proposal, which I suggested at one of these "working groups," was known as the "Boroughs Plan," and was meant to solve the municipal problem within a political context. It was leaked to the press in order to sabotage my chances of attaining a certain public post. The resulting storm brought about my political ostracism for several years. This attempt, however, did not discourage my friend, Teddy Kollek, from his efforts — eventually successful — to have me appointed Deputy Mayor of Jerusalem, or from assigning me the task of assembling a staff to deal with proposals to solve Jerusalem's political problems.

During my search for political solutions, I came to the realization that anyone who wants to play this dangerous game must accept three pre-conditions: first, he must rid himself of all myths; second, he must learn the lessons of the past; and third, he must not set himself up as a judge between the opposing sides.

There is no place which arouses such deep, fanatical feelings as does Jerusalem. The city's atmosphere nurtures an exclusive possessiveness. There is no place where man feels his historical continuity more than in Jerusalem. The feeling that everything has been here since the beginning of time, gives those who live in the eternal city a feeling of modesty and humility. There is no other place where one feels the tragedy of two nations fighting for their homeland more than in Jerusalem. This is the only place in the world today where Jews and Arabs live side by side, and where the struggle is a real, everyday occurrence and not an abstraction. He who decides to judge between the two sides must remember that only in fairy tales is one side all good and the other all bad.

I belong to a nation fighting for its soul, and its soul is Jerusalem. I identify with my nation's longing for Jerusalem. I, too, experienced the transcendental experience of our return to the holiest of our places. At the same time, I am a son of this city and know the meaning of a son's love for it. I cannot, and will not, forget the love, which is as strong as my own, of the Arab residents of Jerusalem for this city.

In the light of this tragic conflict, which has wracked Jerusalem during the past generation, an observer longs for a catharsis, for an end to the damaging myths spread by both sides, and for the transformation of the love that both sides have for this city into a uniting, rather than a dividing, force. Right now, this is only wishful thinking, but perhaps past experiences will help to bring about its realization.

In this spirit I have tried to survey the events and the moods attending them.

This book is dedicated to all Jerusalemites who pray for the mending of this torn city, and above all to Eyal, Yuval, Sharon, Samir, Samira and Hani. I pray that they will succeed in living in brotherhood as adults, much as they play in brotherhood in their youth.

Meron Benvenisti
Giv'at Hananyah-Abu Tor
May 1976

INTRODUCTION

Jerusalem's variegated beauty, atmosphere and attraction are the products of four pairs of co-existing opposites: the arid and the fertile; the holy and the temporal; the East and the West; the Arabs and the Jews.

The dominant element in Jerusalem's natural landscape is the sudden sharp transition from the Mediterranean zone to the arid wilderness. The watershed traverses the city, dividing it into two ecosystems. The green shrubbery of the Mediterranean predominates in the west, having withstood thousands of years of neglect and periodic destruction; while, east of the watershed, the desert predominates, gray-white, together with the bare chalk landscape of the Judean wilderness and its deep canyons, both descending steeply to the Dead Sea. It is this dramatic transformation which endows Jerusalem with its natural variety, its special hues which change with every hour of the day, and the multicolored assortment of its building stones.

Sanctified by three religions, the city is rich endowed with the holy sites and relics of all the peoples who have fought over Jerusalem because of its sacred character. Sanctity and reverence for God are still a dominant element in the day-to-day life of Jerusalem — more so than in any other city. At the same time, its streets jammed with vehicles, high-rise buildings dotting the landscape, and other urban amenities abounding, Jerusalem is a modern city where hundreds of thousands of people live fully secular lives — as in any other city.

But, in Jerusalem, even the secular life is bi-polar. At one extreme, tens of thousands of people maintain an occidental lifestyle, inhabiting multi-storied buildings or garden suburbs, remote from their neighbors, dressing in the latest fashions, shopping at supermarkets and whiling away their time in cafés, with complaints about the leaders whom they repeatedly re-elect in democratic elections. At the other end, tens of thousands, Jews and Arabs, maintain the traditional oriental way of life, boundlessly loyal to their extended family, obedient to the *paterfamilias* who rules them like a biblical patriarch; people who believe that haste is Satan's invention, who live in single-storey houses and feel a mystical bond to the soil.

Jerusalem is also the city of two peoples, and it is loved by each after his own fashion. It is the only city in Israel in which commercial activities do not halt for a single day and whose inhabitants are obliged to converse in two languages; a city in which neither of its two peoples can withdraw into itself; a city which is cosmopolitan and rich in human variety. For the past two generations, the conflict between the two cousin-peoples has been a bloody one. Jerusalem has remained the only city where they live in proximity. And here, more than anywhere else, one can sense the awful tragedy of the conflict between Israeli and Arab.

In some miraculous manner, all these opposites fuse into a single unity. Anyone depriving Jerusalem of these contrasts, anyone upsetting the equilibrium by trying to make any one factor predominant over another, or by trying to prevent the dynamic confrontation of the opposites, would make Jerusalem cease to be herself. For 19 years, a hermetically sealed wall separated these opposites, and Jerusalem did indeed cease to be herself. The barbed-wire fences left the East with the desert, the sanctity, the traditional oriental way of life, and all the Arabs; they left the West with its greenery, its secular aspect, its modern occidental life-style, and all the Jews.

Removing the barriers gave the city back its unity of opposites. For the first time in the chronicles of modern Jerusalem, responsibility for maintaining its character was in Israeli hands. This responsibility has never been a light one, but the conditions created after the Six Day War have made it almost unbearable. Political and economic conditions have sharpened the conflicts, engendering pressures which threaten to upset the delicate balance between them. The city's color and character have progressively changed. The decisive question is: will the city find a renewed equilibrium, or will it be overcome by forces which will totally alter its character?

CHAPTER ONE

WHOSE JERUSALEM?

In December 1947, a meeting which seems quite fantastic today, nearly thirty years later, took place at the Jewish Agency — the executive body representing the Jewish community of Palestine. The meeting followed, by only a few days, the United Nations General Assembly resolution of November 29, 1947, to partition Palestine into an independent Jewish state and an Arab state and to internationalize the city of Jerusalem. The question under discussion was: with the Jewish state due to arise soon, with the termination of the British Mandate, where would the new government establish its seat? Even then, David Ben-Gurion, at the time Chairman of the Agency, regarded the desolate southern Negev as the center of gravity of the state and suggested Kurnub, a short distance from where the town of Dimona was later built. Golda Meir, then head of the Jewish Agency Political Department, wanted it in a new city to be constructed in the northern Carmel forests. Various local councils offered their towns as centers for the future government. It was finally decided, in February 1948, that the government's seat would be in the former German colony of Sharona, a suburb of Tel Aviv.

The fact of this debate is striking testimony that the Jews had accepted the internationalization of Jerusalem, albeit as the lesser of two evils. The Jewish leaders, who had participated in the negotiations which culminated in the 1947 United Nations Partition Resolution, faced a cruel dilemma. On the one hand, there was the oath of a thousand generations of Jews: "If I forget thee, O Jerusalem, let my right hand lose its cunning!" On the other hand, there

1

was the political reality that the chance of establishing a Jewish state in part of Palestine was conditioned on relinquishing Jerusalem and allowing it to become an international city. Faced with a choice of part or nothing, the leaders of the Jewish community chose to accept partition while, at the same time, agreeing among themselves that Jerusalem "was, is and will be the capital of the state." Their choice of an alternate center was only a temporary step until somehow, sometime, Jerusalem would be "redeemed."

The idea of making Jerusalem an international city was not a new one. It had been proposed as early as 1937 by the Palestine Royal Commission, appointed by the British Mandatory Government and headed by Lord Peel, which recommended that with the creation of a Jewish and an Arab state in Palestine, a separate enclave be established embracing Jerusalem and Bethlehem, plus a corridor to the sea including Lydda, Ramle, and Jaffa. The Commission affirmed

> the overriding necessity of keeping the sanctity of Jerusalem and Bethlehem inviolate, and of securing free and safe access to them for all the world ... That ... is 'a sacred trust of civilization' — a trust on behalf not merely of the peoples of Palestine, but of multitudes in other lands to whom those places ... are Holy Places.

The Peel Commission did not believe that the Jews and Arabs of Palestine should be given this "sacred trust" because the conflicts between them would prevent their cooperation. In addition, as an expression of its desire to ensure Christian rule of the Holy Places — and possibly of the Commission's colonialist attitude towards "natives" — it proposed that the Jerusalem enclave be granted the status of a permanent mandate (subject to the League of Nations). Its report specifically stated that

> it is not intended that in the course of time they [the population of Jerusalem] should stand by themselves as a wholly self-governing community.

The essential difference between the Peel Commission's plan and that proposed by the United Nations Special Committee on Palestine (UNSCOP) in 1946, which was adopted by the General Assembly, was only in the name of the controlling power (the Peel Commission had nominated Britain as the mandatory power, while UNSCOP proposed an international regime directly subordinate to the U.N. Trusteeship Council). The principle of giving preference to the

2

religious-universal claim over the right to self-determination and national aspirations was inherent in both. The supporters of the U.N. Partition Resolution evidently believed that ensuring free access and freedom of worship to hundreds of millions of believers was important enough to justify sacrificing the national aspirations of Jerusalem's 150,000 inhabitants. But it would be an oversimplification to state that preference for religious interests over national ones was the sole reason for the adoption of the Resolution. Internationalization may simply have appeared to be the most convenient way to settle the question of which of the two states — the Jewish or the Arab one — should have Jerusalem.

It was possible to partition the country with one set of borders or another; but the problem of what to do with the capital, where the national interests of both warring peoples were focused, defied simple solution. The possible alternatives were (1) the inclusion of Jerusalem in the Jewish state because the city had a Jewish majority — leaving aside the problem of how to maintain the geographical link between the city and the Jewish state via the Arab state; (2) the inclusion of Jerusalem in the Arab state — raising the question of what to do with the city's 100,000 Jews; or (3) the creation of an Arab-Jewish condominium (joint rule) over the city — predicated on the fantastic assumption that it was impossible for Jews and Arabs to live together in the same state but quite possible for them to co-exist in the same city. Of all the impossible alternatives, that of taking the city out of the hands of the two warring sides not only appeared to be the most expedient in theory, but also satisfied the desires of powerful outside interests.

Both the Protestant and Catholic sections of the Christian world united in insisting upon the internationalization of Jerusalem but, not surprisingly, it was the Vatican that was the moving spirit behind the internationalization plan. As explained by Moshe Sharett, who was to become Israel's first Foreign Minister:

> In the Vatican's eyes, internationalization was destined to impose on Jerusalem a Christian regime under the Catholic Church's decisive influence. In other words, to give Christianity a status in Jerusalem that it had not had since the days of the Crusades . . . this historic gain appeared to justify the accommodation with the elevation of the Jewish people to a status of national sovereignty. Indeed, it was because of Vatican influence that the Catholic states

3

voted for the Palestine partition resolution, and several Christian states, which supported the partition plan, made it clear that there was no chance of the majority needed for the plan, if the internationalization of the Holy City were deleted.

The representatives of the Jewish Agency at the U.N. decided to accept the Partition Resolution despite the fact that it fell short of what they wanted. They found a spark of hope concerning Jerusalem in the fact that the draft proposal provided for a referendum, allowing the citizens of Jerusalem to decide whether they wanted a change in the city's status, which would take place ten years after the creation of the international regime. It was hoped that the Jewish majority in Jerusalem would be able to reverse the internationalization decision in that time.

Thus, from the moment the Resolution was adopted, the Jews assisted in its implementation. The fierce fighting in Jerusalem in 1948 did not weaken Jewish support for an international regime there. On the contrary, during moments of depression the Jews thought that internationalization would save their community.

After the creation of the State of Israel on May 14, 1948, no steps were taken to define the legal status of those parts of Jerusalem in Israeli hands. The Government of Israel refrained from doing anything to upset the various international bodies that had interests in Jerusalem. As a result, there was no definition or division of responsibility in the administration of the Jewish part of the city, and various bodies rushed around claiming exclusive rule. As the new Prime Minister, David Ben-Gurion, described it —

One man is appointed, there's a protest. A committee is appointed, another protest. Military government is set up, another protest. If we set up civilian government, there'll be yet another protest.

In fact, Ben-Gurion had no time for political decisions that lacked direct reference to the most important problem of all: waging the War of Independence, then in process —

The question of Jerusalem is, foremost, a question of military capacity. The main thing demanded of us at this moment is, first and foremost, serious military preparations for capturing the road to Jerusalem, and for the complete liberation of the city.

By June 24, 1948, however, during a debate in the Provisional Council of State, it became clear that the political and military events of the previous weeks had left their mark on the Prime Minister's thinking:

Jerusalem is within the bounds of the Jewish Government (to my regret, without the Old City for the moment) just like Tel Aviv; and there is no difference between Jerusalem and Tel Aviv, between Haifa and Hanita. They are all within the boundaries of the Jewish Government.

The decision was not one of principle but an interim one of a practical nature. Israel's acceptance of the internationalization of Jerusalem was still valid, even though events were influencing developments in a different direction.

At the end of June 1948, the United Nations mediator, Count Folke Bernadotte, appointed by the General Assembly one month earlier, shocked the Israelis by proposing a plan which would detach the Negev from the Jewish State, in exchange for the whole of the Galilee. He also suggested that Jerusalem and its environs be included in Arab territory, with municipal autonomy for the Jewish community and a special arrangement for the protection of the Holy Places. The Israel Government's response was sharp and unambiguous: its declaration of July 5, 1948, affirmed that "the people, the government and the Jews of Jerusalem, will oppose the imposition of Arab rule on Jerusalem with all their strength."

The argument against the Bernadotte proposal was not based on Israel's right to have at least the Jewish part of Jerusalem under her sovereignty, but rested on the fact that

the United Nations, after deep and exhaustive study of this question, and as a result of complete unanimity among the Christian nations, have decided to create an international regime in Jerusalem.

In other words, Israel continued to adhere to the decision on internationalization.

At the same time, some of the more perceptive Jewish leaders, notably Moshe Sharett, saw in the Bernadotte proposals an opportunity to re-open the discussion on Jerusalem's future and an opportunity to free Israel of her previous agreement to internationalize the city. In support of his stand, Bernadotte said that the whole matter of international rule was dubious, from the point of view of stability, efficiency, and ability to function. Sharett felt that Israel could seize on this and raise the whole question again.

*   *   *

Fighting in Jerusalem broke out on the morrow of the U.N. vote for partition. It continued to rage fiercely, with thousands of civilian casualties on both sides, until mid-July. For long periods the city was under siege and the Arabs succeeded in cutting it off from the rest of Jewish-held territory. With the declaration of the State of Israel, the Jordanian Arab Legion joined the fighting and, on May 25th, the defenders of the Jewish Quarter of the Old City were forced to surrender. The Israelis, however, held on to the New City and, by constructing a new road through the hills from the coast, managed to break the siege and link Jerusalem to the rest of the country.

On the night of July 16–17, 1948, the Israelis tried to re-capture the Old City but their attack was repulsed. With the enforcement of the truce that followed on the next day, the Israel Government was forced to accept the bitter reality that the Old City would not be in their hands. This acceptance was not at all easy. There were serious doubts, interim decisions, and several switches of policy until the final decision was taken. But the battles in Jerusalem had, in the words of Foreign Minister Sharett,

> willy-nilly re-opened the question of Jerusalem. Morally, we do not regard ourselves as bound by our agreement to the November 29th decision concerning Jerusalem, even though we do not consider the time has come for us to make any clear decision concerning our new position.

Thus, the Government decided to leave all the options open.

On August 2, 1948, Prime Minister and Minister of Defense David Ben-Gurion issued a proclamation stating:

> Whereas the area of Jerusalem . . . is held by the Army of Israel, and whereas it is the duty of the Army in occupied territories to maintain public safety and security and to preserve law and order . . . the laws of the State of Israel apply to this occupied territory.

On the same day, Proclamation Number 2 was issued, appointing Dr. Dov Joseph Military Governor of the occupied area of Jerusalem. As this move was in accordance with the rules of international law, it was accepted without protest by the United Nations. The U.N. representatives and other diplomats soon began to address Dov Josef as "the Military Governor of Israeli-occupied Jerusalem." Still, these two acts came in response to the need to maintain orderly life in the city and did not constitute a formal change in Israel's policy or the question of future rule for Jerusalem.

At the end of August, the Israel Government decided, by a five to four vote, that if the choice was between partition of the city and an international regime, internationalization of the whole of Jerusalem was preferable to handing part of the city over to the Arabs. The feeling of the majority of Israelis, as expressed by Rabbi Meir Bar-Ilan (Berlin), was that

if Jerusalem is not internationalized, the city will be divided into two parts, one Jewish and one Arab. The Old City, with all its holy places, and all the remnants of our glory from ancient times, will fall into their hands, and then Abdallah will be King of Jerusalem, since the Old City is, in reality, Jerusalem. It will be the greatest historical disaster in the chronicles of our people.

In addition to this national and emotional consideration, several members of the Government did not want to initiate a confrontation with the nations of the world over an issue on which nearly all were united.

Still, the Government's August decision was not the end of the affair. The inhabitants of Jerusalem were not prepared to remain outside the boundaries of the State of Israel, and they began to place heavy pressure on the Government to change its decision. The Government met for a further debate on September 26, 1948, and it was at this time that the essence of Israel's policy changed. By a seven to four majority, it was decided that "if partition (of Jerusalem) be essential, our delegation to the United Nations will agree."

The only other proposal brought before the Government was Ben-Gurion's suggestion to renew military efforts that would lead to the fall of the entire city into Israeli hands. This proposal was defeated by a seven to four majority. Years later, Ben-Gurion termed the vote against a military operation "a misfortune for generations."

The reversal in the Israeli position on internationalization also predicated a change in Israel's stance towards Jordan. Sharp opposition to Jordanian rule in the Old City was now replaced by the desire to reach a rapprochement with King Abdallah — who shared control of the city — in order to reach a political settlement. But first the Israelis had to decide whether their partners in a discussion on the future of Jerusalem would be the Jordanians or the Palestinians; the latter, after all, were — at least in theory — their partners in the

7

division of Palestine into an Arab state and a Jewish state. At the end of September 1948 Sharett summed up the Israeli attitude by stating:

> If we could afford a purely theoretical approach to this question, my suggestion would be that we prefer a separate government in the Arab part of Palestine, rather than annexation of that territory to Transjordan.

In practice, however, the Israeli Government's decision to open negotiations with King Abdallah was inevitable. Abdallah was already in complete control of the West Bank, and the Palestinian elements were divided and weak. Moreover, it appeared that the King sincerely wanted to reach a settlement with Israel. Before beginning negotiations, however, Israel took action to consolidate its rule over Jerusalem and turn the city into the Capital of the State, in line with a slogan coined by Prime Minister Ben-Gurion: "Declarations — no; deeds — yes! "

On September 14, 1948, the Supreme Court of the State of Israel was transferred to Jerusalem. On December 1, 1948, the city was visited by the President of the Provisional Council of State, Chaim Weizmann, who declared:

> In addition to the historical connection between us and Jerusalem, in addition to the continuous chain of Jewish occupation of the city, and in addition to the fact that we are a majority here, your exalted courage in defending the city gives us the right to declare that Jerusalem is ours, and ours it will remain!

Meanwhile, when the issue of internationalization came up again in the United Nations General Assembly, at the end of 1948, Israel formally reversed its previous stand, firmly opposed internationalization and demanded United Nations recognition of the city's partition. The Jordanians remained consistent in their anti-internationalization posture.

But that was not the end of the matter, for the Vatican also remained firm. Prior to the Assembly's debate, Pope Pius XII had published an encyclical letter, *In Multiplicibus Curis*, which stated in part:

> It is entirely appropriate to give Jerusalem and its surroundings, where so many precious souvenirs of the life and death of the Saviour are to be found, an international regime, legally established and guaranteed.

The Pope's intervention stemmed not only from a desire to protect the Holy Places but from the assumption that an international regime would permit greater Catholic influence than would national rule by Muslims and Jews.

He also feared that the decline in the Christian population of the city, due to the war, would be permanent if the city remained partitioned and under national rule. Internationalization was the only way to assure the return of the Christian refugees.

On December 11, 1948, ignoring the stands of both Jordan and Israel, the General Assembly resolved that the Jerusalem area

should be accorded special and separate treatment from the rest of Palestine and should be placed under effective United Nations control.

It then established a Conciliation Commission for Palestine (PCC), one of whose tasks was to prepare proposals for a permanent international regime for Jerusalem.

While the PCC was engaged in deliberations, a number of important events occurred. On December 20, reacting to the U.N. General Assembly decision, the Israel Government decided to transfer government institutions to Jerusalem. Eleven days later, the Israeli Jerusalem Municipal Council was constituted. On January 25, 1949, the citizens of Jerusalem joined other Israelis in elections to the new national Constituent Assembly, and on February 2, the Military Government of Jerusalem was disbanded.

Meanwhile, the Vatican stepped up its efforts to achieve internationalization and published a new encyclical letter, on the eve of Easter 1949, reiterating support for the internationalization of Jerusalem and stressing that "it is necessary to preserve intact all rights to the Holy Places which the Catholics have acquired over the centuries."

Finally, the Arab States, with the exception of Jordan, made an abrupt turnabout in their position and came out in support of internationalization. This move had nothing to do with either the Holy Places or respect for United Nations decisions. It was motivated solely by the Arab League's opposition to King Abdallah's rule in the Old City and to the *de facto* partition of Jerusalem between Abdallah and the Israelis.

Most significant, however, was that, from the middle of November 1948 through April 1949, the Jordanians and the Israelis were holding secret negotiations that culminated in the signing of an Armistice Agreement between the two countries on April 3, 1949.

In the negotiations, Israel tacitly accepted King Abdallah's plan to annex the West Bank to his Kingdom, on condition that the actual implementation of the annexation be postponed until the Armistice was signed. On her part, Jordan conceded that the Armistice would be a step towards the opening of negotiations leading to the signing of a full peace treaty. The third major point of agreement was that the Jordanians would temporarily refrain from making any official declaration of their stand on the future of Jerusalem.

As we have seen, by August 1948 the Israel Government had already accepted the principle of partitioning the city, but it still wanted to keep open its options vis-à-vis Jordan. The main obstacle towards reaching complete agreement on the partition of the city was whether the Arab quarters in western Jerusalem should remain in Israeli hands. Abdallah was only interested in keeping his hegemony over the Old City and tended to present the outline of partition in the simplest terms possible: "Old Jerusalem, Arab; the Jewish area in Jewish hands." The Israelis did not question the fact that the Old City should remain in Jordanian hands; any other position would have meant the end of negotiations. But, contrary to the King's clear-cut proposals on the division of the city, his negotiator, Abdallah al-Tal, on his own initiative, insisted that the Arab quarters in the western part of the city be given to Jordan. It was this point that made the Israelis insist upon putting off any final decisions on the future of the city. At the same time, both sides were eager to sign an armistice agreement quickly.

As a compromise both sides agreed to leave outstanding problems regarding Jerusalem to be discussed and settled in a special committee established for this purpose, as outlined in Paragraph 8 of the Armistice Agreement. (The committee met intermittently between April 1949 and November 1950 without arriving at a single tangible result. The partition of Jerusalem, therefore, remained along the cease-fire lines established in November 1948.) What was absolutely clear, however, was that Israel and Jordan had agreed to partition Jerusalem between them and join forces in fighting the move to internationalize the city.

The debate in the Palestine Conciliation Commission lasted for some months, and in September 1949 the PCC put forward a draft statute that departed substantially from the principle of a *corpus separatum*. The Conciliation Commission grasped the fact that it was impossible to implement the November 1947 internationalization decision literally and that it was necessary to find a formula that would take into account the *faits accomplis* created by the war and the partition of the city. The basic points of the draft statute were that: (1) the Jerusalem area would be demilitarized and neutralized permanently; (2) the area would be divided into Israeli and Arab zones; (3) a United Nations commissioner would be appointed, with executive authority in matters of free access, protection of the Holy Places, coordination of public services between the two zones and the solution of legal problems stemming from the existence of the two zones.

Although this was a more realistic proposal than any other, it encountered the opposition of the supporters of full internationalization. A bizarre coalition of the Soviet Union, the Vatican and the Arab States (except Jordan) demanded a return to the original 1947 formula. Among those supporting the proposal of the Conciliation Commission were the Protestant states of Europe — including Britain and part of the British Commonwealth — the United States and Turkey. They stressed that internationalization was simply not practical. In the words of the British delegate: "It could be that, as a theoretical exercise, the plan is excellent, but it is far from reality." The American delegate warned that ratification of the internationalization plan would

> involve the United Nations in innumerable problems to achieve aims, not all of which concern the international community ... The Resolution not only does not take into account the interests of the inhabitants of Jerusalem, but endangers the attainment in Jerusalem of those international rights which most delegates so insistently demand.

Jordan and Israel stated flatly that "internationalization would never come about."

On December 5, 1949, three days before the vote on the Conciliation Commission proposal in the General Assembly, David Ben-Gurion declared in the Knesset:

> We regard it as our duty to declare that Jewish Jerusalem is an organic and inseparable part of the State of Israel, as it is an inseparable part of the history of Israel, of the faith of Israel, and

of the very soul of our people. Jerusalem is the heart of hearts of the State of Israel. . . . We do not imagine that the United Nations Organization will try to tear Jerusalem out of the State of Israel, or to prejudice Israeli sovereignty in the eternal capital of Israel.

But that was precisely what the council of nations was about to do. The decision was taken on December 9, 1949, when, by a majority of 38 to 14, a proposal was adopted in which the General Assembly decided to

restate . . . its intention that Jerusalem should be placed under a permanent international regime . . . the City of Jerusalem shall be established as a corpus separatum *. . . .*

Israel and Jordan responded to the resolution by stepping up their actions to integrate their respective parts of the city into their national frameworks. On December 13, Ben-Gurion told the Knesset that:

This resolution of the United Nations is not in any way capable of implementation, if only because of the energetic and firm opposition of the citizens of Jerusalem.

Three days later the Prime Minister transferred his office to Jerusalem and fixed the beginning of January 1950 as the date for the transfer of all government offices to the city, with the exception of the Foreign Ministry, the Ministry of Defense, and the national police headquarters. On December 28, representatives of Israel and Jordan even met to coordinate their fight against internationalization.

For all that, there were forces in Israel that were dissatisfied with the mere acceptance of the partition of the city and with the elevation of the Israeli part of Jerusalem to the Capital of the State. In the Knesset debate over Jerusalem, held on January 2, 1950, the right-wing Herut party sharply attacked the Government for its policy of "deeds, not declarations" and demanded the enactment of a law declaring "the whole of Jerusalem as the capital of the Nation and of the State." Herut accused the Government of "relinquishing parts of the homeland."

The left-wing Mapam party also attacked the Government for its reconciliatory stance towards Jordan — for completely different reasons. In reply, Ben-Gurion stated:

No conquest can rest on strength alone, least of all the conquest of Jerusalem. We will succeed in Jerusalem — and I believe that we shall succeed — if we respect other people's rights.

"Whose rights? Abdallah's?" shouted a Communist member.
"Yes. Abdallah's too," Ben-Gurion replied.

Considering the open defiance of the two countries that actually controlled Jerusalem, the problem was referred back to the United Nations. By this time the question of Jerusalem had been passed on to the Trusteeship Council, whose chairman put forward yet another compromise proposal. It stipulated that a *corpus separatum* be created but that it be divided into three parts: (1) an Israeli part — including most of the New City — under Israeli sovereignty; (2) a Jordanian part — including the Arab quarters outside the Old City walls, the Temple Mount, and the Muslim Quarter within the Old City — under Jordanian sovereignty; and (3) an international zone, to be taken from both sides equally, which would include all the Holy Places and would be administered by a United Nations representative. This proposal, which tried as far as possible to approximate the political *status quo* and was therefore quite realistic, received the same reception as the plan of the Conciliation Commission. Despite the opposition of Israel and Jordan, as well as the United States and Britain, the Trusteeship Council rejected the proposal of its own chairman and went on to discuss a statute based, with certain changes, on a full and permanent international regime over the whole Jerusalem area. In April 1950, the draft of this statute was sent to Israel and Jordan. Israel replied with a plan for functional internationalization of the Holy Places. Jordan did not reply at all.

Two months later, in June 1950, the Swedish delegation to the United Nations submitted a proposal suggesting functional internationalization as an alternative to territorial internationalization. The main point of this proposal was that the political control of Jerusalem would remain in the hands of Israel and Jordan, and the United Nations would supervise only the Holy Places and access to them. The proposal for functional internationalization was not new. As early as the end of 1949, Israel had proposed that a United Nations representative, with similar powers, be appointed. It was therefore not surprising that the Swedish plan enjoyed Israeli support. Jordan did not oppose the plan in principle, but stated that she could not accept it in its present form. Obviously Jordan, which occupied the Holy Places, was more affected by the Swedish proposal than was Israel, which did not, in fact, hold a single Holy Place in the Jerusalem area. The United States, Denmark, Great Britain, Holland, Uruguay, and other states supported the Swedes.

But the General Assembly Ad Hoc Political Committee discussing the question did not even vote on the Swedish proposal. Instead, a Belgian-sponsored resolution was adopted supporting a renewed attempt "to settle the question in accordance with the principles already adopted by the Assembly" — that is, full territorial internationalization. At the same time, even the enthusiastic supporters of full internationalization had come to the realization that the idea was no more than an intellectual exercise, without foundation in reality. Still, they found it hard to withdraw from their previous positions. Only the Soviet Union announced that it was abandoning the idea.

When the Belgian proposal came up in the General Assembly, it failed to receive the two-thirds majority necessary for adoption. With that, the issue of the internationalization of the city became a dead letter at the United Nations. The General Assembly did discuss the question again in 1952, but again it failed to adopt any resolution.

Most states continued to take the legalistic attitude, according to which they were bound by the last formal decision of the General Assembly — that of December 9, 1949 — confirming the intent to impose an international regime. This stand was adopted not only by the Catholic states that had supported permanent territorial internationalization, but also by states that had opposed it fiercely, such as the United States and Britain. Formally, most states continued to give only *de facto* recognition to Israeli and Jordanian rule in Jerusalem.

This posed a more serious problem for Israel than for Jordan because Jerusalem was Israel's Capital.

As long as Israel's first President, Chaim Weizmann, was alive, the problem of foreign ambassadors presenting their credentials did not arise, because the President lived in the town of Rehovot. But with his death, and the election of Yitzhak Ben-Zvi as President, on December 10, 1952, the President's office was transferred to Jerusalem. At first, foreign representatives continued to present their credentials in Tel Aviv. But on May 4, 1953, the Dutch ambassador presented his credentials at the President's office in Jerusalem, and he was followed by the Chilean ambassador.

In July 1953, Israel took a further step to enhance Jerusalem as its capital and transferred the Foreign Ministry there. The United States

14

and France characterized this decision as being against U.N. resolutions; but the Dutch ambassador was received by the Foreign Minister in Jerusalem on July 17, 1953, and he was followed by the Greek diplomatic representative. Other representatives boycotted the Ministry in Jerusalem at first, but not for long. In December 1953, the Russian ambassador visited the Foreign Minister in Jerusalem and later presented his credentials to the President there, and, since 1954, all the foreign ambassadors have indeed presented their credentials in Jerusalem. Although most of the embassies remained in Tel Aviv, by 1967, 23 embassies were housed in Jerusalem.

Israel agreed to only one concession regarding the status of the consuls in Jerusalem. These consuls, already resident in the city during Mandatory times, did not recognize Israeli and Jordanian rule of the city — only the *de facto* control by these states. The consuls would inform the District Commissioner of both parts of the city of their appointment, but did not present their accreditation to the Foreign Ministry. The Jerusalem consuls were, in addition, not subordinate to their countries' ambassadors, because the city was considered to be outside Israeli and Jordanian sovereignty, and they reported directly to their Foreign Ministries abroad. For the same reason, some consulates in Jerusalem belonged to states that do not recognize Israel at all, such as Spain. All these consulates officially maintained only one residence in the divided city, since they did not recognize its partition. On their documents, the consuls wrote only the name of the city, not of the state.

Thus, by the beginning of 1954, for both Israel and Jordan, the prolonged process of establishing political facts was completed, and the vision of claiming Jerusalem in the name of the brotherhood of nations had clearly died of exhaustion.

CHAPTER TWO

PALACES IN AMMAN

The prolonged debate at the United Nations over the future of Jerusalem and the internal Israeli conflict over relinquishing the Old City to the Arabs, constituted only part of the intricate struggle to determine hegemony over the city. The position of King Abdallah of Transjordan was the most complex and precarious: from most points of view — including that of his Arab compatriots — he had no business being in Jerusalem at all.

When the Arab States rejected the UN Partition Resolution, they decided to go to war against it and the Jewish State. However, King Abdallah ordered his army to intervene in Jerusalem only after desperate appeals for help from the Arab defenders of the city. The Arab Legion's British commander, John Glubb, feared that intervention in Jerusalem would so weaken his forces that he would not be able to defend the Arab parts of Palestine. But an infantry company of the Legion, under the command of a young Arab officer named Abdallah al-Tal, was already stationed in Jerusalem, and, on May 18, King Abdallah went over Glubb's head and ordered al-Tal to "Go and save Jerusalem! "

The Legion's intervention stopped the advance of the Jewish forces and the lines in Jerusalem remained more or less static until they were formalized in the Israel-Jordan Armistice Agreement. During the first month of Transjordanian rule, there was no sign of friction with local citizens. The danger of an Israeli conquest was still a unifying factor. Leaders of the local irregular forces were appoint-

17

ed to key positions and Ahmad Hilmi, Vice-President of the local Arab Higher Committee, was appointed Military Governor of the city on June 10.

But severe conflicts between Palestinians and Transjordanians soon broke out. The fall of Lod and Ramla to the Israelis in July was one of the main reasons for the deteriorating relationship. The Palestinians claimed that the Arab Legion had abandoned the 30,000 inhabitants of the two towns as a result of collusion between King Abdallah, the British and the Israelis. There were bloody riots in Jerusalem and Nablus, and the situation steadily worsened. The Mufti of Jerusalem, the extreme Arab nationalist, Haj Amin al-Husayni, who had spent most of World War II in Berlin, stood at the head of the radical elements, which forcibly opposed Abdallah's attempts to gain political control over Arab Palestine.

In the course of the 1948 War, most of the Arab area of Palestine was occupied by Iraqi and Transjordanian forces, with the Egyptian army overrunning some of the southern part of the country. Within the Jordanian-Iraqi occupation areas, the Palestinian elements were prevented from organizing. But in the Egyptian areas of occupation — Mount Hebron and the Gaza Strip — the Palestinians were encouraged and activity for the creation of a Palestinian entity reached its peak at the end of September 1948, when the Arab Higher Committee met in Gaza. On September 20, the Committee announced the creation of an "All-Palestine Government." The name was decided to stress the "Government's" claim to all Palestinian territory, whether controlled by the Jews or by Abdallah. Haj Amin al-Husayni was elected President of the Palestine National Assembly; Ahmad Hilmi, the Military Governor of Jerusalem, was elected Prime Minister; and another Jerusalem Arab, Anwar Nusaybah, was made Secretary of the Cabinet. A few days after its creation, the all Palestine Government was recognized by all the Arab States then in existence, with the exception of Transjordan.

Abdallah, however, had other plans for those parts of Palestine under the control of his army and declared that he would not permit the All-Palestine Government to function within "the security boundaries of Transjordan," which extended "from Egypt to Lebanon." He speeded up steps to annex the areas of Arab Palestine under his control. The Arab Legion, led by its British commander, disarmed the Mufti's supporters, and many of the Palestinian leaders

18

were thrown into prison. King Abdallah then organized his own meeting of Palestinian leaders.

At the beginning of December 1948, 2,000 Palestinian notables from Transjordanian-occupied territory met in Jericho. Sheikh Muhammad Ali Ja'abari of Hebron, who had been one of the founders of the All-Palestine Government three months earlier, now changed his mind and agreed to serve as chairman of the Jericho conference. All the resolutions had been worded beforehand and were adopted unanimously. The most important of these were:

> *Para. 2: The Arab countries cannot combat the dangers facing them and menacing Palestine unless they achieve national unity. This must begin with the unity of Palestine and Transjordan, as a first step towards complete Arab unity.*
> *Para. 4: The Congress declares His Majesty, King Abdallah, King of all Palestine.*

The resolutions of the Jericho Congress were ratified in the Transjordan Parliament on December 13, 1948.

The Jericho conference, and the decision of the Transjordanian Parliament, aroused furious reactions throughout the Arab world. On December 18, 1948, the Arab League Council convened to discuss the expulsion of Transjordan. The League members stressed that Transjordan's annexation of parts of Palestine contradicted the Arab League Resolution of April 1948, in which all the states about to intervene in Palestine guaranteed that the regions they would capture would remain under their temporary military rule, so that "the country, after its liberation is completed, will be handed to its owners, who will administer it as they choose."

Faced by the fierce opposition of all the Arab States, Abdallah was forced to retreat from his position. At the end of December 1948, his Prime Minister announced that "in view of the international complications, Transjordan would not hurry to annex those parts of Palestine under her control, but would hold a referendum." At the same time, the King stepped up his measures for *de facto* annexation and his fight against the supporters of the Mufti. At the end of December, he took the significant step of appointing Sheikh Husam al-Din Jarallah as Mufti of Jerusalem, thus depriving Haj Amin al-Husayni of the title that had helped him to dominate the

19

Arab political scene for twenty-seven years. The occupied area was divided into three military regions — Jerusalem, Ramallah and Hebron. At the beginning of March 1949, the military governors were replaced by civilian governors, and at the beginning of April, all government offices were transferred to the direct control of ministers resident in Amman.

The Armistice Agreement signed with Israel in April 1949 came as a profound shock to the Palestinians. They regarded it as Jordanian recognition of the State of Israel and as a betrayal of their lands. They were particularly incensed that Jordanian Bedouin officers had fixed the border line with the Israeli representatives, even though they were unfamiliar with the country's topography, land values or water resources. The Palestinians felt that the Jordanians, because of their ignorance, had relinquished stretches of pasture, wells and orchards, leaving the border villages destitute. A refugee leader complained to the King that the Armistice Agreement was "a new Balfour Declaration."

Nevertheless, King Abdallah continued his *de facto* annexation of the West Bank, using a mixture of administrative acts, incentives and repression. In December, customs duties were abolished and the police posts on the Allenby Bridge, which crossed the Jordan River, were withdrawn. The Jordanian Parliament was then dispersed in order to hold general elections on both banks. All the inhabitants of Palestine living on the West Bank became citizens of the Hashemite Kingdom. At the end of December 1949, the post of "Governor-General of the occupied territories in Palestine" was abolished, and civilian administration was placed under the Minister of the Interior in Amman. In January 1950, the Ministry for Refugee Affairs was abolished, on the grounds that the refugees had become citizens of the Hashemite Kingdom.

In April 1950, parliamentary elections were held, with the participation of all the citizens of Transjordan and Palestine. A forty-member parliament was elected with 20 representatives from the East Bank and 20 from the West. Jerusalem and Jericho together delegated three deputies (two Muslims and one Christian). Anwar Nusaybah, who had been Secretary of the Cabinet of the "All-Palestine Government" set up in Gaza, now switched his allegiance to King Abdallah and became a deputy for Jerusalem. After a year of idleness in Gaza and Cairo, the young Palestinian leader had decided, like many of his fellows, that he had no choice other than to compromise with the Hashemite regime.

Following the elections, Abdallah appointed a Government consisting of 12 ministers, five of whom were Palestinians, and a twenty-man Senate, which included seven Palestinians. On April 24, 1950, Abdallah spoke from his throne to the new Parliament, asking it to ratify the unification of the two banks of the Jordan. His proposal stated, in part:

The Jordanian Parliament decides that approval is granted to complete unity between the two banks . . . and their amalgamation in one single state — the Hashemite Kingdom of Jordan, under the crown of His Hashemite Majesty, Abdallah Ibn Husayn, the exalted. This will be upon the basis of parliamentary constitutional rule and complete equality of the rights and duties of all the citizens.

A number of Palestinian deputies left the joint session in protest before the vote; but the bill was passed. Palestinian aspirations to self-determination found their expression in Paragraph 2 of the Law of Unification: ". . . this unity shall in no way be connected with the final settlement of Palestine's just cause, within the framework of national hopes, Arab cooperation and international justice." The Palestinian leaders regarded the unification decision as a temporary step that did not close the door on the idea of their independence in the whole of Palestine. Until their aspirations could be realized, they regarded themselves as tied by bonds of loyalty to the Hashemite regime.

Three days after this decision, Britain recognized the annexation of the West Bank (and simultaneously extended *de jure* recognition to Israel). The decision was accompanied by a reservation concerning Jerusalem, in the following terms: ". . . pending a final determination of the status of [the Jerusalem area] they are unable to recognize Jordan sovereignty over any part of it." The only other state to recognize Jordan's annexation of the West Bank was Pakistan. No other state, Arab or non-Arab, ever recognized it.

In May 1950, the Arab League Council met and again decided that the annexation was a violation of its decision of April 1948. But the dispute ended in a compromise, with the Jordanian Prime Minister declaring that the annexation would not affect the outcome of a final settlement of the Palestine problem. In 1950, therefore, East Jerusalem, together with the rest of the West Bank, became an integral part of the Hashemite Kingdom of Jordan.

Although King Abdallah intervened hesitantly in the fighting in Jerusalem, once his forces had taken control of the Old City and the eastern part of the new city, he was not prepared to share his rule there with anyone else. Even during the first weeks, when the Israelis continued to adhere to the principle of internationalization, Abdallah refused to permit the intervention of the United Nations; and there is no doubt that the British encouraged Abdallah in his firm stand against internationalization. But the King's opposition to international rule did not mean that he wished to strengthen the status of Arab Jerusalem as a political center. On the contrary, as the Hashemite régime improved its standing, Jerusalem's political stature diminished. Abdallah's policy in Jerusalem should be seen against the background of his struggle with the Palestinians.

Jerusalem contained the largest concentration of those elements which contested the King's domination and disrupted attempts to integrate the two banks of the Jordan. Abdallah's regime conducted a bitter struggle against them, disarming them, arresting them and exiling them from the city. Abdallah also cultivated and promoted the Nashashibis and the Khalidis, traditional rivals of the dominant Husaynis, who opposed him. He encouraged the immigration to Jerusalem of citizens from Hebron, now supporters of the regime following the defection of their leader, Sheikh Ali Ja'abari, from the separatist Palestinian cause. The Jordanian regime also deliberately hindered the development of Jerusalem, giving preference to Nablus and Hebron. It felt that strengthening Jerusalem politically, by making it the joint capital of the Kingdom or the capital of the West Bank, would help the Palestinian separatist forces. Accordingly, the Jordanian Government consistently worked to strengthen the standing of Amman as the sole political and economic center of the Kingdom. There was an obvious contradiction between Jordan's desire to downgrade Jerusalem and its wish to strengthen the Arab claim to the city. The Jordanians reconciled these two conflicting aims by continuing to discriminate against Jerusalem in practice while publicly declaring its intentions to strengthen Jerusalem and taking short-lived ostentatious steps.

The inhabitants of Jerusalem watched Abdallah's moves in anger and frustration. Their furious reactions stemmed not only from anxiety over the fate of their city, but were also an indirect expression of their separatist aspirations. In protesting against the impov-

22

erishment of Jerusalem, they were protesting the loss of their political independence as well. They knew that the Hashemite regime could not afford to repress those who were calling for the strengthening of the Holy City.

As has been stated, the Jordanians transferred their government departments to Amman, leaving in Jerusalem only those offices concerned directly with the local population. This decision aroused a wave of protests from the Palestinians, and the Government was forced to issue a denial of its moves, even though it continued to carry them out. A letter sent by Anwar Nusaybah at the end of 1950 was typical of the Palestinians' reactions:

> His Excellency the President [of the Jordanian Parliament] will be surprised to hear that the Jerusalem Municipality is almost the only one of the Kingdom's municipalities, on either bank, which does not receive any encouragement — perhaps the opposite — from the government administration. This is in spite of the fact that Jerusalem is in the forefront of those towns affected by the catastrophe of the Palestinian holocaust.

'Aref al-'Aref, appointed Mayor in August 1950, also complained about the transfer of government offices:

> The city is wrestling with the ruins of destruction, writhing on the embers of poverty and scarcity, and therefore [the Municipality] requests you to abstain from damage to its standing and to the livelihood of its citizens by government departments being moved away to Amman.

Despite these and other protests, the departments were moved to Amman, according to plan.

On July 20, 1951, King Abdallah was assassinated while entering the Mosque of al-Aqsa in Jerusalem. There followed a period of repression and acts of reprisal by the Hashemite regime. The situation in Jerusalem deteriorated to such an extent that 15 members of Parliament, representing the West Bank, met in May 1952 and sent a memorandum to the Government calling for the reopening of government offices in Jerusalem, the establishment of an office to promote tourism, and the granting of more support to the Municipality. They also demanded an end to discrimination against the West Bank in siting government development projects and to the preference given to East Bank Jordanians in government service. Responding to this pressure, in October 1952, the Government restored the post of Deputy Minister of the Interior, resident in Jerusalem. He was granted certain powers to deal with local affairs, and to coordinate the operations of government offices on the West Bank.

The Jordanian regime also tried to sabotage Jerusalem's preeminent status within the Muslim religious establishment. The Higher Muslim Council, which had been established during the British Mandate, was still in existence and remained the bastion of its head, the ex-Mufti, Haj Amin al-Husayni. The Palestinian *waqf* (religious endowments administration), a powerful financial instrument, which had financed the Husaynis for years, also maintained its independence. In order to eliminate the Higher Muslim Council and bring the religious establishment under their control, the Jordanians set up a "Board of 'Ulaymah" in February 1951. Its members were the Jordanian-appointed Mufti, Husam al-Din Jarallah, the head of the *shari'a* courts (Muslim religious courts) on the West Bank, the chief *Qadi* (Religious judge) of Jerusalem, the Mufti of Hebron, and (as a balancing factor) four government officials. The Higher Muslim Council was then dispersed and the central administration of the Palestinian *waqf* was transferred to Amman.

The Government did, however, encourage non-separatist religious activity. In April 1953, the feast of "The Journey and the Ascent" of the Prophet Muhammad from Mecca to the al-Aqsa Mosque took place in Jerusalem for the first time. Delegations from various Muslim countries took part in the assembly, during which violent speeches were made attacking Israel. At its conclusion, the assembly adopted the following resolutions: (1) similar celebrations would be held each year in Jerusalem; (2) Muslims were called upon to work for the salvation of the Holy City and to collect money for the reconstruction of Muslim Jerusalem; (3) efforts were to be made to repair the al-Aqsa Mosque, and (4) a permanent office would be established in Jerusalem.

As a result of these resolutions, a "Muslim Charitable Society for the Reconstruction of Jerusalem" was set up with the purpose of erecting educational institutions, orphanages and hospitals in the city. A number of projects were financed by the Charitable Society, including a hospital on the Mount of Olives (completed in 1969). It is perhaps significant that part of the money was used to finance the erection of anti-sniping walls in the Musrarra and Sheikh Jarah areas in 1954. Apparently, the Jordanian Government did not consider itself to be under any obligation to allocate money from its budget for such a purpose.

The conflict between the Municipality and the Jordanian regime continued, with the Government holding back local development. Even development projects planned in Jerusalem by philanthropic bodies were not always approved. In the early 1960s, the Saudi Arabian Government offered to build a secondary school in Jerusalem and to defray the cost of the whole building. The Government refused, insisting that the school be erected in Amman. The Order of St. John, which had for decades maintained an opthalmic hospital near the railway station in West Jerusalem, decided to erect a new one in East Jerusalem, as most of those in need of its services were Arabs. It sold the old building to the Israel Government and presented to the Arab Municipality of Jerusalem a plan to build a new clinic in Sheikh Jarah. The Government opposed the plan, demanding that the clinic be erected in Amman. The Order, which originated in Jerusalem at the time of the Crusades, firmly refused to leave the city. When the Municipality also demanded the construction of the eye hospital, the Government was forced to give way.

In July 1953, following the transfer of Israel's Foreign Ministry to Jerusalem, the Jordanian Government was forced to take counter-measures. For the first time, it held a meeting in Jerusalem and decided on a number of steps to strengthen the status of the city. The Jordanian Parliament then met in Jerusalem, in the presence of King Husayn. A number of solemn resolutions were adopted, including a recommendation to erect a memorial to the victims who had fallen "in defense of the Arab character of Jerusalem." At the same time, the Jordanian Foreign Minister declared that Jordan was not considering the transfer of her capital to Jerusalem; but branches of the Ministries of Finance, Economic Affairs, Construction, Education, Justice, and Transport, would be opened in the city.

The Government then proceeded to drag its feet in implementing these decisions and, at the end of January 1954, the City Council sent a telegram to the Prime Minister expressing its concern over the non-fulfilment of the Government's promises concerning the status of Jerusalem. The Prime Minister hurried to Jerusalem to quieten the storm. On his arrival, two petitions were handed to him. The first, from the Chamber of Commerce, demanded a reduction of taxes and

25

a redoubled allocation for services and development aid in the city; the second, from schoolchildren, said that the unemployment of their parents was a burden upon them and claimed that most of them lived "in conditions unfit for human beings."

From 1954 to 1957 Jordan passed through a series of severe political crises which threatened the collapse of the Kingdom. King Talal, who succeeded Abdallah, permitted the parties to function and accepted a fairly liberal constitution. His son, King Husayn, who was crowned in May 1953, tried to continue his father's policy. As a result, the radical Palestinian opposition — which had been crushed by King Abdallah — raised its head and began to attack the Government's policy, and even the regime itself. A primary focus of opposition was Jordan's relationship with Britain. The Palestinians regarded Britain as the source of their catastrophe and demanded an end to political, economic and military dependence on her. At that time, the Jordanian economy was overwhelmingly dependent on a British subsidy. Britain also covered all the costs of the Arab Legion. Tension rose as a result of continuous incitement by Egypt and Saudi Arabia, and was exacerbated by Israeli reprisal actions which began in 1953 in response to Arab infiltration and murder. In December 1955, tension reached a peak during Jordan's negotiations to join the pro-Western Baghdad Pact. The Palestinian Ministers resigned from the Government and there were violent demonstrations throughout the country. Only when King Husayn announced that he would not join the Pact did the tension begin to subside.

In March 1956, the King was forced to expel all the British officers serving with the Arab Legion, including its commander, John Glubb, but even this move didn't end the crisis. In October 1956, a new Parliament was elected. It included radical elements that aspired to stronger links with Syria and Egypt, and even to a union between those countries and Jordan. For more than a year King Husayn was locked in a struggle with these extremists, headed by Prime Minister Sulayman Nabulsi. Following bloody riots, and several attempted coups, martial law was declared, followed by widespread arrests and the banning of political parties and trade unions. By the end of 1957, King Husayn had crushed the opposition and restored peace to his Kingdom.

Jerusalem was, naturally, one of the main bastions of the opposition. There were violent demonstrations in the city. The army

26

opened fire a number of times, and dozens of civilians, including women and children, were killed. This was hardly the atmosphere likely to induce the Government to strengthen the status of Jerusalem. The King had, admittedly, informed a delegation from Jerusalem that he intended to take up residence in the city during part of the year; but, at the same time, the Deputy Minister of the Interior, who was to organize the affairs of the West Bank from Jerusalem, resigned his post because he had not received sufficient authority. Complaints about injustice and discrimination against Jerusalem continued during 1956—7, but by then the Government had even abandoned the tactic of issuing declarations on the issue.

Husayn's rivals in the Arab world continued to encourage the idea of a Palestinian entity, forcing him to make a number of ostentatious moves. In August 1959, the Cabinet met in special session in Jerusalem. King Husayn, who presided, declared that this would be the first of a series of Cabinet meetings to be held in Jerusalem, "the second capital of the Kingdom of Jordan." Again, a number of decisions were taken to improve the situation in the city. The King ordered some of his Ministers to spend one day a week in Jerusalem.

The inhabitants of the West Bank, whose standard of economic, social and political development was higher than that of the inhabitants of Eastern Jordan, loathed the primitive — tribal and autocratic — political structure which had been imposed upon them by the unification of the two banks. They felt no loyalty towards the Hashemites; on the contrary, they regarded them as puppets of Britain, the power they blamed for all their troubles. They would not accept the Government institutions nor their mode of functioning; and the repressive methods of the security police revolted them, as did the arrogance of the Arab Legion. They were well aware of their numerical superiority (65% of the Kingdom's population), their technological ability, their educational superiority and their economic power, and they refused to bow to the tutelage of the small oligarchy which lived in the little desert township of Amman.

Nevertheless, the Palestinians found themselves in a terrible dilemma. Jordan was the only state in which they had any chance at all of reaching important positions of power — inferior, perhaps, to those of inhabitants of Eastern Jordan, but positions, nevertheless, as ministers, ambassadors, and members of Parliament. While the Palestinians regarded the unification of the two banks as a unilateral act by an expansion-hungry King, and the conquest by the Arab Legion as an invasion that destroyed their hopes of independence, they had been left in their homes and their towns and the refugees had received Jordanian citizenship — unlike their brethren who had fled to Lebanon or were kept in the refugee camps of the Gaza Strip.

The radical elements, who centered around the supporters of the Mufti and the parties of the left, continued to oppose the Hashemite regime. Their opposition found its expression in violent demonstrations and acts of terror. The city of Jerusalem became the focal point for stormy demonstrations, which were crushed, often with loss of life, by the Legion's soldiers. Tension reached a peak in the years 1955–7, when the city was under martial law.

Towards the end of the 1950s, however, tension gradually decreased. The consistent policy of the Jordanian Government, during its first ten years of rule, was crowned with full success. The East Bank, especially Amman, became the undisputed economic and political center of the Kingdom. It was impossible to reverse the trend. Hundreds of thousands of Palestinians who had moved from the West Bank and Jerusalem to settle in the East Bank and Amman, quickly integrated into the political and economic life there, and the process of enforced assimilation bore fruit. The feelings of frustration, discrimination and injustice did not melt away, but they no longer found political expression. The inhabitants of Jerusalem bowed their heads before forces stronger than themselves. In the struggle between Jerusalem and Amman, the latter emerged victorious. The number of inhabitants of Amman — 61,000 in 1948 — had increased fivefold by 1967, reaching 311,000. During the same period, the population of Arab Jerusalem increased by only fifty percent. Jerusalem turned into a provincial town, with even less influence than Nablus. One of Jerusalem's candidates for the Jordanian parliamentary elections in 1962, summed up the situation in the following words:

> See the palaces which are being built in Amman . . . those palaces should have been built in Jerusalem, but were removed from here, so that Jerusalem would remain not a city, but a kind of village.

In 1962 this was no longer a call for action, but the sad summing-up of a situation that was irreversible. All the same, the Jerusalemites were still left with their pride in their city. No one could take away its world-wide fame and importance. By 1964, the Jordanian regime was so sure of itself that it permitted the convening of an All-Palestinian Conference in Jerusalem. The delegates, who established the Palestine Liberation Organization, did not call for the separation of the West Bank, and did not protest the situation that had been created in the Kingdom of Jordan. They did call on King Husayn to declare Jerusalem "an Arab city" and the capital of Jordan; but there was no reaction from the King and the situation remained unchanged until the outbreak of the Six Day War.

CHAPTER THREE

THE DIVIDED CITY –
THE ISRAELI SIDE

At the end of 1947, on the eve of the outbreak of the War of Independence, 100,000 Jews lived in Jerusalem, but nearly one-quarter of that number abandoned the city during the war. Some returned to the city after the fighting ended in July 1948 and the population was augmented by a thin trickle of immigrants which began to reach Jerusalem. The first census held in the State of Israel, in November 1948, registered some 84,000 inhabitants in Jerusalem. The following year there was a rapid growth in population, and by the end of 1949 it reached over 103,000. Most of the immigrants who arrived in 1949 were accommodated in abandoned Arab houses and, when these were filled, they were housed in transit camps, mainly in a converted British army camp in Talpiot. The Jewish population continued to increase rapidly until 1951. Between 1948 and 1951 the number of inhabitants increased by some 54,000, a growth of 65%. In the years 1952–6, there was a halt in the rate of growth, but it picked up again and the 1961 census showed a Jewish population of 167,000. After 1961 the rate of increase slowed down. On the eve of the Six Day War, the population of Jewish Jerusalem had reached 197,000.

The population of Jerusalem increased more slowly than that of Israel as a whole, resulting in a constant decline in the status of the city. Whereas the Jewish population of Jerusalem comprised 12% of the Jewish population in Israel in 1948, it had declined to 8.2% of the total Jewish population on the eve of the Six Day War.

31

Jerusalem also differed from the rest of the country in demographic make-up. In 1964, half of the city's population were native-born, a quarter were immigrants from the countries of Asia and Africa, and another quarter were from Europe and America. But if we examine continents of origin of the fathers of the native-born population, it transpires that one-third of these were likewise native-born, over a third were born in Africa and Asia, and less than a third were from Europe and America. Jerusalem was therefore to a large extent a city of second-generation *sabras* (the Hebrew term for native-born Israelis). The proportion of third-generation *sabras* in Jerusalem, on the eve of the Six Day War, was three times as large as in the rest of the country (17% in Jerusalem, 6% in the State as a whole). The number of inhabitants originating in Asia and Africa (including first-generation *sabra* offspring) came to 45% of the city's population.

It may, therefore, be said that the overwhelming majority of the Jewish inhabitants of Jerusalem (first-, second-, and third-generation *sabras*, and those born in Asia and Africa) were acquainted with the ways of the Arab population from childhood. Only one-third of the city's population came from abroad, and became acquainted with the Arab population and its ways for the first time in their lives in Jerusalem.

Despite the enormous growth in population, Jerusalem remained a mosaic of neighborhoods, each possessing a clearly defined character, way of life, and communal composition. It was this patchwork structure that permitted the co-existence of communities that adhered to differing social, economic, and religious ways. For the most part, the older Jewish quarters maintained their pre-State character; the abandoned Arab neighborhoods were populated by immigrants from the same country of origin; and in the new quarters the residents were also homogeneous groups. As a result, each neighborhood in the city developed its own special character, while the number of neighborhoods with mixed social features remained small.

Examining the twenty-four (by one count) neighborhoods of Jewish Jerusalem at that time, we find that nine have a majority of Jews of European origin, nine have an Oriental majority, and six are mixed. Twelve of the neighborhoods may be classified as religious, seven are non-religious, and five contain a mixture of religious and non-religious inhabitants. Seven areas enjoy a high economic and social standard, nine are of intermediate economic standard, and eight can be classed as poor neighborhoods. Eight are largely immigrant neighborhoods, while 16 contain native-born inhabitants or immigrants who arrived before 1948. There is also a certain correlation between the characteristics mentioned. All the areas whose inhabitants are mostly of European origin are also of a high or intermediate economic standard. All the areas whose inhabitants are mostly of Oriental origin are of an intermediate or low economic standard. The non-religious areas tend to be European.

This division of the city into neighborhoods possessing clearly defined social characteristics is not only the result of fortuitous circumstances, but indicates the desire of the inhabitants to live in a neighborhood that suits their way of life. In Jerusalem, identification with one's neighborhood finds a characteristic external expression. A Jerusalemite tends to identify his home according to the neighborhood and pinpoint his house in relation to some familiar feature, rather than by giving the postal address. For the inhabitants of Jerusalem, the city is the sum total of its quarters.

Nonetheless, the concentration of inhabitants of similar social and economic characteristics in specified areas did not prevent social friction. Religious citizens protested against traffic on the Sabbath, and there were violent demonstrations by the unemployed; yet social friction was expressed mainly in the prolonged instability of the municipal regime.

The stabilization of municipal government in Jerusalem was a long and painful process. For a year and a half after the breakdown of the joint Arab-Jewish Municipality in May 1948, Jewish Jerusalem was governed by a number of authorities simultaneously — military and civilian alike — and there was no lack of conflict between the various administrations, over the boundaries of their respective control. It was not until November 1950 that the first municipal elections were held for a 21-member council, but even then the state of municipal government was far from satisfactory. Despite the waves of immigration that doubled the population of the city, there was almost no change in the balance of political forces in Jerusalem. A third of the population voted for the religious parties, a third for the labor parties and a third for parties of the right and center. The absence of an absolute majority for any one of the main blocs, and the fierce political competition between the religious parties and the labor parties, gave rise to continual political upheavals in the Municipality, so much so that every now and then the national Government was forced to intervene. In 1952 it appointed a commission of inquiry to investigate the state of the Municipality. When the commission presented its conclusions, the Mayor resigned and another member of his party (the National Religious Party) took over and served amidst continuing crises and further upheavals in the municipal administration until April 1955, when the Government was forced to disperse the City Council and appoint, in its stead, a commission headed by the District Commissioner.

In the 1955 municipal elections, a coalition headed by the Israeli Workers' Party (Mapai) was formed for the first time in the history of the Jerusalem Municipality. It remained intact until the 1965 elections, bringing about a stabilization of the city's government. It also succeeded in implanting proper procedures into the municipal administration and contributed to the city's development.

In the 1965 municipal elections, the entire approach to forming a municipal government underwent a radical change when Teddy Kollek, candidate of Rafi (a party that had split off from Mapai), conducted a campaign based on personal leadership which drew attention away from traditional party loyalties and focused on municipal problems. As a result, Kollek out-polled Mapai in Jerusalem, established a 16-member coalition in the Municipal Council together with the right-wing Herut movement (which had until then been in opposition) and the religious parties, and left Mapai in the opposition for the first time since 1955.

The stocky, blond, Vienna-born Kollek was a dynamo of energy with a remarkable talent for public relations and ramified political and personal connections, both inside the country and abroad. Free of dogmatic political concepts, Kollek soon brought a new breath of life into the Municipality. The petty squabbling between the coalition parties ceased; the municipal bureaucracy, which had suffered from over-centralization, was decentralized; but at the same time coordination between the different branches of the Municipality slackened, and the decision-making process ran into difficulties. Nonetheless, Kollek's personal drawing power was to provide greater stability — under what were to prove more difficult conditions, from 1967 onwards, than ever before — than Jerusalem had known since the British Mandate.

34

Jerusalem's special character was also the result of its being the Capital, a university city, a spiritual and religious center and a city isolated from the centers of population and economy in the coastal plain. More than half of the population, at the begining of 1967, was employed in service branches; more than half of those employed belonged to the liberal professions and less than a third were manual workers. Although Jerusalem did not benefit, as much as it might have, from its status as the Capital of Israel — despite the pressures of the city-fathers to enhance this aspect of the city's nature — the Government was the largest employer in the city and, together with the Hebrew University, Hadassah Hospital and the Jewish Agency, employed over 30% of all wage-earners. Industry was less important than in other cities.

As a result of all these features, Jerusalem had the quality of a tranquil, introverted provincial city; its social life concentrated in its neighborhoods, within the framework of closed social groups. There were relatively few cars and the children played in the streets.

It was a city of contrasts. On the one hand, there was a unique concentration of intellectuals and scientists, on the other, many illiterate relief workers. Modern residential quarters were surrounded by slums almost unfit for human habitation. One-third of the city's population occupied substandard housing. Although most Jerusalemites identified with their city and kept faith with it, hundreds of the city's youngsters left and moved down to the coast, because of difficulties in finding housing and a livelihood.

Just before the Six Day War, Jewish Jerusalem began to emerge from the economic recession which had slowed down the rate of economic growth of the entire country. But because of the special structure of Jerusalem's economy, the city did not suffer from sharp economic fluctuations. It showed neither swift development, nor sharp retreats. The changing trends in the economic situation of Jewish Jerusalem can be seen through changes in the division of employees between 1948 and 1967. Whereas, in 1948, 25% of all employees were engaged in industry and crafts, the proportion fell to 18% by 1967. Those engaged in banking and commerce also decreased proportionally; but the number engaged in services and building rose from 37% in 1948 to 50% in 1967, and from 5% in 1948 to 9% in 1967, respectively.

Most of the industrial concerns in Jerusalem were small, even though over the years there was a trend towards a concentration of larger ones. About half the enterprises were engaged in producing consumer goods (textiles, food, leather and wood) and in diamond polishing and printing. But even in the consumer industries, Jerusalem did not cover the needs of its own population, and more than half of its consumer products were imported from outside. The city had almost no machine industry or factories for production equipment. The influence of the city's scientific institutions was mainly felt in the pharmaceutical, electronic and printing industries. The growth of the building industry resulted not so much from rapid construction of residential housing as from extensive investment in the construction of public buildings and institutions. This development stemmed from the deliberate concentration of government institutions and other public bodies in Jerusalem.

Tourism in Jerusalem, "the City of Pilgrims," did not develop as might have been expected. The percentage of overnight stays in the city's hotels declined. At the beginning of 1967, there were 1,000 hotel rooms in the city and another 250 in the immediate vicinity.

Another problem that the Municipality and residents of Jerusalem had to face was that of the quality of public education. During the British Mandate, Jewish education in Jerusalem was backward in comparison with the educational networks which developed in Tel Aviv and Haifa. This was due to the fact that in the latter cities there were independent Jewish authorities and organized Jewish communities that created highly developed educational systems. In Jerusalem, on the other hand, the mixed Municipality did not give any assistance to the educational system, and the Jewish community was split and divided.

In October 1949, when the primary school network became the responsibility of the Municipality, the number of pupils reached 12,500, in 55 primary schools. A decade later, in 1960, the number of pupils reached 26,000, and their number had passed 40,000 on the eve of the Six Day War.

After the 1948 War, Jerusalem was the only city in Israel without municipal secondary schools. The schools were either private or owned by public bodies other than the Municipality. It was only in the 1960s that some were transferred to municipal management.

The schools were another area in which the gap between the different social and economic backgrounds of Jerusalem's population found its extreme expression. To a worrying extent, the attainments of pupils who came from immigrant families with many children and limited means were lower than those from veteran and wealthy families. The mechanism by which each child supposedly got an equal chance to obtain an education was, therefore, an illusion. In order to help eliminate this gap, a number of projects were initiated, including lengthening the school day, combining cultural activities and homework preparation at school, and inaugurating other activities for those pupils in need of special attention. Despite its initial backwardness, the municipal education system made impressive progress, especially after the beginning of the 1960s. Institutions of learning, culture, and adult education were developed and as a result of these educational efforts the percentage of illiteracy fell to 14% of the population as a whole.

While the standard of education was generally high, Jewish students were taught little, if anything, about the Arabs, their history, language, and culture. Of the 416 hours devoted to teaching history in Jewish secondary schools, only six hours were allocated for the study of Arab history; some 40% of the lessons were devoted to Jewish history, 60% to general history. Even those few lessons in Arab history were taught in connection with world history, and not as a subject in itself. The history of Palestine was taught almost exclusively in connection with the history of its Jews. The Jewish pupil was well learned in the history of the country up to the end of the Talmudic period. But the time between the end of the Byzantine period and the first wave of Jewish immigration to Palestine in the 1880s was studied — if at all — in the most superficial manner. As a result, leading Arab figures, such as Omar Ibn al-Khatab and Saladin were unknown to the average Jewish pupil, even though they had lived in and left their mark on his own land.

No attempt was made to give the Jewish pupil any knowledge of the Muslim or Christian religions. The average Jewish pupil did not read extracts from the Quran or the New Testament, not even as literary classics in the framework of general literature study. Arabic was learned in a few schools, but it was an optional subject, parallel to French, and the number of pupils who chose it was very small. Usually, it was literary, and not spoken, Arabic that was taught. The Jewish-Arab conflict was studied in citizenship classes and within the framework of Jewish history. According to one survey on this matter, the curriculum "avoids increasing hatred and encouraging aggression, but is not free of the type of indoctrination that tends to glorify Israeli society and culture while playing down the value of others." As a result, the average graduate of the Jewish educational system lacked the most basic knowledge of the Arabs, their history, culture, language, and way of life. He was not really aware of their existence; and in as much as he was aware of it, he sensed physical and cultural superiority over them, even though he did not hate them.

*　　*　　*

After the 1948 War and the partition of Jerusalem, the Jewish inhabitants quickly adapted to the existence of walls and barbed wire fences in the heart of the city. Those living near the demarcation lines suffered from shooting incidents and from occasional provocations by Jordanian soldiers; but, on the whole, the inhabitants did not sense the anomaly of living in a divided city. The siege of 1948 had made the inhabitants of Jerusalem psychologically immune to the dangers of life on the border. Men of military age, who served in the reserve Jerusalem Brigade, would come in contact with this aspect of reality during their reserve service: some stood guard on the frontier; others served at the isolated Jewish enclave on Mt. Scopus, and units of the Brigade drilled for defense and attack around the city, in preparation for the possible outbreak of war.

As the years passed, there was a gradual increase in the number of citizens who had no personal knowledge of the Arab sector of the city. The 1,700 refugees from the Jewish Quarter of the Old City put down roots in their new homes. Only for the old-timers, who were adults in 1948 — no more than 20% of the population in 1967 — were the alleyways of the Old City and the way of life of a united Jerusalem a personal memory. Every year, on the anniversaries of the deaths of relatives who were buried on the Mount of Olives and on those Hebrew dates on which it was customary to visit the graves of family, the sensation of separation arose again. For both old-timers and religious immigrants, being cut off from the Western Wall and the ancient synagogues in the Jewish Quarter was an open wound. On every festival they would hold special prayers on the roof of a high building on Mount Zion, from which they could see the area of the Wall. Even from there it was not physically possible to actually see the Wall itself, which was hidden by the ruined Jewish Quarter. Every now and then, Jewish tourists from Western countries would report on the Wall's condition. Their stories were given wide newspaper coverage. On Saturdays, parents would take their small children to observation points, from which the Old City was visible, and describe the places they could see from a distance. But the sadness and the yearning remained on an emotional plane and did not inspire any political initiative to conquer the Old City. The prevailing feeling was that the city's unification would not be achieved in this generation and there was not a single responsible political group which called for a forcible change in the status quo.

This acceptance of the city's partition found notable expression in its physical planning, in the 1950s. Jerusalem's Master Plan, drawn up in 1955 and approved in 1959, moved the city's center of gravity from its historic position — the Old City and the areas around it — to the western part of the city. Jerusalem's face, its representative institutions, and its communications' network were all turned westwards. The planning and development of West Jerusalem were deliberately carried out in isolation from the Old City. The planners neglected the old neighborhoods in the center, which had, in part, become border areas, and allowed them to deteriorate. New areas on the hilltops to the west were developed, and the road network was planned according to the post-war situation, whereby Jerusalem became the terminal of roads from the coast, rather than the meeting place of roads covering the whole length and breadth of Palestine.

The planners cannot be blamed for their westward orientation, in view of the Israeli city's encirclement on three sides by Arab-controlled territory. However, instead of moderating this process, which perpetuated the city's partition, the planners and their political mentors encouraged the process and speeded it up. The Master Plan made no effort to expand the city's commercial center, to build up the vacant areas in the east, or to rebuild the border regions, which were thinly populated before the war and now became slums. Acceptance of the city's partition was also expressed in the siting of prominent public buildings. When a new building to house the Knesset (Israel's Parliament) was planned, the architects wanted to place its facade southwards, facing a magnificent view of the south of the city and the hills of Judaea. Under the influence of security advisors, who feared that the building would be exposed to Jordanian army snipers, stationed only two kilometers away, it was decided that the Knesset would face north, and be lower than its surroundings. This change spoiled both the positioning and the architectural form of the structure.

The geographical center of the western city became the campus of the Hebrew University, an area which was, until 1949, far to the west of Jerusalem's municipal boundary. The demographic center of gravity also moved westwards over the years, as the population of the city's older neighborhoods thinned out. Had this process continued, the outcome could have been the creation of two cities, one in the east and the other in the west, separated by the desolate area of no-man's-land and an extensive belt of run-down and largely abandoned slums. The reunification of the city stopped this process, or seems at least to have moderated it.

Not long before the Six Day War, in response to a request by the Mayor of Jerusalem, the song-writer Naomi Shemer composed "Jerusalem of Gold," later to become famous as the hymn of the war. The tune and words expressed the attitude of Jerusalemites to their divided city as "a captive of its dream, sitting solitary, a wall in its heart," with poignant memories of "the cisterns," "the market square" and "the Old City." But these were longings for the unattainable, for a dream whose realization was remote.

CHAPTER FOUR

THE DIVIDED CITY —
THE JORDANIAN SIDE

By the time the British Mandate ended on May 14, 1948, the Municipality of Jerusalem, which had been composed of an equal number of Arab and Jewish representatives, had split into two distinct bodies. The Jews had established a Jewish Municipal Committee and the Arabs appointed Anton Saffiah, who had been Treasurer of the defunct joint Municipality, to the post of Municipal Director. Before leaving the country, the British Deputy Commissioner handed over two checks: one of £30,000 to the Jewish Municipal Committee and the second, for £27,500, to the Arab National Committee, the supreme Arab body in Jerusalem, which had also taken on municipal functions. The Jews immediately deposited their check in the Anglo-Palestine Bank, while Anton Saffiah placed his check in the municipal safe. Subsequently, the fighting in the city made it impossible for Saffiah to move beyond the Old City walls and the undrawn sum remained in the local branch of Barclays Bank. During the first truce, in July 1948, Saffiah entered the municipality building, then in no-man's-land under U.N. protection, but could not find the check. It was only during the second truce that he managed to travel to Cyprus, where he claimed the money from Barclays Bank and from those responsible for liquidating the Mandatory's debts; but they declared that the money was in the hands of the Jews. In June 1948 the Jewish Municipality decided to use part of the money allocated to its Arab counterpart to pay half of the debts of the joint Municipality. But, after receiving an application from Barclays Bank in Cyprus, the Jewish Municipality forwarded the *balance* of

41

the money to its owners. Anton Saffiah could at long last claim his funds.

Backed by this money, and in the absence of a Municipal Council in East Jerusalem after the war, Saffiah acted on his own until the beginning of 1949, when the Jordanian Military Commander, Abdallah al-Tal, appointed a Municipal Council headed by Anwar al-Khatib. This Council functioned until the middle of 1950, when al-Khatib was dismissed for protesting Jordan's agreement to vacate a number of houses in one of the quarters on the border and hand them over to Israel. Seven of the Council's nine members resigned in protest against the dismissal, and on August 1, 1950, 'Aref al-'Aref was appointed as head of the Municipal Council.

The first municipal elections in Arab Jerusalem were held on July 31, 1951. Twelve members were elected, the largest number of votes going to 'Aref al-'Aref, chairman of the appointed Council. The aged statesman and historian did not, however, last long in the post. During a visit of King Talal to Jerusalem, 'Aref al-'Aref held a dinner in his honor and made a speech of welcome, in which he quoted the greeting uttered by a Bedouin chief to the Caliph Omar ibn al-Khatab: "If we were to see you take a crooked path, we would straighten it out with a sword." The neurotic King took this as an insult, and within two hours the Mayor was informed by phone of his dismissal.

Omar Wa'ari was appointed to replace al-'Aref, but after the elections, held in September, 1955, 'Aref al-'Aref was reappointed. A few months later, however, he agreed to serve as Minister of Public Works in the Jordanian Government. As it happened, the Government was forced to resign within five days, as the result of anti-British and anti-Hashemite disturbances. Al-'Aref wished to return to his previous post, but the Municipal Council refused to elect him as Mayor again. The continual changes at the head of the Jerusalem Municipality came to an end with the appointment of Rauhi al-Khatib as Mayor, on January 15, 1957. He held the post for three terms.

Comparing the state of municipal government in the two halves of the city, we can see that in the early 1950's, both suffered from unstable regimes. However, the reasons for this instabiltiy were different. In Israeli Jerusalem, internal disputes between the parties constituting the Council forced the central Government to intervene and disperse the elected Council, appointing a committee in its stead.

The instability in Jordanian Jerusalem, on the other hand, stemmed from arbitrary intervention by the central Government. In contrast, both parts of the city achieved stable administration in the decade preceeding the Six Day War.

The Jordanian Municipal Elections Law of 1955 specified that Jerusalem would be governed by a Council, of up to 12 members, that would serve four years. After the elections, the Government could appoint two additional members. The Mayor was to be appointed by the Government from among the Council members, including the appointees. Thus, the Government in Amman had decisive influence over the Council's composition and the number of its members. Above all, it had complete control over the choice or dismissal of the Mayor and the dispersal of the Council.

In the 1963 municipal elections, 11,000 voters, out of 60,000 inhabitants, cast their ballots for 11 council members. Fifth on the list, was the Mayor, Rauhi al-Khatib — short and lean, with the look of an ascetic, an excellent administrator. Throughout his public life, al-Khatib managed to maintain a balance between the Jordan Government and the demands of the extremist Palestinian organizations. As Mayor, he did much to improve services, and foster economic development; but he was accused of nepotism and insufficient insistence on the integrity of municipal employees. He was active in the Palestine Liberation Organization (PLO) but nevertheless, in July 1955, he expressed the opinion that Tunisian President Bourgiba's proposal for negotiations with Israel on the basis of the partition plan (a suggestion which aroused a great deal of anger among the Palestinians) was a logical proposal. At the same time he expressed his disappointment in the PLO and its leader, Ahmad Shukeiry. In November 1966, following the Israeli retaliation raid on the village of Samu', he was among those who demanded that the Jordanian Government permit the entry of other Arab forces into Jordan, and allow saboteurs to cross into Israel. Nevertheless, his relations with the Jordanian authorities were excellent, and they appointed him Mayor for the third time.

The Municipality of Arab Jerusalem had no lack of problems to deal with during the 19 years of the city's division. When the cease-fire agreement was signed in July 1948, only 33,000 of the original 64,000 inhabitants remained in the Arab part of Jerusalem; half of the city's Muslim and Christian inhabitants had left the city. These included thousands of the Arab inhabitants of West Jerusalem, most of whom were Christians. Many of them were convinced that their departure was only for a week or two, until the tension subsided. The Christians did not remain in the Old City, but continued their flight to Jordan, Lebanon, and even overseas. Many hundreds of former Hebronites left the city, returning to their farms and houses in the Hebron area. As in other Arab towns, members of the wealthy and aristocratic Muslim families were the first to flee, some finding refuge in their winter residences and orange groves near Jericho. The Arab local authorities, and later the Jordanian military administration, tried to prevent the mass flight; but many bribed officials to acquire permits, while others slipped out of the city without the required permits. According to estimates, there were some 12,000 Christians and 19,000 Muslims among the fugitives.

Despite the mass flight, the Old City was crammed full of refugees. Some were fugitives from modern sections of the city that had been captured by the Israelis, or were in the line of fire, but most were from the villages near the city, including those in the Jerusalem corridor, now in Israeli hands.

The only space in the Old City available for refugees was the Jewish Quarter, whose inhabitants had been evacuated to the west. The poorest and most backward of the refugees were lodged there and the abandoned Quarter was turned into a large refugee camp, administered first by the Red Cross and later by the United Nations.

Living conditions in the Old City were intolerable. The city was cut off from its electricity supply, as the urban power station was in the Jewish area, and the water supply was likewise cut by the Jews. Only the automatic telephone network continued, partially, to function. Many months after the war, several of the lines linking the western part of the city with the east were still in order, and callers who dialled a wrong number were surprised to find themselves being answered in Arabic or Hebrew, as the case may have been.

Throughout the summer of 1948, there was a severe water shortage in the Old City and the inhabitants drank cistern water, mainly from the huge cisterns in the Temple Mount area. In the summer of 1949 the pumps of Ein Fara, northeast of the city, were repaired, but they only supplied a meager quantity. The pumps were improved in 1951, but even then the supply was inadequate. Later, supplementary sources of water were added, but even they did not completely solve the chronic shortage.

Even worse was the fact that the city remained without electricity for over a year. For a long time the population listened to news broadcast by battery-operated loudspeakers placed on the Temple Mount. During the initial period after the signature of the Armistice Agreement in April 1949, there was still hope that the power station in the western part of the city would renew its supply to the Old City. Paragraph 8 of the Armistice Agreement mentions "the provision of electricity for the Old City." But after a year, when it became clear that there would be no agreement on any of the matters listed in paragraph 8 (including free access to the Holy Places and the reopening of the institutions on Mt. Scopus), the British electricity company, which owned the concession, began to supply electricity in small amounts by means of generators. The tardy supply of electricity was a cause for severe complaints by the inhabitants.

Following the signing of the Armistice Agreement, people began to move back to the city. The first to return were those from the Hebron region. The Hebronites, who had settled in Jerusalem between the disturbances of 1929 and 1936 and fled with the beginning of the 1948 fighting, were old-timers in the city. The Grand Mufti, Haj Amin al-Husayni, had encouraged them to move to Jerusalem, because they supported him in his struggle against the rival Jerusalem families, above all the Nashashibis. The Hebronites were diligent, sharp witted, and frugal, traits that earned them the nickname of "Scots." Laborers who found no work too demeaning, or skillful traders, they were deeply religious and loyal to their leader. The Hebronites prospered in Jerusalem. Numerous families, who began as laborers — including the Barakat, Jaulani, and Qawasmi families — accumulated great wealth during the 1940s.

Together with the established Hebronite families, hundreds of families of new Hebronites also reached the city. Anwar al-Khatib, the first Jordanian Mayor, was a member of a prominent Hebron family, and he assisted his fellow Hebronites by giving them jobs in the Municipality. In contrast, only a small minority of the Christians returned to Jerusalem; nor were the leading Jerusalem families — the Husaynis, Nashashibis, and others — in a hurry to return. It is not surprising, therefore, that the Hebronites came to dominate the city's

45

commerce, and, by 1960, owned over 40% of the city's businesses.

By 1951, the city's population had reached some 45,000, and this increase in number brought about a further worsening of the housing situation. Gradually, people started moving into houses in no-man's-land. New housing quarters were built on the slopes of the Ophel (south-east of the Temple Mount) and the eastern side of Mount Zion (Wadi Khilwah). New houses were also built in Abu Tor and there was large-scale building in Wadi Joz and Sheikh Jarah. The loss of the Jewish-Arab commercial center had left the Arab side of Jerusalem without a business area. A new one was developed during the 1950's, facing the Old City walls. It extended from the Damascus Gate northwards to the American Colony and Wadi Joz. Hitherto mainly uninhabited, this area was owned by the Muslim *waqf* and by monasteries and churches. Entrepreneurs rented sites from the *waqf* on 20- to 35-year leases and built shops, offices, and hotels.

All this considerable development activity was restricted to the relatively small area of about one square kilometer. Together with the Old City, which is less than one square kilometer, and the extension to the south (Abu Tor to Silwan), the continuously built-up area did not exceed three square kilometers. The jurisdiction of the Arab Municipality, however, extended to an area of six square kilometers. This meant that only half of the Jerusalem municipal area was built up. There were a number of reasons for this. First was the Municipality's strict adherence to the city's Master Plan, as laid down during the Mandate (the Holliday-Kendall Plan), which banned any building on the western slopes of Mount Scopus and the Mount of Olives and left the Kidron Valley slopes as open space. Pressure to permit building in these areas was great, but was blocked by the counter-pressure of the churches and other Christian bodies, and by the fact that Kendall, the principal planner of Mandatory Jerusalem, continued to serve as the head of the municipal planning panel.

The extensive areas to the north of Sheikh Jarah were not developed either; but here the reason was entirely different. These were unparcelled plots of land, owned in common by dozens of people. Despite repeated demands by the Municipality, the Government was in no hurry to carry out "land settlement" in this area. The few land-settlement teams were kept busy in northern Jordan and the north of the West Bank, reaching Jerusalem only in the mid-1960s. As building on non-apportioned land is legally prohibited, these areas, including some of the best building land in Jerusalem, were not touched. The Government's tardiness in carrying out parcellation led to accusations that it was deliberately delaying the operation in order to hinder the city's development. Some alleged that regulations were not being implemented because there was extensive Jewish-owned land in these areas, and the Government feared that permitting construction on them would endanger the restoration of Arab property left in Israel.

A third reason limiting the built-up area was the extensive purchase of land by Christian groups, which led to pressure for the enactment of a special law forbidding the purchase of land in Jerusalem by Christian organizations.

As a result of the shortage of building land within the city, many people began to build houses outside the municipal boundaries, to the north and east. The new neighborhoods were within the domains of small rural councils, which had no modern planning procedures. As a result, "ribbon development" suburbs appeared along the Ramallah road, without any development in depth or any rational possibility of extending municipal services. In fact, the Arab Municipality of Jerusalem was not interested in incorporating these areas within its municipal boundaries, since this would have changed the disposition of political forces in the city, endangering the hegemony of the dominant Jerusalem-Hebron coalition. As a result, it was precisely the wealthy people, who could afford to purchase land in the suburbs and build luxurious villas, who were released from the obligation of paying Jerusalem municipal taxes.

The failure to extend the municipal boundaries created severe planning problems. In an attempt to solve them, an area of 12 square kilometers (double the municipal area) was proclaimed a "planning zone" for the city. However, this solution was ineffective, as expansion continued beyond this limit. In 1964, it was recommended that Jerusalem's urban planning zone be extended to an area of 75 square kilometers, bounded by the Qalandia airfield in the north and the Bethlehem municipal boundary in the south. But by the time of the Six Day War this recommendation had not yet been implemented.

During the 1950s, the population of East Jerusalem increased by 15,000, bringing the total number to over 60,000. This growth of approximately 3% per annum was the result of four trends: net natural increase, migration into the city, migration from the city to the suburbs and emigration to the East Bank and overseas. It is estimated that the rate of emigration from the West Bank was about half the rate of natural increase. Only a few individuals from the leading families remained. Less than one-tenth of the al-Husayni family and no more than a quarter of the Nashashibis stayed in the city, and a large proportion of the other leading families left. The Dajani family was the only one to make great efforts to reduce emigration, and most of its members remained in the city. On the eve of the Six Day War, a third of the families in Arab Jerusalem had at least one member living outside the borders of Palestine, apart from the many families which had left the city entirely.

These extreme fluctuations in population brought about far-reaching changes in the city's social structure. The absolute rule of the leading families crumbled away, together with the economic and religious power that had been concentrated in their hands. In general, the old hierarchical social stratification was undermined and social mobility was created. Family connections ceased to be identical with economic status, education, or political power. Members of common families and rural immigrants accumulated great wealth, which also gave them political influence. Education spread, even among families which had been illiterate. Above all, a new political elite was formed and enjoyed the favor of the Hashemite regime.

Because of the severe conflict between Husaynis and Hashemites, and because of the contempt the prominent families exhibited for the Bedouin regime, the Jordanians sought support among the non-Jerusalemite families. They cultivated the men of Hebron and Nablus, and it is no mere coincidence that out of eight governors of the Jerusalem region, only one, Anwar Nusaybah, was a Jerusalemite, while five came from Nablus. Hebronites dominated the *shari'a* courts and the local *waqf* department, supplied the heads of the Chamber of Commerce, and constituted one third of the members of the City Council.

Despite their eclipse, the distinguished Jerusalem families did not lose their pride. To be *walad al-balad* (Jerusalem-born), was still a sign of distinction, as opposed to the *Khalaylah* (Hebronites). Even if a Hebronite had resided in Jerusalem for three generations and had accumulated great wealth, he was still considered a *Khalili* by the people of Jerusalem. The exclusive Lion's and Rotary clubs had very few Hebronite members. And while the frugal Hebronites sent their sons to public schools, which were tuition free, the Jerusalem families sent their children to the exclusive Christian schools.

The tension between the population and the authorities, which remained high until 1957, slackened during the last decade of Jordanian rule. But while most Jerusalemites bowed to the inevitable, they maintained their distance from senior Jordanian officials and officers, whom they considered ignorant Bedouin. The prominent Jerusalem families did not encourage their sons to serve as government officials, preferring them to go overseas and study for the liberal professions.

Despite the increase in social mobility, Arab society was still based on clearly defined, hard-and-fast stratification and on privileges for the upper classes. The lower classes accepted this situation without query and did not regard favoritism or privilege for the leading families as unjust. Nepotism and the acceptance of benefits — financial or otherwise — in exchange for services rendered, were not considered immoral or improper. Each family or group boasted a member who had good connections with the authorities and was able to "arrange matters." The key word in this system was the *wasta*, or intervention with the authorities, and there was a clearly defined hierarchy of *wasta*. Some people could arrange matters on a low level, but in order to reach the higher echelons it was necessary to apply to a go-between of a different rank. Election campaigns to the City Council, and even more so to Parliament, were aimed, not so much at achieving political influence, as at achieving a convenient position to exercise *wasta*. The Jordanian Parliament was an institution of very limited political influence, but its members enjoyed distinguished personal status.

As an outcome of this kind of relationship, official interference was only felt among the lower classes and it was only against them that laws were enforced. The privileged classes enjoyed nearly total freedom of action, as there was almost no financial or legal matter that could not be "arranged." Naturally, the authorities exploited the system for their own needs too, making those they favored almost completely dependent upon them. The ever-present scrutiny of the security police, and its power to imprison people without trial, offered opportunities not only for destroying political opponents, but also for settling personal or financial scores. Yet, the atmosphere was not that of a "police state" and the inhabitants did not fear that the authorities would act arbitrarily since the "rules of the game" were known to all and anyone willing to keep to them knew what price he had to pay to achieve his aims. Only those groups or individuals who waged an ideological struggle against the regime — whether they were communist or pan-Arab nationalists — were exposed to the heavy hand of the security police, liable to detention without trial, torture, economic reprisals, or deportation.

Most of the population grew accustomed to the regime and its system, and some even found the way to prosper. Large-scale migration to the East Bank, primarily to Amman, progressively blurred the distinction between the two banks. Matters went so far that the Jerusalemite felt himself closer to happenings in Amman, where many of his relatives were living, than to what was going on in Nablus or Hebron, which were, in theory, parts of his own homeland. The prominent families, especially those favored by the authorities, identified with the Hashemite regime and were interested in its progress and welfare. From this point of view, the regime achieved its aims. Talk of the "artificial" nature of the Hashemite Kingdom, or of the Jordanian "conquest", did not reflect the feelings of a majority of the Kingdom's subjects.

The population continued to clash with the authorities on one overriding issue, however: its attitude to Israel. The vast majority of the population was far more extreme than the Government with regard to Israel. They grumbled over the fact that the Government crushed with severity any attempt to infiltrate into Israel, that it forbade any organization of *fedayeen* (or guerrillas) on Jordanian soil, and that it refrained from arming the border villages. After each Israeli reprisal action, there would be demonstrations calling for the arming of the populace. Sometimes, the army fired upon the demonstrators and some were killed or wounded. But while trying to maintain law and order in the city and prevent provocation of the Israelis, in fear of murderous reprisal raids, the Hashemite regime fostered hatred of Israel through its system of public education.

The 1948 War had engendered a severe crisis in the Arab educational system. As a result of the war, all schools were closed and they only reopened in 1951. By 1957, however, a highly developed network of primary schools ensured six years of free education to all. Less than half of the graduates of primary schools went on to higher education, including governmental secondary schools, and the Government's educational network catered to less than half the pupils in the city. Most of the non-government schools were maintained by various Christian bodies, although there were also some private schools as well as schools for the children of refugees, maintained by UNRWA.

The standard of the government schools was lower than that of the private schools and, as a result of the great differences in standards and curriculum, two different levels of education were created in the city. The Government approved the existence of a network of private schools, thus reducing the burden of its outlay on education; but it tried on a number of occasions to interfere with the curriculum of the Christian schools and to impose a uniform government curriculum. These attempts bore fruit only in the year before the 1967 War, and the outbreak of fighting halted the experiment before it could be determined how the standard of studies in the Christian schools had been affected.

On the eve of the Six Day War, the percentage of the population that had completed at least primary education reached 68%, of whom 20% had also attended secondary school. The proportion of those lacking any schooling whatsoever (one-third of the population) was high mainly because nearly half the women had not been to school. Nonetheless, these figures represent an educational level which was high in comparison with the West Bank as a whole. Jerusalem also contained a relatively high number of people who had received a higher education.

The Jordanian curriculum was distinguished by its extreme nationalistic educational tendencies. Over 50% of the history lessons were devoted to Arab and Jordanian history. Great emphasis was placed on the study of modern Arab literature and poetry, with its strong nationalist motifs. Three lessons a week were devoted to religious instruction. The history of the Jewish people, its culture and tradition, or the Old Testament, were not studied at all. But while the Jewish school curriculum practically ignored the Arab people and its history, the Jordanian equivalent taught its pupils to hate the Jewish people. The study of Zionism was a special subject, and a weekly lesson was devoted to it in the senior class of secondary school. The textbook on this subject, written by the Jordanian Minister of Education, Zuqan al-Handawi, is not only anti-Israeli within the context of the Arab-Jewish conflict, but contains clearly anti-Semitic elements as well. For example, it states that

51

*the Zionist Congress in 1897 approved a complete plan with re-
gard to the aims and methods of the Zionist movement, and most
of the details of this plan are in fact mentioned in the 'Protocols of the Elders of Zion,' approved by said Congress's Supreme
Committee in secret session.*

In another place the book claims to quote David Ben-Gurion as
saying at the time of the declaration of the State of Israel: "This is
not the end of our struggle, but only the beginning. We must continue until we realize the existence of the state we have fought for,
from the Nile to the Euphrates."

The textbooks quote extensively from the anti-Semitic classic,
"Protocols of the Elders of Zion," which describes the Jewish plan
for world domination. They cite statistics to show how Jews dominate "nine out of ten stock exchanges" and control all means of mass
communication: "The French Jew, Marcel Buzaque, is granted a
monopoly on the export of racehorses to the entire world and can
control dozens of French politicians and direct them as he wills."
They state that the Jews are a nation of spies, nurtured on the
Biblical story of the 12 spies that Moses sent "to spy out the land;"
that the Jews are depraved and are responsible for the spread of
cheating, hypocrisy, prostitution, and licentiousness throughout the
world — "The proof is that Jews run most of the dance halls in the
whole world" — that the Jews created the State of Israel and want to
expand in order "to enable it to rule the world." The books end with
the warning that "a considerable part of the recommendations of the
Elders of Zion have, indeed, been implemented. But the remnant is
more important; therefore beware! Awaken, O Arabs! "

The question remains whether such incitement was at all necessary
since the population's clashes with the Hashemite regime, over its
policy towards Israel, were symptomatic of the fact that the city's
partition was not accepted by its Arab inhabitants as a *fait accompli.*
Despite the mass flight of the 1948 refugees, there were still thousands of people in the city with houses in western Jerusalem, and
they did not forget their homes. It is characteristic that many, who
fled without being able to take their movable possessions, had carefully preserved their *tabu* (title deed) certificates, as well as the keys
to their houses. Over the years, the bounds of reality and fancy grew
blurred, so that even the poorest of the refugees spoke of the houses
and the extensive stretches of land they had left behind.

The Mayor of Jerusalem, Rauhi al-Khatib, expressed his view of the division of the city on a number of occasions. In 1965, in a speech to Western visitors, he said: "Historic Jerusalem suffers from a catastrophic partition of a nature more sombre and more drastic than the division of Berlin or any other city." He concluded a review of the Municipality's activities since 1949 by stating: " . . . It is natural that our most important aims are that rights be restored to their owners and the two sections of the city be reunified."

The truth of the matter is that it was the Christian community of Jerusalem that had suffered most from the city's partition, since the Arab quarters in the part of the city captured by Israel had been inhabited mostly by Christian Arabs. At the end of the Mandate, the Christian community in Jerusalem had reached its numerical peak of 31,000 and was at the height of its economic and political power. As a result of the war, however, the Christian population of the city decreased by over 40%. Some of the refugees from the quarters in the Israeli-held city found shelter in the Old City, the Sheikh Jarah quarter or the American Colony; others moved to Christian towns in the vicinity of Jerusalem, such as Bethlehem and Ramallah; the rest emigrated from the country. Statistical data concerning the emigration of Christians from Jerusalem following the 1948 War are no more than rough estimates, but testimony to the relatively high number of Christian refugees can be found in the population census which Israel conducted in September 1967. This census showed that the proportion of refugees was higher among the Christians (37% of all Christians) than among the Muslims (15.6% of all Muslims).

The large number of Christian refugees aroused international Christian bodies to extensive welfare activity. In 1949, the Vatican established a Pontifical Legation in Jerusalem, and placed ample funds at its disposal. The decrease in the number of Christian inhabitants of Jerusalem had also aroused the Vatican to vigorous political activity in favor of internationalizing the city (see Chapter 1), in the belief that Vatican influence in an international city could create conditions that would allow the Christians to prosper, as they had during the Mandate. But efforts by Christian organizations to stop the flow of emigration were not successful. A population census conducted in 1961 found 10,982 Christians in the city — 62% less than in 1948.

The city's division left almost the whole of the Christian community, with most of its holy sites, under Jordanian rule. Only a few hundred Christians, mainly monks and non-Arab citizens, were left in the western city. Thus, after an interval of 30 years, the Christians again found themselves under the rule of a Muslim state. The Ottoman regulations insuring the autonomy of religious institutions, personal jurisdiction and internal communal organization had remained in force during the Mandate. The Jordanian authorities inherited this system and made few changes in it.

The Christian communities watched the creation of the Jordanian regime suspiciously, not so much out of fear of the abolition of their religious autonomy, as out of anxiety about their fate under the rule of a state with a profound attachment to Islam. The Jordanian Constitution, adopted in 1952, declared Islam to be the religion of both the State and the King. At the same time, however, the Constitution recognized the rights of the Christians to maintain an independent educational system, as well as religious courts whose competence was under government supervision, equal to those of the Shari'a courts. In many other matters, however, there was distinct discrimination against the Christian communities. For example, Christian festivals — unlike the Muslim ones — were not considered official holidays, and Christian employees were obliged to refrain from work on Friday, the official day of rest, but they were only allowed to absent themselves from work until 10 o'clock on Sundays.

Far more serious, however, were the laws enacted to restrict Christian activity in three spheres: the purchase of property, freedom of action for Christian charitable organizations, and the organization of communal education.

The first of these was a law enacted as far back as 1953, restricting the purchase of property by "religious and charitable organizations, which constitute branches of a foreign religious body," in other words, Christian bodies. These institutions had to obtain the Government's approval for every piece of property acquired, and they were specifically forbidden to acquire property in the vicinity of Holy Places without government approval. Publication of the law aroused great anger among the Christian organizations, but it was not altered. On the contrary, in 1965 it was made even stricter with regard to Jerusalem, where churches were forbidden to buy land within the Old City walls or to acquire possession of it in any way. Despite the strict application of this law, the churches found a way to bypass it by buying land through Muslim intermediaries. In 1949, the Christian churches possessed 91 commercial plots in East Jerusalem; in 1969, no less than 392 sites were in their possession.

In 1953, another law was enacted imposing strict controls on the activities of Christian charitable organizations. This statute imposed restrictions and proscriptions on the use of the funds of Christian organizations. It kept control of their organizers, their members, and those benefitting from their money. As in the case of the restrictions on buying land, these controls reflected the regime's fear that foreign interests would gain control of Arab land, especially in Jerusalem, as well as the fear that they would expand their influence on the population.

The conflict between the legitimate aspirations of a national state, with strong Muslim attachments, and the legitimate aspirations of the Christian community to maintain its own character, resulted in a severe confrontation on the question of education. The highly developed and progressive Christian educational system continued to operate according to the curriculum in force during the Mandate, whereby the language of instruction was English in the Anglican schools, German in the Lutheran schools, and French in the Catholic schools. Textbooks were European, and the pupils were prepared for European matriculation examinations. As these were missionary schools, Christian religious instruction was also given. If these schools had been restricted to the Christian communities alone — in the same way that the Armenian community had its own schools — the problem would not have been so acute. However, the Christian schools attracted the cream of the Muslim pupils, mostly the children of the rich and educated Muslims. Therefore, it was natural that the Jordanian Government should try to change the curriculum, with the aim of inculcating the pupils with Arab cultural and national values. The problem was not restricted to Jordan alone, but existed in all the Arab States, which, on one level or another, intervened in the establishment of the curriculum of their Christian schools.

In 1955 the Education Law was enacted, laying down that textbooks would be supplied by the Ministry of Education; that Christian schools would teach Arabic, history, geography and Arab national consciousness according to the government curriculum; that the examinations in these subjects would be in Arabic; that it was forbidden to give religious instruction to a pupil not of that religion; and that schools would close on official (Muslim) holidays. The Christian communities could not accept the law's provisions, since changing the language of instruction and their textbooks altered the purpose of the schools, which was aimed at European matriculation examinations. In addition, banning Christian instruction of the Muslim pupils contradicted the *raison d'être* of these schools, which were basically missionary institutions. There were also practical reasons for their opposition, the main one being the wide disparity in the standards between the state schools and the Christian schools. Imposing government textbooks would considerably lower the level of studies, which were based on European textbooks of a superior standard.

Faced with the general opposition of the Christian communities, which was accompanied by political pressure from Catholic bodies, King Husayn, whose throne was insecure at the time, retreated and ordered that the law be frozen. Only ten years later did the Government set about imposing it. During the 1966 academic year, far-reaching changes were made in the Christian educational system, even though the Catholic schools stood firm in their refusal to implement the alterations. However, before the results of the law's implementation could be felt, the Six Day War broke out, and the Christian schools faced a new situation.

The consolidation of a sovereign Arab national entity also accelerated and sharpened an internal crisis within the Christian communities, namely the confrontation between the ecclesiastical hierarchies and the lay congregation of believers. The clash grew out of the fact that in the principal churches, the upper echelons of the hierarchy were non-Arab and alien, while the overwhelming majority of their congregants were Arabs. The concentration of all religious and secular power in the hands of an established ecclesiastical body, most or all of whose members were not local people, while the Arab congregation had no possibility of influencing its activities, caused severe conflicts.

The severity of the inner rift varied from church to church. In the Unitarian churches, such as the Greek Catholic, it did not exist at all, since the whole community, congregation and hierarchy alike, is Arab. Nor did it exist in the Armenian Church, which is not Arab at all. In the Catholic Church it was not severe, because canonical law does not recognize any lay organization of members of the congregation or lay participation in the management of the church, and because of the sensible policy of the Latin Patriarchate, which placed Arab priests on all rungs of the hierarchy. It was in the largest community — the Greek Orthodox — that the confrontation found its severest and most extreme expression. In this venerable church, all spiritual authority, material power, and jurisdiction are concentrated in the hands of a small group of priests of Greek origin, while thousands of Arab members of the congregation are deprived of any influence on the affairs of their community.

The Greek Orthodox community is run by an order of monks known as The Brotherhood of the Holy Sepulcher. Only the members of this Brotherhood may be appointed to senior posts as priests: The Synod (the supreme administrative body of the church, which is responsible for Patriarchate property and the election of the Patriarch) is selected from its members, and only members of the Brotherhood are appointed judges in the community's ecclesiastical courts. The struggle between the Greek Brotherhood and the Arab congregation has been raging fiercely for a hundred years. During the British Mandate, the authorities tried to mediate in the dispute, but without success.

At the beginning of Jordanian rule, the lay members of the congregation thought that the opportune moment had arrived to settle the prolonged conflict with the Brotherhood: After all, they were now living under the rule of an Arab national regime, which must surely exhibit sympathy towards a struggle for the Arabization of the congregation. However, their hopes were dashed. The Brotherhood, which had throughout its long history accommodated both Christian and Muslim rulers, found a way to get along with the new Arab regime, and only two minor changes were effected. The judges in the church courts saw to it that proceedings and verdicts, hitherto published only in Greek, were translated into Arabic and all members of the Brotherhood took Jordanian citizenship. Because of the Jordanian regime's fear of arousing unfavorable reaction in the Christian world should it interfere directly in church affairs and the close personal relationship between King Husayn and the Greek Patriarch, that was all that the Arab members of the congregation got out of Jordan's Hashemite regime.

There was similar tension in the Anglican Church; but in 1957 the

Church hierarchy was reorganized and an Arab bishop was appointed over a diocese including Jordan, Lebanon, and Syria. The lay congregation was fully integrated into the administration of all the community's affairs and property, as well as its courts. By the time of the Six Day War, this small but important church had achieved a model solution of its internal tensions.

Relationships between the Jordanian Government and the Christian community were correct, on the whole. The Christian minority was loyal to the regime, and the Government rewarded it with a tolerant and sympathetic attitude. Every Jordanian Government included at least one Christian Minister — some Governments even as many as three. But for the most part, such representation was no more than tokenism. Because of the ramified Christian educational system, the Christians generally reached a higher lever of education than the Muslims and were, on average, economically better off than the Muslims. As a result, the Christians filled government and municipal posts to an extent exceeding their percentage in the population. But they did not reach the Kingdom's decisive positions of power. Christian members of the Government never held important portfolios, nor were the Christians appointed to posts as district commissioners and ambassadors, or to senior command positions in the army or police. A Christian had to be far better than his Muslim rival in order to gain a post for which the two were competing, and this hidden discrimination engendered feelings of frustration and bitterness.

On the other hand, their status as a minority community forced the Christians into adopting more extremist attitudes than their Muslim compatriots in order to prove their loyalty. This posture found its expression both in their anti-Israel attitude and in their opposition, as Palestinians, to the Hashemite regime. The political activities of the Christians (with the exception of the foreign religious establishment) indicates that, despite their position as a religious minority suffering from hidden discrimination, they identified with Arab national trends and regarded themselves as an integral part of the Arab nation. As a result, there is little significance in distinctions between Muslims and Christians with relation to political questions, whether internal or external.

In 1967, there were 11,000 Christians living in Jerusalem, the same number as in 1961. Taking into account natural increase, this figure means that at least 2,500 left the city between 1961 and 1967. Some moved to the smaller Christian towns within the city's metropolitan bounds, such as Bethlehem and Ramallah; others to the northern suburbs outside the city; still others migrated to Amman and overseas.

In face of all the political and social undercurrents of conflict in Arab Jerusalem, it was imperative that stability be achieved in order for the city's economy to function, since the economic structure of Arab Jerusalem focused on one single activity: tourism. About one-quarter of all employees were directly engaged in this branch of the economy and approximately the same number worked in branches allied to tourism, such as taxis and restaurants. In 1966, some 600,000 tourists visited the city, about 175,000 from Western Countries, and the rest from Arab or other Muslim countries. Around 85% of the West Bank's total income from tourism came from Jerusalem.

The development of tourism was reflected in the extensive construction of hotels. From the one 30-room hotel in East Jerusalem in 1948, the number had increased to 70 hotels, with 2,350 rooms, by 1966. Jerusalem's airport was extended and opened to international traffic in 1965 and, in 1966, 100,000 passengers passed through it. This impressive expansion was accompanied by a small development of industry and crafts, but the city had no industry worthy of the name. Only two concerns employed more than 50 workers (the average workshop employed five workers). Such industry as there was, concentrated on the food, wood, and leather branches and, of course, on the production of souvenirs. Economically, therefore, the city relied almost completely on tourism, whose sensitivity to political and military tensions placed the economy on a very narrow base. Any tension that brought a reduction in the stream of tourists could cause an economic crisis.

The precarious structure of the city's economy was no accident; it was planned by the Jordanian regime. The Government discriminated against enterprises planning to erect factories in the city and its environs and pressed for them to be set up in Amman. A large number of Jerusalem entrepreneurs could not get development loans when they asked for help in establishing concerns in the city, but exceptionally good terms were offered if they would set up the same concerns on the East Bank. Only tourism was fostered by the authorities because it simply could not develop in Amman. The govern-

59

ment-imposed economic policy of "all the eggs in one basket" caused crises and fluctuations, and the 1967 War brought about, at least initially, a severe economic crisis.

Unlike Jewish Jerusalem, which was cut off from its hinterland after 1948, Arab Jerusalem maintained links with the surrounding area, so that in this respect it suffered less from the 1948 War. Together with its suburbs, the city maintained its position as the largest town on the West Bank, and its district included some one-half of the West Bank's inhabitants. Although the Jordanian Government deliberately abolished Jerusalem's status as an administrative center, a number of government institutions were nevertheless concentrated there, together with religious institutions, courts and broadcasting services supplying services to the entire West Bank. There were also nine banks in the city. Although these were only branches of banks whose centers were in Amman, they were the principal branches on the West Bank. On the eve of the Six Day War, 50% of the loans given in the whole of the West Bank were concentrated in these banks, as were 40% of the total deposits. Likewise, wholesalers and importers, most of whom were centered in Jerusalem on the eve of the 1948 War, had moved their head offices to Amman under pressure from the authorities, but they continued to maintain large branches in Jerusalem, which served the whole West Bank. The city also functioned as the medical center of the entire West Bank, supporting ten hospitals with 550 beds.

Jerusalem's economy was massively supported by outside help. Some 12,000 people received assistance from the United Nations Relief and Works Administration (UNRWA), since they had the status of refugees. Some 28% of East Jerusalem's families received support from relatives working abroad. Only 22% of the population were included in the labor force (as against 37% in the west). This low percentage stemmed partially from the fact that most Arab women never worked outside their own households, thus, only 9% of the women of East Jerusalem were in the labor force. On the eve of the 1967 War, the unemployment rate stood at 8%, where it had been steady since 1961.

The enormous differences between the Jewish and Arab cities in way of life, standard of living, residential conditions, and consumption, is vividly illustrated in the following figures. The average number of persons per room was 2.4 in eastern Jerusalem, as against

60

1.6 in the west. Over 59% of the apartments in the east had no water faucet and some 30% had no electricity, while in the west, all apartments had electricity. Only 22% of the Arab families possessed refrigerators, as against 77% of the Jewish households. The number of Arab families owning a car was half that of the Jewish families. In 1965, the average Jewish family paid 30.6% of its expenditure for food and drink, as against 50.4% spent by an Arab family the same year. The Jewish family spent a smaller proportion on clothing; far more on furniture, and more on rent and entertainment.

The large differences in expenditure on food and on consumer hardware are well-tested indicators of large differences in standards of living. Indeed, the average annual income per head in Jewish Jerusalem is estimated to have been four times as high as in the east that year. A comparison of wage levels in identical professions indicates the egalitarian tendencies in Israel, as opposed to the extreme inequality in Jordan. The ratio between the lowest wage-earner and someone at the top of the ladder, was 1:11 in Arab Jerusalem, compared with 1:3 in Israel. The difference between Arab and Jewish wage scales was enormous on the lower rungs, gradually shrinking as one went up the wage scale. At the top, the salaries of engineers, lawyers and senior doctors equalled out, and sometimes pay in eastern Jerusalem was higher than in the west.

The fundamental differences in the tax system of the two countries further increased equality of available income among employees in Israel, in comparison with their Jordanian colleagues. In East Jerusalem, income tax was proportional, at a more or less fixed rate, so that it had no influence on the wage differentials. On the other hand, Israel's progressive income tax and the structure of the cost of living index, effected a further reduction of the gap in incomes, making the scale even more egalitarian.

However, the gap in the standard of living of people working in identical professions in Israel and Jordan was significantly moderated by the great difference in price levels existing in the two parts of the city. The Israeli paid almost three times as much for meat as the Jordanian. The cost of rice was 93% higher in Israel than in Jordan, and in other commodities too, Israeli prices were far higher. It is true that certain items, such as kerosene, edible oil, and flour were cheaper in Israel; but on the whole, the Israeli paid 40—50% more than the Jordanian. In addition, low tariffs caused the markets of the

Arab city to be flooded with consumer products from all over the world at relatively low prices. In Israel, where there is a high tariff on these goods to protect local producers, most consumer articles were locally produced. Foreign, imported food and clothing products were sold in the Old City at less than a quarter of their price in Israel. The price of cars in Israel was double that in Jordan, and electrical products were 50% more expensive in Israel than in Jordan. This gap in the prices of consumer goods was not lost on the inhabitants of Israeli Jerusalem when the city was united and they immediately took advantage of their new-found access to Arab stores and market stalls.

CHAPTER FIVE

THE PROBLEM OF THE HOLY PLACES

Undoubtedly one of the most sensitive problems Jerusalem has faced in the past, faces today and will continue to face in the future, is that of the Holy Places. Just as the sites holy to the world's major religions are inseparable from Jerusalem itself, so the problems they have engendered over the years are as integral to the city's history and future as spires and minarets are to its landscape.

Tens of sites in the city and its environs are considered sacred by Jews, Muslims and Christians. The most important of these are the Western Wall, the mosques of the Temple Mount, and the Church of the Holy Sepulcher.

A survey conducted by the United Nations in November 1949 found thirty Holy Places in Jerusalem; 15 holy to Christians, 11 to Jews and 4 to Muslims. This survey, however, was arbitrary and incomplete since the Jews point to 50 synagogues in the Jewish Quarter of the Old City alone, the Muslims to tens of mosques and the Christians to a similar number of churches. But, in general, the problem of the Holy Places is not one of number or of their division. It is, instead, the dispute over their ownership which was created on the interreligious, interdenominational and international plane.

During the period of Ottoman rule, no problem concerning the Muslim Holy Places existed. The British, similarly, promised in the Mandate for Palestine that "nothing in this mandate shall be construed as conferring upon the Mandatory authority to interfere with the fabric or the management of purely Muslim sacred shrines, the immunities of which are guaranteed," and they acted accordingly.

Thus the problem was narrowed to the Christian Holy Places and the Western Wall, which the British considered sacred to both Jews and Muslims.

With the reunification of Jerusalem, the problem of the Muslim Holy Places came to the forefront, as we shall see, and the problem continues to be a vexing one. In this chapter, however, only the Christian and Jewish Holy Places will be dealt with, since they were the ones which were problematical before 1967.

The Jewish Holy Places

All Israel believes, with perfect faith, that the place of the Temple and the whole of the Temple Mount is the holy and eternal place of Israel, and even if it remains in the hands of others for many days and long years, ultimately it will come into our hands. . . . If we do not enter the Temple Mount, beyond the Western Wall, it is not because we lack rights or a link to this Holy Place, but because of our great link to it . . . for even now it is full of the honor of the Lord God of Israel and His Sanctity, and we do not now have the religious means by which we can purify ourselves in order to stand in this holy place. . . . The Western Wall especially, has survived as a sign and as a token of our redemption and of the certainty of our return to the sacred standing . . . and we feel in this place a very holy and inspiring sensation. All the air above the Wall, up to heaven, is considered by us to be exalted and holy, and our right that we be not deprived of this place, will stand to all eternity. . . . We have no interest in the stones or from which period they date. For us, the main thing is the place and the holy air above it, up to the heights of heaven . . .

In these sentences, the late Chief Rabbi of Palestine, Abraham Yitzhak Hacohen Kook, explained the significance of the Western Wall to the British Military Governor of Jerusalem in 1920.

Throughout the years of the British Mandate, the Western Wall — the remnant of the Temple compound and the most sacred place on earth for the people of Israel — was the place where the Jewish-Arab conflict found its sharpest expression. As long as the Arab nationalist movement was dormant, the Wall was a place where Jews prayed without hindrance. But from the time that the Grand Mufti, Haj Amin al-Husayni, gained control of the Muslim community, the Wall became a means of incitement and political struggle against the Jews.

64

The Arabs tried their best to disrupt prayers at the Wall, to prevent access to it, and even to besmirch it.

The Mufti incited the Arabs by insisting that the prayers of the Jews by the Wall were simply a preface to their attempt to gain control over the Temple Mount and to rebuild the Temple. As one of his papers stated in 1925:

> The Jews' crying at and kissing the Wall does not stem from their love for the Wall itself, but from their heartfelt aspiration to gain control over Haram al-Sharif (the Temple Mount), as is well-known to all.

The Mufti made life difficult for the Jews by demanding that the British authorities preserve the *status quo* in the area in front of the Wall, in other words that Jews be allowed only whatever they were permitted, formally and in writing, during the Ottoman period, which ended in 1917. The Jews, who had in the course of the years managed to gain more rights than those granted in writing by the Ottomans, demanded that these accumulated rights be recognized. The Mandatory Government supported the Arab stand, both because the Mandate obliged it to adhere to the situation that reigned before the First World War in all matters connected with the Holy Places and because it wanted to appease the Mufti.

At the time, the only approach to the Western Wall was along a narrow alleyway, that extended 32 yards in front of the Wall, and was less than four yards wide, a total area of 120 square meters (about 1,290 sq. ft.). Both this alley and the one leading to it were squeezed between the Western Wall to the east, the wall of the courtyard of the old *shari'a* court to the north, and the Mugrabi Quarter to the south and west. (This Quarter, part of which was erected in 1320, was built to serve the needs of North African pilgrims.) The Muslims claimed ownership of both the Western Wall, on the grounds that it was part of the wall of the Temple Mount, "which belongs to the *waqf* of Haram al-Sharif," and the approaches to it, which were a *waqf* consecrated in 1193 by al-Afdal, the son of Saladin.

Muslim ownership of the approaches, undisputed by the Jews, gave the former the chance to complain to the authorities whenever Jews acted in a manner that could be interpreted as suggesting common-law rights to the place. This included the placing of benches, chairs, and a screen in the alleyway and the repairing of its

65

stone paving. To solve the problem the Jews tried to acquire the approaches, as well as the whole Mugrabi Quarter, a number of times, but without success. The last attempt was made in 1919.

In the second half of the 1920s, the Muslims began to claim that it was not only forbidden to place benches and barriers in the alleyway, but even to bring Torah scrolls to the Wall or to hold prayers in public. They demanded that the Mandatory Government judge the issue. When the Government delayed its decision, the Mufti began a series of provocations. The *muazzin* in the nearby mosque would begin his call to prayer precisely at the time of the Jewish prayers. A *Zawiyah* — Muslim place of prayer — was erected nearby and noisy religious ceremonies, accompanied by drumbeats called "Zikr," began to be held there. In addition, the northern wall of the street was opened, providing an approach to the Mugrabi Gate, so that the Wall approaches, which had previously been a dead-end, now became a thoroughfare from the Mugrabi Quarter to the Temple Mount. The Muslims would deliberately lead animals through the alley during the prayers, smoke cigarettes on the Sabbath, and even pour the Quarter's sewage into the alleyway. The Jews, naturally, reacted sharply to these acts.

The rise in tension was the immediate cause of the outbreak of anti-Jewish riots in 1929, during which the Jewish community in Hebron was destroyed and dozens of people were killed or wounded in other places. A Royal Commission established to investigate the causes of the conflict (the Shaw Commission) reached interim conclusions accepting most of the Muslim demands but recommended that a final verdict be given by a committee appointed by the League of Nations according to Paragraph 14 of the Mandate. The League of Nations refused to appoint a commission because of Paragraph 14's connection with the problem of the Christian Holy Places, but it agreed to appoint an *Ad Hoc* International Committee to propose "a final solution of the question of the rights and demands of Jews and Muslims in connection with the Western Wall." Representatives of both sides appeared before the Committee. The Muslims repeated their demands that the Jews be permitted no more than "the right to make a simple visit at the Western Wall," in other words, not to pray in public and, of course, not to bring ritual articles or benches to the Wall. The Jews demanded that they be "permitted to continue their prayers in conditions of decency and decorum without prejudicing the religious rights of others." They also proposed that the Committee

> *approve the plan presented to the Mandatory Government . . . by which appropriate arrangements are to be made for the Mugrabi Quarter to be cleared, and for the Mugrabi* waqf *to receive, in its place, certain new houses, to be built in a suitable place in Jerusalem.*

The Committee duly presented its findings and these became part of Palestinian law by their publication in 1931 as an "Order in Council." According to the Order, the Jews had the right of free entry at all times for the purpose of prayer and were also permitted to bring ritual articles — whose number and size were laid down precisely. To cite two examples, the portable Holy Ark had to be 40 inches high, 20 inches wide, and 12 inches deep; the stand for the Eternal Lamp was permitted to reach a height of 32 inches, a width of 47 inches, and a depth of 27 inches. On the eve of every festival the British District Commissioner would insure the conformity of the ritual objects to their approved dimensions and then stamp them with his seal. It was forbidden to attach the ritual articles to the Wall or to the walls of the houses of the Mugrabi Quarter. The reading of the *Torah* was permitted on official Jewish holidays, but not on the Sabbath. It was forbidden to bring chairs, benches, or barriers; to blow the *shofar* (ceremonial ram's horn); or to sing songs. The Jews were instructed to assemble at the Wall in a manner that did not block the alleyway to inhabitants of the Mugrabi Quarter. The Muslims were forbidden to lead animals through the alley at certain hours or to hold the "Zikr" ceremony near it in such a fashion as to disturb the prayers of the Jews.

The Jews were forced to adapt to these humiliating conditions of prayer right up to the end of the British Mandate. During the High Holidays, when Jews are at prayer all day, old men were forced to stand on their feet because of the ban on chairs and benches. On the Sabbath, Jews would recite the early morning prayer, at the Wall, then go and read the *Torah* in the synagogues in the Jewish Quarter, and finally return to the Wall to complete the service. The *Mussaf* ("additional") prayer could not be said at the Wall on the Jewish New Year because of the ban on blowing the *shofar*. Especially irritating and humiliating was the ban on blowing the *shofar* at the end of the fast of *Yom Kippur* (the Day of Atonement), a vital part of the ceremonies. For all that, the Arab inhabitants continued to pester the worshippers by their loud prayers at the *Zawiyah*, by the *muazzin's* calls during prayers, by dirtying the Wall's approaches with sewage water, and by throwing stones.

The Jewish community took a line of self-restraint and conciliation throughout the years; but some Jews, mainly members of the right-wing youth movement, Betar, refused to tolerate such humiliating conditions and clashed with the authorities. Tension would reach a peak on the eve of the Ninth of Av, the anniversary of the destruction of the First and Second Temples, and during the closing prayers of Yom Kippur. On the eve of the Ninth of Av, thousands of worshippers would come to the Wall to utter the lamentations; thousands of non-religious people came too, setting off to march round the walls of Jerusalem. At the close of Yom Kippur, young Jews would blow the *shofar* and sing *Hatikva*, the Jewish National Anthem. All these actions were forbidden by the regulations.

On Saturday, November 29, 1947, the day the United Nations adopted its resolution on the partition of Palestine, some 1,500 Jews visited the Wall to offer prayers of thanksgiving. They did not know that they would be the last Jews to reach the Wall for over 19 years, with the exception of a few Jewish tourists from western countries.

Throughout the 1948 War, and between the years 1948 and 1967, the Wall was inaccessible to Jews. The Jordanian authorities saw to it that it was kept clean, as it was a tourist attraction. In 1965, the Arab Municipality put up a ceramic street sign reading, "al-Buraq Road," the Arabic name for the Wall, and in brackets "Wailing Wall Road."

The second area of contention was the ancient cemetery on the Mount of Olives, the only Jewish cemetery in Jerusalem. On the eve of the 1948 War, there were some 60,000 graves there. At the beginning of hostilities in the winter of 1948, Jews risked their lives to continue burying their dead on the hill. But with the growth of violence, burial there ceased and "temporary" cemeteries were consecrated in the west of the city. At the end of 1949, Israeli lookouts posted on Mount Zion reported that the Arabs had begun to trespass on the cemetery and to uproot gravestones in order to plough the area. In 1954, an Israeli memorandum sent to the United Nations protested against additional destruction of graves and the ploughing of the area. Two years later, Jordan attempted to pave a road to the top of the hill from the Jericho road. Israel complained, and the Jordanians promised that the work would not be resumed.

At the end of the 1950s, the Jordanian army began to use tombstones as building materials for the erection of army camps. Dozens of tombstones were transferred whole to an army camp erected near al-Azariyah, where they served to pave the tent areas and washrooms. Tombstones were taken to the courtyard of the citadel, where they were smashed and the fragments used as markers for a parade ground. In February 1962, the paving of a dirt road from the direction of the Jericho road to the top of the hill began again. At the same time, the building of a hotel began on the top of the hill, on a vacant plot adjacent to the cemetery. In the middle of July 1963, Israeli lookouts saw Jordanian soldiers busy destroying tombstones. Israel complained about these acts and on July 15 the deeds of destruction ceased, but the laying of the road continued. Israel complained again, and on July 24, a barrier was erected and traffic to the hotel building site was diverted.

Two years later, the road was finally paved and on June 15, 1966, it was inaugurated. Jordan's reply to the Israeli complaint was that "the road did not damage the graves," and the land of the cemetery was registered by Jordan in the name of the "Custodian of Enemy Property." After the Israelis took the area in 1967, they found that some 40,000 tombstones had been desecrated.

Far more complex, however, was the subject of the Jewish Quarter. With the outbreak of hostilities in the winter of 1948, the Jewish Quarter of the Old City was at the smallest size it had been since the end of the 19th century. The Jewish community which, until the anti-Jewish riots of 1929, had occupied an area twice as large, gradually shrunk as a result of the violence in 1929 and in 1936–9, as well as of normal migration to new neighborhoods outside the Old City. At the beginning of 1948, there were some 1,700 inhabitants. The Quarter contained several dozen synagogues and religious seminaries, some of the most important of which were the Hurva Synagogue, the Tiferet Yisrael Synagogue, the Rabban Yochanan Ben Zakkai Synagogue and the Porat Yosef *Yeshiva* (religious seminary).

In the course of the siege of the Jewish Quarter, which ended with its surrender, a large part of the Quarter's buildings were destroyed, including synagogues. Some of the synagogues were destroyed as a direct outcome of hostilities, as the Jewish defenders used them as fortified positions. Other synagogues were destroyed and desecrated by the mob, after the surrender and evacuation of the Quarter.

Arab refugees who had fled from the city and from the surrounding villages as the Israelis advanced, were then housed in the Jewish Quarter under the direction of the Red Cross. In October 1948, Israel complained that acts of destruction were being performed in the Jewish Quarter. In the 1950s, the original refugees were joined by immigrants from Hebron.

At the end of January 1963, the Arab Municipality's planning adviser, H. Kendall, suggested turning the ruined Quarter into a development center, with public buildings and parks. The Israeli delegation to the Mixed Armistice Commission drew the attention of the Jordanian representative to the fact that demolishing the Quarter and converting it into a development area was a violation of Paragraph 8 of the Armistice Agreement. The Jordanian delegate replied that the "newspaper publication was unreliable, and the Jordanian Government guards the Holy Places scrupulously."

In 1964, with the completion of a refugee camp near Shu'afat, the transfer of the 1948 refugees to this camp was begun. Most were moved during 1964; but after some of them refused to move, the Jordanian Government gave the District Commissioner permission to carry out the evacuation by force. On the eve of the 1967 War, the transfer of refugees had been completed, but the ruins of the Jewish Quarter did not remain empty. Migrants from the surrounding villages, especially from the Hebron area, replaced the refugees. A large majority signed leases with the Jordanian Custodian of Enemy Property. On the eve of the Six Day War, some 5,500 inhabitants were living in the Jewish Quarter. Some of them inhabited synagogues which had been converted into living quarters.

In June 1948, at the time of the proclamation of the first truce, the Israeli authorities began to press for Jews to be granted permission to pray at the Western Wall. Abdallah al-Tal even relates that an agreement was reached in this matter, but that he prevented its implementation. The Israel Government was officially informed that the Legion Commander was

> prepared, as far as the matter depends on him, to open the gates of the city to those going to the Wall, but cannot accept responsibility for the prevention of irregular sniping. Accordingly, if the Jews enter the Old City, they do so on their own responsibility, not his.

During the negotiations which resulted in the Armistice Agreement, the question of access was discussed a number of times. At the fourth session of the Rhodes Conference on March 12, 1949, Moshe Dayan, the Jerusalem Area Commander, proposed that free access be guaranteed to the Jewish Holy Places in return for free access for Muslims to those of their holy places in Israeli hands. A member of the Jordanian delegation, Lieutenant-Colonel Jundi, answered that the Jordanians did not disagree in principle to Jewish visits, but they were afraid of clashes between the Arab population and the Jewish visitors. The acting mediator, Dr. Ralph Bunche, raised the question again at the fifth session. He asked the Jordanians to put their position in writing. The Jordanian delegation proposed postponing the discussion till peace was reached. The Israeli delegation made no response.

Finally, at the thirteenth session of the Conference, the two sides agreed that the subjects demanding settlement, including access to the Holy Places, "would be discussed in the framework of the Special Committee to be set up according to Paragraph 8 of the Armistice Agreement." Israel presented to the first meeting of the Special Committee a list of the Holy Places to which it wanted free access, including the Western Wall, the Temple Mount, synagogues in the Old City, the Tower of David, and the Mount of Olives. It also asked that Jews be allowed to walk around the Old City walls on the Sabbath eve. The Israeli proposal was not discussed at this meeting and subsequent sessions only dealt with access to the Holy Places in passing. The problem of insuring the safety of visitors as they passed through a hostile populace was not solved.

In May 1949, Moshe Dayan stated that as long as Jews could not pass through the Armistice Lines on their way to their Holy Places, Israel would not permit Christians such passage. However, the Israelis eventually decided to refrain from this type of pressure and permitted Christians to pass. In December 1950, there were negotiations about the paving of a road from Mount Zion to the Dung Gate, which would have enabled the Jews to reach the Wall without passing through Arab-populated areas. But despite Israel's right to free access to the Holy Places on the strength of Paragraph 8 of the Armistice Agreement, and despite the guardianship she demanded over the Places themselves, by virtue of precedent, not a single Israeli visited the Holy Places during the 19 years of the Armistice.

The Christian Holy Places

The problems posed by the Christian Holy Places arise from different roots entirely. The danger to public order and to safety of the shrines comes from within the Christian communities themselves, with their internal squabbles. Constant disputes over possession of the Holy Places and the rights of worship forced the city's rulers, throughout the years, to intervene, localize conflicts and take a position between the sides. Sometimes the restoration of order was imposed by force. Whoever is responsible for law and order in Jerusalem must move prudently, since every act of omission or commission can stir up the quarrels even more or bring protests about discrimination.

For anyone dealing with the Christian Holy Places, the magic word is the Latin phrase *status quo ante,* "the situation as it was." Rights in the Holy Places, their ownership and use of their parts, were all fixed in accordance with what had been recognized at some previous point in time, and no change was permitted to take place. If the *status quo* had been clearly defined and accepted by all, matters would have been relatively simple; but, in the past, for historical or political reasons, certain arrangements had been settled and then subsequently reversed. Thus emerged "one of the most liquid and inaccurate codes in the world," as a British Mandatory official defined it.

The following, from a passage written by a British district officer for matters of the *status quo*, demonstrates the delicacy and complexity of the matter:

> *Certain fixed principles are followed in the administration of the* status quo. *Thus, authority to repair a roof or floor implies the right to an exclusive possession on the part of the restorers. Again, the right to hang a lamp or picture, or to change a lamp or picture, is a recognition of exclusive possession of a pillar or wall. The right of other communities to cense at a chapel implies that the proprietorship is not absolute.*

To give one concrete example, the steps leading to the Chapel of St. Mary's Agony in the Church of the Holy Sepulcher are the property of the Latin Catholics. But who had the right to clean the lowest step, which is slightly above the level of the commonly-owned front courtyard? In 1901, a bloody dispute between Catholics and Greek Orthodox broke out over this issue. The situation today is that Catholics sweep the step at dawn, while the Greek Orthodox sweep whenever it is their turn to clean the courtyard. Similar petty disputes exist over the columns supporting the rotunda dome. In 1924, there was a dispute over the right to dust the door leading to the Coptic courtyard between Columns 10 and 11. The Armenians claimed full ownership of the section and of the courtyard and, therefore, contended that dusting the doors was their right. The Copts demanded the right to dust the doors. The Mandatory Government ultimately accepted the Armenian contention.

In order to understand the roots of the inter-communal tangle which led to the creation of the concept of *status quo*, we must go back into history. The *status quo* is the result of developments originating with the early days of Christianity. Changes in the situation were influenced by historical conditions in Jerusalem over hundreds of years. The situation reflects not only inter-communal jealousies and religious disputes, but also the diplomatic struggles between the various Christian Powers. Rather than trace the whole complex and often bloodstained history of the Christian Holy Places and their ownership, the following review will only go as far back as the period in which the arrangements in force until today were made.

During the 400 years of Turkish rule, Greek Orthodox power in the Holy Places constantly increased at the expense of the Catholics and the smaller Christian congregations, such as the Armenians, the Copts and others. The Sultan, who regarded the Greeks as his subjects, supported their demands over those of his enemies, the European Powers. Military victories by Europeans, principally the French, over the Ottomans, brought the Catholics some rights, but these were subsequently filched from them. In the meantime, the Greeks found in Russia a powerful international backer. In the 18th and 19th centuries, the problem of the Holy Places in Palestine became a primary international issue. In 1757, while Europe was engaged in the Seven Years' War, the Greek Patriarch of Jerusalem succeeded in obtaining a *firman*, or order by the Sultan, which gave the Greek Orthodox Church superior status in the Holy Places.

For many years, the Catholics tried, with the vigorous support of the European Powers, to annul the *firman* of 1757. In 1850, the French ambassador in Constantinople demanded, in the name of his own country and of Austria, Spain, Sardinia, and Belgium, that the control of parts of the Holy Sepulcher and of other places, be restored to the Catholics. Russia opposed this move vigorously, and

73

the ensuing diplomatic struggle was one of the causes of the Crimean War.

In February 1852, the Turkish Sultan issued a *firman* rejecting Catholic demands for exclusive control, as phrased in 1850, and stating that the *status quo* would be maintained everywhere. Subsequently, in various international agreements, such as the Treaty of Paris (1855) and the Treaty of Berlin (1878), it was expressly agreed that the *status quo* in the Holy Places in Palestine was to be maintained; any change would only be by agreement of all parties.

After the First World War, there was a decisive change in the situation. The Ottoman Empire was defeated; Britain, a Christian Power, ruled the Holy Land; and post-revolutionary Russia was not interested in Holy Places. Things had also changed among the Catholic countries.

Whereas previously the French protectorate over the Catholics of the Ottoman Empire had been generally recognized, it was now Italy that became their principal diplomatic patron. The Vatican's aim was to annul the *status quo* of 1852. In order to achieve this, it demanded the establishment of a commission to investigate the various claims and reach a renewed agreement. Such a commission was called for in the Palestine Mandate.

In 1922 the British Mandate for Palestine was ratified by the League of Nations. The Mandate Charter contained many instructions concerning the Mandatory Power's role with regard to the Holy Places. It bound the British Government to "work for the preservation of existing rights" and to appoint a commission to investigate demands for changes in the *status quo*. The problem, in fact, concerned only the Christian Holy Places because it was expressly stated that the Government was forbidden to interfere in the Muslim Holy Places and the Jews were not represented at the League of Nations. During the Ottoman period, the status of the Jews had been inferior to that of the Muslims and Christians. Their Holy Places were not included within the code of any *status quo*. Nevertheless, the Mandate referred to Holy Places in general. This was to have very serious results with regard to the Jewish sites.

The Mandate also stipulated the establishment of an inquiry commission to study the question of rights for the various religious communities in Palestine. The Vatican demanded that the inquiry commission have a majority of Catholic members and that it should

74

not have jurisdiction over rights already in Catholic hands. In other words: "What's mine is mine; what's yours, we'll see! " Britain did not agree that the commission's composition be such as to sabotage the attempt "to solve, once and for all, justly and without prejudice, all the disputes between the Christian communities officiating in the Holy Places." The British suggested dividing the commission into three sub-committees; one each for Christian, Muslim and Jewish Holy Places. They proposed that the Christian committee include three Catholics, three Greek Orthodox, one Abyssinian, one Copt, with an American Protestant as chairman. The Catholics bitterly opposed this.

When it became clear that there was no chance of reaching agreement on the composition of the commission of inquiry, the British Government took upon itself all responsibility for the Holy Places. As it had guaranteed, under Article 13 of the Mandate, to maintain "existing rights," it interpreted these rights as those recognized by the Turkish Government on the eve of the First World War. As a result, the *firman* of 1852 remained in force. Although, as has been mentioned, it applied only to the Christian Holy Places, the Mandatory Government saw fit to apply the principle of *status quo* to the Western Wall and other sites as well.

As the Mandatory Power did not have the authority to "study, define, and determine rights and claims with regard to the religious communities," it withdrew these matters from the jurisdiction of the Palestinian courts. Disputes and claims with regard to the Holy Places were dealt with by the executive branch, which tried to fulfil its duties according to the precedents of the *status quo*, wherever there were clear precedents. Faced by the varying interpretations given to the *status quo* by members of the different religions, the Mandatory Government endeavored to mediate, postpone or, as a neutral party, take upon itself controversial tasks such as the repair or cleaning of buildings. The Government's responsibility, which the Mandate defined as "maintenance of public order and decorum," was not linked to the *status quo*. In order to ensure order and decorum, the Mandatory Government enacted a special section in the criminal law dealing "with offences against religion and public monuments."

As the end of the British Mandate drew near, the Vatican renewed its efforts to attain what it had not succeeded in gaining 30 years previously. However, rather than demand juridical investigation of the rights of others, it supported the plan for the internationalization of Jerusalem. Internationalization itself did not ensure Catholic interests, as it did not enter into the question of disputes between the Christian churches. But the Vatican relied on its political influence, which was far larger than that of the other churches, and hoped that the international trusteeship in Jerusalem would advance its interests. This intention was not concealed in encyclicals and other official Catholic pronouncements. The other Christian communities regarded the internationalization plan with suspicion, since Vatican intentions were obvious, as were the dangers to their status likely to stem from the internationalization of Jerusalem. Thus, the Greek Orthodox Patriarch, for example, demanded that the principle of *status quo* be safeguarded in the constitution of the international city, and also that the city's governor be a man "whose impartiality shall be beyond any doubt."

As the plan for internationalization foundered in the face of the determined opposition of both Israel and Jordan, once again a Muslim regime was in control of the Christian Holy Places in Jerusalem. It was Jordan's ambition to prove its ability to fulfil the difficult task involved in guarding the Holy Places. For this purpose, King Abdallah created a new post, "Guardian of the Haram al-Sharif and Supreme Custodian of the Holy Places." In his eagerness to satisfy everyone, the King ordered not only that the *status quo* be maintained, but also

> that all the firmans of the Sultans and the traditional rights held by the Patriarchs be examined and registered impartially in special gazettes, for the purpose of documentation, which a man may utilize whenever necessary.

In other words, he was leaving an opening for a judicial investigation similar to the one proposed in 1918. In the end, however, the Christians refused to recognize the Supreme Custodian and later responsibility for the Holy Places reverted to the District Commissioner.

The Jordanian Government was strict in maintaining order and succeeded in keeping the peace in trouble spots, such as the Church of the Holy Sepulcher and the Church of the Nativity in Bethlehem. On festivals, such as Easter, the Jordanians stationed up to 200 soldiers and policemen at the Church of the Holy Sepulcher to maintain order. The only sizeable dispute during the Jordanian regime was the traditional one between Ethiopians and Copts. The

Government decided in favor of the Ethiopians at first, but later, under Egyptian pressure, altered its verdict and decided for the Copts.

The other matter dealt with by the Jordanian authorities was the repair and redecoration of the Church of the Holy Sepulcher. Continual disputes between the Christian communities over responsibility for repairs had created a situation obliging the Mandatory Government's Public Works Department, or in some cases, the Municipality, to carry out urgent work. In 1951, cooperation between the Christian communities was initiated on the subject of repairs, but negotiations went on for 11 years. Only in 1962 did the Catholics, Greek Orthodox, and Armenians set up a joint technical office to start reinforcing and redecorating the building. Work went on slowly, partly owing to its delicate character and the lack of access for vehicles, but also due to mutual suspicions. The unification of the city found the work still in process.

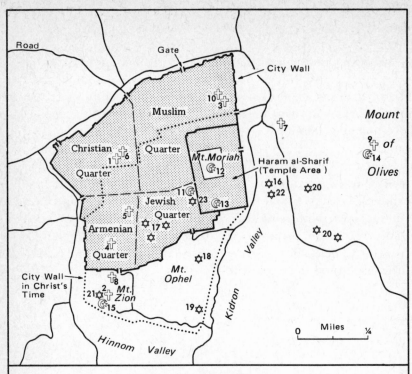

Road

Gate

City Wall

Muslim

10

3

7

Mount

Christian
Quarter

1 6

Quarter

Mt. Moriah
12

Haram al-Sharif
(Temple Area)

9
7
14

of

16

22

20

Olives

11

Jewish
Quarter

23

13

5

17

Armenian

Quarter

4

20

20

18

City Wall
in Christ's
Time

8

2
Mt.
Zion

21

15

Mt.
Ophel

19

Kidron

Valley

0   Miles   ¼

Hinnom   Valley

Principal Holy Places

CHRISTIAN
✝

1. Church of the Holy
   Sepulchre *

2. Cenacle

3. Church of St. Anne

4. Church of St. James

5. Church of St. Mark

6. Deir al Sultan *

7. Tomb of Virgin and
   Garden of Gethsemane *

8. House of Caiphas

9. Church of the Ascension *

10. Pool of Bethesda

MUSLIM
☾

11. Al Burak al-Sharif

12. Dome of the Rock

13. Al-Aqsa Mosque

14. Mosque of the Ascension

15. Tomb of David

JEWISH
✡

16. Tomb of Absalom

17. Synagogues

18. Bath of Rabbi Ishmael

19. Pool of Siloam

20. Cemetery

21. Tomb of David

22. Tomb of Zachariah

23. Wailing Wall *

* Holy Place to which the Status Quo applies

CHAPTER SIX

WAR AND CONQUEST

At 8:30, on the morning of Monday, June 5, 1967, the lookout posted near regional Staff Headquarters in Israeli Jerusalem noticed that the Arab workers, who had been peacefully engaged in building King Husayn's palace on Tel al-Ful hill, had stopped work and were leaving the area. The lookout also reported that Jordanian soldiers had taken up positions in the Givat Hamivtar area, near the border, on the northern edge of the city. At the same hour, hundreds of the inhabitants of Israeli Jerusalem, armed and in uniform, were converging on prearranged assembly points. These were the reservists of the Jerusalem Brigade, who had been discharged only a few days previously; now, only a quarter of an hour after hearing radio reports about the outbreak of fighting in the south — the beginning of the Six Day War — they had become soldiers again. On both sides of the barbed-wire fence that divided Jerusalem, the city's inhabitants, who had begun their day as usual, felt the tension mounting by the minute. Between 8:30 and 9:00, without anyone instructing them, factory managers and businessmen in East Jerusalem ordered their employees home. Precisely at 9:00, the Jordanian delegation to the Mixed Armistice Commission received orders from the Jordan Army Command to leave the MAC building, which was situated in no-man's-land. In West Jerusalem, most of the citizens were at work, the pupils in their classrooms. Despite reports of heavy fighting in the south, and of alerts in the coastal cities, the Israeli authorities did not order Jerusalemites to go home.

All over Jordan, cheering crowds gathered immediately after the radio, at 9:00, announced the outbreak of fighting between Israel and Egypt. In East Jerusalem, the atmosphere was relaxed. People were anxious about the future but certain that the war would not engulf Israel and Jordan. Feelings on the Israeli side were similar.

At 9:58, though not a single shot had been fired, Jordan Radio broadcast the following statement: "Israel's end is in your hands. Strike at her everywhere, until victory! " At 10:15, martial law was declared in Jordan. Within two minutes, the sound of small arms' fire was heard in Jerusalem. The shooting spread, and within a few minutes it had encompassed all sectors of the city's front. The firing increased rapidly, and the rattle of machine guns was joined by the hollow explosions of mortars and the crash of artillery shells.

At 10:50, King Husayn broadcast the following appeal:

My brothers and citizens! These are the hours when every one of us will do his duty so as to achieve our aims. Precisely as we had expected, the enemy carried out his aggression this morning and, in our air space, is attacking Arab soil, our airfields, and towns. We expected it. The decisive battle has already begun. We are determined to live honorably or to die honorably in defense of all that is precious to every Arab.

The King announced that command of the army had been transferred to the Egyptian General Abd al-Mun'im Riad.

Around nine o'clock, the United Nations' chief observer in Jerusalem, General Odd Bull, was called to the Israel Foreign Ministry and asked to transmit an urgent message from Prime Minister Levi Eshkol to King Husayn. Eshkol wrote:

We are engaged in a defensive battle in the Egyptian sector, and we will initiate no action in the Jordanian sector unless Jordan attacks us. If Jordan attacks Israel, we will assault her with all our forces.

At 10:20, the message reached Colonel Muhammad Da'ud, head of the Jordanian delegation to the Mixed Armistice Commission, and from there it was immediately transmitted to Amman, reaching King Hussein a few minutes after eleven. No reply was sent. Israel sent two further messages that day; they too remained unanswered. After the war, Husayn was to relate:

On June 5, after hostilities had begun, General Bull conveyed a message from Israel which said that Israel was mainly interested in the attack on Egypt. If we did not intervene, they would save us from consequences, which otherwise were inevitable; but by that time, we no longer had any choice. We were obliged to do every-thing to help our allies.

Until noon, hostilities were confined to exchanges of fire. But at 1 p.m. a Jordanian force crossed the Armistice Line and captured the headquarters of the U.N. observers on Government Hill. This was the point of no return. Jordan and Israel were at war. By the afternoon of Wednesday, June 7, 1967, when the last battle was fought in the city, Israel had surrounded East Jerusalem, entered the Old City, and raised its flag on the Temple Mount.

Eight hundred and forty people lost their lives in the battle for Jerusalem. One hundred and ninety-five, including 14 civilians, were Israelis; six hundred and forty-five, including 249 civilians, were Arabs. The Israeli dead were buried in the city's cemeteries during the fighting; their relatives had yet to be informed of their deaths because of the danger of further casualties if funerals were held amidst the shelling. Israeli soldiers buried the Arab soldiers in com-munications trenches, placing markers over the common graves. Some Arab civilians buried their relatives in their private gardens; but about 180 Arab dead lay in the city streets and in open lots in the east of the city. In the hospitals and first-aid stations lay hundreds of wounded.

On Wednesday morning, both parts of Jerusalem looked forlorn. Shell damage was everywhere — 600 houses had been hit on the Israeli side and 250 on the Arab side. On Monday, the metal dome of the Church of the Dormition had caught fire after having been struck by the Jordanian bombardment, while on Wednesday the roof of the Augusta Victoria Hospital was in flames after being hit by bombs from Israeli planes. In the exchange of fire, several synagogues and mosques were hit, as well as ten churches. The Hadassah Hospital and the St. Joseph's Hospital were shelled, as were the Rockefeller Museum and the Israel Museum, where art treasures were damaged. Eighty-two animals were killed in the West Jerusalem Biblical Zoo.

East Jerusalem's water and electricity supplies were completely cut off. In West Jerusalem, the main water pipe line was damaged and 2,000 telephones were cut off. Burned-out cars littered the streets; display windows were smashed; cables were torn down and trees felled. Most of the houses in the Old City were locked and bolted, with white flags dangling from the windows. Trucks delivered hundreds of Arab soldiers to prisoners' clearing stations on the tennis courts of the Hebrew University, where they lay facedown with out-stretched arms, waiting their turn to enter the interrogation tent.

Up to eleven o'clock on Wednesday morning, most of the inhabitants of West Jerusalem stayed in their shelters. Only when the radio announced the "All Clear" did people go out into the streets. The news of the capture of the Old City circulated by word of mouth. Crowds began to collect on the roads leading to the Mandelbaum Gate, the border crossing between the two halves of the city, watching with great enthusiasm as military convoys passed back and forth through the Gate. Roars of delight greeted soldiers driving Jordanian military vehicles that flew Jordanian flags or displayed pictures of King Husayn. At midday the Israeli flag was hoisted over the Tower of David, in view of thousands of inhabitants. Dozens of people ignored the soldiers' warnings and found a variety of ways to slip through the barbed-wire fences and minefields on their way to the Western Wall; several were to pay for their enthusiasm with their lives.

There was a spirit of elation in the western city, but there was no joy or triumph. The throb of helicopters evacuating casualties continued to plague the city's citizens, whose fathers, sons, and brothers were among the soldiers. Rumor spoke of scores of dead, and everyone prayed for the safety of his dear ones.

The official announcement of the capture of the Old City was a long time in coming. At his command post, on the threshold of the western entrance to the Dome of the Rock, Colonel Mordechai Gur, the commander of the paratroopers who had stormed into the Old City and taken the Temple Mount, asked if the news of the Old City's capture had been announced in the noon news broadcast. The answer was negative. The public had to wait another five hours because the Government needed time to word the announcement carefully; its political significance was enormous. It was finally decided that after the Prime Minister's visit, a recorded description of Eshkol's entry into the Old City, including his declaration and statements by the Minister of Defense and the Chief of Staff, would be broadcast on the five o'clock news in lieu of an official announcement.

The Western Wall attracted people like a magnet. At eleven o'clock, Uzi Narkiss, head of Central Area Command, arrived together with Deputy Chief of Staff, Haim Bar-Lev, and the Chief Rabbi of the Army, General Shlomo Goren. At the time, there were several hundred soldiers in the narrow, shaded alley in front of the Wall. Some were leaning against the Wall and fondling its cool stones, while others squatted on the ground and cried. Everyone was deeply moved. Rabbi Goren began by blowing the *shofar*; others read passages from the Book of Psalms. Then Rabbi Goren read the prayer in memory of the fallen. After that the atmosphere warmed up and some of the soldiers joined in the Rabbi's shouts and started singing and dancing. Other soldiers, whose friends had fallen at their side such a short time before, felt that the shouting and singing were out of place.

Some of the soldiers immediately went to the Jewish Quarter. They were shocked by what they found. None of the Jewish Quarter's prominent features, such as the dome of the Hurva Synagogue or the Tiferet Yisrael Synagogue, was to be seen. When they went to search for the synagogues and public buildings, they found that some had been destroyed and others converted into primitive apartments. About one-third of the buildings were demolished, and the uncleared rubble from 1948 lay about in great heaps. The visitors concentrated at the Hurva Synagogue. Through a green iron door, they entered an open passageway, leading to a yard full of rubble, with only the eastern wall of the Synagogue left standing. The building's dome, and the other walls, had collapsed inwards, creating a great pile of rubble. The main synagogue of Jerusalem's Jews — in which the Chief Rabbis were inaugurated; in which the flags of the Jewish batallions of the First World War were kept; the most important place of worship, barring only the Western Wall — no longer existed. Soldiers who remained dry-eyed at the death of their comrades, burst into bitter tears at sight.

General Narkiss had not been at the Wall for more than a few minutes before he was forced to turn his attention to other matters. Before leaving, he gave orders to barricade the entrance to the Temple Mount and its mosques, lest the Muslim Holy Places be damaged.

Defense Minister Moshe Dayan and Chief of Staff Yitzhak Rabin entered St. Stephen's Gate a few minutes before two o'clock in the afternoon. After leaving their vehicles at the gate, they entered the Temple Mount courtyard accompanied by a large entourage. Someone drew Dayan's attention to the Israeli flag flying over the Dome of the Rock (Mosque of Omar), and he ordered it removed. He then ordered the withdrawal of the paratroop company, which Narkiss had placed in the courtyard to defend the Temple Mount. In doing so, Dayan restored responsibility for protecting the Temple Mount to the *sadana*, the traditional Muslim guards, at the same time sealing it off completely.

Standing beside the Western Wall, Dayan then declared:

This morning the Israeli Defense Forces liberated Jerusalem. We have reunited divided Jerusalem, the dismembered capital of Israel. We have returned to our most holy places; we have returned and we shall never leave them. To our Arab neighbors, we extend, at this time also, especially at this hour, the hand of peace. To members of the other religions, Christians and Muslims, I hereby promise faithfully that their full freedom and all their religious rights will be preserved. We did not come to Jerusalem to conquer the Holy Places of others, nor to hamper the members of other religions, but to ensure its integrity and to live in brotherhood with others.

From the Western Wall, Dayan returned to the command post, where he again ordered Narkiss to immediately open all the gates in the walls of the Old City and to remove all the barriers and barbed-wire fences separating the two halves of the city. He had first ordered Narkiss to do so at eleven o'clock that morning, immediately after the capture of the Western Wall. It seems that by this act the Defense Minister wished to ensure the physical reunification of Jerusalem in case the U.N. should intervene and demand that the barbed-wire fences, the symbol of the city's partition, remain. Throughout the coming days, Dayan was to demand the fulfillment of this order, showing impatience as its implementation encountered delays because of enormous technical difficulties.

At 5:30 that same Wednesday afternoon, June 7, Prime Minister Levi Eshkol reached the Western Wall. His declaration was prudently non-political:

It is a great historic privilege for me to stand here now, beside the Western Wall, the remnant of our sacred temple and of our historic past. I regard myself as the emissary of the entire people, as the emissary of the many generations of our people who pined for Jerusalem and its holiness. To the inhabitants of Jerusalem who suffered greatly in 1948 and who have, during the past days, faced wicked bombardment with heroism and utter calm, I would say: may the victories of the Israel Defense Forces, which have re-

moved the dangers from the capital of Israel, be a source of en-
couragement and comfort to you and to all of us. In the comfort
of Jerusalem, may you be comforted. And from Jerusalem, the
eternal capital of Israel, greetings of peace and security to all the
citizens of Israel and to our Jewish brethren wherever they are.

He then uttered the traditional thanksgiving prayer: "Blessed be He
who has preserved us, and sustained us, and brought us to this
time."

A military administration for the conquered city had to be organized as quickly as possible. That morning, the Military Governor
of the West Bank, General Chaim Herzog, was ordered

to take control of the area already conquered and to impose order
there; to take supreme care of religious institutions; to make sure
there is no looting; and to set up a regular administrative structure.

Herzog had been appointed to the then theoretical post of "Military Governor of the West Bank" in 1963, when the Israeli army
organized military government units to control the conquered areas
in the event that war should break out. The experience of the first
weeks of the occupation of the Gaza Strip, after the Sinai Campaign
in 1956, had proved that control of captured territory cannot be a
matter of improvisation; trained staff must be prepared ahead of
time. All the elements necessary for the work of these military
government units were prepared beforehand, including decrees, procedures, and briefings. In addition, files were prepared and updated
from time to time, with data on the size of the population, its
leaders, the economic and social structure, and other useful information. Every now and then, maneuvers and courses were held for the
men of these units. But in the tranquil mid-1960s, when the possibility of war seemed remote, the needs of these units were placed on
a very low level of priority.

Despite the increased tension in May 1967, preparations for the
establishment of a Military Government were not stepped up. When
Israel mobilized its reserves and the Israel Defense Forces went over
to a high state of alert, no orders were given to mobilize the military
government units. Only on the morning of Monday, June 5, when
artillery fire had already been exchanged between Israel and Jordan,
was the military government unit for the West Bank called up. On
Tuesday, June 6, the military government units began to assemble,
but they lacked transport and administrative facilities; on the other

85

hand, by that time, Israeli forces had already taken all of the northern quarters of East Jerusalem.

The official appointment of General Herzog as Military Governor of the West Bank was only issued on Wednesday, and it was not until then that the military government units began to move up to Jerusalem. It had already been decided that the Military Government's staff would be quartered in the Ambassador Hotel in the Sheikh Jarah quarter, on the road to the Mount of Olives. Because the tall building dominated its surroundings, General Narkiss believed that "the hotel was . . . a symbol; whoever occupies it, controls the whole of the eastern city." At the assembly point, one of the officers expressed his indignation at being sent to rule a city he knew nothing about. "Don't worry," his friend said, "all you need is a little common sense."

By mid-day on Wednesday the Military Government's ability to function was still very limited; but it was impossible to wait until the Military Governor got organized. In the city were dozens of Jordanian soldiers who had stripped off their uniforms and gone into hiding in private houses, public buildings, and even the basements of the churches and monasteries. The Israelis were concerned lest the enormous quantities of arms and ammunition rumored to be in the city had been distributed to the inhabitants. There were reports of looting, mainly by civilians who had slipped through the barbed-wire border fence. And there was anxiety about the Holy Places. It was essential to tackle all these matters immediately; the establishment of a regular administrative structure and the return of civilian life to normal could wait.

Reserve units were, therefore, ordered into the eastern sector of the city and intelligence men fanned out, arresting several hundred people, according to lists that had been prepared earlier. Special units enclosed the Holy Places with barbed-wire fences, marked them "Holy Place — No Entry," and set up machine guns to protect them. Israeli soldiers began house-to-house searches, banging on locked doors and, when they were opened, bursting in with weapons ready. The male occupants were ordered to raise their hands and turn to the wall while their clothes were searched. Subsequently, everybody was taken outside and the house itself was thoroughly searched. Cupboards were opened, beds overturned, attics checked. The manner of the search, and the behavior of the soldiers, varied from section to section. Most behaved politely, reassuring the terror-stricken inhabitants; but a minority acted roughly, deliberately smashing china and breaking windows. In a few cases, soldiers pocketed articles of value.

After the searches ended, the adult males were ordered to leave their houses and accompany the soldiers. The inhabitants were convinced that the men were being taken off to execution. Men and women embraced each other for what they thought was the last time. The men were taken on foot to the wire-fenced assembly points and ordered to squat with their hands raised. One by one, they were called by the interrogation teams, who ordered them to identify themselves. Here, too, the treatment they received depended on the character of the individual Israeli soldier: some soldiers took the trouble to supply their prisoners with water and cigarettes; others cursed and hit them; a few removed watches and rings.

As their wait at the assembly point dragged on, the prisoners' fears gradually faded, and they began to talk to each other. Hundreds of Arab inhabitants, including the District Commissioner, the Chief of Police and other prominent figures, collected in a shady corner of the Temple Mount. They watched in silence as the Israeli leaders passed by on their way to the Western Wall. In the evening, the Arab men were given permission to return home. Some of them requested — and received — a military escort. Their families received them as men who had returned from the dead.

Cars with loudspeakers cruised through East Jerusalem, reading the "Proclamation of Assumption of Power by the Israel Defense Forces," which stated:

The Israel Defense Force has, today, entered this area and taken into its hands the control and maintenance of security and public order. A house curfew in the entire area is hereby declared. No one may leave his home at any hour of the day. The inhabitants will be able to acquire essential commodities, in their regular places of residence, at times to be made known in special announcements. The movement of vehicles is forbidden. It is forbidden to assemble in the streets or in any other public place. Everyone shall carry with him, at all times, a document bearing his photograph, for purposes of identification. Essential services in the area will function normally, according to instructions which will be given. Anyone contravening these orders shall be punished with all severity, and any attempt to disturb security will be crushed immediately. Israel Defense Force soldiers will ensure the strict enforcement of these instructions.

Shortly after seven that evening, a meeting was convened at General Narkiss' command post. The Military Government's level of organization was not encouraging. There was complete chaos at the Ambassador Hotel. All the military government units due to disperse throughout the various towns of the West Bank were crammed into the Hotel's halls. Senior officers who had not been called up for reserve duty milled round the building, begging to be assigned posts in the Military Government. Some were prepared to take on any post, even the lowliest, just as long as they could "do something."

Into this uproar walked General Shlomo Lahat and Colonel Yaakov Salman, both of whom had just arrived from the United States and been appointed Governor and Deputy Governor of Jerusalem, respectively. Their first decision was to get out of the Ambassador Hotel and find a quieter place for their headquarters. In the course of the next day, Thursday, June 8, they reorganized the garrison force, which was still continuing its searches. Their most pressing problem was to put an end to the looting of shops and houses, which had taken on disturbing dimensions. On that same day a decree was issued, stating that "anyone looting, or breaking into a house, or any other place, to loot, or who knowingly holds loot, will be punished with life imprisonment."

It was also essential to reactivate civilian services and see that the needs of the civilian population were met. Most people possessed some food stocks, but there were shortages of bread, vegetables, and milk for the children. The shops had to be reopened, and this meant lifting the curfew for a few hours a day. The supply of electricity and water had to be renewed, and, above all, the dead had to be buried and the city cleaned up.

The behavior of the Israeli soldiers reassured the populace and to some extent reduced its discomfort. On their own initiative, the soldiers provided the inhabitants with vegetables and bread left over from their rations, helped to convey expectant mothers to hospitals, and calmed the population cooped up in its houses, still in fear of death. Months later, many of the inhabitants of the eastern city retained affectionate memories of some soldier who, unasked, brought a crate of cucumbers or handed out candy to the children. The inhabitants gazed in amazement at the Jewish soldiers, most of

Left: The Western Wall in the 1940s (Photo Barak)

Below: The Mandelbaum Gate which divided Israeli and Jordanian Jerusalem between 1948 and 1967

1948 to 1967 — Near the border (above) and the
walls which divided the city (Zev Radovan)

Above: The Arab Higher Committee with Haj Amin al-Husayni in the center and Rashid Nashashibi and Ahmed Hilmi on the left (Hanna Safieh)

Right: Soldiers of the Arab Legion, the Israel Defense Forces and the United Nations on a tour of the borders

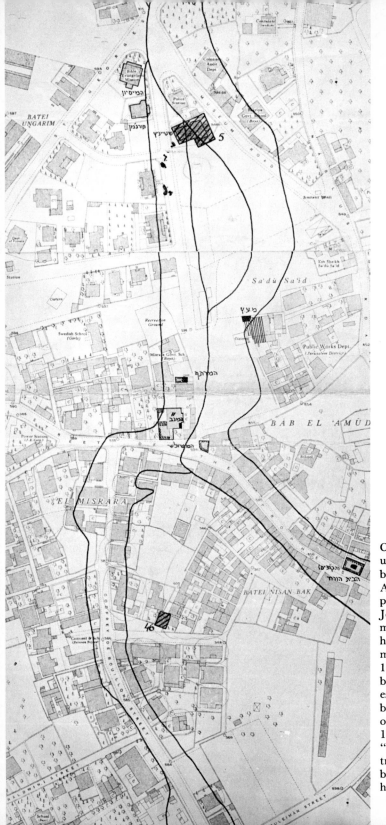

On the map dividing Je
usalem, which was signe
by Moshe Dayan a
Abdallah al-Tal and a
pendixed to the Isra
Jordan Armistice Agre
ment, the borders we
hand-drawn with a chi
marker on a map scal
1:20,000. As a result t
borders were uncle
especially in the dens
built-up areas. The m
on the left, on a scale
1:1,250, shows how t
"thickness of the lir
translated into reali
bisecting buildings a
houses

The Temple Mount patrolled by Israeli soldiers immediately after the Six Day War (Hans H. Pinn)

Mayor Teddy Kollek, with Moshe Dayan to his left and the author to his right, visiting the Old City (Israel Press and Photo Agency)

A street in Jerusalem as it appeared before the city was unified (above) and after (Zev Radovan)

The Municipality—Barclays Bank Building before 1967 (above) and shortly after the Six Day War (Zev Radovan)

The Yochanan Ben Zakkai Synagogue in the Jewish Quarter as it was found by the Israelis in 1967 (above) and as it has been reconstructed since the Six Day War (Photo K. Weiss)

them carelessly dressed veterans of the "Grandfather Corps" in wide-brimmed hats, and their sandalled, unmilitary-looking officers. It was a strange garrison, whose behavior was quite different from what they expected. After years of listening to the propaganda of Arab radio stations, they were sure there would be massacres and torture. When such grim expectations failed to materialize, a tremendous sense of relief enveloped the population, as though their lives had been granted them.

It was impossible to return life to normal, in a city of 60,000 inhabitants, by improvisation alone, and an attempt was made to locate the Arab civic leaders. The first leader discovered by the Israelis was Dr. Ibrahim Tlil, the Mayor's Christian deputy, who said that the only person capable of reorganizing the municipal services was the Mayor himself, Rauhi al-Khatib. Al-Khatib had remained in the Latin Monastery in the Old City, where he had found shelter on Wednesday morning. Captain Aharon Laish, who had been appointed liaison officer with the Municipality, met the Mayor, and it was agreed between them that the Mayor would come to the Municipality building the next day.

Anton Saffiah, the Mayor's chief assistant, was also contacted. He had been treasurer of the joint Municipality until 1948, had organized the Arab Municipality after the city's partition, and had served as head of the municipal administration ever since. A year before the 1967 War, he had reached retirement age but continued in his post at the Mayor's request. Now he was asked to reorganize the Municipality under Jewish rule. The radio broadcast instructions to all municipal employees, as well as policemen, to report for duty the following morning, while the curfew was lifted between 9:00 a.m. and 3:00 p.m.

In their attempts to reactivate the Arab Municipality, the military authorities were acting on the express orders given by Moshe Dayan to the Military Governor of the West Bank the day before. These orders can be summed up as follows:

Don't set up an Israeli administration, reactivate the existing Jordanian ones. Don't make the mistake the Americans made in Vietnam. Be sure that essential services function properly again as quickly as possible, but manned by the Arabs themselves. Let them manage themselves.

Jerusalem, however, was not Nablus or Hebron; not an Arab city, but a divided one that was slated to be reunited immediately. This much was clear from Dayan's other orders to dismantle the barricades. But if the city was to be unified, there was no place for the Arabs to "manage themselves"; the Israeli and Arab Municipalities had to be deployed together.

The decision to bring the Israeli Municipality into the picture was not, at this stage, a well-considered political move, but the result of pressure on the part of the Israeli Mayor of West Jerusalem, Teddy Kollek, whose ambition it was to take responsibility for the reunited city's municipal affairs. On Tuesday, even before the capture of the Old City, he had offered his services to General Narkiss: "We'll get services going again — like nobody's business." But the latter gently refused the offer. By the next day, Kollek already had a complete program for the operation of services: "We are prepared to take responsibility for water, sewage, sanitation, street lighting, garbage collection and all other services the moment we are asked to do so." Faced with such overwhelming readiness, it is easy to understand why the Military Governor was happy to accept. It was agreed that on Friday, June 9, Israeli municipal employees would enter the occupied area and begin to organize services, "contact being maintained between [Kollek's] departments and the parallel departments in the Arab Municipality."

Even after this agreement, the role of the Arab Municipality was still not clear: in which spheres, if any, should the Defense Minister's order about "self-management by Arabs" apply to Jerusalem? The issue was not decided during the first week as Military Governor Lahat was in no hurry to arrive at a clear-cut definition of the Israeli Municipality's mode of operation in the occupied territory. It was only on June 15 that the Mayor agreed with General Narkiss, in writing, that

> the Municipality takes it upon itself to cleanse the Old City of the results of military operations. At this stage, pending any decision about annexation, the Municipality will assist in the current maintenance of municipal services, water supply, street lighting, road repair, etc. For this purpose, the Municipality will also operate the municipal organization existing in the Old City.

The Israeli Municipality was not content to handle just municipal services. It wanted to play a leading role in everything connected with the city — care for the Holy Places, reconstruction of the Jewish

Quarter of the Old City, and preparation of a masterplan. For this purpose the Municipal Council, in festive session, resolved on the establishment of a "Jerusalem Fund" totalling IL 150 million (about $40 million) "to reclaim all parts of the city, restore its historic sites, and build it into the political and spiritual center of the people of Israel."

The Municipality was not the only Israeli body that wanted to operate in East Jerusalem. Its aspirations were shared by all the Israel Government ministries, as well as other public bodies. At midday on Wednesday, several Directors-General and Deputy Ministers were already at the Mandelbaum Gate, trying to enter occupied territory. The Army prevented them from doing so, insisting that they all acquire permits; but on the following days, no one could prevent this influx of men of goodwill in search of fields of activity. Within a short time, as a result, proper administration was impossible.

At 4 o'clock on Thursday afternoon, General Chaim Herzog held a meeting with the heads of the Christian clergy in Jerusalem, during which he stated:

This is a historic day for us. For 19 years we have been deprived of access to our Holy Places in Jerusalem; now we have returned to them. For us, too, this is something of a surprise. We have returned not to harm those places which are holy to all religions, or any other Holy Places, but so that we, too, will have the right to visit the places which are holy to our people . . . We will permit free access and life to members of all religions.

He mentioned Moshe Dayan's declaration of the previous day and the words of the Prime Minister in a meeting he had held the same day with the heads of the Christian communities in Israel. In the practical part of his address, Levi Eshkol had said:

At my request, the Minister of Religious Affairs has given the following instructions:

(1) Arrangements near the Western Wall shall be made by the Israeli Chief Rabbis;

(2) arrangements in the Muslim Holy Places shall be made by a council of Muslim clergy;

(3) arrangements in the Christian Holy Places shall be made by a council of Christian clergy.

This was a far-reaching declaration; but its meaning was not sufficiently clear.

On the whole, however, the Christian clergy were satisfied with the Government's declarations and, above all, were grateful to the military command for the protection given to the Holy Places. The Patriarch Benedictos answered General Herzog in the name of the clergymen, saying:

We are not politicians but clergymen. Our only wish is to be permitted to live according to our beliefs and maintain the precepts of our religion ... I wish to declare my admiration for the fact that the Israel Army did not harm our Holy Places in the course of the battles in Jerusalem.

One of the participants asked, "Why are our colleagues, the heads of the Muslim community, not here with us? " Herzog answered that it had not been possible to locate them and invite them to attend. That day, in fact, the head of the Muslim religious leaders, the *qadis,* Sheikh Abdal-Hamid a-Sayah, was in Jericho. As for the *mufti* and the other *qadis,* some were in the city and others had found refuge elsewhere. Perhaps it was just as well that they were not invited, for the Government had not yet decided how to relate to the Muslim establishment. In a short discussion of the subject a day earlier, the Ministers of Justice and Religious Affairs were in favor of establishing a temporary "Board of Guardians," composed of Muslim *qadis* from Israel, together with several *qadis* from East Jerusalem, to be responsible for arrangements concerning the Temple Mount and the other Muslim Holy Places. They were accustomed to the Muslim religious establishment in Israel and thought that their absolute control of it would safeguard the Israeli link with the Temple Mount. The days to come were to show how different the Muslim establishment of East Jerusalem was.

Before the end of the day, overseas reactions to the capture of the Old City began to be heard. The news agencies reported that "France will not agree to Israel attaching to new Jerusalem those parts of the city in Jordanian hands until now." In a public address, the Pope called for the demilitarization of Jerusalem. The international battle over the future of Jerusalem was thus renewed the moment the shooting ended.

At the end of the first day after the cessation of hostilities, perceptive people discerned a complex set of problems facing the city's new rulers: the return to normalcy; the function of the Arab Municipality and its relationships with the Israeli Municipality; removal of the barriers and the physical unification of the city; the Holy Places — above all, the Temple Mount and the Western Wall; the fate of the Jewish Quarter; the over-enthusiasm of Israeli civilian bodies and their mutual conflicts; the political future of the city, and the international struggle over it. Those responsible for ruling the city were, as yet, spared only one problem, possibly the toughest of all: that of co-existence between the Jewish and Arab populations. An explicit decree, military guards, and barbed-wire fences continued to separate the citizens of the reunited city. Another 20 days were due to pass before the city was to experience its severest test.

CHAPTER SEVEN

PICKING UP THE PIECES

At 9 o'clock on the morning of Friday, June 9, approximately half of the employees of the Arab Municipality reported for work at the municipal offices next to Jaffa Gate. Of the absentees, some had left the city, while others could not get through because of military roadblocks. Rauhi al-Khatib and Anton Saffiah were in charge. The most urgent tasks were to bury the dead and repair the water systems.

Forty-three employees of the Sanitation Department went out into the streets, accompanied by a doctor, to collect the corpses; in the course of the morning they were joined by Jewish employees who brought trucks. Some of the bodies had been lying in the summer sun for three days and were in a state of putrefaction. The employees had to carry out their tasks wearing gas masks. There were difficulties in identifying some of the bodies, and, by agreement between Christian and Muslim clergymen, all the unidentified bodies were taken to the Muslim cemetery near the Damascus Gate, where they were buried in a mass grave. That day 180 corpses were interred; but the work of burying the dead was to last for two weeks, in the course of which some 250 additional bodies were buried. After the formal reunification of the city, the Muslim *waqf* continued the burials, interring a further 224 bodies up to September 1967.

The water supply system had been put out of action on Tuesday, June 6, by damage to the main pipelines and pumping stations and the cutting off of the electricity supply. Crews from the Water Department, joined by Israeli engineers and workmen, repaired some of the pumping stations; but, because of the pipeline damage, the water did not reach the city. On June 15, after the pipes were replaced, the pump motors were repaired, and the electricity supply was restored, 2,500 cubic meters of water per day were supplied to East Jerusalem. This too, however, was insufficient, and the eastern city was connected to the western water system in three places, in effect unifying Jerusalem's water supply.

Another top priority was the restoration of the electricity supply. The Mayor, who was also Chairman of the Board of Directors of the electric company, went to the company offices and ordered the employees to begin repairing the network immediately. The Military Governor asked for help from the Israeli Electric Company, which assigned some 80 employees to the task. Crews from both companies began intensive repair operations, and, as a result, the electric current was renewed the next day, Saturday, June 10.

If normal life was to be restored, shops had to be opened and the inhabitants given a chance to purchase food. Although the curfew was lifted between 9 a.m. and 3 p.m., the authorities were worried that the shops would remain shut. Mayor al-Khatib and the director of the Chamber of Commerce were requested to bring their influence to bear on the shopkeepers. At first, the shops did not open, but the Mayor walked through the streets, accompanied by an Israeli officer, calling on the shopkeepers to open. One after another, most of the stores were opened; some, however, remained closed because their proprietors had left the city. The shops had stocks of all types of food, except fresh produce. At the Military Governor's request, the bakeries in the west of the city delivered bread. Flour and milk were also supplied. The shopkeepers continued to sell at prewar prices and did not limit sales. They were afraid of looting and wanted to get rid of their stocks as quickly as possible; but there was no panic buying in the city, and the inhabitants only bought what they needed.

Despite the fact that Israelis were strictly forbidden to enter the eastern city, hundreds of soldiers and civilians were roaming the streets. On that Friday morning a decree was published forbidding anyone not belonging to the local population from buying any object or commodity. At that time, the Government intended to maintain total economic segregation between Israel and the West Bank, maintaining the West Bank as a closed economic unit. The dinar was to remain legal tender, and an entirely separate system of taxation was to be put into operation. It was, therefore, strictly forbidden to use Israel pounds in East Jerusalem or the West Bank. But this economic plan proved impossible to implement. The severe shortage of cash in the eastern sector of the city, and the Israelis' tremendous hunger for commodities — both imported and locally produced — made the Israel pound the principal currency of East Jerusalem within a few days.

The Military Government directed all its efforts towards the opening of the city's businesses, with the exception of the banks, which were forbidden — by special decree — to reopen. There were branches of nine banks in East Jerusalem, seven local and two foreign. An inspection showed that their vaults held only 218,687 dinars. On the eve of the war, the banks had transferred all their cash to the main offices in Amman, and, therefore, they could not meet obligations to their Jerusalem clients, whose deposits totalled 5.7 million dinars.

In order to forestall chaos, the Military Governor published a decree stating that "all the banks and credit institutions . . . shall be closed until a subsequent decree is issued." In addition, the local branches were forbidden to "operate or hold contacts or negotiations with any banks or branches outside of the area" — in other words, to contact their head offices in Amman. This ban remained in force even after the application of Israeli law. As a result of the banks' closure, East Jerusalemites lost 60% of their liquid assets, creating a severe shortage of ready money that was initially filled by Israeli purchases in Israeli currency. After the abolition of the Military Government, certain other measures were taken, as we shall see.

After the success of the first steps aimed at bringing life back to normal, the Military Government decided to continue to make use of the Arab Municipality. The authorities were concerned that Jordanian soldiers were still hiding in the city and that arms and ammunition were concealed in the homes of the inhabitants. Army units continued to search houses and also began inspecting ecclesiastical buildings, where a number of Legionaries were found hiding. Notices were posted, ordering the inhabitants to give up any arms and forbidding them to give shelter to regular or irregular soldiers, or failing to report knowledge of the same, under a penalty of up to 15 years' imprisonment or a fine of IL 5,000. Anyone carrying firearms or ammunition, a bomb, or a hand grenade faced life imprisonment.

The Military Governor decided to summon Mayor Rauhi al-Khatib and make him responsible for the surrender of arms. When the Mayor reported at military government headquarters, he was not even asked to sit down. The Governor informed him that "he had reliable information indicating that many of the inhabitants had arms and ammunition in their possession" and that he regarded

> the Mayor and the City Council, as elected representatives, responsible for informing the inhabitants of the necessity of handing in the arms and for convincing them to do so with all dispatch. If there is no response, severe measures will be taken against the Mayor and the Council, and against all the inhabitants.

When the Mayor tried to explain that, while he was prepared to assist the authorities, he could not take personal responsibility for the arms being handed in, he was rudely interrupted by the Governor, who raised his voice and rebuked him. Al-Khatib left the headquarters and informed his liaison officer that he would rather go to prison than be treated with a lack of respect. He calmed down later; but from that time on there was a significant change in his behavior and his readiness to cooperate with the Israelis. Nevertheless, he agreed to broadcast a radio message to the citizens.

Feeling that he had to get the backing of the members of the Council for all that he had done, so as not to be accused of "collaboration with the conqueror," al-Khatib also utilized the radio to call for an emergency meeting of the Jerusalem Municipal Council. The meeting took place on Tuesday, June 13, with eight out of the 12 council members present. They heard a report from the Mayor and decided unanimously to approve all his actions. It was also decided to ask the Military Government for help in the following areas:

> Ensuring protection in all quarters, especially in the commercial areas; food supplies for men and live-stock; help in finding shelter for refugees whose houses have been demolished; cooperation with the welfare associations to supply food and clothing for the refugees.

The Council then passed a resolution asking the Mayor "to clarify the Municipal Council's status with the military authorities and inquire whether it is recognized."

This question had bothered al-Khatib earlier, when he had asked an Israeli officer what the Israelis intended to do with him and his colleagues. His misgivings about his status stemmed from the fact that, since Friday, June 9, employees of the Israeli Municipality had entered all the departments of his Municipality.

Many of the Israelis were veterans who had worked together with the senior Arab employees in the Mandatory Municipality. The encounter was very friendly. One employee described it as follows:

> We arrived at the Municipality and were received by the Arab Deputy Mayor and senior officials. After the greetings, the hugs and kisses from officials who knew me from Mandatory times, we went on to the office. . . . The next day I took two Department employees and we went down to the office to begin organizing the job. I should point out that they haven't made any progress at all in administration. It's the same now as when I left them 20 years ago, worse maybe.

The Jewish officials asked for data and plans and made notes. Al-Khatib gave his employees instructions to hand over all material in their possession and to hide nothing. In the face of all this activity on the part of the Israeli Municipal employees, it was natural that al-Khatib should be suspicious of official intentions.

The resolutions of the Council's emergency session were handed to the Israeli liaison officer. The officer reiterated the Israeli demand for the surrender of arms, declaring that the Military Government held "every Council member present responsible for the whole city, and especially for the area where he lives," but he did not respond to the council members' questions about their status and future, because he did not have an answer. Even at this stage, a week after the constitution of the Military Government, the fate of the Arab Municipality had yet to be decided.

Demands for the surrender of weapons, as well as arms searches, continued throughout the period of the Military Government, but Israeli concern was exaggerated. The severe ban on the possession of arms during Jordanian rule resulted in the almost total lack of arms by the population. On Sunday, June 4, the Jordan Army had transferred a quantity of rifles and ammunition to be distributed to different parts of the city; but the inhabitants, to whom the arms had been issued, returned them, without even removing the grease. Most of the arms found by the Israelis were in public buildings and military emplacements, where they had been left by the retreating army.

The Arab Mayor's cooperation with the Military Government was not confined to resuming services and bringing life back to normal. The Military Government also asked the Mayor to cooperate in the evacuation of Arabs living in synagogues, and he tried to persuade these inhabitants to move out. He saw to it that their possessions were moved to the empty houses where they were billeted. Not all of them agreed to leave their houses voluntarily, whereupon pressure and intimidation were employed. Some of the people ousted found shelter with relatives; others joined those expelled from the Mugrabi Quarter, who had been housed in empty public buildings and in an unfinished school building. The Military Government moved a number of families into abandoned houses in the Silwan and Ras al-'Amud neighborhoods, but some of the owners of these houses soon returned home, and the Jewish Quarter refugees had to move again.

In most spheres, however, the Military Government succeeded in acting alone. When the stocks of food were exhausted, flour, sugar, rice, and fuel were supplied wholesale from the western part of the city at Israeli prices. Because the city was suffering from severe unemployment, and the poor had been left without means of sustenance, the Military Government reopened the Welfare Office and contacted voluntary welfare associations.

In the first few days after the war, the movement of civilians was still limited by a tough regime of transit permits, exchanged every few days. On June 13, however, a decree was issued permitting Jerusalemites to travel to the West Bank or to Jordan. They were required to sign statements that they were leaving of their own free will and were provided with transport to the Allenby Bridge on the Jordan River. During the first days, some six hundred people left the city daily.

Armed robberies continued, mainly during curfew hours, with the thieves posing as soldiers searching for arms. As a result, the Military Government halted night-time searches and informed inhabitants that they were not obliged to open their doors during the hours of darkness. It also set up checkpoints to search Israelis who had spent time in the eastern city. Anyone caught with loot in his possession was tried before a summary tribunal and sentenced to a fine or imprisonment. On June 21, a military spokesman disclosed that dozens of persons suspected of possessing loot had been arrested.

Eight had been sentenced to prison terms of up to six months, and fines of hundreds of Israeli pounds had been imposed.

On Saturday, June 17, Dayan visited Jerusalem and ordered that responsibility for the Temple Mount be restored to Muslim hands and that all Muslims from Israel and the West Bank be permitted to pray there. On Friday, June 23, 5,000 people prayed in the al-Aqsa Mosque, including 1,000 Muslims from Israel who had been forbidden to worship there during the rule of the Jordanian regime. As a precaution, tanks were deployed at the approaches to the Temple Mount. After the service, the Mayor complained that many non-Muslims, among them photographers, had entered the Mosque and wandered among the worshippers. The army acted to remove them and promised to ban the entry of non-worshippers into the mosques during services. Because of the large number of Jewish visitors in the churches, a decree was issued banning the entry of non-worshippers without a special permit; but Christians from all parts of Israel and the West Bank were permitted to enter the city for prayers every Sunday.

All this time, the Israel Cabinet continued to discuss the legal aspects of the annexation of Jerusalem, the demarcation of boundaries, and transition arrangements. On June 21, the draft law of annexation and the maps were ready. Reports of the Government's intentions to unite Jerusalem under the municipal authority of the Israeli Municipality of Jerusalem had already appeared in the press on June 16, two days after the Government's decision in principle on unification. However, the formal step was postponed for a week, because of the emergency session of the United Nations General Assembly, and was fixed for Wednesday, June 28.

Rauhi al-Khatib's officials informed him of the Israeli press disclosures, and he wondered what was to become of him and his Municipality. He told his friends that a possible solution was a unification of services, while leaving the Arab Municipality intact to cooperate with the Israeli one. On June 21, he was told that Israel Radio had announced that the Mayor of the Israeli city was about to visit the municipality building at 2 o'clock that afternoon, accompanied by his deputies, department heads and the Military Governor. The Israeli flag would be hoisted over the municipality building and "the city would be declared unified, as it had been in the past." That same evening, he relates, "I myself heard on the BBC that the British

Ambassador in Israel had visited the Tel Aviv leaders and informed them of the British Government's opposition to any change in the status of Arab Jerusalem."

Rauhi al-Khatib tried to find out if any of his subordinates knew of the visit. His chief assistant, Anton Saffiah, informed him that the Israeli Town Clerk, Yaakov Marash, had indeed contacted him to inform him of the intended visit. The Jewish official had assured him that "this is a friendly visit, to establish acquaintanceship between the two Mayors, and that their flag will only be flown over the municipality building during their presence there." It was stressed that it was the municipal banner which was referred to, not the Israeli flag. The Mayor demanded that the members of the Council convene one hour before the scheduled visit. Four council members arrived in response to his call.

At 1:30 that afternoon, Teddy Kollek reached the building of the Arab Municipality, together with his deputies and the department heads of the Israeli Municipality, and they were warmly received. Some time later, the Military Governor, Shlomo Lahat, also arrived. The executives of the Israeli Municipality had met previously and were officially informed of the boundaries of the municipal area following annexation. Therefore, to the Israeli participants, at least, it was clear that their hosts were about to be removed from their posts. Nevertheless, it appears that Teddy Kollek and his colleagues were unaware of the artificial character of the gathering and of the illusions it fostered. When they entered the council hall, Rauhi al-Khatib offered his chair to Teddy Kollek. The latter refused, saying "No, under no circumstances. I'm only a guest," and took his place at the Arab Mayor's right hand. The symbolic nature of this gesture did not escape the Arabs, who are strict about ceremony. After the meeting al-Khatib was to mention Kollek's gesture as a sign that the Jews did not want to oust him.

The host initiated proceedings by thanking Kollek for the help the Israeli Municipality had given in restoring services. He also thanked the Governor for his work in returning daily life to normal. He concluded by saying that they were all working "in the service of the inhabitants, in order to safeguard their welfare and that of the city."

The Israeli Mayor replied, saying that

cities do not make war, and certainly not the two parts of Jeru-salem. Despite the partition of the city, we sensed, throughout the years, that this is one city. Despite the bombardment by Arab forces, we took the initiative in extending help, restoring services, supplying food, and any assistance needed.

He continued: "The two Municipalities must work in fraternity, for they are siblings." Cooperation would be facilitated, he said, because many of the employees on both sides had worked together, for many years, during the British Mandate.

After al-Khatib had again expressed his gratitude, coffee was served. Dr. Rashid Nashashibi, a council member, brought up the problem of the continuing thefts and looting. He asked the Israelis to have this stopped. To this, Kollek replied that the behavior of the Israel Defense Forces had been exemplary and asked Nashashibi "what would have happened if the outcome of the war had been the reverse?" The ceremony ended and the Israelis left the building, while the Arab Council members remained in session with the Military Governor on current matters.

This meeting of the Mayors confused the Arabs. All indications pointed to the dispersal of their Municipality. But in that case, how were they to interpret Kollek's words and the visit as a whole? They wanted to believe that a way would indeed be found to perpetuate their existence as a separate Municipality, and the visit tended to support this illusion. However, on Sunday, June 25, al-Khatib knew that the days of the Arab Municipality were numbered, and he dictated his last official declaration, asking each employee of his Municipality

to continue to dedicate his efforts and to devote himself to his work within the framework of his duty and responsibility for carrying out the services resting on our shoulders, keeping our spirits firm and the deep faith in our love and devotion to our homeland and to our sacred city, to its inhabitants and visitors, holding on patiently and taking part in relieving the sufferings of all.

He also requested that detailed reports be presented to him within two days on all that had been done from the end of the fighting up to June 26, on the damage inflicted, on the help extended by the authorities, on the time needed to restore matters to normal, and on any other matter that they wished to bring to his attention. He concluded with "many thanks to all of you. May God bless you and all your brethren, the family of the Municipality."

On June 27, the Knesset adopted the set of laws that enabled the Government, on the following day, to issue a decree establishing Israeli law in East Jerusalem, and including it within the municipal area of the Jewish city. On the morning of June 28, the Arab department heads were handed a circular letter to pass on to their employees. The circular, from the Israeli Jerusalem Municipality, stated:

Those wishing to work for the Municipality should report for work at 7:30 a.m., Thursday, June 29. This employment is temporary. Those wishing to receive permanent employment are requested to present their applications in writing.

The circular was carefully phrased so as not to create legal continuity between the Israeli Municipality and the dispersed Arab Municipality. When the circular was distributed, Rauhi al-Khatib was still in his office. Asked by his employees what they should do, he replied:

We are serving the city, and this is a continuation of that service. I suggest that all of you sign. If you continue to work, you will help to maintain the Arab character of the city.

Al-Khatib carried on his business as usual. He called the Council members to a regular meeting on June 29. However, the meeting which convened that day was not at his invitation; the session was extraordinary in the extreme. Military policemen appeared at the homes of the Mayor and the Council members, ushering them into cars that took them to the municipality building, where they met the Deputy Military Governor, Yaakov Salman, and his assistant, David Farhi. The key to the Municipality could not be located, so the meeting was held at the nearby Gloria Hotel. There, the Deputy Governor read to the council members the text of a statement he had prepared in his office:

In the name of the Israel Defense Forces, I have the honor to inform Mr. Rauhi al-Khatib, and the members of the Jerusalem Municipal Council, that the Jerusalem Municipal Council is hereby dispersed. The Municipality's administrative and technical employees will from now on be considered as temporary employees of the Jewish Municipality of Jerusalem until their appointment is confirmed by the Municipality on the strength of applications they shall present in writing. In the name of the Israel Defense Forces I request the municipal employees to continue to supply the services required for the maintenance of the normal life of the

104

population. I hereby thank Mr. Rauhi al-Khatib, and the members
of the Council, for their services during the transition period from
the city's capture by the Israel Defense Forces up to the present
day.

Salman refrained from addressing al-Khatib as Mayor. In the copy of
the statement he had prepared in his own writing, the title precedes
Rauhi's name, but apparently on second thought, Salman crossed it
out.

The Arab Mayor did not respond, but instead asked for the declaration in writing. Farhi took one of the hotel's paper napkins, wrote
out an Arabic translation of the announcement, and handed it to
al-Khatib. The Council members were then taken back to their
homes.

This ceremony lacked any legal value, for according to the laws
adopted by the Knesset two days before, the Arab Municipal Council
was not dispersed; it had simply ceased to exist. From the moment
that Israel law was applied to the annexed area, the Council ceased to
have any municipal status. The Municipal Council disappeared, so
that legally it was as if it had never existed. Therefore, there was no
significance to the Deputy Governor's statement that the Council
was "hereby dispersed." He was addressing a body which, according
to Israel law, did not exist. It was, of course, in place to bid farewell
to the Mayor who had cooperated loyally with the Military Government during 21 difficult days; and it was also necessary to explain
the legal changes which had taken place in the city to the council
members. But this was not done. The form of the ceremony was not
appropriate to the importance of the matter. The feelings of bitterness and humiliation felt by the members of the now defunct
Council did not stem from the content of the statement they had
heard — they were prepared for that — but from the hasty and
undignified form of the ceremony.

The soldiers were not to blame. They had received an order to
dismiss all the Council members, and to put an end to the existence
of the Jordanian Municipality of Jerusalem. Upon receiving the order
from the Central Command's General Uzi Narkiss, shortly before the
meeting was convened, Yaakov Salman had asked in embarrassment:
"How does one do that? "

"Are you asking me? " responded Narkiss.

It was not the army that had asked for the ceremony, but Teddy

Kollek. On June 28, he had requested one of his assistants to remind the army that the Arab Council should be dispersed. The assistant did not see any legal reason to disperse the Council, as it would cease to exist automatically. He was also certain that the Military Government would itself arrange a farewell meeting with Rauhi al-Khatib. Accordingly, he did not comply with the Mayor's request. Twenty-four hours later, when Kollek discovered that the Council had not been dispersed, he phoned the Military Governor and pointed out that a constitutional anomaly had been created, with the Knesset resolving on annexation and the Arab Municipality being left in office. The Military Government, frightened of the implications of this "mistake," ordered Salman and Farhi to correct it immediately.

Teddy Kollek's fear of "a constitutional anomaly" was superfluous. His call to the Military Governor was an expression — unconscious, perhaps — of his ambition to take upon himself, and upon the Municipality he headed, total responsibility for the reunited city, a goal that had guided him in all his steps since the end of the war. And now his ambition was to be realized: the Arab Municipality had ceased to exist.

CHAPTER EIGHT

UNIFICATION

Any study of the developments and decisions taken during the Six Day War will show that the moves leading to Israel's capture of the Old City stemmed from the inner logic of military development, rather than from a preconceived political plan of conquest. The Defense Minister, Moshe Dayan, was hesitant about attacking Jerusalem, even after Jordanian provocations, while other Ministers were keen to order the attack. However, following the capture of the city, Moshe Dayan's attitude underwent a typical dialectical change. Now he, more than any of his colleagues in the Cabinet, wished to create *faits accomplis* regarding Jerusalem. His first order following the city's capture — an order reiterated several times that day and afterwards — was that all the gates be opened immediately and all the barriers removed, erasing the border between the two halves of the city. His aim was to create physical facts before anyone could try to restore the *status quo ante bellum*. On the other hand, Prime Minister Levi Eshkol, who had supported those pressing for a decision on the city's capture, very carefully worded his statement delivered in the Old City, giving no hint of his intentions, now that the city was captured.

The differences between the declarations of the Prime Minister and of the Defense Minister stemmed more from differences of character and of temperament than from a basic divergence of views. The Defense Minister, a pronounced pragmatist, tackled issues as he encountered them; he was too preoccupied to wrestle with hypothetical questions. As far as he was concerned, the next move was up to the Arabs. On June 13, he declared that he was waiting for a phone call from the Arabs, and that "we won't make any move. We are perfectly satisfied with what we have attained. If the Arabs want the situation changed, they should contact us." The Prime Minister, on the other hand, was worried about the fate of the occupied territory after Israel's withdrawal. He called a special meeting of top experts on Arab affairs to discuss the matter. The experts, all of whom had considerable experience in dealing with the Arabs, both before and after the 1948 War of Independence, presented the same divergent views they had put forward 19 years earlier. Some looked to a Palestinian solution; others saw the Kingdom of Jordan as the representative of all the Palestinian Arabs; still others envisaged an "Israeli-Palestinian-Hashemite" confederation. The meeting did not reach a unified position. But all those who attended were agreed on a policy of "first things first", and the first thing was to make peace.

A few days after the cease-fire, the former Jordanian Military Governor of Jerusalem, Anwar al-Khatib, presented himself to the Israeli Military Governor and offered to organize a meeting of Palestinian leaders in an East Jerusalem cinema, where the creation of a Palestinian entity on the West Bank would be proclaimed. The Governor rejected the proposal.

This was the beginning of a process whereby the purpose of the war was transformed retroactively, or, at least, there was a change in the evaluation of its significance. It is only natural that the first expression of this change in attitude was in regard to Jerusalem. No power on earth could give the order to withdraw from Jerusalem, and arriving at a decision regarding the destiny of the city took very little time.

On June 11, 1967, the Government met to decide upon the future of East Jerusalem. In unofficial consultations, Prime Minister Levi Eshkol expressed the opinion that the eastern sector of Jerusalem should be annexed at once. He felt that whether or not East Jerusalem was annexed "the possibilities for peace were equal." Most of the Ministers backed annexation, even though there were various opinions concerning the practical and legal steps to be taken. Only a minority of the Ministers favored delaying the decision. When it became clear that a majority favored immediate action, the Ministerial Committee was asked to prepare a detailed proposal which would solve the legal and administrative problems. The proposals were then

108

crystallized into three draft laws and tabled before the Government on June 21. Based upon this proposal the decision was to take effect within a week, but implementation was, in fact, postponed for another week, at the request of the Israeli delegation to the United Nations, in view of the forthcoming emergency session of the General Assembly.

Following the decision to annex East Jerusalem, four problems presented themselves: the legal form of the annexation; the boundaries of the unified city; the municipal status of the annexed area, and the legal provision for the Holy Sites.

The Government, for various reasons, decided to carry out the annexation by means of an amendment to the "Law and Administration Ordinance," Israel's first constitutional law, supplementing it with a paragraph stating that "the State's law, jurisdiction and administration shall apply to any area of the Land of Israel which the Government shall designate by order." In the order issued on the strength of this amendment, the Government ordered that "those areas of the Land of Israel described in the schedule are hereby determined as areas where the State's laws, jurisdiction, and administration apply." The schedule specifies the demarcation line of the annexed territory but the law of annexation does not mention Jerusalem by name, nor even hint at it. The demarcation line is specified not by a map, but by listing imaginary lines between reference points on an ordnance survey map.

The desire to camouflage the act of annexation is evident in the wording of the law and the decree. It also characterized the whole process of discussion and ratification. For example, the Government avoided using the word "annexation." Its official declarations, as well as Foreign Ministry explanations, spoke of "unification" or "reunification." Following the unification of the city, Israel stressed that use of the term "annexation" concerning municipal and administrative steps was "inappropriate."

Within a short time, a vigorous debate on the meaning and legality of the Israeli steps developed among experts on international law. The overwhelming majority of experts agreed that the Israeli conquest was legitimate, being the outcome of a defensive war, and the fact that the United Nations did not denounce Israel as an aggressor (July 4, 1967) indicated that most states considered the Israeli conquest to be "belligerent occupation," valid till the signature of peace agreements. "Belligerent occupation," however, gave Israel a hold but no title. Annexation, or the granting of an absolute title, could only be executed by a peace agreement, which put an end to the state of war, or by "superannuation," after the passing of many years of undisputed Israeli rule. As to the legal steps taken in Jerusalem, a minority of the jurists held that these were in accord with Israeli possession, stemming from "belligerent occupation," while a majority held that they exceeded Israel's competence. A number of jurists tried to prove that Israeli legislation constituted full, legal annexation. According to them, the Jordanian conquest was illegal, since the Transjordanian invasion of Palestine in 1948 was in contradiction to United Nations resolutions. Jerusalem and the West Bank had never been under Jordanian sovereignty: since the end of the Mandate, a "vacuum of sovereignty" had existed there. Having expelled the unlawful invader, Israel had prior claim to fill the vacuum of sovereignty by taking possession of these areas, as she had in Jerusalem.

Other jurists countered this by saying that, by virtue of the same Partition Resolution, and the same right to self-determination by which the State of Israel was created, the Palestinian Arabs had also been granted the right to create a state of their own. Accordingly, in those parts of Palestine which had not been included in the State of Israel, there was no "vacuum of sovereignty" but a Palestinian "potential sovereignty" that had never been achieved in practice due to Jordanian annexation. Jordan, they claimed, had indeed conquered these areas illegally, so that she had no title to them; but this fact did not make them "no-man's-land." Accordingly, it was proposed that, while Israel's claim may be greater than Jordan's, the test of Israel's claim is not in relation to that of Jordan, but to that of the Palestinians who inhabited these areas.

The Israel Government assumed an ambiguous position. Outwardly, it stressed that the steps taken did not constitute annexation, while for internal consumption it emphasized that annexation was full and complete. On a number of occasions, when referring to the issue, Israeli courts handed down verdicts stating that "united Jerusalem is an inseparable part of Israel," or mentioning "the annexation of East Jerusalem."

The effect of the Government's legislation, however, was not in the least ambiguous. The law of annexation clearly applied Israeli law, jurisdiction, and administration to the annexed area. Nor did the process permit selective or gradual application of Israeli law; it enforced a revolutionary change from one day to the next. It did not even lay down transitional arrangements that would have ensured some kind of jurisdictional and administrative continuity. The resulting situation was legally absurd. All the inhabitants of East Jerusalem became "enemy aliens" according to Israeli law, with all the consequences that this implied for their personal status, their commercial contacts, and their property. According to international law, they remained citizens of the Kingdom of Jordan. According to the Israeli Law of Absentees' Property, they had all become "absentees." Enacted in 1950, this law stated that any person who, at any time after November 29, 1947, had been a citizen of any Arab state, or an inhabitant of one of them or of any part of Palestine outside the boundaries of the State of Israel, was an "absentee," and his property was entrusted to the Custodian of Absentee Property. Since the inhabitants of East Jerusalem had for 19 years been "outside the boundaries of the State of Israel" and were still citizens of one of the Arab states, they had ceased to be the legal owners of their property as soon as Israeli law was applied. Every company or corporation which had been incorporated by Jordanian law was suddenly without status; every form of licensed business, from a grocery store to a bus company, which had operated on the basis of Jordanian licenses, was now operating without authorization. Lawyers, doctors and others who needed licences, could no longer legally practice their professions. Every legal action, whether completed or not, as well as all documents issued or authorized before the law of annexation, became null and void.

The proposers of the law were not unaware of its absurdities. It seems, however, that they considered it preferable to carry out the annexation unambiguously and without complicated legal niceties. This move was also an expression of the desire to avoid giving East Jerusalem a special status, which might indicate Israeli readiness to accept a special status for all Jerusalem. The absurd legal situation was to be solved in the first stage by administrative orders and, later, by laws and regulations that would permit juridical continuity and a gradual transition. For example, immediately after annexation, the Minister of Justice instructed the Custodian of Absentee Property not to treat as absentees those inhabitants of East Jerusalem who remained within the annexed area, and the Civil Service Commissioner ordered that Jordanian citizens could be employees of the State of Israel. All corporations and businesses were permitted to continue their operations. In practice, also, most Israeli authorities did not try to enforce Israeli law fully in the annexed area; however, some official bodies were in a hurry to impose their authority, not because they wished to harass the inhabitants, but because they wished to operate in the annexed area and take an active part in the historic act of unifying the city. As far as they were concerned, East Jerusalem had simply become a part of Israel, to be treated like Tel Aviv or Haifa. Naturally, this haste caused friction, confrontation and bitterness, which actually impeded the process of unifying the two halves of the city.

The moderation shown by most authorities in imposing Israeli law was no substitute for a law to straighten out the severe legal injustices created by the law of annexation. Some time after the annexation, such a law was drafted, but its presentation to the Knesset was held up for eight months because the Israel Foreign Ministry was concerned about the international repercussions. Only in August 1968 was the "Law of Legal and Administrative Arrangements" adopted, ironing out most, though not all, of the difficulties.

Once the legal procedure for annexation was settled, it remained to determine the boundaries of the annexed area. This matter was debated by a committee headed by the Deputy Minister of the Interior, with the participation of representatives of the Planning Department and the Army. Every now and then, differences of opinion were settled by Ministers, either individually or in meetings of ministerial committees. The debate was fierce, since those engaged in it were convinced that the boundaries they were marking out would, in fact, be the border of the State of Israel. At that time, the West Bank was carefully kept separate from Israel, and the "Green Line" (the 1949 Armistice Line) still possessed great practical and, above all, psychological importance.

According to the Committee's assumption, the area annexed was to be connected in every way to Israel and totally detached from the West Bank. The economic separation thus foreseen, led to a cigarette factory and an Arak distillery being excluded from the annexed area, so that they could continue to supply the West Bank. The Army representatives, however, thought in terms of a border that could be

112

defended and proposed that it include all the hilltops around Jerusalem "so that the city would never again be at the mercy of enemy artillery batteries." As a result of the armistice years, the tradition of a hermetically sealed border was so strong that there was a long debate concerning the construction of a road joining the northern part of the West Bank with the south, which would by-pass Jerusalem.

Once again it was Moshe Dayan who foresaw future developments and refused to regard the demarcation line of the annexed area as a dividing line. When representatives of the religious parties demanded that Rachel's Tomb be included in the Jerusalem area, the Defense Minister disagreed, apparently because he wanted Jews to cross the border in order to visit "the holiest of our Holy Places." In his thinking, the expression "we have returned" was not identical with "we have annexed."

During the Committee's discussions, its members divided into "maximalists" and "minimalists." The former proposed a boundary enclosing an area of 50,000 acres. In addition to East Jerusalem, it encompassed 22 villages, and the total number of Arab inhabitants was about 100,000. The minimalists proposed a much smaller area, and in the end a compromise was reached. One of the considerations in restricting the area was the desire to limit the number of Arab citizens to be attached to Jerusalem, so as to maintain a large Jewish majority in the city. For this reason, populated suburbs like Abu Dis and al-Azariyah were excluded from the annexed area. In the north, the boundary line was drawn 50 meters to the east of the Jerusalem—Ramallah road, excluding urban suburbs and refugee camps beside the road to the east, which were an inseparable part of the built-up area of the city.

The precise line was drawn according to clear tactical criteria, ensuring control of hilltops and passing through defensible valleys. The area annexed encompassed a total of 18,000 acres, of which only 1,500 acres were within the boundaries of Jerusalem's Arab Municipality. The rest belonged to 28 villages, some of which were totally annexed, the majority of which were only partially annexed. The annexed territory also incorporated areas which had been included within the municipal boundaries of al-Bira, Beit Jallah and Bethlehem.

The basic political assumption was that the whole of the annexed area would be attached to the municipal area of Jerusalem. Making the state boundaries identical with the city boundaries caused conflicts between the dictates of security, demography, and urban needs. If future developments had been foreseen at the time of these debates, greater weight might have been given to urban considerations. But one of the main considerations was a "defensible border" or "a border that would impede mobility of Arab labor into the annexed territory." As a result, the boundary line drawn was, from the purely urban point of view, inappropriate. On the one hand, it was too restrictive and did not ensure sufficient reserves of land for urban development. An examination by the Jerusalem Master Plan Office recommended redefining the border by moving the frontier four to six kilometers eastwards and by adding areas to the west. Not only did the municipal area not include all the metropolitan area, but it also left out populated neighborhoods that were an integral part of Jerusalem. On the other hand, the area was too extensive and hetero-geneous to allow for a rational and centralized development of mu-nicipal services. On June 21, when the members of the City Council were informed of the new area for which they were responsible, they demanded that the Government provide a grant for services, otherwise they could not be responsible for such an extensive area. Subsequently, however, the city's boundaries acquired the same political and sym-bolic significance as the unification decree, and, like the latter, they became part of a national myth which could not be questioned.

The third problem facing the men drawing up the annexation laws was the question of the area's municipal status. The annexation decree automatically abrogated the existence of all legal municipal bodies, and the annexed area lost its municipal status. Therefore, an amendment (No. 7) was drafted to the Municipal Corporation Ordinance which gave the Interior Minister the right to expand the area under the juris-diction of the local authority affected by the decree; in other words, the annexed area. The Interior Minister's proclamation then placed it within the municipal boundaries of the Israeli Jerusalem Municipal-ity, which became the municipal authority of the unified city.

The third of the Unification Laws, the Law for the Protection of the Holy Places, will be dealt with in another chapter.

For the legislators of the democratic State of Israel, it was incon-ceivable that the inhabitants of the annexed zone should not be represented in the municipal council of the united Municipality. Accordingly, a further paragraph was added, stating that the Minister was "entitled to nominate, by decree, additional members of the

Council, from among the inhabitants of the area." The question of representation arose before the principles of annexation had been clearly settled. In view of Mayor Rauhi al-Khatib's readiness to find ways to cooperate with the Israeli Municipality, while maintaining the independence of the Municipal Council he headed, the liaison officer in day-to-day contact thought there was room to seek a formula for such cooperation. When the officer suggested something on these lines to Teddy Kollek, he claims that the Mayor replied: "They'll get in the way of my work."

Following his meeting with the Arab Mayor, when one of the Arab Council members complained of looting, Kollek adopted a policy of opposing the cooption of Arab members. His reaction was:

I'm opposed to such an approach. Today, we visited the Old City Municipality for a talk with the Mayor, and they talked of looting. Tomorrow, they'll be members sitting in [our] Municipality, and they'll be saying all kinds of things. Our meetings are open, and they will be addressing foreign bodies and hostile elements. I suggest that we treat the annexed area as a neighborhood, and that some of the local inhabitants serve as members of an advisory committee.

He repeated his view in a newspaper interview:

Jerusalem is one city, and will have one Municipality. During the transition period, I propose that the liberated area of Jerusalem be divided, in the same way that large neighborhoods or regions are administered abroad. An independent administration will be set up, whose heads will work under the department heads of the Jerusalem Municipality.

The Government did not accept this view. As in other matters related to annexation, it did not want to create, as one Minister put it, "the seed of anything else within the city." The proposal to coopt Arab members was approved and included in the amendment to the Municipalities' Ordinance, but even after the annexation, debate on this issue continued.

The draft laws were presented to the Government on Sunday, June 25, and approved. Within 48 hours, they were presented to the Knesset. But before the Knesset assembled to discuss them, some further administrative steps were taken. On Monday, June 26, a population census was held in all those sections of the city to be annexed. The census was carried out, by the Ministry of the Interior, to determine which citizens would be entitled to Israeli identity cards following annexation; but, due to insufficient preparation, hundreds of families were not reached by the census teams.

It was also necessary to decide how responsibility would be transferred from the military authorities to their civilian counterparts. The problem was not a complicated one, as the Israeli Municipality was already providing services, and the ministries were already operating in East Jerusalem. On June 21, a Ministerial Committee for Jerusalem, headed by the Prime Minister, nominated a "Committee of Directors-General" for Jerusalem to coordinate the operations of the ministries and to solve the enormous tangle of administrative problems expected after unification. A few days after this appointment, another coordinating body was appointed, this time under the Mayor. This committee only survived one meeting. The Committee of Directors-General did not fare much better. It met for a number of sessions, but never became a coordinating and organizing body. The various ministries were jealous of their authority, and each worked energetically in its own field. Most regarded the coordinating committee as an impediment that interfered in their affairs. The results of this lack of coordination were not slow to appear.

On the eve of the Knesset debate, final arrangements for annexation were made. Bureaus were set up for the exchange of dinars into Israel pounds. Teams of customs officials were alerted to impose surcharges on stock, so that customs' duties in the annexed area would be equal to those in Israel. The supply of food, and of industrial and agricultural products, was ensured. Only one single issue remained unresolved: would the barriers between the two halves of the city be completely removed, permitting free passage of Jews and Arabs in both parts, or would restrictions be retained? This was only settled after the ratification of the annexation laws, and not without arguments and hesitation.

The Knesset met at 4 o'clock on June 27, to discuss the three draft laws. The Knesset Members were not officially informed of the agenda. Nothing was written on the notice boards. Contrary to custom, the draft laws had not been placed on their desks. The Knesset Steering Committee, convened secretly, had allocated three hours for the debate; but the coalition parties had agreed not to take part in the debate, so as to shorten it and insure its conclusion that same evening. The Prime Minister and many of his colleagues were not present in the chamber. Only when the debate began were the draft laws handed out to the legislators.

At 7:30 that evening, the laws were adopted with only the two Communist parties voting against. They went into force "on the day of their adoption by the Knesset," and not, as is the custom, on their publication. Thus, secretly, and with a considerable effort to reduce tension and minimize the drama, the Knesset passed the laws that permitted the Government to meet the next day and order "the application of Israeli law, jurisdiction, and administration" in East Jerusalem. Ministers and public figures were forbidden to make declarations or give newspaper interviews. Mayor Teddy Kollek was not present in the Knesset hall but was invited to drink a toast in the Interior Committee's office, where the Interior Minister told him: "As of tonight, you are Mayor of the whole of Jerusalem."/Formally, Kollek had to wait for the publication of the order and of the Interior Minister's proclamation on the following morning. At midday on June 28, the Interior Minister handed the Jerusalem proclamation to the Mayor, saying "I hope that all of us, both the Jewish and the Arab citizens, will be happy. We will see to it that peace reigns between us, and that there is mutual understanding." In reply, Kollek said: "I am overawed by the great historic responsibility which has befallen us. We have yet to appreciate its enormity." At first, they had even thought of doing without this modest ceremony, but changed their minds since "it is impossible to bypass such an historic moment."

The sole official notification given to the population of East Jerusalem of the revolutionary change in their lives was affixed to walls and notice boards on the morning of June 28. It was neither the annexation order, nor any kind of proclamation, but a simple Finance Ministry notice of the obligation to exchange Jordanian dinars for Israel pounds. The citizens learned formally of the unification in this manner, since the first sentence said: "As by law . . . the laws of the State of Israel have been applied to the areas detailed . . ."

As rumors spread that Israel intended to annex East Jerusalem, an increasing number of statements by various world leaders warned against such a step. As might have been expected, the first came from Pope Paul VI. He did not connect his statement with the rumors of annexation, but expressed his concern about the safety of Jerusalem

117

and the hope that it would at long last become the City of Peace —
reiterating the Vatican view that it should be internationalized. On
June 15, the French Government declared that: "Nothing which has
happened in the region concerning border-alterations, and changes in
the status of citizens, is a *fait accompli.*" On June 19, President
Johnson declared that "There must be adequate recognition of the
special interest of three great religions in the Holy Places of Jerusalem." Unofficially, the President demanded that Israel take no unilateral step concerning the city's status before consultations with
religious leaders and other concerned bodies. Finally, at the request
of the Soviet Union, a special emergency session of the United
Nations General Assembly was convened, and the Israeli delegation
to the U.N. sent a telegram to the Israel Government suggesting
postponement of the annexation order until after the emergency
session.

The issue of annexation was first raised at the Assembly by the
British Foreign Minister, George Brown, on June 21. He called on the
Israelis not to take any steps to change the status of Jerusalem.
Foreign Minister Abba Eban chose to answer Brown immediately. He
did not conceal Israel's intentions, although he did not dwell upon
them at length:

> All I shall say is that our policy is the preservation of the unity of
> Jerusalem, the elevation of its material and cultural life, free access
> to the Holy Places of all faiths and perfect respect for religious
> interests.

Since the President of the emergency session of the Assembly intended to end the debate on June 30, the Israel Delegation thought
that adoption of the annexation laws on June 27, and publication of
the decree the following day, would not cause too drastic a reaction
at the Assembly. They were right. On June 28, the Jerusalem problem was mentioned by the representatives of Ecuador, Spain, and
Brazil, not in relation to the day's events, but in connection with the
internationalization plan of 1947. The Lebanese delegate mentioned
annexation, as a fact, but did not adopt any position regarding it. It
was the Yugoslav delegate who was the first to relate directly to the
annexation and its implications. He demanded that his proposal, calling for an immediate and total Israeli withdrawal from all the territories she had conquered, be carried out immediately, since, in his
opinion, Israel's decision to annex Jerusalem made this essential. The

Pakistani Chairman replied that the question of new developments in Jerusalem was not yet before the Assembly.

But although annexation was received calmly by the Assembly, there was a vigorous reaction throughout the world. The American State Department issued a short declaration stating:

The hasty administrative action taken by Israel today cannot be regarded as determining the future of the Holy Places or the status of Jerusalem in relation to them. The United States has never recognized such unilateral action by any of the states in the area as governing the international status of Jerusalem.

The Vatican did not issue any official statement, but informed sources had already expressed their reservations about the annexation and stated "that the Vatican believes that the only desirable solution is the internationalization of the Holy Places, as decided upon by the United Nations in 1947." The Arab states issued sharp statements and called for a "holy war."

On the next day, June 29, there was still no sense of urgency at the U.N. The delegates of Peru and Cyprus touched briefly on the act of annexation; but the first to devote his whole speech to the issue of Jerusalem was none other than Israeli Foreign Minister Abba Eban. The course of the debate did not call for Israeli intervention at this stage, and it is hard to know what induced him to deal with the subject at length. He may have decided to exploit the Assembly podium to reply to statements made on the previous day.

Eban's speech set out the Israeli line of argument that would be followed throughout the coming debates.

The attacks on the Israeli step, Eban said, originated in "a basic misunderstanding," since the administrative legislation "contained no new political statement and concerned itself exclusively with the urgent necessities of repairing the ravages and dislocation arising from the division of the city's life." The purpose of this legislation was "to assure for the inhabitants of all parts of the city, social, municipal, and fiscal services on a basis of equality and non-discrimination." He extended this point in his speech of July 3, adding that a Pakistani proposal

would have us re-install the barbed wire and minefields which have been removed. It assumes that the United Nations has a vested interest in division, separation and embattled confrontations.

Furthermore, claimed the Foreign Minister, the Israeli legislation had another aim: to safeguard the Holy Places and free access to them. Israel's steps did not bar the way to a settlement of this question; on the contrary, they opened it. On July 4, he could say

these words of reassurance. Discussions are now going forward, and will continue with the interests involved, in order to elaborate a satisfactory agreement for the protection of the Holy Places.

As for Jordan, said Eban, she had conquered Jerusalem in 1948 and carried out an explicit annexation in 1950. She had done what she wished in Jerusalem, and her wishes included the destruction of ancient houses of prayer and a criminal obstruction of free access to the most ancient Holy Place in the world, the Western Wall. It was Israeli policy to distinguish between sacred and secular aspects of the life of the city.

It would be farfetched to assert that the existence of this specific universal issue requires that some of Jerusalem's citizens remain artificially cut off from the social services and municipal facilities which others enjoy.

A comparison of Israeli arguments in 1967 with the ones offered in 1949 on the Jerusalem issue is instructive. In 1949, the State of Israel had demanded Jewish Jerusalem, by virtue of historic claims and the right to self-determination of its Jewish citizens. This position was expressed in the most forceful terms, with no attempt to hide behind altruistic arguments. Israel knew that she was confronted by Christian religious interests, but considered that these could be met under Israeli sovereignty in the city. In 1967, the purpose of annexation had suddenly become an act of goodwill and desire to improve the standard of living of the Arabs. The steps taken were administrative and municipal and no political significance should be attached to them. Unifying the city would remove the barriers on the road to neighborly relations between Jews and Arabs. All these were altruistic aims. Conspicuous in its absence, especially in view of the arguments of 1949, was any reference to the Israeli national element, the Israeli title to the whole of Jerusalem. The only point that the arguments of 1949 and of 1967 share in common concerned Israel's ability to find a solution to the question of Christian religious interests under her sovereignty.

Israel was now trying to blur the national conflict over Jerusalem, whereas in 1949 she had tried to define it more sharply, in opposition to Christian religious interests. The reason for the change is clear. In 1949, two national states, one Jewish and the other Arab, had reached temporary agreement regarding partition of the city and had worked in cooperation to frustrate the attempt of some Christian States (in conjunction with other forces, some of which were Arab) to impose an international solution on the city. In 1967, however, one of the national states had upset the equilibrium in Jerusalem, and, due to a strategic error, had lost control of its section of the city. The other partner now remained in control of the whole city. In her triumph, however, Israel now faced a double battle: with Christian religious forces, as in 1949, *and*, unlike 1949, with Arab national interests. Eban deliberately avoided the specific national problem that had now been created.

This evasion made sense from Israel's point of view. She had something to offer the Christian states, with whom she could enter into a dialogue leading to a settlement. But there was no point in arguing with the Arab States; the only way of satisfying them was by returning to the *status quo ante*, to the previous compromise of partition, which was no longer acceptable to Israel.

Of course, as a result of this line, Israel's enemies indulged in heavy sarcasm: "Now we know why Israel went to war: to bring water to the parched lips of the Arabs of Jerusalem, and to open schools for their children," or "The claim of an improved standard of living of the inhabitants has been used by all the imperialists to justify their rule in the colonies." It was only when Eban was severely provoked by the Soviet representative that he abandoned his restraint and expressed the fundamental Israeli view:

It is very easy for Mr. Fedorenko to sneer at Israel's traditional concept of body and head, Israel as the body and Jerusalem as the head. This is a concept which lies beyond and above, before and after, all political and secular considerations . . . the eternal link between Israel and Jerusalem [is] a link more ancient, more potent, and more passionate than any other link between any people and any place . . . therefore Israel will continue to pray, yearn, and work for Jerusalem's unity and for Jerusalem's peace.

But this was the only outburst of its kind.

There was an important distinction between Israel's opponents in this debate. The Arab-Soviet bloc wanted "the elimination of the results of aggression," namely immediate Israeli withdrawal from the territories she had occupied, including Jerusalem. For them, the crucial point was Jordan's expulsion from the city and the necessity to have the Israeli occupation declared illegal. States friendly to Israel, however, as well as other independent ones, recognized Israel's right to belligerent occupation until the signing of peace treaties, as recognized by international law. States such as Britain and the United States did not, therefore, cast any doubt on the legality of Israel's steps prior to annexation. As far as they were concerned, the military occupation of Jerusalem could go on as long as necessary.

Israel's annexation of East Jerusalem gave the Arabs an opportunity to try to gain the support of states that had recognized Israel's right of occupation. Although Israel anticipated a large majority for a resolution against annexation, she was nonetheless unable to change her decision regarding annexation. It was not Unification Day that was the turning point, but the day the city was captured. The moment the Israel Army controlled the whole city, Israel came under the influence of forces "beyond and above, before and after, all political and secular considerations." These forces created a situation from which there was no return. The annexation laws were no more than a legal step to define the situation created the moment the city was captured. The demand to abrogate these laws was interpreted as renunciation of the return "to the holiest of our Holy Places." On the day of their promulgation, the annexation laws, together with the annexed area, became part of the national myth. Accordingly, Israel could take notice neither of the counsel of her friends nor of the warnings of her enemies.

On July 4, 1967, the U.N. General Assembly decided, by a vote of 90 to none, with 20 abstentions, that Israel's steps were invalid; called on Israel to repeal them; and commissioned the Secretary-General to report within a week on the implementation of the resolution. Secretary-General U Thant requested Israel's reply, which was delivered on July 10. It contained the same elements as Eban's speeches:

> The term 'annexation,' . . . is out of place. The measures adopted related to the integration of Jerusalem in the administrative and municipal spheres and furnish a legal basis for the protection of the Holy Places. These steps are aimed at improving the lives of the inhabitants, rebuilding the ruins, at civic cooperation, and at safeguarding the Holy Places and ensuring free access to them.

When the Secretary-General's report was laid before the General Assembly, opposition to Israel's policy came from the Pakistani and Kuwaiti delegates. They said that it didn't matter how Israel defined her acts in Jerusalem; Israel could not impose her definition on the world. The acts amounted to the annexation of territory belonging to another member-State, and were therefore invalid. Israel defended annexation by referring to its aims and results, but that was not the question. The Assembly had called on Israel to refrain from steps which could alter the status of Jerusalem, and any Israeli declaration about the results of her steps, even if true, is not a relevant reply to the Assembly resolution. The British Delegate stressed the juridical view: "The Israeli measures . . . were invalid because they went beyond the competence of an occupying Power as defined by international law."

The least hostile view, for Israel, was that of the United States. The Americans "insisted that the steps taken cannot be interpreted as other than temporary and intermediate and do not predetermine the final and permanent status of Jerusalem." In other words, even if Israel said the opposite, this was the way the United States viewed the legislation. Privately, the Americans advised their Israeli friends more or less as follows: do what you like in Jerusalem, but for Heaven's sake, don't make a fuss and don't pass laws! Israel accepted this advice and a heavy curtain of secrecy descended on Israeli activity in East Jerusalem. The Israel Foreign Ministry tried to delay or postpone any act involving the publication of laws or decrees. When the Law of Legal and Administrative Arrangements was published, even the United States was obliged to vote for the Arab proposal, which reiterated in the most severe terms that Israel's steps were illegal and null and void. During the years 1967–71, six similar resolutions were adopted.

The question of whether or not the barriers that separated the Jewish and Arab population should be removed, was still pending. The civil, police, and security authorities grappled with the problem, their main concern being security. They feared that there would be serious disturbances; that Jews who had been forced out of the Old City would come into conflict with the Arab occupants of the Jewish Quarter; that Arabs who had lived in the neighborhoods of Qatamon and Bak'a would go to their old houses and resent their Jewish occupants; and that the resulting chaos would provide an excellent

123

opportunity for hostile elements to carry out sabotage and murder. Apart from security, there were a number of severe practical problems. Roads between the two halves of the city had not been paved; no-man's land was still full of scattered abandoned buildings, barbed-wire fences, barriers, and communications trenches. Mines and unexploded shells had yet to be removed. The City Engineer, traffic officials and the police were sure that there would be chaos when hundreds of Israeli cars tried to cross to the east, which lacked any parking facilities. All those concerned planned physical unification as a process to extend over several weeks. As late as the morning of June 28, one of the Mayor's assistants reported that removing the barriers and preparing transit points would take two weeks. The planners proposed, but one man disposed — differently.

The Defense Minister had stuck to his view since the capture of the city: the deed had to be carried out to its conclusion. His first order on the day of the city's capture was also his last. On the formal ending of the occupation he repeated: "Open the city; remove the barriers! " He took no notice of appeals by army or police officers. His reply rested on a formality:

> If Teddy [Kollek] wants the army to stay in the city, he should apply to the Interior Minister. East Jerusalem is Israeli, and his application has to go to the Government.

In other words, only by removing the barriers and allowing Jews and Arabs to intermingle would the Government's intentions concerning the city's future remain credible.

Military and civilian leaders tried to persuade Moshe Dayan to change his view; but he took no notice of them, and his order remained in force: free movement in both directions would be permitted from mid-day, Thursday, June 29.

The orders to remove the barriers and fences between the two parts of the city, placed a huge burden on the army. There was more than one-and-a-half miles of fortified frontier between the two parts of the city. Along this border were 55 fortified emplacements (36 Jordanian and 19 Israeli), tens of miles of barbed wire fences, and massive defensive ramparts. Within no-man's-land, which covered 45 acres, there were 150 buildings in ruins since 1948. Three of the gates to the Old City (the New Gate, Jaffa Gate and Zion Gate) were blocked by reinforced concrete walls. Tens of thousands of mines had been laid all over the whole area by both sides. Admittedly, the minefields were marked, but the precise placement of the mines within the fields was not known, since they had been laid over many years, without charts.

The Israel Corps of Engineers cleared the minefields, demolished the emplacements, and opened the gates of the Old City. Mine-clearing was very difficult and dangerous. The sappers were troubled by layers of Chinese-made plastic mines, resembling match boxes, which had been laid by the Jordanians and could not be dismantled. The men of the Engineers Corps were forced to uncover them by using jets of compressed air to peel off fine layers of soil, and several men were wounded in the course of the operation.

Teddy Kollek offered to carry out the clearing of no-man's-land. On June 15, he wrote to General Narkiss that, in accordance with the latter's request, the Municipality was taking upon itself the prepara-tion of access routes for the clearing of ruins.

The employees of the municipal Maintenance Department worked day and night to demolish the remnants of buildings, and to remove vast amounts of rubble from the city. Altogether, 145 buildings were cleared from the entire no-man's-land area. At the beginning of July, the job of demolishing all the Jordanian emplacements at the top of the Old City walls was completed. The gates were opened, no-man's-land areas were cleared, and the roads revealed beneath the rubble were re-surfaced. Near Jaffa Gate, a large public lavatory, discovered under the ruins, was rebuilt and put back into use.

Only one Israeli emplacement was left unaltered for the sake of posterity. This was the position in the Turjeman building, south of the Mandelbaum Gate. The Gate itself became an ordinary road junc-tion, with pedestrian crossings and safety barriers. Visitors who gazed at it could not believe that this was the famous Mandelbaum Gate that had served as the transit point between Israel and the Arabs for 19 years.

The barriers dividing the city of Jerusalem came down on June 29, without the issuing of any specific order. The Israeli authorities had decided to open the city at mid-day; but the army and police guards had already stopped demanding permits in the morning, and soon abandoned the barriers completely. What took place during the fol-lowing hours has been variously described as a "peace festival," or "mutual invasion" — thousands of Jews poured into the alleyways of the Old City, completely blocking them; hundreds of Arabs, in groups of various sizes, made their way through the streets of the Jewish city.

The Jews swooped down on the shops and market-stalls of the Old City, buying anything they could lay their hands on. Veteran Israelis fell on the piles of Arab cakes and pastries and drank *suss* and *tamarhindi* poured from the ornamental copper jugs carried by vendors, and licked the Oriental ice-cream that stretches like chewing gum. They filled restaurants to eat delicacies they had not tasted for 19 years. Others gazed in amazement at the shelves, loaded with imported foodstuffs — bottles of French wine, canned meats, chocolates, and cheeses, the likes of which could not be found in West Jerusalem. Some bought more durable commodities — sets of china, tableware, and electric goods — for a third of the price that they would have paid in Israel. Everybody bought souvenirs. All the displayed goods were snatched up within a few hours, but they were soon replaced. The Arab traders had seemingly inexhaustible stocks.

There was a mood of exhilaration, a carnival atmosphere. Jews and Arabs conversed in broken Arabic, in English, or with gestures. Human contacts were somewhat hesitant; people were shy but polite. However, there was no hostility. A thin trickle left the turbulent flood of Jews that poured down David Street in the Old City and turned right into the Suq al-Hussur. These were inhabitants of the Jewish Quarter who had left in 1948. There were emotional reunions with neighbors of a generation ago: fathers introduced their children; cameras clicked. Those whose former houses had not been destroyed knocked politely on the doors and asked the present occupants to let them see the inside of the houses.

The Arab visitors in West Jerusalem were more hesitant. They walked the streets slowly, hand in hand; whole families dressed in festive attire, gazed in all directions. When they saw the traffic lights and the pedestrian crossings, they halted for a moment and applauded. A few went into shops and enquired about prices, but none bought anything; prices in the western sector were more than double those in East Jerusalem. The older ones stopped near the landmarks they had not seen for nineteen years: the Municipality, the Post Office, the Y.M.C.A. and the King David Hotel. Fathers stopped in front of shops and whispered to their children: "This used to be grandpa's store." Cars with Jordanian licence plates caused traffic jams; but Jewish drivers, usually tense and excitable, behaved with unaccustomed politeness.

Many of the Arabs were not, however, interested in the city center. They took their children and grandchildren to the residential suburbs of Qatamon, Bak'a and Talbiya. Several of the families brought the keys with which they had locked up their homes nineteen years earlier. Most of them stood in silence, staring at their houses. Very few plucked up the courage to ask the Jewish occupants for permission to look inside. A middle-aged Arab woman dressed in black reproached a Jewish housewife: "Why didn't you look after the garden? " But there was no hatred or hostility here either.

There were no complaints registered that day in Jerusalem's police stations. The fears expressed on the previous day, concerning the dangers involved in a sudden meeting of the two peoples, did not materialize. When evening fell, everyone returned home. That night Jerusalem was quieter than usual. A heavy air of nostalgia permeated both parts of the city. The day had been characterized by a yearning for the past. The people had tried to rid their minds of the wars, the suffering, the dead, the hostility and the fear of the future. Even the sweetness of victory and the bitterness of defeat were momentarily forgotten. The past — before the 1948 War — suddenly seemed idyllic and happy, when Jews and Arabs lived together in peace, when people used to go down to the Old City on Saturday afternoons and lilies grew in the gardens of Qatamon. Suddenly, there were no victors and no vanquished, only human beings in search of security and peace. Several observers of the scene were quick to draw conclusions: "This was a short-cut to normalization and peace," one person said. "Within a day or two, it will become apparent to everyone that a majority of the Arab citizens of Jerusalem want to see the united city as the Capital of Israel," enthused another. "Perhaps this is the peace we have been longing for? " asked a third. The days that followed, however, were to show that the road to peace and brotherhood was a long one.

CHAPTER NINE

IMMEDIATE CONSEQUENCES

The transfer of formal responsibility for the municipal affairs of the reunited city raised a whole series of questions, both theoretical and practical. Most of the problems were not new, since the Israeli Municipality had become involved in East Jerusalem's municipal services within a day or two of the city's capture. However, working of one's own free will, being free to choose what problems to tackle, is quite unlike day-to-day work and total responsibility. At first, everything had a political taint, even garbage collection. Each question was approached primarily from its political aspect, and only then was the practical side considered.

The political guidelines followed by all Israeli bodies dealing with East Jerusalem led them to dismantle any form of independent Arab organization, while refraining from the creation of any special body to deal with East Jerusalem, so as to reinforce the *fait accompli* of total and unambiguous annexation. The Municipality generally kept to these guidelines, but set up a headquarters, with a small staff, to coordinate operations in East Jerusalem.

As soon as the Arab Municipality was dispersed, it was decided to transfer its employees to the parallel departments of the Israeli Municipality. Due to shortages of office space and other administrative problems, this move took several weeks to complete. The documents comprising the Arab Municipality archives (including most of the Mandatory archives), untidily stored in a basement, were loaded into sacks and taken, in the same disorder, to basements in West Jerusalem. Salah Jarallah, the veteran Municipal Secretary, refused to

129

part with his desk and papers. He personally packaged the papers with loving care, guarding them strictly, until they were deposited in his new office in West Jerusalem. When he arrived, he found that he had been given the very same room he had left in April 1948.

Anton Saffiah was the only Arab employee who refused to continue his employment. In a conversation held a few days after the Council's dispersal, Saffiah said that he had faithfully served two regimes, but that, at his age, he did not have the strength to serve a third. The man who had created the Arab Municipality out of nothing in 1948, endangering his life to provide the money for its operations, was broken-hearted to see it dissolved and could not join the organization that had swallowed it up. There were few who could not understand his motivation.

A few days after the officials of the Water Department and the City Engineer had been transferred to their new offices, an urgent meeting was called at the request of the Department heads to discuss a serious problem. The Arab employees were now able to see all the maps: water system, telephones, electricity grid, even shelters. This was classified material and involved a security risk. After a long discussion, the participants concluded that there was no choice. "If the Municipality is unified, then it's unified! "

The unified Municipality now employed Jews, Christians and Muslims, and problems arose concerning time-off for the weekly day of rest and religious festivals. The representatives of the religious parties on the Municipal Council demanded that all Municipal offices close on the Sabbath. They claimed that they did not mind non-Jews working on Saturday, but this would result in the desecration of the Sabbath, since Jewish senior employees would be obliged to work as well. The religious councillors were told that, if their proposal was to be accepted, non-Jewish employees would be obliged to work on *their* day of rest or to absent themselves from work on two days a week. It was finally decided that offices in the Jewish zone would close on Saturday, while those in the Arab area would remain open. Employees working in offices in the Arab area would take Friday or Sunday off as their day of rest. Non-Jewish employees working in offices in the Jewish area would be off work on Saturday, while leaving work early on the rest-day of their faith. Muslim religious sages were asked if this arrangement was satisfactory, with regard to Friday. The reply was that Islam did not make it obligatory that

Friday be a day of rest, but participation in mid-day prayers was essential. Since these were held at approximately 12 o'clock, the Muslim employees were released an hour earlier. There were no problems with regard to festivals, as these are official holidays for the minorities in Israel. And one holiday not celebrated by Israeli Muslims, "The Journey and the Ascent" festival, was added to the list of "optional holidays," from which all Israeli employees may choose two a year.

Language, at first, loomed as a very severe problem. Very few of the Arab employees understood Hebrew, although quite a few of the Jewish employees spoke Arabic. Luckily, the majority of both understood English. During the first few months, English again became the predominant language between Jewish and Arab municipal employees, but both sides were quick to learn to converse in each other's language. The Municipality sent dozens of Arab employees to Hebrew courses, where they studied together with new Jewish immigrants.

Before the day of annexation, the Arab employees were informed that their new employment would be temporary. All of the 370 permanent Arab employees came to work and thus became temporary employees of the unified Jerusalem Municipality. As an intermediary step, it was decided that they would be employed at a daily wage, on a monthly basis. Wages were fixed according to the instructions of the Accountant-General of the Finance Ministry and were altered from month to month, according to a key relating to price increases. This arrangement naturally caused resentment among the Arab employees, who demanded permanent postings and salaries. The matter was discussed at length until it was decided, in April 1968, to grant permanent tenure to all those who had been permanent employees of the Arab Municipality.

These workers were appointed to regular posts and their salaries were equalized retroactively to unification day.

With the Arab employees integrated into their departments, their wages equalized and their pension problems solved, integration was outwardly complete. But inwardly it was far from an accomplished fact. The sanitary and maintenance workers and technicians continued to work under the control of Jewish foremen; but most of the white-collar officials lacked employment. Everything was strange to them: the language, the procedures, and the public. Those Arabs who

131

had been Department heads had been appointed deputies to Jewish directors, but they were not granted any clearly defined authority. No Arab headed a unit that included Jewish employees. (Only in 1972 were a few Arab officials appointed to deal with mixed areas.) The Jewish employees therefore kept all the positions of power and the administrative posts, with Arabs restricted to lower, secondary positions. This is not surprising, considering that there were five times as many Jewish as Arab employees, and that the Jews had greater professional expertise. What is surprising, however, is that the Arab employees were not, in the main, embittered or frustrated by their situation. There was no lack of ambitious men among them, and many were capable and highly-trained. If conditions had been normal, no doubt there would have been tension over the lack of balance in dividing authority; but conditions were abnormal, because of the political situation.

The Arab employees reported for work after annexation remembering the words of their Mayor, Rauhi al-Khatib, that they were not betraying their people by doing so, but, on the contrary, were helping to safeguard the Arab character of their city. However, doing one's duty is not the same as whole-hearted devotion to one's work. Most of the employees considered their work merely as a duty. One morning, a pair of municipal inspectors — a Jew and an Arab — went out on a tour in the Old City. When the Arab inspector saw an Arab trader who was violating a by-law, he glanced over his shoulder to see whether the Jewish inspector had noticed. Seeing that the Jew was not looking, he winked at the trader and walked on. When they came upon another merchant and the Jewish inspector noticed the violation, the Arab pulled out his notebook and wrote a charge. In the evening, the inspector came to the trader's house and handed him a receipt. After finishing his work, he had gone to pay the fine on the charge that he himself had written.

With the integration of Arab employees accomplished, the Municipality was able to turn its attention to preparing its operational plans and its first budget for the annexed area. The first problem was the accumulation of information about the annexed area. The Jordanian Municipality's archives were orderly, and easily accessible, but they only provided information about the urban section of Jerusalem and about those services that had been supplied by the Arab Municipality. When the planners tried to find material belonging to Jordanian ministries or other bodies, they discovered that it had been scattered to the winds. Jordanian archives and files had been destroyed; material of priceless value, such as land registers and original maps, had been taken as war souvenirs by Israeli soldiers.

Despite the destruction, there was still some material left. Part of it was transferred to the State Archives, but not before the nimble Israeli ministries had laid their hands on the material concerning their fields. In a metting held in the Municipality, the various bodies were asked to bring the material together in one place; but most of them refused to part with what they had taken. In the end, they agreed to cooperate in preparing a list of the available material and its whereabouts. It was the lack of basic data that obliged the Municipality of Jerusalem — through the Central Bureau of Statistics — to carry out, at its own expense, a population and residence census, in September 1967.

Meanwhile, the municipal planners tried to construct a plan on the basis of what little material they had. On July 15, 1967, they presented a budget of over IL 13 million for the remaining nine months of the 1967/8 fiscal year, and another IL 8.7 million development budget for basic investments. The Jordanian budget for the previous year was less than a quarter of these sums, but the figures were not comparable, since the annexed area included extensive sections that had not been under the jurisdiction of the Arab Municipality; furthermore, the budget included services that had been provided by the central Government under the Jordanian regime. Nevertheless, the municipal officials planned a revolutionary change in the standard and extent of services — bringing them up to the level of those in West Jerusalem.

The Municipality's operational plan was, however, too ambitious. It was impossible to achieve the equalization of services within nine months. The Finance Ministry, which had guaranteed to finance all municipal expenditure in East Jerusalem, cut the budget from IL 13 million to IL 5 million for ordinary services and from IL 8.7 million to IL 8 million for investment, and even these sums were not spent. The process of equalizing services was gradual and spread over years.

Achievements during the first six months were, none the less, impressive: more than 13.6 miles of roads were constructed or repaired; most of the ruined buildings in no-man's-land were demolished;

street lamps were repaired and put into operation; 6,000 saplings were planted; private septic tanks and water cisterns were marked and examined; the slaughterhouse was restored and put into operation; refuse collection was improved; almost nine miles of waterpipes were laid; all water-users were registered; water consumption increased by 50% and six youth clubs and sports teams were organized; school children underwent medical examinations and food rations were distributed to the needy; 28 school buildings were repaired and a municipal library opened; the city's walls and gates were cleaned and repairs were begun on damaged sections of the walls; the citadel was cleaned and opened to public visits; 2,500 businesses were inspected for tax purposes; house-numbers were affixed in the Old City, alleyways were named, and Hebrew street signs were added to the existing ones in Arabic and English; a census was held and 2,000 families were registered with the Welfare Department.

At first, the Directors-General Committee for Jerusalem decided that Israel would not extend its highly developed welfare system to East Jerusalem but would leave the quite different Jordanian system in effect in the annexed area. This hasty and unconsidered decision could not be implemented technically; moreover, it was in violation of the spirit of the unification order, which had turned East Jerusalem into an inseparable part of Israel. The Government finally accepted the Municipality's view and instructed the Directors-General Committee to alter its decision. On July 16, 1967 the Committee declared that "services shall be provided on the same level as in Israel. The Ministries concerned must make the effort to equalize the provision of legally-prescribed services, as early as possible." The decision was important to the Municipality not only because of its overall political direction, but principally because it meant that the Government had committed itself to finance full-scale municipal services in East Jerusalem.

Most of these were ordinary municipal activities. But in united Jerusalem, every activity seemed out of the ordinary. For example, the Municipality was responsible for such diverse matters as the funeral expenses of pilgrims who died destitute, and the firing of a cannon to mark the onset of Muslim religious festivals, such as the beginning and the end of the fast of Ramadan. The cannon, a Turkish weapon captured by the British during the First World War and subsequently presented to the Municipality, stands in the old

Muslim cemetery opposite the Damascus Gate. As luck would have it, on one of the first festivals after reunification, the gunpowder slot became blocked. Attempts were made to repair the fault, but without success. There was nothing left but to call in the Israel Army's Artillery Corps. The unit commander called upon to help saw nothing strange in the request. At the appointed time and place, a gun crew appeared with a 25-pounder. The Israeli officer awaited the orders of the Arab official in charge of the operation and, at his command, three salvoes were fired. The next day, the ancient cannon was repaired and continued to fulfil its function. None of the inhabitants noticed any difference.

One morning in the summer of 1969, two inhabitants of one of the city's southern suburbs walked into the Municipality building, entered the office of the Commissioner for East Jerusalem, and laid a bundle of Jordanian banknotes on his desk.

"What's this? " he asked in surprise.

"The money arrived from Amman," they answered. "It's the Government grant for our village. We get our services from you now so we don't need the money. Take it and use it for anything you want."

The official accepted the money and wrote out a receipt. Then he asked his visitors what they would like the Municipality to do with the money.

"For years," they said "we have wanted to repair the cemetery wall and the roof of our mosque, but we never had the money to do so."

The Jewish official promptly phoned the Ministry of Religious Affairs to ask for a further contribution. The Ministry agreed, and with money from the Government of Israel and the Government of Jordan, the mosque and the cemetery were restored.

The municipal authorities of Jerusalem have always had to grapple with the problem of supplying water to the parched city. After the success of their efforts to restore the war-damaged water supply, Water Department officials began a thorough examination of the situation. The findings showed that sixty percent of the households in East Jerusalem had no running water, but drew their supplies from rainwater cisterns.

The various springs tapped by the Jordanians supplied less than 2 million cubic meters of water annually — one-sixth of the quantity

135

piped to West Jerusalem in 1967. Within a short time, Israeli sources were supplying most of the water consumed in the eastern sector of the city and Israeli Water Department officials sought ways to replace the existing expensive and out-dated sources. Without any sentimental regard for history, they started with Solomon's Pools to the south, originally constructed by King Herod in the 1st century B.C.E., and promptly agreed to the request of the Bethlehem Municipality for all the water from the Pools, even consenting to place the pumps at Bethlehem's disposal. At this point, the Arab officials in Jerusalem intervened. One of them told his Jewish colleague angrily: "If you took our city, you're responsible for everything we fought for. Solomon's Pools must not be given to Bethlehem; they belong to us." When his colleague remarked that the quantities of water under discussion were of no value now, he replied: "That doesn't matter. The honor of the city is at stake. That's why the Council resigned in 1958." The Jewish co-worker paid his respects to historical continuity by going to the Water Department and getting the plan officially shelved.

In East Jerusalem, there were four or five "water contractors" who received a certain amount of water from the Arab Municipality and, having laid pipelines at their own expense, then sold the water to the consumers at inflated prices. The contractors were called to the Municipality, one at a time, and the value of their pipelines was calculated. They were paid compensation, including the value of their "goodwill," and the contracts were terminated. All the water contractors were thus eliminated, with one exception.

Northern Jerusalem received its water supply from the Jordanian National Water Authority. The Jerusalem Municipality did not want other organisations supplying water within its boundaries, nor could it agree to prices 70% higher than its own. The Municipality held prolonged negotiations with the Authority, which had been taken over by the Israeli Military Government but was still administered by the same Jordanian officials. As time passed without an agreement being reached, the Municipality decided to sever the main pipeline. At this point, however, it met the resistance of a superior force. The Military Government proclaimed: "Do not touch our waterworks! If you try to cut the pipeline, we'll call out the Military Police." The Municipality retreated from its position but demanded that, at the very least, charges be reduced. This was conceded by the "Jordanian" Authority, and water charges were equalized throughout the city.

The water supply caused severe drainage and sewage problems because East Jerusalem lacked a central sewage system. Only the Old City had a sewage system, which dated back to the days of King Herod. In addition, in many places vegetables were irrigated with sewage water. East Jerusalem's main sewage pipe traversed the Kidron Valley, ending two miles south of the Old City. The local farmers would block the pipe and irrigate their vegetable gardens with the water that leaked out of the manholes. Representatives of the local population were called in to the Municipality to discuss the matter. After the responsible official had explained the sanitary dangers involved in irrigating vegetables with sewage water (which was, in fact, one of the causes for the outbreak of cholera in the city in 1970), one old man stood up and said:

I'm 75 now. Five years before the First World War, when the pipe only went as far as Silwan, the Turkish Governor called us in and threatened to burn our gardens if we used the sewage. After the war, the British came along; they lengthened the pipe, and threatened to burn our gardens. Then the Jordanians came, they also lengthened the pipe and threatened us. Now, you've come . . .

He did not continue, but one of the young men added, impudently: "And we'll survive you as well! "

The Municipality promptly prepared plans for a sewage purification plant, which, when it is completed, will enable the farmers to use the sewage water without ill effects.

CHAPTER TEN

ATTEMPTS AT BUILDING BRIDGES

In order to carry out its practical plans, the Municipality decided to extend its contacts with the population through the *mukhtars* of the various neighborhoods and communities.

The post of *mukhtar* is an ancient one, dating back as far as the time of the Crusades, and possibly even earlier. It is, essentially, the position of a village elder, whose task is to represent the population to the authorities, and vice-versa. During the British Mandate and the Jordanian period, the importance of the *mukhtar* decreased, especially in those areas where local councils were established. Nevertheless, the *mukhtar* continued to fulfil his traditional role; he had legal authority to register births and deaths, register land proprietorship in those areas where there was no land settlement, keep registers of ownership, etc. The principal task of urban *mukhtars* was the notarization of documents. Each *mukhtar* kept a seal for this purpose, and without his signature the authorities would not issue official documents, such as passports.

Contact with the *mukhtars* enabled the Municipality to gauge the needs of the inhabitants, keep abreast of their opinions, and transmit its own opinions and demands on municipal issues. The *mukhtar*'s collaboration with the authorities was not regarded by the Arabs as treason, since his task was non-political. After the war, the Municipality reappointed all the *mukhtars* who had served during the Jordanian period, but it was forced to appoint additional ones in response to the demands of communities that did not have a *mukhtar* under the previous regime. Every *mukhtar* was appointed for a six-month period, his appointment being renewed almost auto-matically. In a few isolated cases, when a *mukhtar* did not appear at the Municipality for an extended period, and it transpired that he was neglecting his duties, his appointment would not be renewed. In return for his pains, the Municipality paid each *mukhtar* "representa-tion fees," which were equal to half of the expenses paid to a munic-ipal councillor. The 44 *mukhtars* included representatives of communities such as the African congregation (originally pilgrims from Africa), the gypsies, the city's three Bedouin tribes, the Chris-tian communities, as well as representatives of all of the city's neigh-borhoods.

The *mukhtar* system was not a democratic one, and was regarded by some as "colonialist," but lacking any alternative, the Munic-ipality seized on it as a direct institutionalized contact with the population. In all, contacts with the *mukhtars*, cooperation with the Arab municipal employees, and close personal links between the Jewish officials dealing with the Arab sector and Arabs of all classes, made the Municipality a familiar and even popular body. Although the Arabs regarded the Municipality as foreign, it proved that it was prepared to listen to them, to help without demanding political iden-tification, and to represent them loyally to the Israeli authorities. As a result of their confidence in the Municipality, Arabs would turn to it concerning a whole range of matters which were beyond its author-ity and range of operations.

The Municipality guidelines in dealing with the affairs of its Arab citizens have been defined approximately as follows: "In matters which relate solely to Arabs, act as though you were an Arab. In any Israeli—Arab confrontation, try to mediate and compromise. Be a loyal representative of the Israeli authority and its policies among the Arabs, but at the same time, be a loyal representative of the Arab view before the Israeli authorities." These guidelines, which essential-ly turned the Municipality's officials dealing with Arab affairs into intermediaries, inevitably met with criticism and hostility from both sides. However, the importance of the link between the Municipality and the Arab citizens was proven, time and time again.

While these contacts with the local citizens brought much pro-gress, it was strongly felt that more should be done to bring the Arabs of Jerusalem into a full partnership with the Jews. The Interior Minister was legally entitled to supplement the Municipal Council with additional members from the population of the annexed area, but Mayor Teddy Kollek feared that the addition of Arab members to the Council would make it into a platform for anti-Israel propaganda. He favored, instead, the establishment of an advisory committee. In the summer of 1967 the Ministry of the Interior invited seven former members of the Arab Municipality to a meeting to discuss their co-option to the Council; but they refused to come. They replied: "In 1963, we were elected to our posts by the inhabitants of Arab Jerusalem. They did not delegate us to be their representatives in the Israeli Municipal Council."

At the same time, Teddy Kollek, together with a group of experts on Arab affairs, continued his efforts to establish an advisory committee. A Municipality representative negotiated with former Mayor Rauhi al-Khatib (who had not been summoned by the Interior Ministry), former Jordanian Defense Minister Anwar Nusaybah and three others; but they also refused to cooperate.

The failure of both attempts led to mutual accusations, which found their way into the press. The Interior Ministry alleged that the Arabs refused to join the Council because of Teddy Kollek's public opposition; the Mayor accused the Ministry of causing political damage to Israel. He claimed that were it not for the Ministry's intervention, he would have succeeded in establishing the advisory committee. Both sides thought that the problem concerned only the *form* of representation to be granted to the Arabs. It never entered their minds to ask the Arabs whether they wanted any form of representation at all, not were they alone in this attitude.

At the same time, a conflict arose between the three merchants' associations in Israel as to which of them was to adopt the East Jerusalem Chamber of Commerce. No one asked the Arab merchants, or their Chamber of Commerce. When the Jewish organizations finally approached them, the Arabs declared that they did not want to join any organization; they were content with their own.

The Jordanian Government, which obviously had not recognized the annexation of Jerusalem or the dispersal of the Arab Municipal Council, continued to behave as though the Arab Municipality was still in existence. Each year, its budget would be published in Jordanian official publications. Salaries continued to be paid to the Arab employees, who already received salaries from the Israeli Municipality. The Arab Municipality councillors continued to meet regularly. When Rauhi al-Khatib was expelled from Israel in 1968, the Jordanian Municipality appointed his Christian deputy, Dr. Ibrahim Tlil, as Acting Mayor. Meetings of the Arab Council were then held in Tlil's home.

In the summer of 1968, drawn-out secret negotiations almost led to an agreement, whereby an Arab "Municipal Committee" would receive certain executive powers concerning the eastern area, while overall responsibility would remain with the Israeli Municipality. Before the details could be worked out, however, Rauhi al-Khatib announced from Amman that he was against even discussing the matter, since it was a political question and not a local one. He demanded the repeal of the annexation decrees and restoration of the Arab Municipal Council, refusing to hear of any sort of tie with the Israeli Municipality. The negotiations were broken off and never renewed.

Approximately a year and a half before the municipal elections, which were due to be held in October 1969, the Interior Ministry agreed to include all Arabs of voting age in the list of municipal voters. The Knesset passed an amendment permitting them to be included automatically. In this way, some 35,000 Arabs were included in the voting register. It was assumed that the Arabs would, for the most part, boycott the voting and, in order to make this abstention less conspicuous, it was decided that the Arabs would vote at polling booths placed in the former Jewish border sections.

As the date of the municipal elections approached, East Jerusalem leaders began to fear that Arab participation would be on a large scale. In a statement issued in May 1969, several of them claimed that the city could not be reunited by means of legislation and that it was impossible to force the inhabitants to vote. Of course, it was easy to find "quislings," they said, but the Arab population had the right to its own independent, elected council. They proposed that parallel elections be held, for separate Jewish and Arab councils, which would then cooperate with each other.

A few weeks before the elections, the general feeling among both Jews and Arabs was that only a few hundred Arabs would turn out to vote. The Labor Party wanted to place two Arabs high enough on its list to make their election likely, but when it proved impossible to find candidates of suitable stature, the Party decided not to put forward any Arab candidates. At the same time, dozens of *mukhtars* and heads of clans were being canvassed by campaign officials on behalf of Teddy Kollek's Labor Party. These activities were not publicized, nor were election pamphlets distributed, to minimize counter-propaganda by the Amman Government and the P.L.O. Arab propaganda against the elections was, in fact, relatively limited.

One day before the elections, on October 2, 1969, the Labor Party issued a pamphlet which included the following message:

We know that the Arab voter feels sensitive about these elections. Nevertheless, we call on you to elect the body by which the city and its institutions shall be administered. We are certain that there is no one who is not concerned about the education of his children, the beautification of his city and the development of his neighborhood. We do not, therefore, imagine that any one will abstain from participating in the elections to the Municipality. . . . We shall not promise you anything on the eve of the elections, for we, and our deeds, are well known to you . . . today, on the eve of the elections, all we can say is that we will continue the path we have taken so far, according to the principle of justice, mutual tolerance and respect for the rights of the individual, irrespective of his nationality or religion. . . . You can put your faith in the list headed by Teddy Kollek, which also includes some of your old friends. . . .

No other party was active in East Jerusalem.

A few days before the elections, it became clear that some 6,000 Arabs were likely to vote. Consequently, the official in charge informed the chairman of the Election Committee that the polling committees should be reinforced. The Election Committee did not accept this assessment, however, and the staffs of the polling stations were not increased. On the eve of the elections, the campaign manager of the Labor Party visited the editorial offices of the East Jerusalem newspaper, *al-Kuds,* and asked how many Arab voters they expected. Everyone replied that the number would not exceed 1,000, all of whom would be municipal employees or employees of other Israeli bodies. A bet was made, on the spot, for several bottles of whisky.

On election day, there was an enormous stream of Arab voters, transported by buses and taxis according to pre-arranged plans, and within a few hours there were long lines outside the polling stations. Hundreds of Arabs milled around the information center looking for their polling stations. Rumors were spread that anyone not voting — and whose identity card was accordingly not stamped — would not find employment. The stream of voters grew, reaching thousands. At the end of the day, hundreds of Arabs were still lining-up outside the polling stations.

When the ballots were counted, it transpired that 7,500 Arabs had cast their votes. A further 2,000 had been unable to vote because, by error, their names were not included on the registry. Some 6,500 Arab votes had gone to the Labor Party, giving it an absolute majority, with 16 councillors out of a total of 31. After the elections, Arab participation was extolled by some Israelis who regarded it as a sign of acceptance of the city's reunification. Those with a more intimate knowledge of the Arab population knew that no far-reaching political significance could be attached to the relatively heavy poll.

The true situation refuted the optimists. Immediately after the elections, 12 Arabs agreed to join the municipal committees; but a few days before their appointment, every single one of them withdrew. One broadcast from the Fatah Radio sufficed to prevent them from cooperating with the Israeli Municipality. The unwillingness of Arab candidates to stand for election left about one-third of the population without elected representatives. The Jewish majority could continue identifying its political aims and national interests with the interests of the whole city, without having to take legitimate Arab demands into consideration.

From the Arab political point of view, a refusal to stand for election was inevitable. One who does not recognize the unification of Jerusalem and regards the dispersal of the Arab Municipality as an illegal act cannot stand for election to the united Municipal Council in accordance with Israeli law. Arab agreement to become a candidate would have given Israel a highly valuable propaganda tool. If Arab councillors, elected in general elections, had taken part in the work of the united Jerusalem Municipal Council, it would be very difficult, if not impossible, for Jordan to claim that the Arabs of East Jerusalem did not accept the city's unification under Israeli sovereignty.

However, the price paid by the Arabs for adhering to their uncompromising insistence on principle was a heavy one. They were forced to rely on a small minority of Jews who took it upon themselves to serve as a channel for conveying their demands. These Jews

144

fulfilled this task, but they encountered increasing opposition from Jewish circles, and their effectiveness decreased progressively. Neither Jewish public opinion — nor its representatives — could accept the strange set-up by which Jewish delegates represented the views of the Arab population. The majority of Jews were unable to distinguish between conveying Arab views and agreeing with Arab views. Jewish extremists regarded the representation of Arabs by Jews as high treason; moderates, while recognizing its value, were only prepared to take it into account in marginal matters.

Because of its lack of representation, the Arab population progressively conceded political and economic positions. They did not think that they were sacrificing their short and middle-term interests in favor of a long-term political aim, however, in practice the boycott was detrimental to the basic Arab objective. After years of pinning their hopes on diplomatic activity at the United Nations and on sending petitions to the Israel Government, to no avail, the Arabs came to recognize that the only political trump they held was the fact of their presence in Jerusalem. The Arab inhabitants of the city were a factor that could not be overlooked, particularly if they found means of independent political expression.

The Government of Israel had given 40,000 Arabs the right to vote for the Municipal Council. If they decided to put up an Arab national slate, they could have become the second largest party in the Jerusalem Municipal Council. With the Municipal Government structured on coalitions, such an Arab party could acquire great power; in fact, it would be almost impossible to maintain a stable regime without it. The existence of Arab councillors in the Municipality would have been far more than an Israeli political victory. As long as they worked within the law, no one could prevent the Arab representatives from expressing their political opinions on any subject, including even their refusal to accept Israeli annexation. Besides facilitating the representation of their legitimate interests, the renewed political activity, even if restricted to municipal affairs, could have made the Arabs into an independent political force.

Arab journalists faced a similiar dilemma when they wanted to publish a newspaper in Jerusalem. The application to the Israeli authorities for a licence would, of itself, constitute recognition of the unification of the city. However, in this case they decided differently. The chance to establish an independent Arab vehicle of ex-

145

pression appeared more important than the application. The Israeli licence was granted and the first Arabic newspaper, *al-Kuds,* appeared, stressing in its very first editorial that the editors did not recognize the unification of Jerusalem. Gradually *al-Kuds* became the Arab voice. Arab nationalists, who had regarded the application for a licence, and publication of the paper in Israeli-occupied Jerusalem, as treason, began to use it to propagate their views. After five years of publication, the paper's political value was universally recognized. Following the success of this paper, another three newspapers were granted licences.

The editorial stand of the Arab newspapers was not uniform. There were those that backed the pro-Husayn line and those that were followers of the P.L.O. When these Arab papers began appearing in Israel, they came under the Israeli censorship laws which affect only matters of defense, and not under the Jordanian censorship laws (still applicable in the administered areas) affecting political matters as well. Some papers used this freedom of speech in order to launch bitter attacks against Israel, the sharpness of which increased after the Yom Kippur War.

The city's Arab leadership, however, did not see the analogy between *al-Kuds* and the municipal elections; it adhered to its uncompromising stand, to the detriment of Arab interests. Although the Jewish leaders tried to coax the Arabs into making use of their democratic rights, few of them realised that Arab participation in the united Municipal Council would cause a basic change in the relationships between the capital's two peoples. The paternalistic regime of "Advisers for Arab Affairs" would have given way to a pressure group, competing on equal terms with other pressure groups over the allocation of financial resources and the satisfaction of political, social, educational, and cultural needs. One-way intervention in Arab municipal affairs would have disappeared. In the same way that Jewish councillors voted for roads to be paved in the Arab areas, and for money to be allocated to Arab schools, Arab councillors would vote for roads in Jewish areas; if the Arabs wanted to, they could even vote on the budget allocated to the Jewish Religious Council. The Jewish majority would then, for the first time, be forced to relate to the Arabs as a group with legitimate social and political interests that had to be met within the framework of a united city.

Such a development did not come about, however; nor is anyone

146

prepared to prophesy when and if it will. If it ever does happen, it will be the beginning of an exciting chapter in Jewish-Arab relationships in Jerusalem.

Although all these speculations are limited to the field of Jerusalem's municipal politics, the truth of the matter is that they are linked to, and influenced by, the general political context of the Arab-Israeli conflict, of which they are an integral part.

On the eve of the Yom Kippur War there were many indications that the municipal-political development of the Arab population in Jerusalem would be similar to that of the Arab minority in Israel as a whole. In other words, the Arabs of East Jerusalem would be absorbed into Jewish Israeli politics and most of them would vote for Jewish parties and Jewish candidates, while only a minority would express their national opposition by voting for the Communist Party.

In the years 1972–73, a number of Jewish political parties, which were united under the banner of opposition to territorial concessions, opened offices in Jerusalem and began enlisting supporters. There was no doubt that, in the municipal elections to take place in October 1973, several Jewish parties would be competing for the 40,000 Arab votes and the Labor Party's complete control over the Arab electorate would be put to a serious test.

But the Yom Kippur War, which broke out while the campaign was still underway, overturned the cards even on the Jerusalem municipal level. All the estimates and predictions as to the future political expression of the Arabs in East Jerusalem were proven wrong.

As a result of the War, the elections were postponed until the end of December. On election day great efforts were made by the Labor Party and the "Likud" (a coalition of parties whose mutual base is opposition to territorial compromise) to enlist the maximum number of Arab voters. The two parties based their forecasts on the assumption that the number of voters would be at least as many as in 1969, if not more.

But when the ballots were counted, it became clear that the number of Arab voters who turned out for the 1973 elections came to only about half as many as in 1969. The Arab votes, which had given Teddy Kollek's platform its 16th mandate and provided an absolute majority in the City Council in 1969, were drastically reduced. This was one of the reasons that the Labor Party lost its overwhelming majority in the City Council.

147

The 1973 elections, however, taught an even more important lesson. The Yom Kippur War created a new reality in the Israel-Arab conflict. All the political processes, which prevailed until October 1973, ceased, and new processes began in their place. We will deal with the post-October 1973 Arab mood later, but as far as their municipal-political expression is concerned, it should be mentioned that the limited readiness of East Jerusalem Arabs to accept the moves to unify the city, as expressed in the 1969 elections, changed after the War into a belief that the unification process would disappear altogether and therefore there could be no need to sacrifice short-term considerations for the sake of long-term ones.

Since the 1973 elections, a definite stagnation has begun in the efforts to find a temporary or permanent solution to the problem of the representation of East Jerusalem Arabs within the municipal system. Within the new reality, neither side has allowed itself to seek such a positive path.

CHAPTER ELEVEN

EXTENDING AND ENFORCING THE LAW

One of the problems automatically created by the Law of Unification was an intricate legal tangle, referred to earlier. With a stroke of the pen, an entire legal and administrative system had ceased to exist and was replaced by another, without transitory regulations or insured continuity. The situation was so absurd that the only way to act was to ignore the legal change and carry on with business as usual, the new legal and administrative superstructure remaining purely theoretical.

Day-to-day life followed its usual course. The citizens continued making property deals, even though legally they were "absentees" whose property had been transferred to the Custodian of Absentee Property. All professionals whose occupations required Israeli licences continued to work, although they were, in theory, breaking the law. Arab companies continued to do business despite the fact that they were not registered in Israel. The juridical tangle did make life slightly more difficult, as property transfers were not entered in the Land Registry, banks refused loans to limited liability companies, and civil cases were not continued in the courts. Nonetheless, if it had been up to the citizens, the absurd situation could have gone on forever. And most Government authorities did not impose Israeli law and administration, not only because of their liberal views and their desire to avoid burdening the inhabitants without cause, but also because they realized that applying the law was simply impossible. Lawyers and bureaucrats, however, could not tolerate the continuation of a situation that was illegal and, in their opinion, abnormal.

A draft law was prepared to settle the "legal anomaly," but its presentation to the Knesset was put off month by month because the Foreign Ministry feared that the world would regard it as a further step in the annexation of East Jerusalem. The proposed "Law of Legal and Administrative Arrangements" was finally laid before the Knesset at the end of July 1968. In presenting the Law, the Justice Minister stated that its aim was to "remove the injustices burdening the inhabitants of East Jerusalem, which limit them in the free use of their property, in the free practice of their professions, in their crafts and commerce." His approach was a further expression of the newly born Israeli custom of guessing the desires and problems of the Arab inhabitants and trying to make life easier for them. The motivation was admirable; but the Arabs were not asked for their opinions.

There can be no doubt that the new law intended to make life easier for the citizens of East Jerusalem by creating the proper legal conditions to enable companies and professionals to continue their operations. But the citizens of East Jerusalem saw it quite differently. In their view, the proposed law was yet another move by the Israel Government to impose unification, and a deliberate attempt to gain control of the city's economy. The misunderstanding was total, as it was rooted in the totally opposed viewpoints of the two sides.

The conflict can best be illustrated by those articles of the law concerning legal practice. Article 16 says that "an inhabitant of the area in which the law applies . . . [who] officiated in that area as a civil magistrate or was a lawyer, shall become a member of the [Israeli] Bar Association . . ." The intention was to make things as easy as possible for lawyers to continue to practise their profession; but the Arab lawyers saw it as "forcing lawyers and judges, against their wishes, to become members of the Israeli Bar, with the intention of imposing upon them loyalty to Israeli objectives." Their point of departure was the *status quo* created during the year since unification, when the authorities had left them alone, not troubling about legal niceties. The new law intended to alter the practical *status quo*, and therefore they considered it as another step in the process of annexation.

When the Israeli officials learned of the opposition to it, they did not understand Arab motivations and accused the East Jerusalemites

150

of ingratitude. The Law had left it up to the Arabs to register their companies and businesses, erroneously assuming that the statute would be well received by the Arabs, who would promptly make use of its concessions. However, the Arabs, sharply critical of the Law, refused to obey its provisions. As long as the six-month period of grace lasted, there were no problems. When it transpired that the period had passed without the Arabs taking any initiative, the Government extended the final date for applications by another three months. The problem of business licences was finally solved by the Jerusalem Municipality, by automatically renewing the licences of all businesses existing prior to 1967.

The professionals remained defiant, and so did those who owned companies. One month before the end of the grace period, in April 1969, the authorities were facing the same problem as they did before the adoption of the new Law — Arab companies and professionals continued to operate illegally. The authorities now had to decide whether to apply the Law, thus eliminating the Arab businesses, or whether to admit their mistaken judgement and find a legal settlement differing from the rather naive and optimistic ones proposed by the new Law.

At the end of April 1969, the Government decided to empower the Justice Minister to issue emergency regulations permitting the automatic registration of all companies established under Jordanian Law, that had possessed registered offices in East Jerusalem before June 28 and had not taken steps for registration in Israel. Another order was issued dealing with the automatic registration of all professionals whose practice required licencing and registration. At the same time, the Government extended the date for registration and licencing by another six months.

Both the jurists and the Arabs were content with this compromise. The Israelis felt that with the solution of the juridical anomaly, order had been restored; the Arabs did not care if someone else registered them. The important point was that they themselves had not taken any initiative towards registration, nor had they in any way changed their way of life or occupations.

The Law of Legal and Administrative Arrangements was typical of the Israel Government's management of the Arab population's life. The Government would initiate some legislative action based on political objectives, without consulting the Arabs or considering their reaction. After the step was taken, the authorities would encounter Arab opposition based on a totally different point of view, and a confrontation would result. Hesitating to force its will on the Arabs, the Government would then withdraw from its original intentions and find a more or less honorable compromise.

The new Law itself created many legal problems. While putting an end to the "absentee" status of the inhabitants of East Jerusalem, it did not change this status for inhabitants of the West Bank, many of whom owned property in the city, and were still regarded as "absentees." An administrative order was passed down not to enforce the Law with respect to landed property, but the order did not apply to the rights of West Bank residents as shareholders in companies automatically registered in Israel. A complex administrative decision had to be effected before these residents were permitted to continue to hold their shares.

A far more complicated problem arose when it transpired that the exact geographical boundaries of the area where the Law was in force were not clear. The problem centered around the area that had formerly been no-man's land. Since the conquest of East Jerusalem, the armistice lines had been eradicated and the ruins and military positions had been cleared from no-man's land. But the land remained, and the question was, to whom did it belong? The question could only be answered by deciding whether these areas had or had not been under Israeli sovereignty before 1967. If they had been under Israeli sovereignty, the Law of Absentee Property applied, their Arab owners (most of the area had been under Arab ownership prior to 1948) were considered absentees, and their property would be given over to the Custodian — in other words, the Government. If they had not been under Israeli sovereignty, the Law of Absentee Property did not apply, and consequently the property would now return to its East Jerusalem owners, after 20 years.

The problem was far from an easy one. The area under dispute was over 700 acres, some of it in the center of the reunited city. In 1968, it was valued at several million Israel pounds. The ambiguity about ownership brought about violent clashes between Jews and Arabs in the Abu Tor Quarter, which lies to the south of the Old City. Up to 1967, the Quarter had been divided between Israel, which held the top of the hill, and Jordan, which held its eastern slopes. Seventeen of its buildings were in no-man's-land, some of which had been abandoned in 1948, while others had been abandoned during the course of the armistice period as a result of shooting incidents. After the 1967 War, a number of Israelis took over these abandoned buildings on the strength of rather questionable authorization. When the Israelis had been evicted, the buildings were declared "absentee property" and were handed over to the Custodian of Absentee Property. A public committee allocated the houses to Jewish occupants, but the Arabs who had left them and were living in other houses in the Quarter opposed their entry, and in a few cases there were clashes that required police intervention.

The Arabs insisted on being permitted to return to their homes, while the Israel Lands Authority maintained that the property belonged to absentees and had been legally leased to Jews. There was a great public outcry among the Jews. The Lands Authority's action was described as "robbing the poor," "grabbing," and "feudalism." On July 19, 1968, the Government decided to restore the Abu Tor houses to their Arab owners. A similar decision with regard to other areas was only adopted at the end of August 1969, after much argument.

The key to the problem was in the hands of the Foreign Ministry, which is, by law, authorized to determine whether a specific area is within Israeli sovereignty. However, the Foreign Ministry refused to issue such a document, in view of express Israeli declarations throughout the years conceding that the area was not under her sovereignty. In the absence of a Foreign Ministry affidavit, it was resolved that the Law for Adjustment of Jurisdiction and Administration applied to no-man's-land, and that the land would be restored to its Arab owners. This was not the end of the affair, however. A few months after this decision, most of the area of no-man's-land was taken away from its owners. One part, bordering on the Old City wall, was made into a national park, while the large area on the hill of the High Commissioner's Residence served for the construction of a large housing project.

Another aspect of the question concerning property was the settlement of ownership claims by Jews and Arabs who had lost their property in the course of the 1948 War. A considerable amount of Jewish property was left in Jordanian-controlled Jerusalem, including some of the buildings of the Jewish Quarter, as well as areas in the northern and southern parts of the city. The amount of Arab property left in the Israeli-controlled part of the city was enormous, including entire neighborhoods, as well as thousands of acres of agricultural and building land. There were several hundred Jewish claimants to property in East Jerusalem, while the number of Arab claimants to property left in the west ran into the thousands. Some 1,700 Jews who had lived in East Jerusalem left their homes as a result of the 1948 War. The number of Arabs who had abandoned their homes in West Jerusalem was over 20,000. In September 1967, there were over 10,000 people living in East Jerusalem who were born in West Jerusalem before 1948.

Both Israeli and Jordanian authorities had delivered the abandoned property into the care of Government custodians. The Jordanian custodian was called the "Custodian of Enemy Property," while his Israeli counterpart was termed the "Custodian of Absentee Property." The Israeli custodian sold all the property to a development authority that was empowered to develop it or to offer it for sale. In 1958, the development authority was merged with the Israel Lands Authority. A large part of the property was sold to private purchasers or public bodies, while the rest remained the property of the Lands Authority, which rented it out. The Jordanian custodian maintained possession of most of his property, and rented it out, though he also sold some of it to private and public purchasers.

The excitement of both Arabs and Jews as a result of their renewed encounters with their homes and property did not fade away after unification day. Jewish owners promptly tried to regain possession of their property, both by legal steps and by taking physical possession, primarily in the Jewish Quarter. The Arab refugees did not make any such attempts. The authorities soon put a stop to the illegal actions of the Jewish property-owners, promising that the matter would be settled as quickly as possible. It was in fact settled by the Law for the Adjustment of Jurisdiction and Administration, for property that remained in the possession of the Jordanian custodian was returned to its Jewish owners, although property that had been legally sold to a third party was not returned. Even so, not all the Jewish property-owners were able to benefit from their status, since Israel expropriated the Jewish Quarter and the Ramat Eshkol area, which included much private Jewish property.

The problem of the Arab absentees was not solved. At the beginning of 1968, certain Israeli circles called on the Government to work towards a solution, claiming that thousands of people bore a sense of frustration and injustice at the sight of their homes in the hands of others. The perpetuation of such feelings, they said, was a barrier to coexistence and rapprochement between the two peoples, and dissolving them would remove a large stumbling block from the path to reunification of the city. The fact that Jews were settling in East Jerusalem and having their property returned, only increased the sense of injustice.

As in other matters, those who favored a settlement of the property problem did not speak for the Arabs, but rather for their own consciences and out of Israeli political considerations. The Arabs did not express an opinion on the subject, and there were conflicting views among them. They had always demanded a solution to the refugee problem, but were never precise as to what solution they favored within the present context. The Israelis who clamored for a solution were united in their view that the answer was to be found in generous financial compensation, rather than in the restoration of property to its Arab owners. It would have been impossible to return the houses and property as such. A generation had passed since the Arabs had left their homes, and during that time the city had been altered beyond recognition. New quarters had been constructed; the Jewish inhabitants had struck root in their places of residence and raised families there. Many of them had purchased their dwellings from the development authority, and it was impossible to dispossess them. It was impossible, claimed the Israelis, to turn the clock back. Any attempt to solve the injustice in this way would have engendered new suffering and injustice.

Those who raised the problem were isolated, at first. The majority of Jewish opinion was only prepared to consider steps towards solution of the refugee problem in the context of an overall peace settlement and on condition that a solution also be found for the property of hundreds of thousands of Jews from the Arab countries who had been driven from their homes and had had their property confiscated. The number of supporters for the idea gradually increased, but they were still in the minority. The Justice Minister ordered a team to prepare a draft proposal. The proposed law was published in the summer or 1971, after the Prime Minister and Finance Minister had agreed to it in principle. At no stage in the law's preparation were Arab representatives consulted.

The law was based on the principle of monetary compensation, and the key for compensation payments was based on the value of the property — as valuated for tax purposes — on the eve of the outbreak of hostilities in 1947. The value in Palestine pounds was converted into Israeli pounds, according to the 1971 rate of exchange. The basic sum was augmented by a further amount to cover annual interest. The law's proposers believed that total compensation would exceed IL 300 million and that the Treasury would not be able to support such a burden if payment were made at once. Inflationary pressures would also be a threat if such a large cash sum were paid out. Accordingly, it was proposed that compensation be paid in the form of non-transferable bonds for a 17-year period; after a certain time, they would be converted into bearer bonds. The bonds were to bear low interest and to be linked to the cost-of-living index, or to the American dollar.

The publication of the compensation bill was received with mixed feelings in Israel. The Arabs refrained from expressing any official opinion, but did express their views unofficially. Politically oriented circles rejected the basic principle of compensation, rather than restoration of property, believing that "there is no financial compensation for the loss of one's home and homeland." Like some Israelis, they also connected the solution of the refugee problem to an overall settlement of the conflict. Agreeing to a settlement in Jerusalem would, in their view, be making a separate deal, while hundreds of thousands of their brethren continued to struggle for the restoration of their rights. Non-political circles were prepared to accept the principle of monetary compensation but complained that the proposal under discussion was unjust. "Why," they asked, "are you ready to give us compensation according to 1947 values, when land values have increased dozens and perhaps even hundreds of times over? " The needy refugees, who may have been prepared to accept what was offered, complained of having to wait many years before they could make use of their money. The situation was summed up by one Arab leader:

I am opposed in principle to accepting compensation in place of property, as well as to a minority of the refugees solving their own problems while hundreds of thousands are left in exile, destitute. But I can afford to insist on principles; I have a livelihood and am not in need of money. All the time I was afraid that you would

*make such a generous offer that most of my brethren would stand
in line to get your compensation. But you made such a mean offer
that I no longer fear that. What I don't understand is why you,
who are clever people, did not think of the political advantages
that could have been gained if you had been truly generous. You
wanted to purchase political advantages, as well as peace of conscience, at rock-bottom prices.*

In the face of such criticism, redrafting was begun on the proposed
law, this time with private and personal consultation with a number
of Arab citizens. An amended and far more generous proposal was
completed in the middle of 1972; this, too, however, was based on
the principle of the value of property before the 1948 War. The
Israeli view was that the refugees were not entitled to benefit from
the increase in property value that resulted from a generation of
development. The Arabs did not pay the taxes with which the State
of Israel developed Jerusalem; nor did they deserve to benefit from
the investments and contributions made by Jews from all over the
world. They left their homes without anyone driving them out, and
all they deserved was the value of their property on the day they left
it, with the addition of interest. If they were debited with their
relative share of the State's outlay, as against the improvements
created, they would get less than they were being offered.

The draft law was approved by the Government in December
1972, and was passed by the Knesset in the spring of 1973. But
before practical preparations could be made for implementing the
law, the Yom Kippur War broke out. The political climate following
the War made the possibilities for implementing the law that much
more difficult. Nevertheless, a special office was opened which began
handling tens of claims. However, by the beginning of 1976, not even
one claim had been paid in terms of restitution for Arab property
abandoned by the 1948 refugees. Even if compensation is paid in the
future, this will not mean that the refugees will also relinquish their
political demands. Many years will pass before a solution is found for
this problem, one of the most complex and difficult in the overall
Israeli—Arab conflict; perhaps, indeed, such a solution will not come
before peace is attained.

The extension of Israeli law to East Jerusalem also brought about
developments in the more mundane fields of law enforcement.
Before retreating, the Jordanian authorities opened the gates of the

local prison, and its 150 inmates gained an unexpected amnesty. Some of them fled after the retreating army, as did most of the Jordanian police officers and many of the policemen. Only 37 policemen, including seven officers, remained in the city. It is not surprising that most of the police force left the city, as it was composed mainly of residents of the East Bank of the Jordan. Those who remained were all residents of Jerusalem and the West Bank. A few days after reunification, it was decided to recruit local policemen. At first, 24 Jordanian policemen were recruited; by February 1968 their number grew to 80, including four officers. Two years later, there were 200. The young men of East Jerusalem did not seem to consider service in the Israeli police as an anti-national act; on the contrary, the number of applicants was far greater than the need.

The Israeli police began operations in East Jerusalem the day after the establishment of the Military Government. The crime scene reflected by Jordanian police documents was extremely vague. Due to a lack of data, the police were obliged to set up an entirely new criminal file.

When military government ended, the police also became responsible for security. The authorities saw to it that the fight against terrorism and disobedience was waged by the police and not by the army, in order to make it clear that there was no military government, only an ordinary civilian administration in Jerusalem. Only in cases of extreme tension was the army brought to the city, but even then they were under police command.

During the years 1967—70, the principal operations of the police were in the field of preventing terrorism. East Jerusalem, however, also presented routine police problems, principally in drug trafficking and prostitution. Just after the war, there were large quantities of hashish in East Jerusalem, and active trading was soon under way. The Jews also discovered the location of the many drug dens concealed in the alleyways of the Old City and its surroundings. Prostitution likewise flourished and some Jewish prostitutes, finding that they were acquiring Arab clients, transferred their activities from West Jerusalem to the east. In other criminal fields, too, including theft, burglaries and dealing in stolen property, close Jewish—Arab cooperation was soon created.

In June 1968, the Muslim religious bodies initiated a vigorous public campaign in protest against "the conversion of East Jerusalem into a city of vice." They blamed Israel for this "moral degeneration," claiming that it was a deliberate Israeli plot aimed at "eradicating the city's Arab character." On June 28, 1968, the chief preacher of the al-Aqsa Mosque stated in a sermon:

> *Jerusalem was a devout Muslim city, distinguished for its virtue. Today, prostitution and crimes against morals are spreading. Jerusalem has become a city of vice. The city must not be allowed to sink into depravity. The Muslim world is neglecting the Holy City, its source of religious inspiration. Jerusalem must be saved, and its sanctity restored.*

The Muslim Council and the Union of Arab Women issued statements accusing Israel of encouraging crime and prostitution and called on the Jewish religious communities, such as the ultra-Orthodox "Neturei Karta" movement, to join them in the struggle against crime and vice. Specific charges were not restricted to prostitution, but included nightclubs, stripshows, the sale of alcoholic beverages (which Islam forbids) and "inappropriate behavior" at the Holy Places.

The wide reverberations roused by the Muslim complaints caused the police to take vigorous action. Their first step was to examine the files of the Jordanian security police, which showed that during Jordanian rule there were seven semi-official brothels operating in the city. At the time of the occupation, a number of Austrian and German prostitutes, discovered in expensive Jerusalem hotels, were deported. Within the Jordanian municipal boundaries, there were no nightclubs where one could dance, nor was there belly dancing or striptease. Anyone seeking entertainment of this kind was obliged to go to Ramallah. Jerusalem contained seventeen bars, supposedly for light drinks only; no licence for the sale of alcoholic beverages was issued to any proprietor who was Muslim. In the Christian Quarter, there were five licenced saloons. The ban on the sale of alcoholic drinks was only theoretical; in practice, drinks of every kind were available everywhere. The Arab authorities fulfilled their religious obligations by not issuing licences, but no attempt was ever made to prevent sales.

After reunification, Jewish prostitutes began to operate in East Jerusalem and ten bars were opened, some as Arab—Jewish partnerships. Two of them had dance orchestras, but there were no shows. The entertainment and amusement business flourished in East Jerusalem mainly because all the cafés and clubs in West Jerusalem were closed on Friday evenings, and dozens of people, young and old, were looking for a place to spend the evening of their weekly day of rest.

The Israeli police decided to take drastic steps. Within a month, prostitution in the streets had been eliminated completely. Policemen stationed on Temple Mount turned away any visitor who was improperly dressed, or who behaved improperly. The problem of alcohol was more difficult to solve, since the Municipality had no less than 210 applications from Arab proprietors of hotels, grocery stores, cafés and bars, for licences to sell alcoholic drinks. It was impossible to withold a licence for religious reasons, especially as the applications came from Muslims who demanded "no religious coercion." It was therefore decided to renew the licences of the Christian saloons and to grant licences to all the bars and hotels that had sold hard liquor during the Jordanian regime. At the same time, it was decided that sales would not be permitted in the Muslim Quarter of the Old City, nor on the streets leading to the Temple Mount.

To suppress the political campaign, the heads of the Muslim community were called in and warned that if they continued their incitement, the Government would publish all the information in its hands concerning the situation before reunification. It was explained that most of their complaints did not stem from the improper behavior of Jews but from the fact that members of their own community were demanding the sale of alcoholic drinks and the services of Jewish prostitutes. At the end of August 1968, the Chairman of the Muslim Council admitted that the situation had greatly improved and thanked the police especially for its vigorous action concerning the behavior of Jewish visitors on Temple Mount. The moral storm died down, and the situation returned to normal.

Aside from theft, drugs, and prostitution, the police were kept busy with traffic problems. Traffic was especially heavy on the Sabbath and Jewish holidays, when the Old City was blocked off to traffic and policemen were stationed at crossroads to direct the enormous flow.

One day, an Arab approached a Jewish colleague and told him: "I know for certain you don't intend to remain in East Jerusalem."

"How do you know? " asked the Jew.

"The fact is that you haven't installed even a single traffic light in

East Jerusalem. If you were intending to stay, you would have installed traffic lights long ago."

The astounded Jew immediately contacted a friend, who was head of the Municipal Traffic Department, and asked him to install at least one traffic light.

"But the volume of traffic doesn't justify it," said the traffic official.

"Never mind," he was told, "this is a matter of politics, not of traffic."

Within a month, a traffic light was installed at the Damascus Gate.

The increase in traffic naturally led to an increase in tickets. At first, these were only written in Hebrew, but when complaints were made, they were printed in Arabic as well. One day, a policemam stopped a driver who had just gone through a red light at the Damascus Gate. The Arab driver looked at the policeman and said, in Hebrew: "Leave me alone. I work for your [Israeli] intelligence."

"Could be," said the policeman in Arabic, "but I happen to be an Arab policeman," and he continued writing out the ticket.

CHAPTER TWELVE

LIVING THE WAY
THE OTHER HALF LIVES

Although they were residents, and not citizens, of the State of Israel, the population of East Jerusalem could hardly avoid being absorbed into the bureaucracy of Israel. On the eve of the publication of the unification ordinance, the Interior Ministry held a population census, the purpose of which was to determine who was entitled to an Israeli identity card and, thus, to be considered a resident of the State of Israel, as opposed to a resident of the West Bank. The census, therefore, took on far more importance than the mere accumulation of statistical data. Conditions at the time of the census did not permit an exact counting of all the houses in East Jerusalem, and the census officials missed hundreds of homes and groups of buildings. A total of 57,996 persons were counted on census day, each one receiving a registration slip to be exchanged for an identity card.

On the next day, thousands of inhabitants who had been missed by the census poured into the Interior Ministry and demanded registration slips. In the face of this uproar, the Interior Ministry officials decided to permit inhabitants to register during the course of the next ten days. Another 10,000 persons registered during this period, at least half of whom were not inhabitants of the city, but of the West Bank, who wished to be included among the citizens of Jerusalem. Even after registration ended, however, there were still thousands of inhabitants who did not manage to register and, therefore, lacked registration slips.

When the distribution of identity cards began, enormous lines formed outside the offices of the Interior Ministry. Cards were issued at a snail's pace, so that six months later less than half had been processed. In the meantime, a lively trade in registration slips had begun. They became a commodity in the market places of Amman, where they were purchased by refugees who wished to return to the West Bank.

In September 1967, another population and housing census was held, this time by the Central Bureau of Statistics at the request of the Municipality. First, however, every house throughout the annexed area was charted and marked. The number of inhabitants counted in this census was 65,857, more than 2,000 less than in the previous one. The figures were close enough, but it transpired that at least 6,000 persons who had been counted in the second census did not appear in the first.

The Interior Ministry refused to accept that its June census was incomplete. For reasons of prestige, it refused to issue identity cards to inhabitants who had been registered in the Municipality census. An interdepartmental feud developed, complete with accusations and counteraccusations, while the distribution of identity cards came to an end, and thousands of inhabitants were left without official status. Some were fired from their jobs, and the Employment Service refused to register them since they were not Israeli residents. They were also turned away by the National Insurance Institute. Some were even arrested in police sweeps because they could not exhibit identity documents. It was only in September 1968 that the Government decided to recognize the Municipality's census, thereby solving the problem.

But the Interior Ministry's troubles were not over yet. Being in charge of entry into and exit from the country, it was also responsible for applications dealing with the reunion of families, as well as for approving requests for visits to the East Bank. A political decision adopted a few weeks after reunification laid down strict criteria for the reunion of families resident in Jerusalem. These criteria were far more severe than those applying to the West Bank, as Israel was not interested in increasing the number of Arab residents of Jerusalem. Thousands of applications for the return of relatives who had left to study or work before the 1967 War, and now wished to return home, reached the Ministry. One third of the households in Jerusalem had close relatives temporarily away from home at the time of the war. Long lists of applicants were screened by special committees, and most were not approved. As the Military Government approved such applications from West Bank residents with greater facility, residents of Jerusalem circumvented the refusals by applying through relatives living in the West Bank, and a good number of them succeeded in getting their relatives back home.

Israel's "open bridges" policy enabled inhabitants of the West Bank to visit the East Bank of the Jordan, but residents of Jerusalem were not, at first, permitted to take advantage of this policy. It was only at the beginning of February 1968 that the privilege which inhabitants of the West Bank had been enjoying for several months was extended to them. In the area administered by the Military Government, most of the office work involving the receipt and classification of applications was done by the municipalities. In Jerusalem, however, the Interior Ministry insisted that each permit be presented to it for approval. As a result, there were, again, enormous lines outside the Interior Ministry. Weeks would pass from the time an application was submitted until it was approved. If a man wanted a permit to go to his son's wedding, he usually got it after the ceremony was over.

No issue caused as much irritation among the Arabs as that of the permits. In its defense, the Interior Ministry claimed that the lists of applicants had to undergo security clearance, but the security bodies denied that applications were being held up by them. The delays and difficulties led to the emergence of special offices that specialized in acquiring permits for visits and family reunions. In addition to severe complaints of favoritism, the Interior Ministry refused to issue permits for visits of more than a week, which was especially burdensome for those who wanted to study in Arab countries.

It was only in 1971 that the process of approving visits was facilitated by procedures ensuring that only three or four days passed between the application and the issue of a permit. Permission was also given for longer periods. Eventually, it became easier for Arabs from Jerusalem to visit Arab countries than for Israelis to visit Europe. At the end of 1972, travel permits to Jordan were abolished altogether.

The freedom of movement that they enjoyed was of decisive value to the Arabs. The uninterrupted existence of family, commercial, cultural and even political ties with the Arab world gave the inhabitants a feeling of normalcy. The "open bridges" policy, maintained

165

despite the security risks it created, was the single most important factor making life under Israeli rule tolerable. However, freedom of movement and commerce required the establishment of a system of administrative arrangements not only by Israel, but by the Jordanian authorities.

At first sight, there was no formal problem from the Jordanian side concerning people and commodities crossing the Jordan River. The Arab inhabitants had remained Jordanian citizens, and, in the view of the Amman Government, their journey was within the boundaries of the Hashemite Kingdom. Nevertheless, anyone crossing the bridges was required to present a Jordanian identity card or passport, and not all the inhabitants of Jerusalem possessed such documents. The transfer of commodities from Jordan to the west was not hampered by any Jordanian formalities, only by Israeli customs duties. But Jordan did not permit articles to be brought into its territory unless there was a document confirming that they had been produced in the "occupied West Bank," including Jerusalem, because of the Arab boycott of Israeli produce.

What was needed to facilitate matters was an official Arab body whose documents would be recognized by the Jordanian Government. In the areas under the Military Government, the municipalities fulfilled this role. In East Jerusalem, where no independent Arab political body remained, the Arab Chamber of Commerce took the task upon itself. Procedures that were temporary at first, became institutionalized at the end of 1969, and the Chamber of Commerce became, in practice, the Jordanian Consulate in Jerusalem. It gave quasi-notarised verification for almost every purpose. Its seal verified signatures on checks, powers of attorney, bills of sale for cars (which had parallel Jordanian and Israeli licences), as well as the diplomas of pupils applying for Arab universities. It confirmed that export commodities had indeed been manufactured in "Arab Jerusalem," and undersigned land-sale contracts for their registration in Jordanian Land Registries (which paralleled their recording in Israeli Land Registries). It confirmed the declarations of Arab inhabitants wishing to receive Jordanian identity cards and passports. All the documents issued by the Chamber of Commerce were recognized by the Amman Government.

The Chamber of Commerce's activities were no secret; yet, according to Israeli law, they were illegal, since they were not authorized.

But then, the whole "open bridges" policy was, from a formalistic and legalistic point of view, illegal because Israeli law forbids travel to an enemy country or maintaining commercial relations with the enemy. The services of the Chamber of Commerce were essential to maintain free transit between Israel and Jordan, which was in the interests of both sides, so the Israeli authorities did not interfere in the Chamber's activities. On the contrary, they helped to improve the Chamber's standing by allowing it to deal with certain tasks that made the Arab inhabitants dependent upon it, not only because of its contacts with Amman, but also because of its contacts with Israel.

All the *de facto* arrangements which permitted relatively free transit were effective and satisfactory for day-to-day needs. However, at certain crucial moments, the Arabs of East Jerusalem felt how far conditions were from peace. None the less, ironic situations resulted from the extraordinary policy. During the Jordanian civil war (the "Black September" of 1970), shipments of food, clothing, and blankets were organized by groups and individuals in East Jerusalem for the thousands of Palestinian refugees affected by Jordan Army actions. One of the groups comprised the Arab employees of the Jerusalem Municipality, who contributed part of their salaries (an equal sum being added by the Employees' Committee) to buy food and blankets. Men who had accompanied previous shipments related that the Jordan Army was confiscating the food and destroying any can with an Israeli label. The Hebrew labels were removed, and it was decided to send two senior municipality employees with the trucks to make sure that the goods reached their destination. They were also asked to collect information about the dead and the wounded, among whom, it was rumored, there were many Jerusalemites.

The employees drove off, distributed the food, and returned safely. On their return, dozens of Arab municipality employees surrounded them to hear what was happening. A Jewish employee who was also listening was especially impressed with the end of the description, when one of the men said: "The atmosphere in Amman is terrible. The army is shooting at any civilian in the streets. Amman is truly a conquered city. You have no idea how much I wanted to get back home to Jerusalem! "

Such sentiments, however, were the products of exceptional times. In the normal course of events, there was much in Jerusalem to complain about. Two blocks away from the Interior Ministry, for example, was the office most hated by the Arab inhabitants of East Jerusalem — the branch office of the Income Tax Division. To the Arabs, this body represented not only the regime that had been imposed upon them against their will, but the financial price they had to pay to live under its wing. However, politics was not the reason for Arab discontent. The main reason for their discontent was the basic difference between the Jordanian and the Israeli tax systems. Among the changes to which the East Jerusalemites had to adjust was the change from the simple Jordanian fiscal system to the Israeli system, possibly the most highly developed and most burdensome in the world.

Israel has highly developed social services, whereas Jordan lacks state welfare services. When the Military Government entered the Jordanian income-tax office, there were only 500 files of Jerusalem taxpayers, mostly at different stages of legal action. Most of the Jordan Government's revenue came from indirect taxation, and only 8% from income tax. In Israel, the proportions were reversed.

The Israeli burden of taxation, as well as its methods of tax collection, astounded the inhabitants of East Jerusalem. At first, various Arab bodies tried to organize tax boycotts, but they were unsuccessful. Businesses, companies, and individuals were slowly brought into the ranks of taxpayers, and revenues from direct taxation increased every year. In 1968, over IL1 million was collected; in 1969, about IL3 million and in 1974 over IL10 million. Some people paid without coercion, but action was taken against others, including the impounding of moveable possessions. The political bodies responsible for East Jerusalem called for moderation and ruled that their approval had to be given for forced payments; such approval for the impounding of property was only given in exceptional cases.

The method adopted by the tax authorities was identical to that used in West Jerusalem. At the beginning of every fiscal year, tax estimates were sent out, together with demands for advance payment on account of the taxes due. From experience, the Jewish taxpayer knew that this demand was a point of departure for negotiations, and that it could be bargained down. The Arabs were accustomed to bargaining in the marketplace, but they stood in awe of an official demand for payment, not daring to question it. Every year, when the demands were sent, there was a renewed outcry.

The outcry turned into fury in May 1970, when, in addition to especially high demands for advance payments, inhabitants of East Jerusalem were also required to pay a defense tax and an obligatory defense loan. Until then, the defense loan, initiated on the eve of the Six Day War, had been voluntary. The obligation to underwrite the Israeli war effort was regarded by the Arabs as an attempt to force them into committing treason. "After all," they claimed, "we have remained Jordanian citizens, and yet you are forcing us to pay for the war against the state of which we are citizens." Their anger grew when a rumor was circulated concerning an Arab shopkeeper who complained of the high taxes and the Jewish income tax official who responded: "Have you any idea how much every Phantom fighter-plane costs? "

The merchants demonstrated their anger in the customary manner — on May 28, 1970, there was a partial shut-down of the stores in East Jerusalem, which, two days later, became a full strike. The authorities did not react as they did on other occasions, since the economic grounds for the strike were obvious. On the contrary, they took action to persuade the tax authorities to reduce the advance payments. Some Israelis accepted the complaint about the defense tax and regarded its imposition as inconsiderate. According to Israeli custom, a new "Jewish civil war" broke out, with the bodies responsible for East Jerusalem on one side, and the Income Tax authorities on the other. The Arabs made it harder for their champions by adding political elements to their resistance. In the end, a so-called compromise was reached, which in fact gave the tax men a free hand. The Arabs were required to pay the tax in full, but the demand did not expressly state that part of the tax was for defense revenue. Complaints against the income tax did not diminish, but neither did the situation develop into a major crisis. The population got used to the tax as to a necessary evil. The tax officials reported a tax rate of 60% of that originally planned, which, under the circumstances, was an exceedingly high rate.

Another body demanding high taxes was the Municipality. At the end of 1967, it decided that municipal taxes would be imposed on East Jerusalem in stages, and only after the passage of four years would full municipal taxes be paid. However, even this gradual taxation was a heavy burden on the population, which was accustomed to paying extremely low municipal taxes. Even though the municipal tax was, mainly, for actual services, it also aroused political resistance.

One day, an official of the Municipality who dealt with the Arab population was called to an urgent meeting with an Arab leader. When the official arrived, the Arab said: "I have received notice that I must pay municipal taxes for last year, and that if I don't pay, my possessions will be impounded. As you know, I am able to pay, but I don't want to do so, on principle. If I pay, it will be an admission that you are the legal Municipality."

The Jewish official thought for a moment and then asked: "Do you want to receive services for nothing? "

"No," said the Arab leader, "I don't want any favors from you."

"In that case," said the Jew, "you should pay for the services you've received."

"I have a better solution," said the Arab, "I will now pay you the sum I would have had to pay the Arab Municipality. I will also pay you the difference between this sum and the higher one you're demanding, as a deposit which you will hold until the Arab Municipality is restored. You will then pay this sum to the Arab Municipality, and it will be credited on account of the taxes I will then owe my Municipality."

The Jewish official agreed and received the full amount of tax money, together with the letter listing the two sections of the payment. Honor and principles had been kept, and the law was carried out. But when the official handed over the money and the letter, his colleagues asked: "How could you agree to accept the money on such conditions? Are you prepared to admit that our demand is illegal, and that the Arab Municipality will be restored? "

"Give me back the letter," he replied, "and make out a receipt for the money — that's the only thing that should interest you. You deal with money, but I deal in politics."

Not far from the Income Tax Offices stood another bastion of Israeli power in East Jerusalem: the offices of the National Insurance Institute. The Institute was opened on December 4, 1967, and began to pay pensions and birth grants and make industrial-insurance payments. After the legally prescribed period, it also began to pay maternity-leave allowances for women; most important, it began to pay allowances to families with a large number of children. Within less than six months, 20% of East Jerusalem families were receiving National Insurance allowances. Three years later, the number had risen to 50%. Within a short time, the total sum paid out to those entitled to National Insurance allowances in East Jerusalem exceeded the amount collected as income tax. The Israeli policy of encouraging large families — which was, of course, intended to increase the Jewish birth rate — was being applied equally to the Arab population, whose birth rate was already double that of the Jews.

Under the Israeli procedure, birth grants and allowances for children are paid directly to the wife. Some of the Arab women refused to hand the money over to their husbands, insisting that it was theirs, and using it to buy jewelry. For the first time, housewives possessed an independent income.

In June 1972, five years after unification, old-age pensions began to be paid, as the law provides, thereby completing the National Insurance system in East Jerusalem.

In 1975 the National Insurance Institute paid about IL70 million to the residents of East Jerusalem. In that same year, the residents paid the Institute a little over one-tenth that amount.

The public health and welfare departments also built up a ramified system of services in East Jerusalem. The Municipal Welfare Department registered thousands of families that were entitled to welfare by Israeli criteria, even though their economic and social condition was only slightly below the average living standard in their part of the city. By gradual stages, welfare assistance was extended to all those entitled to receive it, their number growing from 70 in 1967 to over 1,000 in 1971. Payments were also increased by stages. At first, welfare allowances were one-half of the amount paid to Jewish welfare cases. When the money to equalize allowances was obtained, it transpired that the total welfare allowance paid to a typical East Jerusalem family would be 10% higher than the average wage earned in the Arab sector. Several welfare workers warned that this would stop people from going to work but, in fact, salary levels rose faster than welfare payments and this danger was avoided. The Municipal Welfare Department was not the only body operating in this field in East Jerusalem. Ecclesiastical welfare bodies, and, above all, UNRWA, continued to maintain a ramified system of social services, including distribution of food rations and free medical assistance.

At the end of the summer of 1967, the East Jerusalem branch of the Histadrut, the National Labor Federation, was inaugurated. More than many other Israeli public or governmental bodies, this organization represented official Israel in East Jerusalem. Its actions

171

were, in the eyes of the population, an integral part of the Israel Government's overall activities to gain its political objectives. The decision to open a branch of the Histadrut was founded on a number of considerations. Above all, the Histadrut, like other Israeli bodies and associations, wished to take part in the historic act of unifying the city. Its leaders aspired to organize thousands of Arab workers and to improve their working conditions. In a meeting with Arab trade union officials, the Histadrut Secretary-General said:

There is, admittedly, a large discrepancy between the standards and conditions of the Israeli worker and those of his colleague in the Old City, but it is to be hoped and expected that gradually, in keeping with economic possibilities, we shall endeavor to reduce the existing gap, for the benefit of both workers and the economy.

The Histadrut leaders did not deny that equalizing wage conditions was essential, not only for the Arab workers, but also, and perhaps above all, in order to maintain the working conditions attained by the Jewish workers. As one of them put it: "The Histadrut will not permit competition between Jewish and Arab workers . . . and will strive to equalize work and pay conditions."

During July–October 1967, West Jerusalem was still in the last stage of the recession that had hit the country before the war. According to official figures, the number of Jewish unemployed was very small; but in fact, far more people were out of work than the statistics showed. In the main, unemployment was relatively high in the construction industry, and Arab workers began to infiltrate Jewish places of employment, prepared to work for half the wage of an unskilled Jewish worker. Jewish employers, whose ecnomic state was insecure as a result of the prolonged recession, hired many of them. In doing so, they broke the law that forbids the employment of workers other than by means of the Labor Exchange, and without paying social benefits and National Insurance dues.

When the number of Arab workers reached several hundred, Jewish workers demanded that the Labor Ministry intervene and send out inspectors to remove Arab workers who had not been sent by the Labor Exchange. The trade unions also sent out inspectors, and threatened to call strikes in all concerns employing "unorganized labor." The only way to prevent the Jewish labor market from being flooded with cheap Arab labor was to equalize Arab workers' pay with that of Jews, ensuring that Arabs were sent to work by means of the Government's Labor Exchanges, and organizing them in the Histadrut Labor Federation.

With the adoption of these principles, the way was open for the Arab workers employed in the Jewish economic sector, as well as in government and municipal bodies, to be organized in the Histadrut. When he was sent to an organized place of employment by means of the Labor Exchange, the Arab worker was certain of wage scales and social conditions equal to those of a Jew. At the same time, he was automatically enrolled as a member of the Histadrut, and a membership card was issued. He could, admittedly, give up his membership and have his dues refunded, but only a small number of Arab workers did so. The number of Arab workers who were members of the Histadrut grew progressively with the increase in the number of Arabs working in the Jewish sector, reaching 1,300 in April 1968, and 5,000 in July 1969. The Histadrut's East Jerusalem branch was headed by a Jewish official, assisted by a member of Arab trade-union secretaries who had been active in Jerusalem before the 1967 War.

The veterans among the Arab trade-unionists knew the Histadrut well, from the days of the British Mandate. At that time, there had been no room for an Arab worker in the Histadrut, whose Zionist ideology was expressed in the principle of "Jewish labor in the Jewish economy." During Mandatory times, the Histadrut tried to organize Arab workers in the "Union of Palestinian Workers," but its efforts were unsuccessful.

Arab trade unions had always been weak and unstable. Towards the end of the Mandate, the Palestinian Arab Workers' Union emerged as the largest and most stable of the Arab workers' organizations, and on the eve of the 1948 War, its membership reached some 8,000. The Union waged an effective fight and managed to improve the working conditions of the Arabs employed in the Mandatory Government and Army. Its organizers adopted a policy of separating their campaign from political activities, even though they were personally involved in the Arab political struggle. On the eve of the war, they declared themselves anti-Hussayni. The Union's Chairman, Sami Taha, paid with his life for his moderate views. He was murdered in September 1947 by the hired assassins of the Grand Mufti.

After the 1948 War, the Union transferred its center to Nablus,

173

and in 1952 the Jordanian authorities disbanded it. In 1953, the Jordan Government enacted the Workers' Organizations' Law, which ensured almost complete governmental control of organizations established under it. Those organizations that were established did not maintain trade union activity worthy of the name, mainly because of governmental interference.

When the Histadrut branch was inaugurated, it was joined by some of the officials of the smaller unions, but not by officials or rank-and-file members of the larger and stronger ones, such as that of the Electric Company's employees or of the restaurant and hotel workers. As long as the Histadrut limited itself to organizing Arabs working in the Jewish sector, there were no problems. But in March 1968, it resolved to penetrate the Arab sector as well. Picking the hotel industry, it began to organize employees in East Jerusalem. This action was badly timed. During that period, there was a severe recession in the local hotel business, but the Histadrut failed to take the objective situation into consideration and demanded improved working conditions. The employers' reaction was prompt: active members of the Histadrut were fired.

The struggle had become a test of prestige. "We must show the workers that we have the strength to protect our activities," said the head of the local branch. In his eyes, the Histadrut was engaged in a class conflict; but the employers saw its moves as a further Israeli attempt to interfere in their internal affairs — a deliberate attempt by the Israel Government to harm the Arab economic sector, as a step towards gaining control of it.

The Histadrut then asked the Government for help. On November 18, 1968, the Labor Minister issued a decree whereby the collective wage agreement between the Histadrut and the hotels of West Jerusalem was extended to apply to the hotels in East Jerusalem. The Histadrut was now able to enforce its demands on the Arab hotel proprietors. No attempt was made to impose the "extension order" on all the hotels, but a small hotel in the Old City was chosen as a test case. When its owner refused to sign a new wage agreement, the Histadrut called a strike. This resulted in a strong protest from the Jewish bodies responsible for security, which were worried about the political implications. The Government backed them in forbidding Arab strikes, whereupon the Histadrut accused the Government of being "effendi-oriented," claiming that the ban on calling strikes forestalled any chance of taking action against employers and undermined the Histadrut's standing in the city. In response, it was advised to forgo trade disputes in the larger concerns, for the time being, and to concentrate on bettering the conditions of youths who were still working long hours in workshops for minimal daily wages.

The Histadrut did not stop its trade union activities, and the internal Israeli debate continued. The Arabs, however, refrained from reacting to the whole matter. Then, in October 1971, a new labor dispute erupted, this time in the *al-Kuds* newspaper. The Histadrut demanded that a labor contract be signed; the editor refused. The Histadrut threatened that "if you do not inform us immediately of your readiness to sign a contract, we will take all steps we consider fit, including a strike." The editor of the independent Arab organ did not panic. His editorial on October 21, 1971 stated:

This [the Histadrut's] penetration into the heart of every Arab institution is not aimed at the welfare of our Arab workers. We declare that its aim is to paralyze our institutions and sabotage their work . . . We of this paper wish to say to those responsible . . . that our economy is in danger, and that sooner or later a blow will descend upon it and devastate it. The Arab workers are our breath of life whom we love . . . and raising their standard of living would make us happy. But it is painful that temptations bring them to a point where they lose faith in their place of work.

The Arabs refused, therefore, to consider the matter as a trade dispute over improvements in the working conditions of Arab employees. They accused the Histadrut, "and all those who control the Histadrut," of trying to eliminate the Arab economic sector by presenting insupportable demands, attempting to divert the Arab labor force into the manpower-starved Jewish sector.

The governmental security bodies were horrified at the conflagration and launched a sharp attack on the Histadrut. The Histadrut, in turn, complained to the Government about the unauthorized intervention in its internal affairs. Official governmental bodies were forced to intervene. They pressed the editor to negotiate and, in the end, a labor contract was signed.

The only positive outcome of this confrontation was that all sides finally realized that the political situation would overshadow any trade union activities for a long time to come. The Histadrut official, however devoted he may be to the cause of raising the wage levels of the exploited Arab worker, will continue to be considered an instrument of the Israeli regime, and his motives will continue to be interpreted within the context of the overall conflict. And, in the final analysis, this view of the Histadrut is symptomatic of the general Arab approach to all Israeli institutions that have attempted to enter their sphere of life.

CHAPTER THIRTEEN

EARNING A LIVING

The Israeli authorities found East Jerusalem in a deep economic crisis as a result of the war. Over a third of the work force was unemployed; all the hotels, the city's main source of income, were closed; the banks had not been opened; travel restrictions between Jerusalem and the West Bank had disrupted commerce with the hinterland; dislocation from Jordan and other Arab countries prevented the flow of money. The uncertainty with regard to the future, the lack of liquidity, and the absence of income brought investments to a halt. The economic crisis was accompanied by sharp price rises, due to contact with the Israeli economy.

To the Israeli officials in charge, the situation seemed desperate, and their first step was to create a few hundred jobs in relief work projects. However, help in solving the crisis came from an unexpected direction. The buying spree of the Jews of West Jerusalem, which started with the occupation and increased after unification, continued unchecked until all the stocks of imported goods ran out. It is estimated that during July and August 1967, purchases ran to IL 2 million per day. This unceasing flow of cash increased the liquidity in East Jerusalem, and the improvement in commerce and services also affected the workshops turning out souvenirs, food products, clothing and footwear, as well as the garages.

On the other hand, hotels did not open, at first, principally because of the continued curfew and the reluctance of Jewish tourists to stay at hotels in East Jerusalem. None of the Arab building contractors picked up work where it had been left off, so that the

177

majority of building workers were unemployed. Concerns connected with the construction industry, which constituted a sizable part of the city's workshops (carpentry, metal workshops, building materials), were also at a standstill. Because of restrictions on travel to the West Bank, to Jordan, and to Israel, most of the taxis, and dozens of buses and trucks, stood idle.

In September 1967, there was still no significant improvement in the employment situation, with 7,500 unemployed. A survey showed that half of the unemployed had not even looked for work. Unemployment was especially severe among white-collar workers. In September 1967, one third of all professionals were out of work, including all lawyers, teachers, engineers and bank employees, most company officials, and some government officials.

The Israeli authorities made efforts to improve the economic situation in the Arab sector by trying to overcome tourists' reluctance to stay at Arab hotels. The Jerusalem Municipality began publishing its tenders in Arabic, with the aim of interesting Arab traders and craftsmen. Restrictions on commerce with the hinterland were abolished, and trade with the East Bank increased with the development of the "open bridges" policy. Money transfers from Jordan were permitted, so that 300,000 Jordanian dinars, both from private and from governmental sources, flowed into the city by January 1968. Also by January, unemployment had decreased by 3,000, although only about half this number had found regular employment, the other half being engaged on relief projects. Most of the unemployed who found new jobs found them in the Jewish sector.

By the end of 1968, employment had almost returned to its prewar level and there was a shortage of manpower, with the majority of the postwar unemployed engaged in work in West Jerusalem. This shift of manpower did not mean that there had been a drastic reduction in overall economic activity in East Jerusalem. Some businesses did deteriorate, but most expanded. The manpower for this increase consisted of workers brought in from the West Bank. From the beginning of 1969 onward, any extension of economic activity in either sector in Jerusalem was bound to increase the number of employees from the West Bank. The Arab employees from outside Jerusalem — whose number reached over 10,000 at the end of 1975 — stayed in the city throughout the week, returning home only once a fortnight or once a month. The West Bank workers increased the

178

number of the city's Arab inhabitants to well above the official figures, which only included bearers of Israeli-issued identity cards.

Despite the growth of employment, some white-collar workers still remained jobless. Mostly high-school or university graduates, they refused to take manual labor, preferring to be supported by relatives. Some received monthly allowances from Amman. In 1968, the Kingdom of Jordan paid salaries to guides, lawyers, unemployed judges and journalists. Employees of the closed banks and jobless government employees also received monthly allocations. These payments were cut off from time to time, but they were always renewed. The Israeli authorities could not, for the most part, offer the white-collar workers employment in their own professions. They tried to solve the problem by developing programs for job retraining, but this could only constitute a solution for a minority of Arab graduates. As this group was also the most politically conscious and the most nationalistic, the Israelis were faced with a severe problem.

As early as August 1968, it had been decided that Arab workers would receive pay equal to that of Jewish employees of the same grade. As a result, in many cases the nominal wage of Arab workers who had moved into the Jewish sector was doubled, while the pay of those who remained in the Arab sector remained unchanged. Incessant pressure for pay increases, and the fear of Arab employers that their workers would transfer to Jewish enterprises, brought some increase in pay for those who remained in the Arab sector. In 1969, the average basic pay for an industrial worker in West Jerusalem was 450 Israel pounds; in the east, it was IL 350. Arab employees in commerce and services in the Jewish sector earned IL 425 a month, as opposed to IL 215 in the Arab sector.

What prevented the total flight of Arab workers to manpower-hungry West Jerusalem? The relative lack of mobility can be explained by the Arab workers' fear of losing the severance pay that had accumulated with his Arab employer, and, above all, his preference for an Arab employer over a Jewish one. He continued to feel economic and social security in Arab employment, and was prepared, in return for this security, to accept a lower wage.

At the time of annexation, there were 2,600 active businesses in East Jerusalem. In the first two or three months after the city's unification, commerce and personal services flourished, but slowly, and more long-range economic trends began to operate. There was a sharp decline in the turn-over of importers, electrical-goods suppliers, textile and clothing shops, and travel agencies, while there was a considerable increase in the business done by restaurants, shoemakers, food stores and garages. In the middle of 1969, it was estimated that about one half of all businesses were marking time or had declined, while the other half had undergone considerable development. The tourist industry only returned to its former prosperity in 1971. Travel agencies, too, were in very difficult straits.

In 1970, and even more so in 1971, considerable improvement was made in the retarded branches of the economy. The Jewish demand for accommodation and vehicle repairs did not decrease and the considerable rise in the living standards of the Arab workers increased the demand for consumer goods. Tourism recovered, reaching a peak in 1971 that had no precedent even in the years before the war. There was a considerable growth of Christian tourism, the speciality of the Arab travel agencies. There was also an enormous increase in the sale of building materials, furniture, metalwork and home supplies, due to the construction of thousands of apartments in the Jewish sector. Arab contractors, who had refrained from working in the Jewish sector before 1969, now began to compete for public tenders, gaining contracts for millions of Israel pounds in Jerusalem and in the coastal plain as well. By the end of 1971, East Jerusalem enjoyed unprecedented economic prosperity.

This prosperity continued until the outbreak of the Yom Kippur War. The immediate impact of the 1973 War was felt mainly in tourism, building, the retail trade and personal services.

Such is the importance of the tourist trade that the steep decline in the number of tourists, which continued until mid-1975, left its mark on all sectors of the economy. The shortage of transport equipment, most of which had been mobilized for the military effort, paralyzed the public building industry. As a result, thousands of Arab workers were laid off. The hoarding of food, which lasted for several weeks, eventually affected the regular retail trade. The decrease in demand on the part of Jewish customers for personal services — due to the call-up of family heads — also hurt the service and car repair branches.

It should be pointed out that the impact of the Yom Kippur War on the economy of the Arab sectors was less severe than on the Jewish sector. This was due to the greater ability of the Arab sector to stand up to drastic changes because it was less complex. In addition, the Arab work force was not drafted and Arab transport equipment was not mobilized. Moreover, economic recovery was faster in the Arab than in the Jewish sector. The unemployed Arab construction workers began building their own homes. In the winter of 1975, work began, all at once, on hundreds of one-family houses all over the Arab sector. This private building reached unprecedented levels and created difficult planning problems. The post-war economic recovery resulted in staggering price rises. The galloping inflation, which reached a rate of over 50% in one year, created new problems, both social and economic.

*　　*　　*

In the short term, the unification of Jerusalem brought a complete integration of the city's economic system, and the general economic prosperity was divided evenly between the two halves of the city. The Arab population's purchasing power (including the Arabs of the surrounding area) increased by 50%. The city also benefitted from the relatively high purchasing power of 250,000 Jewish citizens, and of hundreds of thousands more from the coastal plain who continued to pour in on Saturdays and holidays. The price of this benefit, however, was that the Arab sector was swallowed up within the Jewish economic system and lost its independent staying power. Thousands of Arab workers employed in West Jerusalem remained in the lower grades of their trades, and, as a result, were in danger of dismissal in the event of a recession. Moreover, the Arab sector's economic basis, which was very narrow due to the policies of the Jordanian Government, did not broaden. Consequently, any decrease in tourism or reduction in Jewish demand was likely to engender a crisis that would, of necessity, be more severe than in the Jewish sector.

No effort was made to establish Arab industrial or construction concerns capable of competing with Jewish concerns for the West Bank or the Jewish market. The Arab entrepreneur was not able to take advantage of his superior potential for labor-intensive enterprises. The blame for the absence of a balanced development of the city prior to the war lies squarely on the Jordan Government, which deliberately prevented it. After the war, the blame fell equally on Arab entrepreneurs and the Israel Government. The entrepreneurs refrained from long-term capital investments, even though they were capable of them. The Israel Government, at first, saw as its principal task the elimination of unemployment. Later, when a manpower shortage developed, the Israeli authorities were interested in making maximum use of Arab labor in Jewish concerns and did not devote sufficient efforts to establishing Arab enterprises in the city.

On the eve of the 1967 war, as we have seen, there were major differences in wage levels, price levels, articles of consumption and purchasing power between West and East Jerusalem. In the early days after unification, when food products began to flow into the city from the Israeli side, price increases were yet to be fully felt, owing to the considerable stocks both in the stores and in the possession of the citizens themselves. When stocks ran out, prices increased, reaching a peak in October 1967. Since then, prices have stabilized at a level some 10–15% below those of the Israeli market. The difference stems from the readiness of East Jerusalem merchants to make do with a smaller profit margin. None the less, between May 1967 and October 1968, food prices rose by 57%, accommodation rose by 19%, and clothing and footwear by 43%, while other commodities and services (transportation, health, education, tobacco and cigarettes) became 37% more expensive.

It is easy to imagine how amazed the inhabitants were when faced with such sharp price increases within such a short time. In one survey, people were asked how much they thought prices had risen; an overwhelming majority claimed that prices were ten times as high as before the war. In the short term, these sudden price increases created numerous difficulties. Many families were unable to maintain their standard of living and were forced to cut their consumption drastically. High unemployment and the loss of all savings through the closure of the banks made the situation even worse, and many families were on the verge of starvation.

Two years after the war, however, wage increases had caught up with price increases. From 1969 to 1973, real income grew even more, including all wage-earners to varying degrees. The inflation which came in the wake of the Yom Kippur War resulted, to a degree, in a decrease of real income for many groups. But on this point, the Arab population was no different from the Jewish population.

*   *   *

The effects of unification were especially evident in the changes in distribution of income between different groups of wage earners. Here, a complete revolution had taken place. Adjusting Jordanian wage scales, with their high differentials, to their relatively egalitarian Israeli equivalents, caused those at the bottom of the wage scale to double and even treble their income, in real terms, while those at the top of the scale suffered a decrease in real terms. This drastic change had far-reaching economic, social, and political effects. Large numbers of wage earners began to acquire consumer goods, such as television sets, refrigerators, washing machines and cars — things that had been the stuff of dreams before the war. The rise in living standards also found its expression in improved food and dress, in hospitality and in travelling. Many citizens bought land, built additional rooms onto their houses (mostly without building licenses), acquired jewelry, and invested in gold and foreign currency. After their war experience, the inhabitants did not believe in the banking system, and very few opened bank accounts.

Socially, there was increased self-respect in those classes that had previously been retarded or impoverished. Social mobility increased, and the patriarchal framework — which had been based on financial dependence on the head of the family — was partially dislocated. On the other hand, for those at the top of the socio-economic scale, the freeze in incomes and prolonged unemployment engendered feelings of frustration and bitterness, enhanced by the total loss of political power that followed unification. This important group, the principal political force in Arab society, which had access to mass media, maintained its hostility to Israeli rule and managed to spread its opinions by means of the local and international press.

Unification, which produced such far-reaching changes in the Arab economic system, also forced the Jews to examine their own system. Despite the power of the Israeli economy, some Jews feared that Arab competition, characterized by lower prices resulting from smaller profits and lower wages, would harm Jewish commerce. Others did not fear Arab competition, but simply wished to extend their businesses as far as possible and gain control of the Arab market. Jewish economic interests did not hesitate to take advantage of the Military Government, making use of such ambiguities as "security reasons" and "national interests."

The attitude of the Israeli authorities to the problem of Jewish—

Arab economic relations went through various stages of development. Immediately after the war, the authorities treated Arab claims with suspicion and were prepared to submit to Jewish economic pressures at the expense of Arab interests. The Arabs did not give in and pressured for decisions to be changed to their advantage, making use of various Jewish bodies, above all the Municipality. As a result of this counterpressure, the Israeli authorities became less one-sided. The game of pressures and counterpressures finally produced a less biased, in many cases even a balanced, attitude, at least when the subject was purely economic.

However, under conditions of hostility and mistrust, every matter appeared to be political at first. If the Jews tried to exploit political considerations to promote commercial interests, the Arabs were guilty of exploiting economic problems as a means of incitement. At first, most decisions were taken in accordance with what were understood to be Israeli political interests. Slowly, both sides learned to distinguish economics from politics, mistrust was reduced, and relationships were stabilized. Naturally, the balance tended to favor the Jewish sector, not because of prejudice or discrimination against the Arab sector, but simply because of the power and connections of the Jews. This thesis is illustrated by the following examples.

A few days before the abrogation of the Military Government, one of Israel's bus cooperatives, Egged, received permission to take possession of half the platforms in the central bus station in East Jerusalem, as well as the offices of the Arab bus companies. On Sunday July 2, 1967, nine bus routes were put into operation by the Israeli company, some connecting East and West Jerusalem, and others, in the east, operating on routes parallel to those of Arab public transport. The step was justified as a renewal of bus routes operated by Jewish buses before the establishment of the State. Unofficially, it was explained that Israeli public transport ensured Israeli control of the roads. The Jerusalem Municipality protested against this arbitrary step, which, in view of the adequate number of Arab buses, was quite unnecessary. When the Arab bus companies asked for permission to use the direct road to Bethlehem (they did not dare to ask for the renewal of the routes which *they* had operated before the establishment of Israel, such as those to Jaffa, Ein Karem and Qatamon), Egged applied heavy pressure on the Government to prevent it from agreeing.

184

It was only a few months later that the Government managed to pass a resolution permitting Arab buses to use the old Bethlehem Road, which passes through a Jewish residential area. Under Egged pressure, passengers on Arab buses using this route were not even permitted to alight west of the old Armistice Line. Only when it became clear that travel on this route was growing beyond Egged's capacity, were Arab buses permitted to pick up passengers and let them off. As to the platforms and offices which had been taken over, an Arab bus company finally went to court, and received the verdict that Egged's occupation of the offices was illegal. The Egged claim about the political importance of Jewish bus routes was proved on one occasion only. When, in August 1967, the Arab buses held a political strike, Egged buses maintained transport in the city.

Before the war, there were some 270 taxis operating in East Jerusalem, mainly engaged in conveying tourists to historic sites throughout the West Bank and Jordan. At the same time, there were some 150 Jewish taxis in West Jerusalem. When the city was unified the Jewish taxi drivers demanded that Arab taxis be forbidden to operate in West Jerusalem, while demanding that Jewish taxis operate in both parts of the city without restriction. At first, the Transport Ministry accepted the claim, restricting the Arab taxis to East Jerusalem and the West Bank, while there were no restrictions on Jewish taxis. The discrimination aroused great anger in East Jerusalem. After intervention by the Municipality, the Transport Ministry agreed to make 45 of the 270 Arab taxis into "Israeli taxis." The number was determined by the proportion of taxis to population. But this arrangement proved unsatisfactory, since it left 200 taxi drivers unemployed. In the spring of 1968, a new arrangement was made, permitting Arab taxis to traverse West Jerusalem, but not to pick up passengers there. Only at the end of 1969 did the Arab taxis gain the right to operate throughout the city.

*   *   *

The number of hotel beds in East Jerusalem was more than double that in the western sector. In many cases, the hotels in the Arab sector were superior and provided better service, in addition to being considerably cheaper. During the first month after the war, all the eastern hotels were occupied by the army; but following unification, the military continued to occupy only two of them. Early in July, the Israeli Ministry of Tourism conducted a survey to determine the hotels' grades. The Ministry was under heavy pressure from Jewish hotel owners, who demanded that the Arab hotels raise their prices. The Israeli Hotel-Owners' Association also approached the Arab hotel owners directly, explaining that, for their own good, they should be interested in raising prices as high as possible, since their expenditures would soon rise to Israeli levels, and, if they did not get government approval for higher prices now, they would not get it in the future.

The Arab hotel owners, acting innocently, agreed to fix prices 50% higher than their previous rates. For about a year these prices remained theoretical, since Jewish tourists refrained from staying at Arab hotels and Christian tourists had yet to arrive. At the same time, the Jewish hotels were full to overflowing. In 1968, even at Christmas and New Year, the Arab hotels were only one-third full. If the Arab hotel owners had stood firm and not raised their prices, there would have been a considerable inducement for groups of tourists to stay in their establishments. Only in 1970 did the occupancy rate in the East Jerusalem hotels reach a reasonable level.

*　　*　　*

The supply of agricultural produce, from the West Bank to Jerusalem, was a problem from the first day after the war. Initially, the policy of separating the West Bank from Israel, economically, was in force; but the ban on bringing in agricultural produce was ineffective, as it was mostly brought by donkey over dirt tracks. Early in July, the Israeli authorities decided that suppliers of produce from the West Bank could continue to market their produce in Jerusalem. As a result, Jerusalem markets were flooded with produce from the West Bank, which also reached markets in West Jerusalem and even Tel Aviv. Prices were half of those for Israeli agricultural products. After a break of 20 years, Arab peasants reappeared in the streets of Jerusalem, driving donkeys laden with fruit and vegetables, and weighing produce on primitive scales made of rope and cans. Prices fell, so that the vegetables-and-fruit price index was lower in the summer of 1967 than it had been four years earlier. Jewish farmers, wholesalers and shopkeepers suffered considerable losses, and pressure was applied on the Military Government and on the Ministry of Agriculture to ban the import of West Bank agricultural products into Jerusalem.

The ban was imposed in September 1967. Peddlers caught in the city were driven out and their produce destroyed, sometimes with an excessive use of force. Now the Arab farmers and traders began to complain of discrimination. The prices in East Jerusalem markets rose considerably, to the detriment of the poorer classes. After some months, a compromise was worked out, permitting the delivery of produce from the West Bank, "in the quantities brought to East Jerusalem before the war," with licences issued for these quantities. The varieties allowed were, theoretically, dependent on the availability of Israeli produce, but no severe restrictions were imposed in practice. These permits enriched several Arab merchants, since they paid the West Bank farmers between a quarter and a half of the prices of Jewish produce. At peak periods, such as before Passover, profits reached several hundred percent.

*   *   *

Initially, unification caused a severe crisis for Arab importers and wholesalers, who were cut off from their sources of supply. High protective tariffs and purchase taxes imposed on goods imported into Israel, and the availability of Israeli-produced substitutes, made importing unprofitable. East Jerusalem importers, who had benefitted from low Jordanian duties, were now obliged to liquidate their businesses or to become agents of Israeli suppliers. Two additional factors made the position of durable goods importers difficult: Because of the Arab boycott, they had tended to import products that were not available in Israel. After unification, however, these contacts could not be maintained. Importers who had served as agents of foreign concerns that traded with Israel as well, found their business transferred to the sole Israeli agents, as the foreign companies preferred to maintain their contacts with the Jewish agents, whose businesses were larger.

After selling the stock in their stores, the importers and wholesalers found themselves sitting in empty shops. Israeli wholesalers contacted Arab retailers directly, and the once rich, politically influential merchants who had ruled the Arab Chamber of Commerce were left impoverished. This situation did not last long, however. Some of the importers and wholesalers transferred to other businesses; others agreed to become agents for Jewish wholesalers. Their success in increasing sales persuaded Jewish manufacturers that it was better to work through them. A year after unification, most of the Arab wholesale businesses were flourishing again, with their marketing networks covering the whole of the West Bank. The narrow profit margin of the Arab wholesalers was another factor that induced Jewish retailers to join with them. The "open bridges" policy permitted a limited renewal of trade connections with the East Bank and the Arab countries, which made a further contribution to improving the situation.

The greatest crisis in the economic sphere, engendered by unification, affected the very base of the entire economic system: the banks. The transfer of all the cash in the vaults of East Jerusalem banks to the Central Bank in Amman on the eve of the war, made it impossible to reopen the banks afterwards, and the public lost a large part of its liquid assets. Settling the monetary problems between Israel and Jordan, and reopening the banks, was important for both countries, so that negotiations towards the reopening of the banks began as early as the end of June, through the auspices of the International Monetary Fund. However, no progress was made, and, on June 30, five Israeli banks opened branches in East Jerusalem and began normal banking activities. But since the scope of their activities was very limited, as only Israeli bodies made use of their services, another attempt was made to solve the problem of the Arab banks through the mediation of the U.S. Embassy.

On August 16, 1967, a delegation composed of a representative of the Arab banks, and another representing the foreign banks with branches in the West Bank and Jerusalem, arrived in the city. After three days of negotiations, the representatives from Amman and of the Bank of Israel had reached a 29-paragraph agreement stipulating that the banks in Jerusalem and the West Bank be restored to the direction of the banks in Amman, on condition that the latter's instructions conform to those of the Bank of Israel; that Israel Law be in force in East Jerusalem; and that two million dinars be channeled from the Central Bank to the branches in Jerusalem and the West Bank. Arrangements were also made to facilitate commerce between the banks in the different sectors, and for clearing facilities. The parties initialled the memorandum and returned home to receive final approval.

Unfortunately, such approval was not forthcoming. It is not clear which Government is to blame for thwarting this highly important agreement. One authoritative source relates that when the agreement came to the attention of the Israel Government, it was opposed by the Minister of Defense, Moshe Dayan, and the Minister of Justice, Ya'akov Shimshon Shapira. The latter said that a banking agreement between two belligerent states was unheard of and inconceivable. Restoring the branches to the direction of the head offices meant giving economic control over the West Bank to Amman. The Defense Minister adhered to this opinion, and the Israel Government did not, therefore, ratify the agreement; for reasons of its own, neither did the Jordan Government.

In January 1968, another attempt was made to reopen the Jordanian banks, with the Israeli suggestion that the Arab banks work as independent authorities, without formal ties to Amman. The position of the Arab banks in Jerusalem would, thus, be similar to that of foreign banks and they would be subject to Israeli Law. This proposal was immediately rejected by Jordan.

In June 1969, a new proposal was made, under which the local headquarters of the banks would be moved from Jerusalem to Ramallah, where Jordanian law is still in effect, albeit under the supervision of the Israel Military Government. According to this plan, Jordanian authority would be imposed on the banks by regular visits on the part of Jordanian supervisors. The fate of this proposal, however, was the same as that of its predecessor.

At the end of 1971, another change took place in the Israeli approach. Israel now agreed to a direct link between the local bank branches and the central offices in Amman, on condition that the Jerusalem branches operate according to Israeli Law.

The two opposing positions had come so close that an agreement seemed imminent, but it was continuously postponed for political reasons.

From time to time, after the Yom Kippur War, optimistic announcements were made regarding the reopening of the Arab banks. However, by the beginning of 1976 not a single Arab bank had opened its doors. The major stands of the two sides — the Israeli unwillingness to compromise on the principle of Israeli sovereignty in East Jerusalem, and the Jordanian refusal to agree, even by implication, to this principle — prevented an agreement which could have led to the normalization of relations in this most important and complex issue.

With the failure of the attempt to reopen the Arab banks, the Israel Government had to deal with the problems of liquidity and credits for the inhabitants of East Jerusalem and the West Bank. At the end of August 1967, the Government decided to establish a fund of ten million Israeli pounds, to advance working-capital loans to West Bank inhabitants. Through the intervention of the Municipality, IL 1 million was allocated to East Jerusalem. The loans were advanced through Israeli banks, with government guarantees. When it transpired that IL 1 million was insufficient for East Jerusalem, the sum was doubled, with government guarantees exceeding IL 3 million. Loans were given at 9% interest, and almost all the businesses in East Jerusalem benefitted from the fund. But larger sums, although needed, were not forthcoming.

* * *

The most important Arab economic institution in East Jerusalem is the "Jordan Jerusalem Electric Corporation," which also supplied electricity to extensive areas around Jerusalem. The company is the successor of a British Mandatory company. Its concession, dating back to the Turkish period, and renewed during the Mandate, covered "a radius of 20 kilometers from the top of the Rotunda of the Church of the Holy Sepulcher," and was granted "for 40 years and another 14 years, on condition that the High Commissioner has the authority to grant the extension." At the end of March 1948, the High Commissioner extended the company's concession until 1998. However, the 1948 War intervened, and with the partition of Jerusalem the electricity networks were likewise divided, although the same company continued to supply electricity to both parts of the city from different sources.

After negotiations, in which the British company acted as an intermediary, the Israeli Electricity Company bought the shares of the British company in 1954, and it was agreed that the latter would liquidate its operations in Jordan. The agreement was reached with the sanction of the Israel and Jordan Governments. Then, in 1956, the six municipalities of the Jordanian region of Jerusalem founded the Electric Company for the Jordanian Region of Jerusalem (later they were joined by the Jericho Municipality). The moving spirit in the establishment of the company was Rauhi al-Khatib, who also served as its chairman. It was a public company, with a paid-up capital of 750,000 dinars. With 20% of its shares belonging to the municipalities, the other 80% belong to hundreds of private shareholders. In 1957, the Jordan Government bought the remainder of the concession and all its assets from the original British company and transferred them to the new electric company, which operated efficiently and was financially sound.

Following the 1967 War, the Israeli Electric Company was asked to repair the East Jerusalem power station and put it into operation. However, it only agreed to help with repairs, and, after the electricity supply was renewed, it stopped interfering in the activities of the Arab company.

Unification raised a number of practical problems (for example, supply of fuel; and the fact that the Arab company's rates were much higher than those in force in West Jerusalem), and political problems. At the end of 1967, the Israeli Municipality decided to appoint two representatives to the board of directors of the Arab electricity company. One was a Jew and the other was an Arab who had previously served as a representative of the Arab Municipality. This step, by the Israeli Municipality, was based on the assumption that it was the legal successor of the Arab Municipality.

Three months after receiving notification of the Municipality's decision, the company chairman, Rauhi al-Khatib, wrote to Mayor Teddy Kollek that "according to the opinion of the Company's legal advisers, there is no legal possibility, according to company regulations, to meet this request." Legally, al-Khatib was right; and the Israeli Ministry of Justice had reached a similar conclusion, namely, that the Israeli Municipality was not the legal successor of the Jordanian Municipality. But the problem was not a purely legal one. Co-opting representatives of the Israeli Municipality of Jerusalem, was a political test case. By agreeing to co-opt them, the Arab company would have recognized the legality of the Arab Municipality's dispersal and of unification. None of the board members could agree to this, least of all the deposed Mayor, Rauhi al-Khatib. The legal shortcomings of the application gave the Arabs the chance to achieve their ends without having to relate to the political question. The Israeli Municipality did not react to the rejection of its request, preferring to keep it secret. But Rauhi al-Khatib wished to make political capital of the matter and had the rejection letter published in Jordanian newspapers. His statement there did not quote his legalistic answer, but boasted of "forestalling the Israeli scheme to gain control of the Arab Electric Company." He added that the Israeli Municipality had threatened that refusal would lead to a Jewish takeover of the whole company. The publication of al-Khatib's allegations was one of the reasons for the Government's decision to banish him from the city. After this incident, the electricity company continued to operate without disturbance. When the Custodian of Absentee Property tried to get his hands on those of the company's shares owned by absentees, the Municipality intervened and persuaded the Government to leave the company alone. The electricity company's management adopted a realistic policy in its relations with the Israel Government. In August 1968, it applied to the authorised bodies concerning the fixing of electricity rates, as the law requires.

The problem of the company's continued operation arose when Jewish housing was built to the east of the previous Armistice Line and those in charge of construction asked the Government with which electrical network they should link up, the Arab or the Jewish? Legally, there was no doubt that the area to the east of the Armistice Line was within the Arab concession, since the Israeli company had only bought that part of the concession within Israeli territory in 1954. Furthermore, the concession was in force according to Israeli law, since annexation could not legally alter property rights, and the Mandatory order granting the concession was still the law in Israel.

It all seemed clear on paper. But on a political level, it was another matter entirely. The Government was planning to erect tens of thousands of apartments in East Jerusalem, and the notion that Jews should consume "Arab electricity" appeared fantastic. All kinds of political and military arguments were raised to shore up the argument that Jewish housing be connected to "Jewish electricity." It was, indeed, the first time that Israelis were asked to place their needs in the hands of an Arab company, precisely in the sensitive sphere of their power supply. Mistrust and the very novelty of the situation gave rise to a plethora of proposals. In the end, it was decided, in December 1968, to demand that the Arab company agree that the Israeli company supply electricity to all the Jewish housing to be erected to the east of the demarcation line. In exchange for this permission, the Israeli company would make fixed payments, to be negotiated, to the Arab company. The decision was "Jewish electricity to Jewish consumers." The Arab company, however, vigorously refused even to negotiate giving up any part of its concession.

The Israelis had numerous means available to force the Arab company to capitulate, but they refrained from using them for a number of reasons. In principle, they recognized the legality of the Arabs' concession, and they were afraid that the Arabs would appeal to the courts in Israel or even to the International Court in The Hague. Among the Israeli negotiators, some did not consider it totally unreasonable that "Arab electricity" be supplied to Jewish consumers. On the contrary, they regarded it as proof of the true unification of the city, and as a test of the possibility of co-existence in equality. After extensive negotiations, the Israelis withdrew their demand, and, in January 1970, it was decided that all Jewish housing and army camps within the area of the Arab concession would be connected to the Arab grid. At the same time, it was agreed that the electricity rates be identical, that the Arab company enjoy all the facilities from which the Israeli company benefitted, and that the company's bills be printed in Hebrew as well as in Arabic. Finally, it was agreed that the two grids be joined together, but that current would only be channeled through the connecting line in times of emergency and with the consent of both companies.

Within a short time of the decision, Arab and Jewish engineers began to coordinate the electric plans of the new Jewish housing, and between 1970 and 1972 thousands of Jewish consumers were linked up to the Arab grid. At the same time, the Municipality and the electric company pursued their four-year plan to connect all the 12,000 Arab houses to the grid. The tremendous growth in consumption forced the Arab company to increase its generating capacity, and in 1971 it received permission to import two new generators, which almost doubled its capacity.

The Jewish consumers were slow to show confidence in the company. Initially, there were many complaints about difficulties in paying bills, which were issued in Arabic; housewives in the new housing were afraid of the company's collectors. But as the sides grew accustomed to each other, the situation became normal. It transpired that "Arab electricity" was odorless and that it gave light and heat, precisely like Jewish electricity.

Everything went well until it became clear that the Arab company was unable to meet the pressures of increased demand. It was not only thousands of new Jewish homes that required electricity; Arab consumers, too, doubled and even trebled their consumption. After less than two years, it again became necessary to double generating capacity; but for certain technical reasons the possibility of enlarging the Diesel-operated Jerusalem power station was limited. The Arab company, finally joined by a Jewish member representing the Municipality, began serious consideration of a revolutionary change — that it cease its own production of electricity and purchase current, in bulk, from the Israeli electricity company. Before any decision could be reached, technical faults disabled the two new East Jerusalem power units, leaving thousands of the company's clients without power. In a swift operation, the grids of the Arab and the Israeli companies were linked, and the Arab company began to buy electricity from the Israelis in bulk.

By the end of 1975, over 10,000 Jewish apartments were connected to the Arab electric company circuits. In other words, almost one half of its customers were Jews. Though half of the power was provided by the Israeli electric company and the task of the Arab company was limited to distribution, the effort needed to keep up with the growing demands placed on the system was great. Because of their desire to "keep the concession" serving Jews in East Jerusalem — which was no more than a political principle — the Arab company neglected the development of an electrical network in the Arab neighborhoods. On a short-term basis, the Arabs derived political benefit from protecting their interests in the previously Jordanian districts; but in the long run, the lapse in services to the Arab neighborhoods resulted in grave damage of both a political and economic nature.

CHAPTER FOURTEEN

EDUCATION

Israel's first steps in East Jerusalem found hundreds of teachers and thousands of schoolchildren on their summer vacation. The most effervescent element among the Arabs, the first in every street demonstration, they brought John Glubb to the conclusion that: "Every riot in Jordan, in fact in the whole Middle East, was always initiated by schoolchildren." The fact that the pupils were at home probably contributed to the lack of reaction to the first Israeli steps. But the preparations for the school year, which began in August 1967, coincided exactly with the eruption of the Arab resistance movement (which will be dealt with in a later chapter). The problem of opening the schools soon became the central issue in the confrontation between the Arab population and the authorities. Matters began with the refusal of school inspectors and employees of the Jordanian Education Department, who had been paid by the Military Government since July, to transfer to employment with the Ministry of Education.

The main confrontation, however, began on August 7, when the Israel Government adopted resolutions on educational matters affecting Jerusalem and the West Bank. It was decided that schools would be opened on September 1, and that, in Jerusalem, the Jordanian curriculum would be totally eliminated and replaced by the curriculum and textbooks followed in the Arab schools in Israel. The proposals originated in the Ministry of Education and were justified by the fact that East Jerusalem had become a part of the State of Israel; its Arab population was therefore in the same position as all other Israeli Arabs.

With regard to the West Bank, the Ministry rejected the use of 81 textbooks in various subjects on the ground that they included anti-Israel material or contained Arab nationalist incitement. In the Ministry's view, 49 of the books were totally unacceptable, and large parts would have to be cut out of 20 more. New books, similar to the ones in use in the Arab educational system in Israel, had been printed to replace them. Only 30 Jordanian school books had survived censorship.

When this decision became known, there was a great outcry in Jerusalem. The Association of Arab Teachers in Jerusalem circulated a pamphlet on Wednesday, August 17, calling upon teachers not to cooperate with the Israeli Ministry of Education. The authors of the pamphlet felt that Arab teachers could not accept the replacement of textbooks, and the Israeli curriculum, because "it is a blow to the professional pride of the teachers, and to the Arab as a human being, and it is aimed at educating children in an anti-Arab spirit." A petition signed by dozens of teachers was sent to the Military Governor. The Amman Government added fuel to the flames by broadcasting calls to teachers and parents to provoke strikes in the schools. It assured the teachers that their salaries would be paid and their social benefits safeguarded. In response, officials of the Arabic Department of the Ministry of Education invited the teachers to explanatory meetings, but no one appeared. The political problem was further complicated by a financial one. Some of the teachers inquired whether the Israeli Ministry of Education would be prepared to recognize their seniority and take responsibility for the pension-rights they had accumulated. The Ministry refused to promise anything. In the last week of August, the teachers announced that they would not return to work unless the old curriculum and textbooks were reinstated, the Education Department of the Jordanian Government re-opened in Jerusalem, and educational problems handled by the Military Government in Jerusalem.

The tension in Jerusalem affected the West Bank, and vice-versa, although the situation in the two areas was notably different. Initially the military government authorities on the West Bank did not interfere in the Ministry of Education's activities there. But when the experts of the Military Government examined the rejected textbooks, they discovered to their amazement that the wholesale rejection included not only passages attacking Israel, but whole chapters of Arab history, as well as legitimate expressions of Arab nationalism. As a result, the Military Government considered the unrest caused by the ban on the textbooks to be justified and sincere and the Defense Minister brought the question to the Cabinet, which decided to set up a new committee to check the textbooks. This committee left 100 books unchanged, censored short passages from 20, and rejected only two.

Thus, the problem was solved on the West Bank, but not in Jerusalem. At a meeting attended by the Minister of Defense, the Minister of Education and the Mayor of Jerusalem it was decided that the Israeli-Arab curriculum would be used in municipal schools, without change. Instructions were not altered, and as late as August 24, the Ministry reported that the schools would open on time, and that it would hold a ramified network of courses to instruct teachers in the application of the new curriculum that they were to adopt.

As the first day of school approached, the optimism of the Education Ministry spokesmen waned. The education experts had discovered a little too late that they were dealing with Arabs unlike those they were used to in Israel. On August 29, the heads of the Ministry of Education admitted for the first time that there were difficulties. The Director-General of the Ministry and the Director of its Arab Education Department announced, at a news conference, that "owing to technical difficulties in opening all the educational institutions simultaneously" schools in East Jerusalem would be opened in stages. On September 1, the Ministry and the Municipality decided that the school opening would be postponed by a fortnight.

Arab public opinion was divided. The extremists called for the school strike to continue, but the moderates, and above all the parents, claimed that halting education would harm the Arabs alone, since the Jews did not care about Arab children missing school — perhaps they even preferred it. Many parents wanted to get their children off the streets after three months of idleness. Some of the leaders even called for a return to school. But Amman's propaganda organs continued their incitement against returning to classes. Officials of the Jordanian Education Department in Jerusalem, as well as a number of school principals, also called on their colleagues to continue the strike, resulting in the arrest of the Jerusalem Director of the Jordanian Education Department and two school principals, at the beginning of September.

The first schools to be opened were those in the suburbs and villages. Six schools were opened on September 18; but the number of pupils who showed up that morning was half the number expected. Only ten of the 71 teachers came to work. The Israeli authorities posted notices in the streets, a few days earlier, calling on teachers who had not worked in the Jordanian educational system to register for placement in schools. The response from qualified teachers and young high school graduates from outside East Jerusalem, was quite large. As a result of this registration, the authorities could replace those teachers who were continuing the strike, even though a considerable proportion of the new teachers lacked both training and experience.

During the course of September and October, all the elementary and preparatory schools opened, one after the other — the last on October 9. By then, attendance had reached about 75% of the registered pupils. Only a dozen of the 300 veteran teachers returned to work at first; but by the end of December some 150 of them were back on the job. At this point, the Ministry dismissed 25 of the new teachers who had helped open the schools at the time of the strike. It was now claimed that 11 of them did not have Jerusalem identity cards, while 14 did not have sufficient professional training. When they were needed, no one had quibbled over their documents; but now that there was no need for them, it was suddenly discovered that they were unsuitable. The Municipality intervened to keep them on the job.

The secondary schools were still closed; the delay in reopening them stemming from both the fear of strikes and financial difficulties. In Israel, the secondary schools belong to the municipalities and pupils pay tuition. The Jerusalem Municipality refused to reopen the secondary schools until the Ministry of Education promised to cover all expenses. Fearing the creation of a precedent, the Ministry demanded that tuition fees be charged, but the Municipality refused to do so, as secondary schooling had been free under the Jordanian regime.

It was only at the end of December that the Municipality reached an agreement with the Ministry of Education and began registration for the three Arab secondary schools (two for boys, one for girls). When registration ended, it transpired that less than half the pupils had decided to renew their studies. As a result, one of the boys' schools was closed and all the pupils were concentrated at the Rashidiyah school. The school year started at the beginning of January 1968, with the number of pupils at the Rashidiyah school reaching 489 (as against 800 in May 1967). The enrollment at the Ma'mumiyah girls' school was 300, as against 350 before the war.

When the attempt to paralyze the schools proved a failure, the Amman Government stopped its incitement. Originally, it had threatened to take measures against any teacher returning to work; but in November 1967, it changed its policy, to avoid having to admit defeat, and renewed payment of teachers' salaries. In 1968 and 1969 many teachers and principals received salaries from both Israel and Jordan.

The strike had failed, but the dispute over the curriculum went on, centering, naturally, on the secondary schools. The Israeli curriculum was followed, more or less, but when the twelfth-grade pupils sat for their Israeli diploma examinations in the summer of 1968, the absurdity of the thoughtless imposition of the Israeli curriculum was proved. Of the 96 twelfth-grade pupils of the Rashidiyah school who took the examination, only four passed, compared with the 70–80% passing rate in the pre-war Jordanian examinations. Both parents and pupils drew their conclusions. In the following school year, eleven pupils registered for the Rashidiyah school. All the others had transferred to private or ecclesiastical schools, which continued to work according to the Jordanian curriculum. The state educational system in East Jerusalem had totally collapsed, owing to the stubbornness of the Ministry of Education in its uncompromising adherence to the unpopular curriculum.

The elementary school system, on the other hand, continued to operate without disturbance. Here the problem of the curriculum was not as severe, since there were no great differences between the Jordanian and the Israeli programs. Approximately the same number of pupils, about 11,000, registered during both the 1968–9 and the 1971–2 school years. The reason for the lack of an increase in the number of pupils, despite the considerable natural population increase, may have been that improved economic conditions permitted many parents to send their children to private schools, where the standard of education was higher.

In the course of 1969, the Municipality made great efforts to convince the Ministry of Education to permit a parallel study course in the upper classes that would prepare those pupils who so wished for the Jordanian diploma examinations. The Ministry refused, for political reasons, to accept this proposal; but the Municipality persevered in its attempts, and, in July 1969, it reached an understanding with East Jerusalem educators that it would be possible to prepare pupils for both the Israeli and the Jordanian examinations by means of an additional nine study periods a week. The necessary supplementary studies were in literature, history, religion, and geography. The disagreement between the Municipality and the Ministry of Education was subjected to the arbitration of the Ministerial Committee for Jerusalem which postponed its decision on the matter.

As the 1969–70 school year was about to begin, there was a real danger that the secondary schools would, once again, stay closed. On August 20, 1969, no decision had yet been reached, whereupon the Municipality's administrator for East Jerusalem wrote to the Arab high school principals, on his own authority, informing them that

> we are prepared to allow supplementary lessons for twelfth-grade pupils, by which those so interested can be prepared for the diploma examinations in force in Judea and Samaria. The number of lessons shall not exceed nine weekly. This permission is given on the express condition that lessons held in the schools according to the Israeli curriculum are not in any way affected.

This announcement by the Municipal official had no legal standing since it was the Government and not the Municipality which was responsible for the school curriculum. Nevertheless, this unilateral step yielded the desired result. The Ministry of Education insisted that it would permit no exception to the curriculum; however, the Government decided to approve the supplementary lessons.

The decision had an immediate effect. The number of pupils increased to 200. At the end of the year, five pupils took the Jordanian examinations and all passed. No one took the Israeli examinations. In the following year, 1971–2, the number of pupils rose to 330.

The school supplementary program was only the first step. With its implementation it became clear that the plan was placing too much of a burden on both students and teachers. In a meeting between the Mayor of Jerusalem and the Minister of Education, it was decided that a committee of Jewish and Arab experts should be established to formulate a joint Israel-Jordan study program. The committee completed its work at the end of the 1972/73 school year and presented a course of study incorporating most of the Jordanian program, with the addition of many hours from the Israeli curriculum. This also proved to be too burdensome, with the practical result that the Arab teachers taught the Jordanian material, extracting only the Hebrew language lessons from the Israeli program.

While all this was going on, efforts were being made on the part of the school principals to spread the Jordanian program to the lower classes as well.

At the end of 1975 it was decided to give in to the demands of the Arab educators. In accordance with this decision, as of the 1976/77 school year there will be two separate study programs in the upper six grades of the Arab schools. The first will adhere to the Jordanian educational program as used in the West Bank, with the addition of classes in Hebrew language and "Israeli civics." The second will follow the curriculum used in Israeli-Arab schools.

Since it was clear to the Ministry of Education that only a small minority would choose the Israeli study program, it was decided to group all those students who so chose into one school. The Jordanian system was incorporated into all other schools.

This decision, authorized by the Government, was joyously received by the Arab educators. The Israeli public received it with almost no reaction at all.

Despite the tension that resulted from the education issue, it should be noted that only half the pupils of East Jerusalem were ever enrolled in the state educational system, while the other half went to private schools. The private schools were divided into three categories: Christian schools, private Muslim schools, and U.N.R.W.A. schools. Most of these schools reopened in September 1967, with a total enrollment of 14,000. A week before the beginning of the school year, the Ministry of Education sent a circular to these schools, informing them that they must replace 78 textbooks. But the schools ignored the circular, especially when the instructions were altered for the West Bank by the Military Government.

At first, the Ministry maintained some kind of control over the schools, by means of visits by a Jewish inspector, but in a short time this contact stopped completely. The Muslim schools continued to teach according to the previous Jordanian curriculum. The Christian schools, on which the Jordanian curriculum had been imposed in 1966, went back to their European study programs. The only restriction imposed on those studying for the Jordanian diploma was that they were forbidden to take the examination in Jerusalem but were obliged to travel to Ramallah or Bethlehem for this purpose. But even this rule was abolished in 1971.

The complete liberty to maintain the previous curriculum in private schools, as opposed to the uncompromising imposition of the Israeli program in state schools, was a strange and inexplicable policy. Whatever its motives, the result was that hundreds of pupils, particularly the overwhelming majority of state secondary-school pupils, moved to the private school system. The Muslim post-elementary schools were greatly extended; and as private schools charged tuition fees, which many of the families whose children had left the state secondary schools could not afford, they were subsidized by the Jordan Government. In 1971, 450 of the pupils of these schools took Jordanian diploma examinations, compared to 15 from the state schools; before the war, the proportion had been the opposite.

The subject of Arab schooling in East Jerusalem had significance that far transcended local events, for the confrontation over the curriculum went to the root of the Arab—Israeli conflict. The dispute was colored by many transitory political elements, as well as by practical ones. There is no doubt that Jordan made use of the school strike as a conventient means of incitement, in order to undermine the stability of Israeli rule and sow disobedience, non-recognition, and non-cooperation. The extremists among the Arab population found, in the alteration of the curriculum, an issue upon which they could unite most of the population in disobedience to the authorities.

Aside from the political consideration, the inhabitants had practical reasons for their opposition to change in the curriculum. They feared that the Israeli curriculum would block the way for their children to acquire a higher education. The curriculum they were required to adopt prepared the pupil for entry to Israeli universities. But the Israeli high school diploma is not recognized in Arab countries, the only place where a young Arab can easily gain admission to a university. The universities in Jordan, Egypt, and Syria had opened their doors to young Palestinians, placing generous scholarships at their disposal (although they later reduced the number of places at the disposal of Palestinian students). What was the point in investing in 12 years of schooling if the pupil, upon graduation, found himself prevented from carrying on to higher studies? If the situation was unclear to anyone, the examination results of the first year clarified it sharply. With only four of the 96 students passing the Israeli examination, parents rightly feared that their children would not only be disqualified from continuing their studies, but would not even obtain a high school diploma. For many parents who could not afford the fees for private schools, the Israeli curriculum seemed to be a deliberate means of depriving their children of an education.

The Israeli educational authorities firmly resisted the adoption of a policy that differed from the one in force in the Arab sector of Israel. Weakness on this issue might, they feared, diminish the credibility of Israel's uncompromising stand with regard to the reunification of Jerusalem. When the matter became a subject of incitement and was linked with disobedience and terror, Israel was obliged to break the strike in order to prove her control of the situation and her ability to achieve the normalization of life in the city.

All these were highly important matters, but over and above them was a basic disagreement over educational content, which should not be confused with short-term political considerations. The Arabs rebelled against the fact that Israelis were imposing a program of studies that did not do justice to their national aspirations, language and culture, traditions, religion, and history. This allegation contained a large measure of truth. An objective survey conducted by Israeli researchers found that the curriculum in use in Israeli Arab schools had indeed "fallen victim of a trend toward blurring Arab nationality and [encouraging] self-abasement in front of the Jewish majority." According to the survey, these tendencies were manifested in two ways: firstly, a tendency to define the aims of teaching various subjects without taking into account the national elements in the identity of the Arab pupil; and secondly, a tendency to require of the Arab pupil profound and extensive knowledge of purely Jewish subjects at the expense of his own culture.

In the sphere of history, for example, the Arab pupil in Israel studies Arab and Jewish history for an equal number of hours. The Jordanian pupil, on the other hand, devotes half his time to Arab history. The Israeli curriculum does not include Arab national poetry or Palestinian poetry, which is not all anti-Israel. On the other hand, the Arab pupil was required to learn modern Hebrew poetry, most of which is Jewish-nationalistic. In religious studies, the situation is even worse. The Arab pupil was required to learn the Bible, *Mishna,* and Jewish legends for 156 hours, while only 30 hours were given to study of the Quran — to which the Jordanian study program devotes 360 hours.

At the end of 1971, a committee appointed by Education Minister Yigal Allon completed its work and presented recommendations for certain changes in the guidelines of Arab education. The changes were not revolutionary, but for the first time the need was stressed for education to "crystallize the characteristics of Israeli Arabs." It was also recommended that the number of hours devoted to the study of Jewish history be cut. With that, the committee ruled that Arab history, language, and literature be studied "in the light of the history of the Middle East and its contribution to world culture, with emphasis on Islamic values" — in other words, without relating to Arab national elements. Committees of teachers were asked to prepare detailed programs of study.

Another committee of experts, which submitted its recommendations in April 1975, suggested an even further expansion of the subjects expressing Arab nationalism.

In a general and superficial way, it may be said that the former program reflected the attitude to the Arab minority during the early years of Israel's existence. This approach included the belief that every Arab is a citizen with equal rights, but every independent expression of Arab nationalism, even if it was not hostile, was anti-Israel by definition, since Arab nationalism was the opposite of Jewish nationalism. Israel wished to isolate the Israeli Arabs from the hostile Arab world surrounding her, and to prevent them from identifying with pan-Arab nationalist aspirations by blurring their identity. It is hardly surprising, therefore, that those responsible for Arab education in Israel considered it their duty to impose the same educational standards on the inhabitants of the West Bank and of Jerusalem after the War, just as it is no wonder that the Arab population refused to accept a program of studies founded on such standards.

In the West Bank, the Military Government decided to permit the old syllabus to remain. Textbooks containing sentences such as: "I shall not forget thee, Jaffa, as long as I live," seemed, by comparison with the Israeli books, to be incitement of the worst kind, which called for censorship. But Military Government officials, who were free of the traditional approach, regarded them as legitimate expressions of nationalism, and they were, accordingly, left in. Understandably, books full of hatred and vengeance, which did exist within the Jordanian program of studies, were sifted out and banned. But the Arab population of the West Bank saw nothing provocative in this ban, after having been convinced that the Israelis did not intend to work against those educational values they held dear.

In East Jerusalem there was no Military Government, and there was a special political interest in having the Jordanian syllabus changed. Here too, however, like in most other conflicts of this kind, a compromise, founded on respect and encouragement for Arab national identity, without incitement, and within an Israeli national framework, was eventually arrived at. The Israeli curriculum was kept in the elementary schools, the Jordanian program was preserved in the secondary schools, and private schools maintained the *status quo ante*.

CHAPTER FIFTEEN

RESISTANCE

Throughout the period of military government, and for nearly a month after East Jerusalem was annexed, the Arab population made no attempt to create any anti-Israeli political organization. Most observers described this as "the period of shock." The Jews seemed to be overcome with a feeling of complacency that stemmed from the scenes of fraternization on unification day and on the days following it. At this time, most official spokesmen enthused that

a fantastic thing has happened here . . . the Jews have accepted the Arabs, and the Arabs have come toward us, after having been taught for 20 years to slaughter Jews. That's why they were shaken by the friendly reception they got from us.

During the third week of July, however, a number of events heralded the start of a new period. Members of the dispersed Municipal Council rejected a proposal that they join the Israeli Municipality. The Muslim Council was established, and leaflets calling for opposition to the occupation were distributed in the city. Arab lawyers sent a memorandum on their opposition to annexation; the Chamber of Commerce announced its refusal to pay taxes or customs' duties in accordance with Israeli law; and the teachers refused to cooperate in preparations for the forthcoming school year. At first, these protests were regarded only as the reservations of a few notables, who were trying to stir up emotion and turn again to enmity and vindictiveness. On August 6, however, leaflets were distributed in the city, calling for a commercial shut-down on the next day. The leaflets, signed by the Committee for the Protection of the Arab Nature of Jerusalem, contained the following message:

We have called for a general strike so that your call may be heard throughout the world, and so that you can show that you are firm in your refusal [to accept] the plans and laws made by the Zionists and that you belong to the Arab people on both banks of the Jordan. Long live Jordan, on both banks! Long live Arab Jerusalem!

The Israeli security authorities had dismissed the possibility of a general strike taking place; but on August 7, East Jerusalem was totally paralyzed. All the shops remained closed, the buses and taxis did not operate, and a large proportion of officials did not show up at work. Attempts to induce the traders to open their shops failed, and things only returned to normal on the following day.

Before the strike, many Israelis refused to believe in the existence of widespread anti-Israeli feeling. Now they went to the other extreme, demanding "far-reaching conclusions as far as dealing with East Jerusalem is concerned." They suggested that it was impossible to use ordinary civilian methods, and the restoration, at least in part, of military government was to be expected, for the shutdown was not a demonstrative step by individuals or by a group of notables, but a hostile act that included almost the entire population. The Government did not accept this line, nor did it change its policy. In retaliation for the shut-down, it contented itself with closing four shops and revoking the licences of one bus service.

However, the security authorities began to keep a close check on the activities of the heads of the resistance movement. In August 1967, a National Guidance Committee was established in Jerusalem, under the leadership of Sheikh Abd al-Hamid al-Sayah, Chairman of the Muslim Council, and it took charge of organizing acts of disobedience and resistance. Various circles that were not represented on it — such as notables from outside Jerusalem — demanded to join and threatened to establish a rival committee.

One of the first actions of the new Committee was the calling of a general strike on the day that the U.N. Secretary-General's representative, Ambassador Ernesto Thalman, arrived. This time, the security services were prepared. On August 21, Jerusalem witnessed a struggle that was to be repeated many times. It was a conflict (covert but none the less real) between the security forces and the strike's organizers as to who would sway the traders of East Jerusalem. Both sides used threats and made demonstrations of force. Arab youths treatened to set fire to the shops of strike breakers. Large forces of paratroopers and police began patrolling the city's commercial districts. The decisive moment came at about 7:30 in the morning. The traders stood in front of their locked shops, twirling their keys, looking at each other and then at the Israeli patrol. Indecision lasted for a quarter of an hour. Suddenly one of the traders turned, stuck his key in the lock and, with a sharp movement, opened the shutter. He had decided that this time there was more to fear from the Israelis. Within a few minutes, all the shops in the vicinity were open; then, all the shops in the city. The shutdown had failed.

The National Guidance Committee called another strike, which was to take place on September 19. This time the Committee's members were not content with distributing leaflets and verbal appeals: their call was broadcast on Amman Radio. Israeli security forces repeated their demonstrative presence and, as a result, the shops were open by mid-morning.

It was this attempted strike, as well as the incitement that accompanied it, that induced the Government to expel Sheikh Abd al-Hamid al-Sayah to Jordan. He was deported at dawn on September 22, leaving both the Muslim Council and the National Guidance Committee without a chairman.

Sheikh al-Sayah's banishment paralyzed the Committee's activities, resulting in a temporary cessation of the attempts to organize commercial strikes. There were disputes between the moderates, who favored passive resistance and protest memoranda, and the extremists, who demanded active protests. Widening frustration led several of the extremists to make public accusations of betrayal against the moderates, who were also blamed for the fact that many activists were abandoning their political work in despair.

Some of the local leaders were aware that the National Guidance Committee was an illegal organization that the authorities regarded as subversive. They felt the lack of an open political body which would represent the Arab population to the authorities, and for this reason they formed the National Committee in December 1967. But because of extremist pressures, personal rivalry and jealousy, the National Committee dispersed before it began to function.

At the beginning of 1968, the National Guidance Committee was headed by the former Mayor, Rauhi al-Khatib, who tried to introduce order into its activities and to establish sub-committees for political, economic, and legal affairs. Al-Khatib believed that his principal task was the campaign against land expropriation and the construction of Jewish housing estates in East Jerusalem.

He proposed organizing groups of inhabitants to lie down in front of the bulldozers preparing new roads over the confiscated land. But his suggestion was not accepted. It was decided to make do with a protest memorandum to the Prime Minister. At the beginning of March 1968, Rauhi al-Khatib suffered the same fate as his predecessor at the head of the Committee and was exiled to Jordan by the authorities.

Al-Khatib's deportation was a heavy blow to the city's Arab leadership. The National Guidance Committee's work was disrupted at a critical time, when Israeli construction plans were beginning to be implemented and when Israel was starting preparations for its Independence Day parade, which was to traverse East Jerusalem. The feebleness of the veteran leadership led to intensified activity by anti-establishment bodies.

Beginning in the spring of 1968, two organizations stood at the forefront of the resistance. One was the Union of Palestinian Pupils on the West Bank, and the other was the Union of Arab Women. In November 1967, the founding conference of the Union of Palestinian Pupils distributed a leaflet that called for a struggle against the "loathsome Zionist conquest" and proclaimed: "It cannot be believed that there is a single Arab soul prepared to accept the fact that Jerusalem is the property of the Jews." This body regarded its main task as disrupting the reopening of the schools. When they were opened, it tried to organize street demonstrations and student strikes on memorial days. The organization was connected wih the Popular Front for the Liberation of Palestine, and its members, who had leftist leanings, despised the veteran political establishment. The Union of Palestine Pupils was responsible for a long series of strikes, demonstrations, and student riots throughout the West Bank and in Jerusalem, that reached a peak at the end of 1968. These actions did not have the approval of the National Guidance Committee. Some members of the Pupils' Union engaged in sabotage activities, and this is what brought about the organization's downfall. The activities of the Union were terminated in the middle of 1969, when dozens of its members, organized in sabotage networks, were arrested.

The second organization, the Union of Arab Women, had been established in 1965, and during the period of Jordanian rule it engaged in social, educational, and cultural activities, even though it had anti-Hashemite inclinations from the start. In the spring of 1968, in coordination with the National Guidance Committee, it became the chief standard bearer of disobedience among the Arabs, with activities reaching a peak on the eve of the Israeli Independence Day military parade. On April 18, 152 women signed a letter to the Prime Minister, stating that Israel's decision to hold the parade in East Jerusalem

> *reveals a very ugly picture of provocation and hurts the feelings of thousands of Arab inhabitants, both Muslim and Christian, who live in Arab Jerusalem. . . . We, who have no other way of expressing our protest against this parade, beside presenting this petition, still hope that good sense will prevail and that the Israeli authorities will refrain from holding it.*

On April 25, some 300 women demonstrated in the city's streets. Preparations for the demonstration were made secretly, without the police taking notice until the women assembled at Herod's Gate. According to information that was received later, the demonstration was staged with the aid of the National Guidance Committee, and advance notification was sent to the consulates of foreign countries that had encouraged the organizers. The women carried posters in Arabic: "Long live Arab Jerusalem! " "The Women of Jerusalem oppose the military parade! " "The military parade is a provocation against Arab feelings! "

A police patrol noticed the women assembling and called for large reinforcements. The officers ordered the women to disperse, but the latter refused, obliging the police to use force. Eleven women and two men were arrested. The use of force by the police was welcomed by the organizers of the demonstration. Foreign press photographers, and officials of Western consulates, took pictures of the arrests. In the afternoon, the arrested women were released and driven home. Arab propaganda organs, as well as foreign reporters, spread the tale of Israeli policemen beating Arab women.

In view of their success, the Women's Union planned further actions. On May 15, the anniversary of the establishment of the State of Israel, the Pupils' Union and the Women's Union joined in a protest effort. Their attempts to bring about a commercial shutdown failed, though most pupils absented themselves from school. The next historic date was June 5, the first anniversary of the outbreak of the Six Day War. Both organizations took a very active part in organizing a full commercial shutdown, as well as in erecting memorials to the Arabs who had fallen in the war. They also held mourning processions on the 5th and on the following two days. Women's organizations also took an active part in the commercial strike held on August 22, 1968, in response to attacks by Jewish hooligans after "The Night of the Grenades," which is described below.

The resistance movement reached its peak in the summer of 1968, with all sections of the Arab population — ranging from pro-Hashemites to Communists — participating. This unusual unity was brought about by a combination of various issues. Construction work on Jewish housing, in the northern part of the city, was started. Excavations at the Western Wall were in full swing, the Jewish Quarter was expropriated, and the burden of taxation began to be felt. There were calls for overall civil disobedience, a tax strike, the resignation of municipal officials, demonstrations and shut-downs. Despite the escalation, the heads of the National Guidance Committee continued to oppose sabotage activities. But the growth of the non-violent civil-disobedience movement coincided with the increase of terrorist activity, which reached a peak on "The Night of the Grenades" on August 18.

At that time, the flow of money from Jordan had reached considerable dimensions. The Jordan Government, which was receiving enormous grants from the oil-producing countries to finance its campaign against Israel, sent increasingly large sums to Jerusalem and the West Bank. These sums were paid to government employees and municipalities, as well as organizations, in order to maintain their dependence on Amman. The money was also used to support acts of disobedience and protest against Israel. But although the large-scale transfer of money was maintaining the West Bank's links with the Jordan Government, and upholding Amman's influence, the Israel Government did not take any steps to impede it. The authorities did not consider the political and security dangers intolerable, while the economic advantages were very great.

Faced with growing disobedience, the authorities again resorted to deportation, expelling the heads of the National Guidance Committee and the Women's Union. This time, however, the deportations

212

did not result in any decrease of acts of disobedience. On the contrary, disobedience was at its highest level since the occupation. A show of force by Israeli paratroopers managed to prevent a commercial shutdown on October 24, but the strike took place three days later. On November 2, 1968, the anniversary of the Balfour Declaration, there was another general commercial strike, despite vigorous attempts by the authorities to prevent it. After the first day of the shutdown, the authorities confiscated 15 shops in retaliation and as a deterrent. This caused the strike to continue for two more days, ending only when the Minister of Police announced "unofficially" that he would recommend that the Government return the shops if the strike ceased.

After this peak of protest activity, the strikes took on a routine form. Before each of the historic dates, leaflets would be distributed calling for a strike; the authorities would call the notables together and warn them against holding the strike; the notables would reply that they opposed the strike but they could not be held responsible, since they did not control the situation. The next morning, strong police and army patrols would make the rounds of the city. The traders would arrive at the appointed time, twirling their keys and weighing who was to be feared more, the police or the organizers. If one shopkeeper opened up, the strike would fail; it not, the city remained closed. Full or partial commercial shutdowns took place in Jerusalem on May 15 and June 5, 1969, and on June 5, 1970.

After 1969, the influence of the National Guidance Committee decreased. Extremist circles, principally the Communists and the Popular Front for the Liberation of Palestine, continued to incite strikes and demonstrations, while the old leadership tried to curb disobedience and even opposed the strikes. After two years of activity by the supposedly "secret" National Guidance Committee, the proposal to set up a "political committee" that would openly represent the Arab population to the authorities was again aired; but once again it failed for personal as well as political reasons.

Political disunity and personal conflicts were only forgotten during exceptional events, when the whole Arab population closed ranks to display unity and excellent organizational ability. One such event was the death of Egypt's President Nasser. The news of Nasser's death caused deep mourning, with lament turning into mass hysteria. On Tuesday, September 29, 1970, there were clashes with security

213

forces. The demonstrators threw stones, and the police had to use force to disperse them.

The Arab leadership convened and decided not to let the situation deteriorate. Representatives of all the professional and political bodies in the city were invited to the meeting at which mourning arrangements were discussed. At the end of the meeting, the following statement was issued:

> Sorrow and grief have descended upon the Arab nation at the death of its leader, the symbol of its unity, the initiator of its reawakening, the martyr for Palestine, the great warrior, President Gamal Abdul Nasser. As a sign of esteem for the beloved deceased ... who died for Jerusalem and Palestine, it has been decided that all the inhabitants of Arab Jerusalem ... shall take part in a peaceful popular procession and a general memorial ceremony ... We call upon all the participants to show deference to the procession and to respect the memory of the beloved deceased by maintaining order and calm.

A delegation appeared at police headquarters and requested permission to close businesses and hold a mourning procession. After a discussion at the highest political level, the Israelis decided to permit the procession to take place, on condition that the local leadership undertook to maintain order.

On Thursday, October 1, Jerusalem witnessed a fantastic spectacle: the city's entire adult Arab population, plus school children, some 20,000 people, assembled in a quiet and orderly manner at the prearranged meeting place, each group — professional organization or secondary school — gathering round placards and signs which had been prepared beforehand. Stewards with armbands directed people to their places. The procession set off after a slight delay, headed by the entire leadership, except for two or three who had stayed at home in fear of disturbances. The thousands of men, women, and children marched in closed ranks carrying slogans, black-draped pictures of the dead President, and palm fronds, as is customary at Muslim funerals. Hundreds of young stewards safeguarded the procession by holding hands at its sides. Not a single anti-Israeli slogan was voiced; no one stepped out of line.

From the roof of the post office building opposite Herod's Gate, the procession was watched by Police Minister Shlomo Hillel. As planned, no soldiers or police were to be seen in the streets. In perfect order, the procession entered the Old City and went on to the Temple Mount courtyard. After the midday prayers and prayers for the deceased, the crowd dispersed in a quiet and orderly manner. From the roof of a building opposite the Temple Mount courtyard, the Defense Minister followed the proceedings. After the procession, a senior police officer remarked: "When they want to, they control their people, and they know very well how to organize them." The mourning procession for Israel's greatest enemy went off without disturbance under the protection of Jewish soldiers and police.

The day of Nasser's funeral initiated a new period in Jerusalem. There were no more strikes or demonstrations in the years 1971 and 1972. On the third and fourth anniversaries of the war, groups of women and students marched to the memorial opposite the Rockefeller Museum and laid wreaths; there were memorial services at the cemetery. The period of organized disobedience seemed to have ended.

The period of calm did not last very long. On April 10, 1973, the Israel Defense Forces struck Fatah bases in Beirut. In the course of the attack, three Fatah leaders were killed, including P.L.O. spokesman Kamal Nasser, a Christian resident of the village of Bir Zeit. The death of Nasser and his compatriots awakened an unprecedented wave of Palestinian nationalist feelings in the West Bank and Jerusalem. Mourning ceremonies and memorial services were held. The East Jerusalem newspapers called for Arab unity and a continuation of the struggle against the Israeli occupiers. The Muslim Council in Jerusalem published a notice in memory of "the martyrs to the Arab nation and the Palestinian peoples who gave their lives for a just cause and a sacred homeland."

The reaction shocked the Israelis, who wanted to believe that the period of opposition had ended. In response they arrested two newspaper editors and issued warnings to public leaders. On June 5, 1973, the familiar scenes of the 1968—69 period were re-enacted: most stores in East Jerusalem refused to open; police and army units patrolled the streets and became involved in a "power struggle" with the strike organizers. By afternoon, after several store owners had been arrested, the merchants decided that the Israelis presented the greater threat and re-opened their stores.

The political awakening which began in the spring of 1973 increased after the Yom Kippur War. It reached an unprecedented peak in November 1974. After Yassir Arafat's speech in the U.N. and the Rabat Conference naming the P.L.O. as the only legal representative of the Palestinians, demonstrations and riots began in Jerusalem and the West Bank. In answer to the inciting articles in the Arab press, the Government deported a newspaper editor and three public figures. In November there were violent riots and strikes.

The strikes reached a new peak in early 1976 when tension built up over the Temple Mount, an issue which will be dealt with elsewhere.

The Arab civil disobedience movement in Jerusalem did not attain its objectives. It did not shake Israel's complete control, nor induce her to change her policy toward Jerusalem. Unlike the conflicts over education and religious organization, which were severe disputes on matters of principle but still open to a compromise solution, here the confrontation was total and uncompromising. Both the old leadership and the extremist organizations challenged Israel's very presence in East Jerusalem and tried to undermine her rule. The old Arab establishment, experienced and, on the whole, moderate, lost control. This process was speeded up when the confrontation with the authorities grew sharper, as a result of political steps aimed at buttressing Israeli rule in East Jerusalem. Anti-establishment organizations, such as the Communists, extreme left- and right-wing parties, and students, gained control of the situation. It was only when they were crushed by superior Israeli force, that partial control returned to the moderate elements. By then, however, the moderates had lost their power to act. An inevitable outcome of total confrontation, this was a further blow to the prestige of the Arab leadership and a weakening of its influence. The decline of the established leadership was proven time and again. But the internal clash between P.L.O. backers, extreme leftist Palestinian groups and Hashemite supporters prevented any possibility of creating a leadership supported by a majority of the population.

As a result, the Arabs of East Jerusalem, united in their opposition to Israeli rule, have been unable to establish an organization which could express this opposition for them. —

At about 9 o'clock in the evening, on September 19, 1967, the center of Jerusalem was shaken by a powerful explosion. It was quickly traced to the Fast Hotel, a large ramshackle building that had been in no-man's-land until the 1967 War, opposite the northwestern

216

corner of the Old City walls. The explosion destroyed a printing press and damaged a number of apartments; seven people were injured. The security authorities noted that "the perpetrators possessed knowhow in sabotage." Jerusalem had enjoyed three months of quiet, but the citizens were now to become accustomed to living with, and in the shadow of, terror, directed against civilians and choosing its victims indiscriminately.

The explosion at the Fast Hotel was part of the first series of attacks organized by the Fatah terrorist organization after the war, to herald the start of what it called "the armed popular revolution." At the end of the 1967 War, the Fatah had decided "to transfer the command to the occupied territories" and to create a network of sabotage cells that would, after a period of organization and consolidation, start operations against Israeli civilian and military targets. By September 1967, there were hundreds of well-armed and equipped members in the areas under Israeli control. Some of them had crossed the Jordan River, which was yet to be sealed off by the Israel Defense Forces; some had been recruited on the West Bank. The Fatah men were poorly trained, and their motivation was weak. They were not strict about secrecy, and their coordination and control were defective. As a result, the Israeli secret service easily succeeded in infiltrating their ranks and arresting dozens of them before they took any action. At that time, the chief Fatah commander, Yassir Arafat, was in Nablus.

In Jerusalem, Omar 'Audah Khalil, or "Dr. Nur," as he was called in the underground, a Palestinian refugee from Lebanon, was organizing a sabotage cell of some 30 members. This group was typical in its composition and history. Its members included a number of black women belonging to Jerusalem's African community and East Jerusalem citizens of varying occupations, most of whom were illiterate, as well as a number of saboteurs who had undergone basic training in Syria and had crossed the Jordan when operations began. They did not conceal their movements, travelled by taxi, and found refuge for themselves, their weapons, and sabotage equipment in the homes of the Arab inhabitants of Jerusalem.

Following the explosion in the Fast Hotel, the cell began to organize a far more serious operation. On the evening of October 8, two young black women and an Arab man entered the Zion movie theater and left before the end of the first performance. As the hall

217

filled for the second showing, one of the moviegoers noticed a black plastic bag lying on the floor in the row next to him. He asked two boys sitting there about the bag, and when they said it was not theirs, he asked them to give it to the attendant outside the hall. The attendant opened the bag and found an alarm clock with two wires attached to it, whereupon he gave it to a policeman who was on patrol outside. The policeman ran to the Jerusalem Central Police Station, some 200 yards away, where he laid the bag in a clump of trees nearby. At 8:50, the charge exploded with a loud blast. Had it blown up inside the hall, with its 800 spectators, it would have caused a major disaster.

Within 21 hours, the culprits were in the hands of the security forces. It was the color of the girls' skin that gave them away. Police investigators were swift in reaching the 300-strong African community in the Old City, which consisted of pilgrims who had settled in Jerusalem. In the room belonging to one of the girls they found the network's leader, "Dr. Nur," with a loaded revolver in his pocket.

The first detainees began to talk, and that night, three arms dumps were found, as well as explosives and five vehicles. Dozens of suspects were arrested; the last members of the cell were caught the next day. The arsenal of weapons in their possession included a mortar, a bazooka, ten sub-machine guns, two rifles, five revolvers, hundreds of kilograms of explosives, detonators and ammunition. They also had food supplies, leaflets, and a typewriter. The prisoners cooperated fully with their interrogators and revealed the names of their comrades and their whereabouts. They provided precise information about their training in Syria, their infiltration routes, and the organization of other cells in the West Bank, as well as the plans for other attacks which they had prepared.

The elimination of "Dr. Nur's" network restored peace and quiet to Jerusalem. For six months there were no acts of sabotage in the city. At the end of 1967, a new group was formed, but all its members were caught in January 1968 before they had carried out a single operation.

At the beginning of 1968, the "command of the Jerusalem area" was taken over by Kamal Namari, an engineer whose mother was Jewish and whose family had moved back and forth between Jerusalem and Kuwait. He commanded a group that infiltrated from the East Bank and took cover in a wood near Ramallah. Unlike the

218

previous groups, all the members of the Namari cell were ideologically motivated intellectuals. On Saturday, March 2, 1968, a Druze who was guarding road construction equipment near the village of Abu Gosh, some 10 miles to the west of Jerusalem, was brutally murdered. The following day, the entire troup was captured. During their interrogation, the prisoners related that they had planned further attacks.

Soon after the elimination of the Namari cell, a new group began operations in Jerusalem. Between March and June 1968, it carried out seven attacks, which, although they caused only slight damage and no casualties, had the security authorities seriously worried because, initially, the perpetrators could not be found. The mystery was solved on June 22, 1968, when an explosion occurred near the Ambassador Hotel in East Jerusalem. The shattered body of a dead child was found there, while another lay badly injured. Both the children, 13-year-olds, were pupils of a municipal school. The injured child related that on their way home from school they had found a parcel with "three pieces of soap and a pencil." When his friend pulled at the pencil, there was an explosion. Police investigators found the safety pin of a detonator in the pocket of the dead child. Under renewed interrogation, the wounded child admitted carrying out all the attacks in Jerusalem in recent months. The explosion at the Ambassador Hotel had occurred as they were trying to get to the headquarters of the West Bank Military Government, then housed in the Hotel. All the attacks had been carried out by these two children and a 15-year-old friend.

It transpired that the organizer of the "children's cell" was the dead child's elder brother, Abd al-Rahim Jaber of Hebron, who supplied the children with explosives but left the choice of targets up to them. Jaber disappeared from his Hebron home, together with his family, and began organizing a new network, which carried out eight attacks during August, while he himself carried out additional ones in the Hebron region.

On September 4, 1968, an explosive charge blew up at the Tel Aviv Central Bus Station, killing one man and injuring 72. Among the 150 Arabs arrested at the scene of the explosion were two of the four perpetrators. Under interrogation, they led the police to their colleagues in Jerusalem and Hebron. Within two days, all the members of the network were under arrest. Jaber again managed to get away, but was caught later when he was wounded by a mine while trying to cross the Jordanian border near Naot Hakikar, south of the Dead Sea.

On Friday, November 22, 1968, a car filled with a quarter of a ton of explosives blew up at the West Jerusalem vegetable and fruit market in Mahaneh Yehudah. The explosion took place at midday, when the market was teeming with thousands of shoppers making their purchases for the Sabbath. It killed 12 people and wounded another 54. Nine shops, six apartments, ten market stalls and nine vehicles were destroyed. A curfew was imposed on the Old City and dozens of suspects were arrested, but the perpetrators succeeded in getting away. It was only two years later that the culprit was caught and confessed to the deed.

In 1969, there were two serious acts of sabotage. In February, an explosive charge went off in a supermarket, causing the deaths of two people; the perpetrators were captured within three days. In March 1969, a demolition charge exploded in the cafeteria of the National Library at the Hebrew University, wounding 26 and causing considerable damage. The culprits were caught within a short time.

Terrorist activities reached a peak in 1969. That same year, 30 incidents were recorded in Jerusalem, as a result of which there were 46 casualties. In 1970, there was a slight decline, with only 21 incidents.

The destruction of the Fatah bases in Jordan (by the Jordanians) in September 1970 ("Black September") brought about a period of calm in Jerusalem as well. In 1971, only ten terrorist incidents occurred, and, in 1972, the number declined to only three.

In the years after the Yom Kippur War, terrorism increased again, as did the number of casualties. In 1973, there were 24 casualties, and, in 1974, 65. In 1975, there were 73 casualties, more than in any year since the Six-Day War.

As we have seen, an overwhelming majority of the perpetrators were caught within a short time of carrying out their acts. Usually the sabotage cells were captured in their entirety. The prisoners did not hesitate to denounce their comrades, and there was no need for severe interrogation to induce them to talk. In consequence, networks with dozens of members were eliminated. In the spring of 1969, 150 members of sabotage organizations were arrested simultaneously. All together, between 1967–1975, more than 400 persons responsible for terrorist acts were arrested in Jerusalem.

The city suffered from terrorist activity more than any other Jewish city in the country. There were a number of reasons for this. Primarily, the organizations wished to combat the annexation of Jerusalem and to weaken Israel's resolution to hold on to the united city. Jerusalem is the showcase of Palestine, and whatever happens there gets worldwide publicity. Acts of sabotage in Jerusalem brought international reverberations, and, in the opinion of the terrorist organizations, demonstrated the Palestinians' readiness to fight Israel. The terrorists were also interested in stirring up intercommunal rioting, which would prove that Jewish–Arab coexistence was out of the question. They hoped that Jewish retaliation, whether official or by private individuals or groups, would increase the fears and frustrations of the Arabs and thereby step up their readiness for insurrection.

There were also operational reasons for the large number of acts of sabotage in Jerusalem. Unlike other areas that did not have mixed populations, both the home-base and places of concealment in Jerusalem were very close to the objective. There were also convenient approach routes from the Jordan through the Judean Desert.

It was hard to take deterrent action in Jerusalem. For both political and practical reasons, it was impossible to use the same methods in Jerusalem as in Nablus, Hebron, or Gaza. Curfews could not be imposed (except for a few hours in exceptional cases) and the Old City alleyways could not be blockaded, as was done to the *casbah* of Nablus. The prevention of free access or the imposition of economic restrictions was also impractical. As we shall see, the readiness of the political echelons to use the extreme deterrent of demolishing houses was limited. In consequence, Jerusalem became a refuge for the remnants of terrorist groups hunted out of the West Bank.

The Arab population's attitude to terror activity, and its sympathy for the sabotage organizations, underwent several changes. The first terrorist cells persuaded the local population to help in concealment, intelligence, communications and transport, and the first acts of sabotage were sympathetically received. However, the hope of the Fatah leaders that many sabotage networks would be formed by Jerusalem residents did not materialize; nor did the terrorist acts bring about a popular uprising. Although the cells were concealed by the population, they still remained isolated. The swift elimination of the terrorist groups resulted in long intervals between acts of sabo-

221

tage. Israeli retaliation, such as the demolition or confiscation of houses and the arrest of collaborators, reduced the population's readiness to help new groups. Until the end of 1968, most of the attacks were perpetrated by refugees, or, at any rate, by people from outside Jerusalem.

Most of the local leadership did not cooperate with the terrorists because they did not believe that they could gain by force objectives that had been beyond the capability of the Arab States and their armies. They believed that sabotage activity would not produce any positive results, and the principal victims would be the Arabs themselves, as Israeli retaliation and deterrents would upset the Arab population's day-to-day life with many Arabs leaving the city as a consequence. The leadership believed that passive resistance, demonstrations, strikes, and propaganda through foreign correspondents, was a more effective means of opposing Israeli rule. At the same time, the saboteurs did enjoy great prestige and the passive sympathy of all classes of society, who regarded their actions as an expression of the Palestinians' firm resolve to "take their fate into their own hands." As long as there was a reasonable *modus vivendi* in Jordan between the King and the terrorists, the pro-Hashemite elements were not faced with the dilemma of where to direct their sympathies.

At the beginning of 1969, the situation changed somewhat, as local elements from prosperous and educated circles began to take an increasing part in sabotage activities. They were connected to George Habash's Popular Front for the Liberation of Palestine, an organization whose ideology was extremely leftist and whose members were politically motivated. These groups operated on two planes: subversive political activity and sabotage. They were responsible for a series of demonstrations and disturbances, as well as for acts of sabotage. They needed neither help nor concealment, since they continued to live at home and operated with the knowledge of their families; but their fate was no better than that of the Fatah groups that had preceded them, and they were quickly captured. Among other factors, they were undone by their dangerous combination of semi-overt political activity and sabotage actions, which had to be clandestine if they were to be successful. In the spring of 1969, the number of Jerusalem inhabitants under arrest for belonging to Popular Front groups ran into the dozens, including doctors, priests, teachers, university graduates, high school pupils and other professionals.

Despite the failure of this group, the terrorist organizations continued to enjoy great prestige among the population, which was not dependent on actual results. None of the Arab population believed their boastful claims, which inflated every action to fantastic dimensions. They also saw how quickly and efficiently all the sabotage networks were disrupted by arrests and other Israeli actions. At the same time, the Arab population was deeply impressed by the wide extent of the terrorists' activity and by the sympathy and respect which the "guerillas" gained in certain western circles. The series of agreements that King Husayn was forced to sign with the terrorist organizations and their influence on inter-Arab policy, made the *fedayeen* into the standard-bearers of the Palestinian nation. With all its fears and reservations, the Arab population could not remain indifferent to the fact that for the first time since 1948 "the Palestinians have taken their fate into their own hands." But however strong these sympathetic feelings were, they brought no practical results. The population remained passive, despite the continual incitement broadcast morning and night by the terrorist radio stations and the media of certain Arab states.

King Husayn's campaign against the terrorists, which reached its peak in the "Black September" War of 1970, at first caused the feelings of identification with the *fedayeen* movement to grow stronger, and caused hatred for the Hashemite regime. But when the movement was liquidated in Jordan, a sobering-up occurred. As time went by, the Jordan Army's acts of repression, and the killings of guerillas and Palestinian residents of the East Bank, were forgotten. The liquidation of the *fedayeen* movement in Jordan, and the resulting damage to its strength and image, almost completely removed its influence on the local population.

At the end of 1972, there was a general feeling that the phase of rebellion and terror had ended. The calm, and the declining influence of the Palestinian organizations, continued almost until the outbreak of the Yom Kippur War.

The 1973 War and its outcome drastically changed the situation. Although during the course of the war itself there were no incidents within the city, there was no doubt that the political polarization which began in its aftermath would bring a new wave of violence. Respect for the Palestinian organizations grew and reached its peak in the fall of 1974 after the Rabat Conference, which confirmed the

P.L.O. as the only legitimate representative of the Palestinians. The cycle of violence in the city re-escalated and in 1975 reached a new high in number of incidents.

The political violence which had accompanied Jerusalem for its eight years of unification continued. Residents of the city learned to live with it, and even stopped predicting its termination.

The Israeli security authorities were ready to deal effectively with anti-Israel elements and with anti-establishment groups. Information which had been collected before the war, as well as the archives of the Jordanian security police, seized in their entirety after the war, permitted a close watch to be kept on the activities of these bodies. Most of the members were left free, but a few were put in preventive detention. The organization and consolidation of the first Fatah cells did not escape the scrutiny of the security services. Thanks to an efficient intelligence system, and to the amateurish methods of the terrorists, the overwhelming majority were captured very soon after carrying out their attacks. The readiness of the prisoners to disclose the names of their comrades permitted the elimination of entire networks. The main effort was directed at eliminating networks before they could carry out their operational plans. For this purpose, a special effort was made to plant informers in terrorist bases in Jordan and to infiltrate them into networks operating inside Israel-administered territories. So successful were the security services that, in the later stages of terrorist activity, even the timing of an attack was known to the security services beforehand. Sometimes, if they did not want to reveal the identity of their agent, they contented themselves with making sure that the attack did not cause any damage.

Despite the unusual success in capturing the perpetrators of sabotage actions, new networks were formed and succeeded in carrying out further sabotage actions. The security services, therefore, faced the problem of defending the Jewish population. For this purpose, security officers were trained to take charge of public and government buildings. While sentries were stationed at essential installations, the main burden of defense from attacks fell upon the Civil Defense Service. Armed Civil Defense personnel in green berets patrolled the streets and watched the entrances of cinemas and stores. After the bomb attack at the Zion movie theater, the Civil Defense guards searched the handbags of movie-goers. Similar checks were made of people entering public buildings. Large sums of money

224

were invested in erecting fences around schools and lighting unlit areas. After the explosion in the National Library cafeteria at the Hebrew University, the whole campus was enclosed by a high fence, with guards at each entrance. Police officers visited schools, instructing the children on security precautions.

In the years 1973–4, when the problems of security intensified, the police, in cooperation with the Municipality, organized the "civil guard." This organization is made up of volunteers who serve as guards, usually in addition to their regular military service and reserve duties. After the terrorists' murderous attacks on schools and residential buildings, parents were enlisted for guard duty at schools and kindergartens. The security door and safety lock industry in the city flourished.

On the whole, the Jewish population behaved in a calm and self-confident manner. After all, they were experienced at living near a border. The many incidents between 1949 and 1967, and the Wars of 1948 and 1967, had made the whole population security conscious. Moreover, the security, Civil Defense, and medical services were well trained and experienced in the effective treatment of sudden incidents. The continuing terror had a cumulative psychological effect. Yet the tension did not express itself in feelings of hatred or revenge towards the Arab population. The general public accepted the searches and even the deaths as a necessary evil. There were, however, exceptions.

One of the hardest problems was the control of marginal elements after an attack took place. This problem arose after the attempted bomb attack at the Zion movie theater. When news of the attack became known, a number of the younger inhabitants of the old border quarters set off for the Arab sections and began to carry out wild "reprisal" actions. Car and shop windows were smashed and Arab passers-by were beaten. The police arrested the rioters and warned that they would not permit "any acts of disorder or revenge." The standing police orders for emergencies were extended to include instructions for the setting up of barriers between the Arab and the Jewish quarters, in order to prevent retaliation against the Arab population. There were, however, other cases of people taking the law into their own hands and carrying out acts of revenge. On August 1, 1968, there was an explosion in a café in the center of Jerusalem. Arab passers-by were caught and subjected to murderous beatings. The police intervened at once to rescue the Arabs; but a mob surrounded the police car, threatening to overturn it and shouting "Kill them! " "Hang them! " Dozens of Arabs working in Jewish quarters were rescued and brought home safely. At the same time, in accordance with standing orders, barriers were set up at the transit points to East Jerusalem, and not a single Jewish thug succeeded in getting past.

On August 18, 1968, after "the Night of the Grenades," when demolition charges exploded at several points in the center of the city, causing a considerable number of casualties, the retaliatory acts took on the character of a pogrom. The angry mob beat up a Jew, who had been wounded in the explosion, because they thought that he was an Arab. Dozens of Arabs who were in West Jerusalem at the time were severely beaten. Hundreds of young men began to pour into the Arab quarters. They broke through the police barricades, and began to throw stones at shop windows and attack passers-by. They caused considerable damage to Arab cafés, and the police were forced to fire into the air and use their sticks to disperse the rioters. Reinforcements were sent to drive off the hooligans. It was only in the early morning hours that the city calmed down. That night, 40 Arab businesses were attacked, and the damage was estimated at IL 50,000. The next day, heavy police patrols toured East Jerusalem, but there were no further incidents.

Israeli public opinion was shocked; a feeling of shame and anxiety encompassed the whole Jewish population. The Defense Minister cancelled all his appointments and hurried to Jerusalem, where he conducted a prolonged tour through the Old City streets, accompanied by the Mayor. In a radio interview, he termed the rioting "criminal hooliganism, which is as good as collaboration with the Fatah saboteurs." He warned against letting the situation deteriorate, as it had in Cyprus where the Turkish and Greek communities were incapable of living together. "If we don't control ourselves and avoid lynch-like deeds, we will be doing what the terrorists want." The Jerusalem Municipality issued a leaflet in Hebrew and in Arabic denouncing both the saboteurs and the rioters, who "by their irresponsible deeds helped those circles interested in undermining the coexistence of the city's inhabitants." The Arab population was shocked and frightened. A few reacted moderately. One Arab citizen said:

226

If I knew Hebrew I would write a long article on this affair. I would like to make it clear to the Jewish people that we are not responsible for the acts of the fedayeen *who come from outside, and we will not agree to have this responsibility imposed on us.*

Others were more extreme: "I don't think that it is possible to let this shocking deed pass by without a word; the inhabitants of Arab Jerusalem must, in my opinion, draw the appropriate conclusions and take steps." Three days later, the Arabs responded with a full shutdown of shops.

Shock at the deeds of the hooligans, together with the sharp reactions of Israel's leaders, had a deep and lasting effect on the Jewish population of Jerusalem. On November 22, 1968, when a car full of explosives blew up at the Machaneh Yehudah market, causing many fatalities, similar deeds of hooliganism were not repeated. There were a few instances of Arabs being beaten up in West Jerusalem; but there were far more cases of Jews inviting Arab passers-by into their homes until the tension died down.

Once again, the army and the police set up barricades at the transit points to the Arab quarters, to prevent Jews from entering them. The security authorities also decided to impose an evening curfew on East Jerusalem, not so much to facilitate the search for the attackers as to prevent incidents on the following day, which was a Saturday, when, as they did every Sabbath, thousands of Jews would visit the Old City. There were no further attacks by Jewish rowdies.

The virtual end to terrorist acts between 1971 and 1973 also saw an end to hooliganism. However, at the beginning of 1975, when a terrorist bomb exploded in Zion Square, causing heavy loss of life, Jewish hooligans again attacked Arab shops. The security forces took immediate stringent action and quickly and effectively stopped the attacks. Compensation was paid to the owners of the damaged shops.

The security forces knew that the free movement of Arabs into all parts of the city, and, in fact, all of Israel, greatly facilitated terrorist actions. The risk could have been considerably reduced by setting up control points between the two parts of the city. However, such barriers were inconceivable for political reasons, since this would have been tantamount to a renewed partition of the city. The security forces were compelled to use other means, such as surprise inspections, issuing a special series of licence numbers to Arab vehicles, and imposing certain restrictions on Arab vehicles from outside Jerusalem, preventing them from entering the western part of the city. This was in addition to guarding and fortifying buildings, and improving street-lighting. Naturally, these measures required a considerable financial investment and much manpower.

Whenever terrorist attacks were stepped up in Jerusalem, and a number of sabotage groups were uncovered, the Israeli authorities increased the severity of their countermeasures. On the West Bank, the authorities had been blowing up the houses of terrorists and their collaborators ever since August 1967. This was a very drastic retaliatory method, in the eyes of the Arabs, who attached a great, almost mystical, value to their homes and land. The Arabic curse, *'yahre-betak'* (may your house be destroyed), is one of the strongest curses that Arabs can use.

The demolition of houses was a punishment used by the British during the 1936–39 disturbances. The legal basis for demolition was Paragraph 119(1) in the "Defense Regulations (Emergency) 1945." This regulation, enacted by the British against the Jewish community in Palestine, was now used by the Jews to combat the terror directed against them.

For over six months the authorities refrained from demolishing houses in Jerusalem. However, early in March 1968, the Fatah Jerusalem Commander, Kamal Namari, was captured after his group had carried out the Abu Gosh murder. This time, on the authority of the Defense Minister, it was decided to demolish his house in the Wadi Joz quarter. The decision was taken by a military security body, without consulting civilian advisers. On the evening of March 6, 1968, the Wadi Joz area was blocked off by army and police. Neighbors were warned to leave their homes. Israeli students living in one of the apartments in Namari's house removed their possessions. Two explosive charges were ignited, and the two-storey house, with all its furniture, was blown up. The explosion was heard throughout the northern part of the city, and due to a mistake in calculating the amount of explosives, 20 other apartments were damaged, as well as a school and an archeological institute. The explosion occurred in the evening in a densely populated quarter, and it is a miracle that none of the inhabitants was injured by the blast.

This deed provoked severe criticism, which is unusual in Israel on defense matters. Reservations were expressed, indirectly, by the

228

Mayor, as well as by several Cabinet Ministers. The main contention was that what was permissible on the West Bank under military rule was not permissible in Jerusalem, which was part of Israel. The army apologized for the damage caused, girl soldiers gave out candy to the children, the Municipality sent in a bulldozer to clean up the rubble, and compensation was paid to the owners of the damaged apartments. For a number of months there were no further suggestions that houses in Jerusalem be demolished, despite the detection of a number of additional sabotage networks.

In September 1968, a Fatah unit that had been responsible for a number of attacks, including "The Night of the Grenades," was captured. Most of its members were residents of Jerusalem. The military authorities recommended that a number of houses, where some of the captured terrorists had lived or where arms had been found, be blown up. Several of the houses were near the Temple Mount. This time the decision came before the Israeli Cabinet, which decided that there would be no more demolition of houses in Jerusalem. At the same time, permission was given to confiscate the houses in accordance with Paragraph 119(1) of the Defense Regulations. On October 28, 1968, four houses (three in the Old City and one in Abu Tor) were seized, cleared, and sealed up.

Following the discovery of new sabotage networks and the increase of terrorist attacks in the city, the security authorities came to the conclusion that the absence of a uniform policy of deterrents and punishments for the West Bank and Jerusalem was turning the latter into a refuge for the terrorists. This was confirmed by the interrogation of captured terrorists. As a result, the Government was asked to alter its decision and to permit the demolition of houses in Jerusalem. As this recommendation came from the security agencies, it was accepted, and on March 8, 1969, two buildings, containing six apartments, were demolished. This time the demolition was carried out by bulldozers, with the assistance of laborers, and explosives were not used. Ten days later, another four homes were demolished in the same way. These were the last houses to be demolished in Jerusalem for several years.

From 1969 to 1974, no house was demolished in Jerusalem. The military authorities recommended the demolition of additional houses but the Government did not approve the request. However, in June 1974, the security forces again felt the need to resort to this extreme measure. Army bulldozers demolished the home of three brothers who had murdered a Jewish taxi driver, booby-trapped his car, and left it in the center of the city. Luckily the taxi did not explode.

All in all, nine houses were demolished and 11 were seized; and in 1970 permission was given to several of the owners to rebuild their houses.

The security bodies responsible for combatting and catching the terrorists, safeguarding the Jewish neighborhoods, and taking deterrent and punitive action, also cooperated with civilian bodies in countering disobedience. The Jerusalem Police Chief, Shaul Rosolio, coordinated a military-civilian group whose task was defined as dealing with problems with security aspects, in the widest sense of the term. Due to the total political confrontation, there was almost no subject affecting the Arab population that did not have its security aspect. Views were coordinated and policy laid down on all kinds of subjects, but the main task was to combat overt civil disobedience. Efforts were mainly directed at preventing demonstrations and strikes. For this purpose, talks were held with notables and heads of associations, and warnings were issued to school principals and teachers. In exceptional cases, agitators were put under preventive detention. On a morning when a strike was due to take place, large units of army and police would put on a show of force with motorized and foot patrols. If a strike occurred despite warnings and deterrent actions, the matter would be ignored, unless it was accompanied by additional disturbances, such as demonstrations. In three cases, the first shutdown of businesses (August 7, 1967), the prolonged shutdown (November 1968), and in 1973, the authorities closed a number of shops. Uncooperative tradesmen were also penalized by economic means, such as the withdrawal of their import licences and travel permits to Jordan. These steps, which were effective in military government areas, were totally ineffective in Jerusalem, where the traders enjoyed full economic freedom.

The authorities made a clear distinction between strikes of a political, anti-Israel character and strikes which were provoked by other reasons. Thus, for instance, the authorities did not intervene in the strike after the fire at the al-Aqsa Mosque, the business shutdown in response to the increased tax burden, or that during President Nasser's funeral. Unauthorised demonstrations were never permitted.

In dispersing them, the police would use truncheons and "water cannon" to hose the demonstrators with colored water. Prior to the Yom Kippur War the security forces were never forced to disperse demonstrators by firing warning shots into the air and there was no loss of life during any demonstration. The situation changed, however, at the end of 1975 and in 1976. Violent clashes took place between stone-throwing demonstrators, who set tires on fire and threatened the lives of individual soldiers, and soldiers who were forced to fire into the air. During these clashes there were casualties on both sides. The situation worsened when three Arab youths were killed by warning shots of the soldiers. Tension increased, as did the number of demonstrations. Nevertheless processions of pupils, or women, going to lay wreaths on the graves of war dead, were sanctioned on condition that they stayed on the pavements and did not disturb traffic. During the school pupils' riots, police patrols guarded school entrances to prevent pupils from going out into the streets to demonstrate; but they did not interfere with what was going on in the school courtyard. Only in a few cases was it decided to close schools whose pupils had rioted, and even then they were only closed for a day or two.

Agitators who overstepped the bounds would be put under administrative detention, usually for a month, though some stayed in prison for longer periods. The most drastic personal punishments were banishment or deportation. At the end of July 1967, four Jerusalem leaders were banished to Israeli provincial towns. After September 1967, the authorities began deportations to Jordan. The three heads of the National Guidance Committee were deported in this manner. Administrative detainees who expressed the desire to leave the country were allowed to do so in a number of cases, as were some convicts. Deportations were only carried out with government approval, which was given very infrequently. Some further deportations took place in 1973 and 1974.

The local authorities, both civilian and military, bore a heavy burden of responsibility. Their omissions and commissions not only affected human lives, but had a decisive influence on the form and future of intercommunal relations. They possessed power that was as great as their responsibility, but did not abuse it. The authorities were guided by one practical consideration: how to attain their aims while limiting themselves to a minimum of force and suffering. Despite the prolonged confrontation and the difficult experiences they underwent, the security people did not lose sight of the moral yardstick, which is so often ignored by those who hold absolute power and are faced with extreme situations. They took no notice of those who counselled tougher treatment. They adopted liberal positions and held to them, even when the public raised loud objections. Thus, for example, these bodies gave their full backing to the decisions about the erection of Arab war monuments (which we will deal with later) and the change in the school curriculum.

Although they cannot claim credit for succeeding in putting an end to terrorism and civil disobedience, they can credit themselves with the absence of an atmosphere of oppression. Nobody could change the political antagonisms that caused the confrontation; but it was the task of the authorities to prevent political feelings and views from finding unlawful expression. During the years of civil disobedience, the Arabs succeeded in giving their political views sharp and unambiguous expression. The struggle between them and the Israeli authorities had been overt and, at times, violent; but the opposing positions of the two sides did not change. There was one encouraging outcome to this struggle: after almost ten years of occupation, relationships between the two sides were no worse than at the beginning. The vicious circle of disobedience and terror, followed by countermeasures and punishment, did not aggravate the basic conflict, although it was, of course, still there.

CHAPTER SIXTEEN

FAITS ACCOMPLIS

Even before the sounds of battle had died down, calls were heard for Jewish colonization of the occupied areas. The first to make such a demand in public was former Prime Minister David Ben-Gurion, in an address to the Secretariat of his Rafi Party on June 8, when he said:

> Members of this generation who were inhabitants of the Old City, of Hebron, and the Etzion region should be among those returning to those areas to mark the continuity of Jewish [settlement] in those areas, before the beginning of political pressures to make Israel leave these.

On the same day, representatives of the Jerusalem Municipality appeared before the Prime Minister to inform him that the previous inhabitants of the Jewish Quarter had expressed the wish to return to their homes. At its meeting on June 11, a week before the annexation decision, the Government decided to accept "responsibility for the renovation of the Capital." The Prime Minister asked the Acting Finance Minister for "an immediate allocation of IL 10 million for the renovation and construction of the Capital."

Calls for the colonization of East Jerusalem were heard on all sides. On June 19, Mayor Teddy Kollek announced that the Hadassah Medical Organization and the Hebrew University had promised to operate hospitals on Mount Scopus and in the Old City. The Municipality began to register applicants for housing in the Old City, and there were soon hundreds of Jewish applications, with the executive of the National Religious Party calling on its members to take up residence there. The Hebrew University began practical discussions of

233

plans for the renovation of the Mount Scopus campus. On June 24, the President of the University announced that

it is [our] aim to transfer several of the humanities' departments to Mount Scopus . . . priority will be given to Judaica and Oriental studies, for historical and emotional, as well as practical, reasons.

Along with these declarations, various public bodies tried to assume responsibility for their implementation. Following the Government's decision to take responsibility for restoring the city, it established a committee to "prepare restoration plans." The committee was headed by the Military Governor (who left it at the time of the unification) and its members included representatives of the Ministries of Religious Affairs, Interior, Labor, and Housing. The establishment of this committee did not prevent the Jerusalem Municipality from setting up its own planning commission, however. The Mayor announced that the Municipality's engineers were working on the master plan for the Old City as a continuation of the one drawn up 40 years before by the British. And a seven-man committee appointed by the Labor Alignment Party branch in Jerusalem had a "detailed development plan" ready by July 10, 1967.

All this time, individual Jews were attempting to take up quarters in abandoned houses on the old demarcation line and beyond. Owners of property in the Jewish Quarter — primarily religious and educational bodies — were trying to establish possession of their property, parts of which were occupied by Arabs. Faced with this confusion, Prime Minister Eshkol decided to take over responsibility and establish order. On August 13, the Cabinet decided to empower the Prime Minister to speed up the construction and population of "Greater Jerusalem." A few days later, Yehudah Tamir was appointed to take charge of "populating the Old City of Jerusalem." But Jewish settlement in the Old City created severe problems that could not be solved by ringing declarations.

The first question to arise was that of land. The Israel Lands Authority conducted a thorough survey which revealed that, while "Greater Jerusalem" contained several thousand acres under state ownership, only a few hundred acres were in areas that could be considered for Jewish settlement — and even these were dispersed and partly occupied. These properties, which had been registered as belonging to the Kingdom of Jordan, were transferred to the State of Israel after the Government's Legal Adviser declared, on January 24,

1968, that there was nothing to prevent them being registered in the State's name in the Land Registry. Attempts were made to acquire land from Arab owners. At first, several Arabs expressed their readiness to sell their land, and Lands Authority officials managed to get together about 75 acres. However, by the time they got the necessary allocation from the Treasury, the prospective sellers had changed their minds.

Accordingly, those in charge of settling Jews in East Jerusalem found that Jewish settlement could not be envisaged without large-scale expropriation of land. There was no doubt as to the location of the new Jewish housing. The first in degree of importance was the Jewish Quarter, followed by an unbuilt area in the northeast, stretching from the Sanhedria quarter to Mount Scopus. While the planning teams were beginning to outline the area to be expropriated in the north, urgent action on the Jewish Quarter was required to stop Jews from taking possession of buildings there and to stop the Arab inhabitants from making property deals.

Accordingly, the Minister of Finance issued an order by which he set aside the area of the Jewish Quarter for one year, for the purpose of planning and surveying. This was not expropriation but an interim step that did no harm to the Arab inhabitants, only to those Jewish bodies that were trying to create *faits accomplis* in the Quarter. Representatives of the latter protested loudly, but in vain. On October 27, 1967, the official in charge of settlement in the Jewish Quarter reported that, to date, 19 residential rooms had been restored, and a *yeshiva* (religious college) established. Within three months, another 40 to 60 rooms would be renovated. The rate of renovation would depend on investigation of the situation by engineers. There were three technical teams at work. Within a month of practical operations beginning in the Jewish Quarter, it was clear that the job was going to be difficult and slow. Before anything else, it was necessary to design an overall plan to preserve the Quarter's original character, to conduct a survey of the buildings and to make plans for their renovation. Above all, it was necessary to evict the Arabs who lived there in great density.

With regard to northern Jerusalem, a 60-man team was organized and given the task of outlining the land to be expropriated. They were to prepare a detailed master plan and estimate the basic investment. At first, 1,250 acres were marked out between the former

Armistice Line and the road leading to the Mount of Olives. The area was later reduced by some 500 acres. While planning was going on, the men in charge wished to create *faits accomplis* by installing Jewish settlers immediately. Jewish families that found apartments for rent in Arab neighborhoods received grants and loans. Hotels were also rented for students. By December 1967, the number of Jews living in East Jerusalem had reached some 200. Some people felt, however, that the rate of settlement was too slow. As long as criticism was limited to newspaper articles, the Government kept to its prudent and cautious path. But then, "the old lion" roared again. Ben-Gurion criticized the Government severely for its omissions in populating East Jerusalem, and demanded the creation of *faits accomplis* in the form of thousands of wooden huts in the annexed area.

Levi Eshkol could not remain indifferent to the attacks of his great rival who, ever since 1965, had not missed an opportunity to criticize the Prime Minister and his colleagues. In response to the attack, Eshkol convened the Ministerial Committee for Jerusalem for a special meeting in the Jewish Quarter. Until then, all the planning had been done in complete secrecy. Now, the whole plan for populating Jerusalem was made public and in great detail. According to the announcement, the immediate plan included the construction of 7,000 housing units in the north of Jerusalem, the doubling of the number of Hebrew University campus buildings on Mount Scopus, and the building of government offices, as well as of commercial centers in that part of the city. At a meeting held on December 27, 1967, it was resolved to expropriate the necessary area in northern Jerusalem; the Housing Ministry, which had not yet managed to design the types of buildings to be built, was ordered to do so quickly, so as to ensure the completion of at least 1,000 units during 1968. The building designs that the Ministry had available were of the standard, four-storey concrete-frame type, like the buildings constructed elsewhere in Israel. To prevent ruining the view, it was decided that all units of the first housing project would be built at the back of a slope facing the Old City, so that they would not disfigure the skyline when observed from the Old City. The planners were also ordered to add "Jerusalem elements" to the designs, which they did by adding stone facing and ceramic-faced arches to conceal concrete columns.

On January 11, 1969, the Finance Minister issued an order in accordance with the Lands Ordinance (acquisition for Public Purposes) 1943, expropriating an area of some 840 acres. The area included the former no-man's-land, a strip of land on both sides of the Ramallah Road as far as the houses of Sheikh Jarah, and the whole area belonging to the Hebrew University and Hadassah on Mount Scopus. In addition, the slopes of Mount Scopus and the northern slopes of the Mount of Olives were included. The area included 326 lots, belonging to 1,500 owners. Most of the area belonged to Arabs, though there were also considerable portions in Jewish possession. Some of the buildings inhabited by Arabs were spared from expropriation, though some others were not.

The expropriation struck the Arab population like a thunderbolt. On January 14, 1968, 46 Arab leaders sent a letter to the Prime Minister, stating:

We are shocked and saddened, because we were under the impression that the Israeli authorities would not take such a drastic step, which is a blow at world public opinion. . . . We wish to inform the Israeli authorities of our profound concern over the plan. . . . This step confirms our worst fears that Israel is implementing a policy of expansion and aggression, and that the talk of peace is nothing more than a mask to cover their true intention [which is] expansion . . . [this step] will destroy any of the possibilities of peace now being examined by various bodies . . . it is in violation of United Nations' resolutions, infringing on the rights of another sovereign state. . . . The severity of the situation is not diminished by declarations that these houses [to be built on the confiscated area] will be put at the disposal of the whole population, irrespective of religion or race. That is nothing but a mask to hide the true intentions of the authorities.

They expressed the hope that the authorities would repudiate a plan that would "erase and disfigure the true face of Arab Jerusalem."

On the same day, the U.S. State Department issued a statement that it had "forwarded a request to Israel to receive information about the expropriation." The Israeli Embassy informed the Americans that the expropriation was, in fact, the implementation of a town plan put forward in Mandatory times by a British town planner; that it was aimed at urban development for the whole population; and that the Arab property-owners would be paid full compensation.

The U.S. Government refrained from public criticism, but, in private, the American diplomats said that it wasn't Israel's act that they were angry about, but the publicity accompanying an act that was, in fact, totally routine and ordinary.

The authorities did not respond to the Arab leaders' memorandum, whereupon Rauhi al-Khatib, then Chairman of the National Guidance Committee, proposed taking drastic steps, such as lying down in front of the bulldozers clearing roads through the expropriated area. His colleagues refused to take any steps beyond sending memoranda. The Jordan Government considered appealing to the Security Council, but decided against this.

At first, the Israel Government did not pay any attention to the American warning to avoid publicizing its actions in East Jerusalem. The subject was of great internal political importance, and those involved could not overcome the temptation to make political capital out of it. The Housing Minister not only gave full details of the immediate plans, but also sketched an extensive housing program to be carried out in the future. Slowly, and with some difficulty, the Foreign Ministry succeeded in its efforts to get the matter off the front pages; but censorship took on grotesque dimensions when the Foreign Ministry, with the approval of the Prime Minister, prevented the publication of a notice about the registration of applicants for a new housing project. Also suppressed was an announcement of the terms under which part of the land in the expropriated area that had been set aside for private building could be leased. On March 10, the following advertisement was published: "It is brought to the attention of the public that the construction of residential housing has begun *in all parts of Jerusalem.* . . ." Within a week, 3,000 people had applied for the 250 plots set aside for private building, and another 1,000 for apartments in the four-storey blocks.

At the beginning of March 1968, the officials in charge of populating East Jerusalem completed their plans for the expropriation of two more areas: the Jewish Quarter and the former Jewish villages of Neve Ya'akov to the north of the city. The Government put off its decision several times until, at the beginning of April, it decided to put the expropriation into immediate effect. There was discussion over the form of publication, and the Government decided to follow the same procedure as in the previous expropriation, namely, to list the areas to be expropriated and to stress that there would be no infringement on church property or on mosque buildings. Figures would be issued to show that a considerable part of the property had belonged to Jews; compensation would be paid to the Arab property-owners.

The area expropriated in the Jewish Quarter encompassed 29 acres, and included the Western Wall area (with the exception of the Wall itself), the Jewish Quarter as it was constituted after the 1929 Arab riots, and smaller sections that, historically, belonged to the Armenian Quarter but were in fact inhabited by Arabs. The Jewish Quarter contained 1,740 rooms and 116 shops, as well as stores and workshops; there were 5,500 persons living there. Fifty-seven buildings that had served as synagogues or had housed Jewish bodies had already been cleared. Most of the property was owned by Arabs who belonged to the city's leading families. For hundreds of years, these families had been renting their property out to Jews for extremely low rents. Thus, although ownership was Arab, legal possession, until 1948, had been Jewish. When the Quarter was captured by the Arabs in 1948, the Jordanian custodian took possession of those buildings which had become vacant and rented them out. The Jewish-owned property before 1948 comprised about 20% of the Quarter. The land confiscated in Neve Ya'akov belonged, for the most part, to the village's Jewish inhabitants who left it in May 1948.

The expropriation of the Jewish Quarter provoked a wave of protests from a part of the Jewish community. Those who owned property in the Jewish Quarter feared that the Government would put their property to secular use. The Deputy Mayor, Rabbi Menachem Porush, declared:

> As a Jew born in Jerusalem and as a member of the Municipal Executive, I protest at this slight to the religious community and express its opposition to the Government's decision. . . . It is a burning insult to the Jewish people that yeshivot are confiscated, while churches are not!

This was the beginning of a conflict over the character of the restored Jewish Quarter. Jerusalem's Arabs did not voice any reaction to the expropriation: their comment was to be sent only in June 1968. But Jordan raised the issue in the framework of its complaint over the annexation steps being taken by Israel, which was debated in the Security Council in May 1968.

After the expropriation of these three sections in East Jerusalem, those in charge of Jewish settlement thought they had solved the problem of land. Now, at long last, they could get down to work. Most of the task was given to the Housing Ministry, which began vigorous activity in the northern areas. In the Jewish Quarter, operations began with the eviction of the inhabitants, cleaning and renovation.

At the end of May 1968, the *New York Times'* Jerusalem correspondent published an article in which he pointed out that Israel had yet to start preparing the expropriated land for building purposes. He quoted "diplomatic observers" who said that Israel had not begun work because of "difficulties in locating the Arab owners" and also because Israel had been persuaded by the Western powers not to start building, as this would cause a deterioration in the political situation. This article embarrassed the Government, which was extremely sensitive to any criticism in the foreign press. It was also quoted in the Israeli press, with the addition of sharply critical comments. On May 30, the Prime Minister was asked, in an interview, why so little had been done to consolidate Jewish settlement in East Jerusalem. His reply was:

> To the best of my knowledge . . . everything that can be done has been done at maximum speed; but it transpired that we didn't have land there . . . it was also necessary to work out plans. . . . Nevertheless, things are moving . . . you can't say that we have done less than was possible in settling [Jews] in Jerusalem.

However, the Ministerial Committee for Jerusalem was convened and it adopted a proposal by the Prime Minister to erect 11 prefabricated structures at the edge of the expropriated area. Informed sources said that the structures were being erected in order to catch up with delays in ordinary building and to speed up the process of making the whole of Jerusalem Jewish. The Interior Minister, who was responsible for planning, objected to the construction of the ugly buildings at a sensitive spot that could be seen from all parts of the city, but his objections were overruled. From then on, the conflict between rapid building for political purposes and the maintenance of the beauty of the landscape and the city, would accompany all of the efforts to settle Jews in East Jerusalem.

The decision to erect the prefabricated houses did not impress David Ben-Gurion, who repeated his attacks. Tension grew, and to refute criticisms the Prime Minister conducted a tour of the various

240

building sites, during which he personally attacked the Housing Ministry officials for their tardiness and brushed off their explanations with the comment "old wives' tales." The embattled Housing Minister, whose Ministry had made desperate efforts to overcome delays caused by the need to clear mine fields and pave roads over rocky hillsides, defended himself with the remark: "Houses aren't muffins."

Public opinion was not prepared to accept any explanations, demanding that East Jerusalem be populated immediately. The Minister of Religious Affairs, for example, demanded that hundreds of Jews take up residence in the ruins of the Jewish Quarter, irrespective of the state of the houses and the lack of the most elementary amenities. The Housing Ministry's planners were to some extent affected by this nervousness, but Yehudah Tamir did not budge from his view that the Jewish Quarter should only be rebuilt and populated after precise planning and careful renovation.

The first families did not move into the new quarter in the northeast of the city (named, after the Prime Minister's death, "Ramat Eshkol") until September 1969, a year-and-a-half after work had begun. Construction also began on French Hill, the northwesterly continuation of the Mount Scopus ridge. To the east, the University erected matchbox-like stone structures to house students. The new buildings on the University campus, which were to cater to 10,000 students, also began to protrude above the elevated skyline of Mount Scopus. On the slope of the hill, near the Arab neighborhood, 28 apartments were constructed for Arabs. Spokesmen for the Housing Ministry and the Municipality promised that these apartments were only the first stage of a plan to build dozens of additional apartments for Arabs; but, in fact, no additional apartments for Arabs were constructed on expropriated lands.

The expropriated area began to fill up with houses and residents. Officials of the Israel Lands Authority began to mark out new construction areas. They turned to the area of the High Commissioner's Residence which was, in their opinion, inside Israeli territory and did not, therefore, need to be expropriated. When it transpired that they had erred, they began to press the Government to expropriate additional land; but the Government was in no hurry to agree.

In the meantime, the renovation of the Jewish Quarter was progressing slowly. The master plan for renovation allocated two-thirds of the area to buildings, leaving the remaining third for open spaces, roads, and plazas. Half of the built-up area was to house 600 families, while the second half was set aside for public institutions. Sites were also allocated for 400 shops and galleries. The major task in the first stage was the removal of vast quantities of rubble and the clearing of extensive ruins. Only when the ruins of the houses destroyed in 1948 had been removed could they begin renovating the remaining buildings and start construction of new ones.

The rate of reconstruction depended mainly on the rate at which the Arab population was moved out. At first, the Arab inhabitants of the Quarter agreed to leave of their own volition, after receiving compensation. The houses were quickly vacated and compensation was relatively low. However, after the removal of those residents who were living in ruins and substandard apartments, an increasing number resisted moving. Some of them agreed to vacate their houses after being offered increased compensation; others were evicted by means of legal coercion. Compensation was only paid for the inhabitants' right of possession, and not a single house-owner applied for compensation. The houses were photographed, measured, and evaluated by a government assessor. The material was then collected and filed away until such time as the proprietors might agree to accept compensation. In other expropriated areas, too, the proprietors did not agree to accept compensation. They would not recognize the legality of expropriation and refused, as they put it, "to sell their homeland."

With 2,500 apartments completed or under construction in East Jerusalem, feverish discussions began about the location of new housing projects. The Municipality demanded that a considerable proportion of this new construction be channeled to West Jerusalem, in order to fill up the empty spaces between the widely dispersed neighborhoods in that part of the city. This demand was based on a master plan that had recommended the city be built compactly. However, political considerations tilted the balance and the overwhelming majority of the new housing were to be built on the other side of the Armistice Line. An interdepartmental committee considered the matter for several weeks and in May 1970 submitted a plan for the expropriation of 4,200 acres in seven sections. The Ministerial Committee sent the plan back to a commission of experts, requesting that it make amendments. The Foreign Ministry pressed

242

for the expropriation to be delayed in view of the political climate. The cease-fire between Israel and Egypt, the prospect of indirect peace talks under the auspices of the United Nations envoy, Gunnar Jarring, and the possibility that the United States might impose a settlement based on the so-called Rogers Plan, increased concern about the fate of the unified city. Hopeful Arabs would take their leave of Israelis with the remark: "See you at the Mandelbaum Gate! "

In December 1969, a short time after resettlement of the Jewish Quarter began, a new diplomatic plan was aired, which was to have a greater influence on the physical planning of Jerusalem than any architectural plan. In a statement of United States policy in the Middle East, the U.S. Secretary of State, William Rogers, declared that his Government's policy was for Jerusalem to remain united, while its administration would have to consider the interests of all of its inhabitants and of all of the religious communities. He also said that the United States supported the reconstitution of "some kind of Jordanian presence" in the united city. "Any alterations taking place," said Rogers, "must not reflect the fruits of conquest and must be limited to minor changes essential for mutual security."

The Rogers Plan dealt with the Arab—Israel conflict generally and was vigorously rejected in Israel. The reaction was especially sharp with regard to Jerusalem. On December 29, 1969, Prime Minister Golda Meir said that Jordan had never had any rights in Jerusalem and had ruled there by force of her conquest in 1948. Jordan was the only state in history which forbade Jews access to the Holy Places. In 1967, it attacked the city for the second time. Unified Jerusalem, said Mrs. Meir, would remain the Capital of Israel.

Israel's real opposition, however, found its expression in deeds. Faithful to the old Zionist policy that Israel's borders were marked by Jewish settlements and that facts possess overwhelming political significance, the Israelis initiated a series of drastic actions in Jerusalem, some of which were over-hasty. All budgetary restrictions were removed from construction work in the Jewish Quarter, and an emergency program was initiated to carry out two years' work in one. The custom of carrying out archeological excavations before beginning the construction of new houses was discontinued. The Housing Minister, seeking an opportunity for the immediate construction of additional housing units, decided to add two or three

243

stories to the buildings on French Hill, which caused a severe disfiguration of the city's appearance. The Hebrew University took advantage of the opportunity to lay a wide road down the western slope of Mount Scopus, which had previously been rejected by the planning authorities on the grounds that it would spoil the view. The new road, in fact, has caused irreparable damage to this area, which faces the Old City. The main decision, however, was to start building 25,000 apartments, at the rate of 6–8,000 a year.

The technical committees were urged to complete their work immediately and they submitted a final recommendation for the expropriation of some 4,000 acres, mostly Arab-owned. The expropriated area included sections in the center, north, northwest, southeast and southwest of the city. An additional section in the northeast, which would have closed the ring of Jewish settlements around the city, was excluded at the last minute.

Altogether, some 4,200 acres, about 30% of the annexed area, were to be expropriated. The new areas were about half the size of Israeli Jerusalem before 1967, and almost three times the area of Arab Jerusalem at that time. According to the initial plans, it would be possible to accommodate up to 150,000 persons in these areas.

The order was signed on August 20, 1970. Efforts were made to play down the news; but when that was impossible, an official statement was issued explaining that "this confiscation is for development purposes within the framework of the Jerusalem master plan. It is aimed at finding a solution for 5,000 Arab and 4,000 Jewish families living in sub-standard housing." As most of the confiscated land consisted of uninhabited rocky hillsides, only a few dozen houses had to be vacated. The inclusion of the Jewish-inhabited Mamillah area enabled the Government spokesmen to point out that it would be necessary to evict 350 Jewish families, as against 20 Arab families.

The Foreign Ministry awaited sharp reactions from abroad, but none came, for the Powers were afraid of disrupting the Jarring talks. But the Arabs of East Jerusalem reacted sharply. The day following the expropriation, *al-Kuds* published two articles about them. The editorial stated:

Respect for private property is a humane law, which should be implemented everywhere ... even if the land is in occupied territory. ... What kind of peace will there be if land is expropriated in the Holy City? The Rogers initiative has brought about a

244

*cease-fire on all fronts ... so that there is a good atmosphere
which will lead to peace. What is the point of the cease-fire ... if
there is no halt in the work going on in Arab Jerusalem, day and
night? It is possible to understand the expropriation of a small
plot for some public purpose ... but the expropriation of thousands of acres, for the purpose of building houses for people who
do not own the land, is incomprehensible.*

The other article stated:

*It is clear that this entire initiative shows no consideration for the
rights of the Arab inhabitants and will leave them in inferior conditions. The Arab community will work in Jewish concerns, it will
build houses for new immigrants, and will not find [enough] space
on its own land to build houses for the next generation.*

The Muslim Council sent a protest memorandum (the 60th or 70th)
about the expropriations, and described them as "an aggressive plan
whose purpose is to change the character of the Holy City and to
erase the Arab presence there." Mayors of West Bank towns, as well
as other public figures, joined in the protests. However, the storm
died down quickly, for the Palestinians became the objects of a far
greater misfortune, which made them forget the expropriations:
"Black September" (1970), during which hundreds of Palestinian
civilians died in the battles between the Jordan Army and the Palestinian guerillas.

Meanwhile, the Housing Ministry did not waste any time. On September 15, 1970, the Housing Minister announced that his Ministry
was about to begin building, simultaneously, on four sites. Appro-
priately, for a quasi-military operation aimed at gaining strategic control of territory, a heavy curtain of secrecy enveloped the building
plans. Teams of architects were given instructions to plan fast and
not show the plans to anybody.

Those concerned about preserving Jerusalem's beauty were
shocked. At a public meeting called to discuss the new plans, one
protester said: "If a Jewish presence means an ugly blot, that isn't a
Jewish presence. It is even bad politics to forgo the aesthetic aspects
of Jerusalem, for whose preservation the British made such great
efforts." Alongside opposition to unsuitable house designs, urban
considerations of various kinds were also brought up. Public controversy and a wave of protests held up approval of the plans.

Foreign correspondents in Israel sent extensive reports about the

245

plans, connecting urban aesthetic issues with political ones, an unfortunate combination. The Israeli opponents of the plans based their contentions on solely aesthetic and urban reasons. They were unanimous in their desire to keep the city united under Israeli rule, but objected to "enslaving aesthetic sensibility . . . to a superior national dictate." As long as the debate was limited to the aesthetic sides, there remained a chance of making some qualitative changes in the plans. However, the moment that the subject became a test of patriotism, the battle was lost. At the decisive moment — on the eve of the meeting called to approve the plans — a spokesman for the U.S. State Department intervened by expressing his concern over the building plans. This external intervention put an end to any hopes for change. Approving the plans became a patriotic duty. The City Council, which had criticized them fiercely a few weeks earlier, now approved the plans without opposition. The Mayor and one of the Councillors did not raise their hands; but another Councillor called on the Mayor to vote, and the latter did so, albeit with some hesitation. The Councillors now called on the remaining abstainer to "join for history's sake;" but his hand remained lowered.

"Operation Facts" began at a feverish pace. Within a few months, the shells of the new buildings were sprouting on the construction sites. The "Tower and Stockade" settlements of the 1930s, were reconstructed as modern apartment blocks. Israel's leaders showed that they believed that policies of "another goat, another dunam," "a highway used by a Jewish driver is Jewish," and "a settlement where Jewish children play is a guarantee of our land" were still valid, a full generation after the establishment of the sovereign Jewish State. Israel's transformation into a strong Mediterranean power had not caused the slightest change in the old concepts. One writer severely criticised the Government's policy, stating:

> It will not be a housing project of one kind or another, nor a highway, here or there, built with the money of the Israeli taxpayer, that will influence the form of a future political settlement. It will be shaped by the balance of power in the region, by the international situation, and by Israel's diplomatic ability to tack successfully among the rocks. . . . If Israel is too weak, diplomatically or militarily, to hold a unified Jerusalem, neither housing projects nor roads will help us hold on to the areas beyond the old border.

246

The *faits accomplis* created in East Jerusalem have not yet had to stand a political test. The pressures which had been foreseen, and which were to have been withstood with the help of the "strong-points," did not materialize. In the summer of 1972, a Jordanian spokesman was asked if the Israeli housing projects in East Jerusalem had not eliminated any hope of peace between Israel and Jordan. "No," the Jordanian replied, "it's a problem which can be solved in the framework of the compensation payments that we shall have to make to each other."

Ironically enough, the Arabs did not see any close connection between the new housing projects and Jerusalem. The Israelis considered them a part of Jerusalem, since they were part of the annexed area and they had been calling them "unified Jerusalem" ever since 1967. In the Arab mind, Jerusalem remained within its narrow confines, including only the historic city. Neve Ya'akov, three miles away, or the slopes of Nebi Samwil, four miles from the Old City, were no more a part of the city than were Beit-Iksa, or Sharafat, the Arab villages near which the new quarters were set up. As long as they constituted a majority in historic Jerusalem, within the walls and in the immediate vicinity, they did not believe that the thousands of matchbox-like structures sprouting on distant hillsides would speak the last word on the city's future.

The attempts to create settlement facts in East Jerusalem were not limited to the expropriation of lands and the construction of houses on those lands. As early as 1967 certain official Israeli groups attempted to acquire land from private Arab owners. For this purpose a company was set up in Vaduz, which offered large sums of money for immovable property in the eastern sector of the city. But it achieved little. The Arab land-owners understood the political implications of the sale of land to Israelis and most of them resisted the ridiculously high offers, which were far above the regular market price.

In the areas under Israeli law, there is no legal restraint on the transfer of land from Arabs to Jews. But in the West Bank, a military government order forbids the registration of such transfers without the Military Governor's approval of all the details of the agreement. In the first years after the war, private Israeli citizens did not try to acquire land in the West Bank, although official bodies did become involved in such endeavors, especially in the Jordan Valley where a large Jewish settlement was planned.

In the early 1970s, when the construction of Jewish neighborhoods on the expropriated lands began, commercial groups started to acquire land in the Jerusalem metropolitan area. They were supported by political groups advocating the annexation of the entire West Bank.

Early in April 1973, Defense Minister Moshe Dayan proposed cancelling the order which prohibited Israelis from acquiring land in the West Bank. The Government did not accept his proposal. But some groups succeeded in acquiring several hundred acres in the border regions of metropolitan Jerusalem, just outside the annexed area.

As has been noted earlier, the Government, in deciding to annex East Jerusalem, settled for an area much smaller than that suggested by the various "hawkish" factions. The pressure to "create facts" in the entire metropolitan area and not to be satisfied with settling only the annexed area has not let up since 1967. At the close of the 1960s, the Defense Minister decided to "close" an area of 17,500 acres on the eastern side of the annexed zone. In this area, which is as large as the area annexed to Jerusalem in 1967, no Arab building or agricultural work was permitted. In terms of ownership, most of the area belonged to the State. From time to time it was proposed that the area be annexed to Israel, as was done with Jerusalem, but the proposals were rejected. The subject was last discussed three months before the outbreak of the 1973 Yom Kippur War.

Following the 1973 War, the Government decided that definitive action must be taken in settling the entire metropolitan area.

At the end of November 1974, the Government decided to build an industrial area in Adumim — halfway between Jerusalem and Jericho. Although municipal circles — who wanted land for the city's industrial growth — initiated the suggestion to build a new industrial area, the final decision was a political one and implementation of the project began only after the Government gave its approval.

The crux of the debate over Adumim dealt with the building of a "work camp" near the industrial area. By majority vote, the Government decided to approve the "camp," though it was clear to all that the camp was, in fact, a nucleus for the establishment of an urban settlement in Adumim. Supporters of this settlement emphasized the strategic importance of the Jerusalem—Jericho axis. They saw the settlement as a way of negating the possibility of creating an Arab

248

corridor to Jerusalem, an option which had been discussed in the context of a solution to Jerusalem's political problems. The work camp in Adumim was completed in a little over a year, but was not settled until 1976.

At the same time, other settlement arrangements were being made at the initiative of circles which enjoyed the direct and indirect support of various Cabinet Ministers. Northeast of Ramallah, within the metropolitan area, two settlements were established. Similarly, a residential area was planned adjacent to a youth hostel on Mt. Gilo, in the municipal area of the Christian town of Beit Jallah. At the end of 1975, a plan for the establishment of over ten settlements in the Jerusalem area was published. Early in 1976, the Government decided to adopt those portions of the plan affecting the areas northwest and southwest of the city.

Housing Minister Abraham Offer, who initiated the program, explained the strategy behind it. Jerusalem, he felt, was the only area in which Israel had the possibility of effectuating a significant change in the pre-1967 borders. Therefore, the corridor, which had linked the city to the rest of the country until 1967, should be widened. Two new roads should be built: one from Lod via Beit Horon and the biblical Gibeon to the northern part of Jerusalem; and the second one from the southern part of the city, via Beit Jallah and Gush Etzion, to Lachish. He suggested building urban settlements along these two roads, with the first settlement at Gibeon. Various Ministers supported the plan but, at the same time, continued to encourage the establishment of settlements to the east and south of the city, as well.

The metropolitan area of Jerusalem, beyond the annexed area, in which the proposed settlements were planned, covers some 95 square miles. It includes the towns of Ramallah, al-Bira, Bethlehem, Beit Sahur, Beit Jallah, Beit Zayit, Beitunya and more than 20 small villages. Its inhabitants (excluding unified Jerusalem) number about 110,000. As has already been noted, from an urban point of view the municipal boundaries of the city were demarcated in a totally arbitrary fashion. Demography was one of the determining factors — the inclusion of the most land with the fewest number of Arabs. As a result, the Israeli authorities only consider the residents of the annexed area under their jurisdiction, even though from an urban, or even demographic, viewpoint, no logical differentiation can be made between the Arabs living in the metropolitan area and those in the annexed area.

In the entire metropolitan area there are some 220,000 Arabs and about 250,000 Jews (all of whom presently live within the municipal boundaries). The ratio of Jews to Arabs, which is about 75% Jews to 25% Arabs within the city boundaries, including the annexed area, becomes 53% Jews to 47% Arabs in the total metropolitan area, and can easily be reversed, with an Arab majority in the area, because of the Arabs' greater birth rate. The supporters of the settlement plans strove to expand the borders of Israel by "creating facts," but they could not disregard the heavy demographic cost — the loss of the Jewish majority in the region, which is a natural consequence of annexing the entire metropolitan area.

Actually, the test of these population and settlement plans lies not in their design but rather in their implementation. In fact, the desire to create facts quickly has encountered serious implementation problems. The three new communities, whose land expropriation was carried out in 1970, were built slowly. In Ramot (at the foot of Nebi Samwil) and in Gilo (between Jerusalem and Beit Jallah), 18,000 residential units were planned. By the end of 1975 only 1,500 units were occupied; another 2,000 units were still in the process of being built. In East Talpiot (south of Government Hill), 4,500 units were planned; only 600 were actually occupied. By the end of 1975, only 200 families — or one-third of the planned number — were living in the Jewish Quarter of the Old City, the renovation of which began in 1968.

This delay resulted from various implementation difficulties and from a lack of resources. Thus, many people were amazed at the impracticality of announcing plans for the construction of new settlements in and around Jerusalem when the old areas were being built and settled so slowly.

Despite the importance of populating East Jerusalem and its metropolitan area with Jews, it was essential to regard the city as a single integral unit, and to examine all the demographic and ethnic data. Without a significant increase of the *total* Jewish population, the settlement of the new areas would be nothing more than migration from one part of the city to another. The problem, therefore, was not only populating East Jerusalem, but achieving a rapid increase of the Jewish population of the whole city. As soon as the city was reunited, the policy-makers decided that everything must be done to increase the Jewish majority in the united city, or, at least, to maintain the present demographic proportions.

The demographic data available in 1967 were not encouraging. At that time, there were 197,000 Jews in the city, and 68,600 Arabs. The Jews were, therefore, 74% of the population, the Arabs 26%. This proportion was created arbitrarily: when the city's boundaries were marked out, Arab-populated neighborhoods were excluded in order to ensure an overwhelming Jewish majority.

The Jewish rate of natural increase was slightly less than 2%, while the number of immigrants coming to the city only slightly exceeded the number of inhabitants of Jerusalem leaving for the coastal cities. Before the 1967 War, the average rate of population increase was, therefore, just over 2% annually. The rate of natural increase among the Arabs, on the other hand, reached 3% in East Jerusalem. A forecast made in 1967 assumed that the Jewish birthrate would decrease and reach the average among Israeli Jews, which was 1.6% annually. At the same time, the forecast assumed a rise in the Arab birthrate, a trend that was apparent in the Arab population in Israel. On the basis of all these calculations, the forecast warned that Jerusalem's Arabs would increase from one-quarter to one-third of the population within twenty years. To maintain the existing ratio, it would be necessary to increase Jewish immigration to the city (from abroad and from inside Israel). Jewish Jerusalem would need 5,000 newcomers every year. To maintain the existing population ratio, it would be necessary to bring in three Jews for every additional Arab.

This rate of growth seemed unbalanced to the urban experts, who thought that it would involve the city in insoluble problems of transport and services. The authors of the Jerusalem master plan made their own forecast. They accepted the political guidelines requiring maintenance of the numerical ratio between Jews and Arabs, but they stated that an annual rate of growth of up to 2.8% was optimal for balanced urban development. They claimed that the growth of the Jewish and Arab populations would be equal, at the desired rate, namely, 2.6–2.8% annually. They were not unaware of the fact that the Arab rate of natural increase was twice as high as that of the Jews; but they assumed positive Jewish internal migration, and Arab negative migration. In another document, the authors of the master plan claimed that the rate of Arab emigration during the period of

251

the forecast should be fixed at 50% of the growth from natural increase. This was based on data from the Jordanian period, which showed that emigration from the city was two-thirds of the natural increase.

Politicians do not draw up forecasts; they set targets. Any realistic target would seem pessimistic, and anyone setting such a target would be accused of a lack of vision and belief. The national myth requires more and more Jews. A typical example of demographic objectives set in this way is the plan for populating Jerusalem by Shimon Peres, which was published in January 1970. Peres, who was Acting Minister of Immigrant Absorption at the time, proposed to double the city's Jewish population within five years. He wished to channel 80% of all new immigrants to Jerusalem, achieving an annual growth of 50,000 persons. The plan's sponsors said they would simply carry out the master plan in five years instead of 20.

It was easy for experts to prove that the plan could not be implemented, and it was finally shelved when the Finance Ministry announced that it would allocate money only for the balanced development of the city. The Minister of Immigrant Absorption was not the only one in the Cabinet to set far-reaching targets for the city's growth. In 1971, the Housing Minister declared that, in his opinion, the minimal growth rate for Jerusalem should be 6% annually.

In August 1973, the Government determined an "integrated and coordinated growth rate" for the Jewish population of Jerusalem, to be used as both an optimal and a realistic guideline. The rate was set at 3.7% per year, taking into account political factors (the growth rate of the Arab population and the preservation of the demographic balance), budgetary factors, and the ability to carry out housing plans and infrastructure development.

In actual fact, the Jewish population of Jerusalem has grown according to the planned rate, but the rate has not been uniform each year. In 1969, the growth rate was 2.8%. In 1972, it reached a peak of 5.9%, and, in 1975, 3.1%. But from 1967–75, the Jewish population increased by 31%, or an average of 3.5% per year.

During that same period the Arab population grew by almost 4.5% per year, reaching a peak of 7.2% in 1972. The 1974 rate was 5.9%.

Thus, the number of Jewish residents in Jerusalem came to over 260,000 at the beginning of 1976 and the Arab population numbered just under 100,000. The demographic scale had tipped slightly in favor of the Arabs, but the change was very small.

The forecasts about Arab negative migration have proved false. Not only did all the natural increase remain in the city, but there was even large-scale migration into the city, with thousands of West Bank inhabitants, bearing military government identity cards, taking up residence in Jerusalem. The complete freedom of movement enjoyed by all the population of the areas under Israeli control permitted 8,000 persons to take up residence in Jerusalem. Had this internal migration found its expression in statistics, the official numerical ratio of Jews and Arabs would have been shown to be in the latters' favor.

The plan to direct 5,000 immigrants to Jerusalem annually, which had appeared to be so difficult to implement in 1967, was attained; during the years 1967–1975, 35,000 immigrants came to the city. The city proved especially attractive for immigrants from Western countries, as well as for religious people.

If these demographic trends continue, together with the present real rate of growth, the population of Jerusalem in 1985 will reach one-half million persons, of whom slightly more than 360,000 will be Jews, and slightly less than 140,000 will be Arabs.

The growth of the Jewish population was attained as a result of massive government investment. Between 1967 and 1972, construction began on 21,700 apartments, with 15,000 completed by the middle of 1972. Building "starts" in the years 1973–75 reached approximately 4,000 units annually, with construction time at about 20 months. The overwhelming majority were built by the Government, which invested over three billion Israel pounds. The speed-up in the rate of construction after the 1967 War was staggering. In 1971, construction began on 7,000 apartments, eight times as many as before the war. From the end of 1970 onwards, the shortage of housing stopped being an obstacle to the growth of the Jewish population of Jerusalem. The accelerated building, which speeded up from year to year, ceased to reflect the real rate of population growth, which proceeded according to its own logic.

More than enough housing was constructed for the increase in population; but the surplus created was purely theoretical. In practice, there was a severe housing shortage in Jerusalem, and prices rocketed. The surplus flats were snatched up by the existing population, which was steadily improving its living conditions. This might appear to be an important achievement, as there were thousands of families in the city living in substandard housing. However, the vacant flats were not acquired only by needy families, but rather by those with good accommodation, or by people buying additional apartments as investments. Not all those in need could afford the high prices demanded for apartments. In view of the inflation in the country, and the steep rise in the prices of property, an apartment was a promising investment. In a survey conducted at the end of 1972, it transpired that no less than 6,000 of the apartments which had been sold were standing empty or had been rented out for short periods.

The accelerated rate of construction produced effects that ran counter to Israeli policies. All the manpower required for this gigantic construction project came from the West Bank. In 1971, the number of workers from the West Bank employed in Jerusalem reached 8,000. To complete the buildings planned by 1977, 15,000 workers would be needed, all of whom would have to come from the West Bank. For the first time since 1948, Arab emigration from Jerusalem had stopped. Furthermore, thousands who had left Jerusalem during Jordanian times, to seek their fortune in other Arab countries, now wished to return to the city. Therefore, while the construction of Jewish housing facilitated the growth of the percentage of Jewish inhabitants, it also caused a marked increase in the Arab population.

None of the building programs took the Arab population into account. The Arabs needed 300 apartments every year for their natural increase alone. From 1967 to 1972, only 100 apartments were built for the Arab population by the Israeli Government, or with its assistance. Increased demand caused a higher density of occupation, higher rents, and sporadic building, mostly illegal, at the edges of the city. Up to 1969, there was a total standstill in construction by the Arab population, but, in 1970, 50 apartments were added. In 1971, there was a radical change, with no less than 400 apartments being built privately by Arabs. This change indicates a considerable improvement in their standard of living, as does the fact that half of the flats built had five or more rooms. In 1972, too, there was a growing trend for the Arab population to build private apartments, and if full employment persists, such construction will increase even more.

As we have seen, the land expropriations and the construction of

254

new quarters in East Jerusalem provoked Arab complaints of the "Judaization" of Jerusalem. These complaints were taken up and accepted in wide circles all over the world. However, demographic data did not justify such complaints. The massive Israeli efforts only ensured that the growth of the Jewish population of the city did not lag behind that of the Arab community. As in many other areas, the complaints rested not so much on real facts as on the declarations of politicians. The efforts made for the rapid construction and development of the city brought about a relatively swift growth of the Jewish population, but they also brought about a relatively faster growth of the Arab community. Like Siamese twins, the two communities nourished each other, and were obliged to advance at the same pace. The true beneficiary of the efforts directed towards development was not the Jewish community, nor the Arab one, it was the city as a whole.

JERUSALEM

MUNICIPAL BOUNDARIES
BEFORE AND AFTER REUNIFICATION

KAFR AQAB

To Ramallah

JERUSALEM
AIRPORT

JUDEIDA

AR-RAM

AL JIB

BIR NABALA

HIZMA

NABI SAMWIL

BEIT HANINA

BIDDU

SHUFAT

BEIT SURIK

ANATA

BEIT IKSA

MEVASSERET

SANHEDRIA

MT SCOPUS

ISAWIYA

To Tel Aviv

GIVAT SHAUL B'

SHEIKH
JARRAH

HEBREW
UNIVERSITY

MOTZA

OLD
CITY

MT OF OLIVES

BEIT ZAYIT

EL EIZARIYAH

EIN
KEREM

HEBREW
UNIVERSITY

HADASSA
HOSPITAL

KIRYAT
HAYOVEL

SILWAN

Government
House

ABU DIS

KIRYAT
MENAHEM

BEIT
SAFAFA

RAMAT
RAHEL

SHARAFAT

SUR BAHIR

UMM TUBA

To Bethlehem

.... MUNICIPAL BOUNDARY OF EAST JERUSALEM, MAY 1967
--+--+-- PROPOSED TOWN PLANNING LIMITS, EAST JERUSALEM, MAY 1967
--·--·-- ARMISTICE LINE 1949-1967
-------- JERUSALEM (ISRAEL) MUNICIPAL BOUNDARY
━━━━━━ MUNICIPAL BOUNDARY OF UNIFIED JERUSALEM, 28.6.1967

Compiled & Drawn by CARTA , Jerusalem

CHAPTER SEVENTEEN

THE CHRISTIANS AND THEIR HOLY PLACES

The question of the Holy Places in Jerusalem is undoubtedly the problem with the widest ramifications, since, for the first time since the founding of Christianity and Islam, the Jews found themselves responsible for the holy sites of the three great monotheistic religions. The Christian sites present the most complex, if least dangerous, problems.

The first Israeli census conducted in East Jerusalem showed that there were 11,000 Christians in the city, about 17% of the population. They were divided into no less than ten congregations, of which the principal ones were the Greek Orthodox and the Roman Catholics. In addition, there were Armenian Orthodox, Copts, Greek Catholics, Protestants, Anglicans, Syrian Orthodox, Maronites, and members of other Unitary congregations (Armenian Catholics, Syrian Catholics and Assyrians). The Christians were concentrated mostly in the Christian Quarter, the Armenian Quarter, the Muslim Quarter, el-Tur, Wadi Joz, Sheikh Jarah, the American Colony and Beit Hanina. Only 15% had no schooling, as compared to 37% in the Muslim community. A third of all high school graduates and some 40% of university graduates were Christians, although they were only 17% of the total population. Their standard of living was, on average, higher than in the Muslim population. Following the 1967 War, the Christians suffered more unemployment than the Muslims, since they constituted a higher proportion of white-collar workers and found it harder to obtain employment in their professions, even when the Arab sector was at full employment.

The economic conditions and political uncertainty which existed after the war increased Christian emigration, which had been a regular phenomenon since 1948. In 1968, 4,000 Christians left Jerusalem for countries abroad. As the economic situation improved, emigration decreased to 200 a year between 1969 and 1971 — less than in Jordanian times. But the total number of Christians did not decrease; on the contrary, it rose as a result of natural increase.

Relations between the Arab members of the Greek Orthodox community and the Greek ecclesiastical establishment remained uneasy. In addition to the old complaints of waste, corruption, and lack of support for members of the congregation, there was now anger at the Patriarchate's excellent relations with the Israeli authorities. Individual members of the community joined Muslims in acts of disobedience and protest against the authorities. However, with financial and political power concentrated in the hands of the Greek clergy, and because of the clergy's good relations with the authorities, the community as a whole did not take part in the Israeli—Arab political struggle.

The Armenian Orthodox community had never intervened in external problems. As a separate ethnic entity, with its own language, culture and religion, the Armenian congregation had not been assimilated into its Arab surroundings, nor did it participate in its life. Jerusalem's Armenians, whether descendants of families that had settled in the city hundreds of years earlier, or decendants of the First World War refugees who arrived in 1919, maintained a withdrawn life-style, some not even troubling to learn Arabic. Within the community, there were conflicts and disagreements on social and political issues, with the younger generation severely criticizing the ecclesiastical establishment for its way of life and its reluctance to aid the poorer members of the congregation. The Armenian Patriarchate maintained very friendly relations with the Israeli authorities. In 1969, it cooperated with the Israel Museum in exhibiting the Patriarchate treasures, which had previously been strictly guarded and had never before been exhibited. This was the only congregation to institute Hebrew lessons in its schools.

In its relations with the Israeli authorities, the leadership of the Roman Catholic congregation was guided by Vatican policy. The Latin Patriarchate's relationship with the Israeli authorities was cool and reserved. In addition to the political reservations of the European clergy, the numerous Arab priests exhibited an extremely negative attitude towards Israel. Arab priests, and even some European ones, took part in several acts of disobedience and protest organized by the Muslim Council and other Arab bodies.

As might have been foreseen, the most severely anti-Israel activity was centered in the national Arab churches, or in those where the Arabs had been given almost complete independence: the Greek Catholic community and the Anglican congregation. The Greek Catholic congregation, all of whose priests are Arabs, whose liturgical language is Arabic, and whose head resides in Damascus, adopted a sharply anti-Israel position, from unification onwards. The church's Jerusalem head, Archbishop Hilarion Capucci, was active in all the campaigns of protest and disobedience, initiating assemblies and meetings with the heads of the other Christian communities aimed at organizing them to work against Israel.

In mid-August 1974, Capucci was arrested by the Israeli police after they found arms and explosives in his car. The Archbishop admitted that he used his clerical immunity from search at the border to bring in weapons from Lebanon. He was charged with having served as a messenger for the Fatah and having aided the carrying out of several terrorist incidents in Jerusalem, in which a number of persons were killed.

The trial of Capucci ended in December and the Archbishop was sentenced to 12 years' imprisonment.

Various Christian bodies have asked the Israel Government to expel him to one of the Arab countries, but the Government has denied these requests. Capucci was imprisoned, and he went on several hunger strikes.

Bishop Najib Kub'ein, the Anglican Bishop of Jordan, Lebanon and Syria, signed a protest memorandum which Arab leaders in Jerusalem sent to U.N. Ambassador Thalman in September 1967. One of the congregation's priests in Judea and Samaria was caught concealing explosives under his robes. But the non-Arab elements in the congregation, headed first by Archbishop MacKinness and later by Archbishop Appleton, combatted these anti-Israel trends and tried to find ways of cooperating with the authorities. At the end of 1974, for the first time, an Arab archbishop was named head of the Anglican Episcopalian Church, thus completing the process of Arabizing the church, which had begun in the 1950s.

Unlike the Jordanians, the Israelis did not impose any limitations on the activities of Christian educational institutions or charitable associations. With the repeal of the Jordanian law forbidding the acquisition of land, there were increased efforts by Christian bodies to buy land in the city and its vicinity. At the same time, the Armenians and the Greeks sold large tracts of land in West Jerusalem to the Israel Government in agreements totalling millions of dollars. The Israel Government was careful not to expropriate lands belonging to churches or monasteries, but tried to buy land from them in East Jerusalem. The Order of Assumptionist Fathers agreed to sell the enormous Notre Dame de France building to the Hebrew University, and a contract was signed. However, the Vatican regarded the sale as conflicting with its policy of reinforcing the Christian presence in the city and intervened against it on the strength of the authority invested in it by the Order's charter. The Israel Government, not wishing to strain its relations with the Vatican, ordered the University to forfeit the purchase.

The Israelis based their attitude towards the Christian population on the hope that the Christians would be their allies in the struggle against the Arab nationalist elements. They also wished to show the world that Christian congregations could flourish under Israeli rule. There were discussions and plans to halt emigration and improve the economic situation of the Christian population. Especially active in this direction were the Apostolic delegates.

As in other fields of activity, Israeli contacts with the Christian communities suffered from overlapping and lack of coordination between different authorities. At least four Israeli bodies competed for the prestigious contacts with the various Patriarchs. In the course of a single week, the Patriarchs' offices received the visiting cards of representatives of the Foreign Ministry, the Ministry of Religious Affairs, the District Commissioner, the Prime Minister's Office and the Jerusalem Municipality. Needless to say, the Israel Government's prestige did not increase in direct proportion to the number of officials who came courting.

According to a list prepared by the U.N. in 1949, there were 11 Christian holy sites in Jerusalem, in addition to a large number of churches, monasteries, and other ecclesiastical institutions. The 1967 War caused relatively little damage to the Christian Holy Places; considering the heavy fighting and the mutual bombardment, it is surprising how little damage resulted. On several occasions, Christian clergymen expressed their feelings of gratitude and relief that the belligerent sides had taken care to leave the Holy Places alone.

When no-man's-land was cleared of its mines and barbed-wire fences in 1967, it was possible for the first time to estimate the extent of the damage caused to the Holy Places in the 1948 War. It was discovered that the cemeteries on Mount Zion had suffered the most. The Armenian cemetery, between the Israeli and Jordanian lines on Mount Zion, had been completely destroyed, including the graves of 12 Armenian patriarchs. No-man's-land also contained a monastery that had been destroyed and looted in the 1948 War. A similar fate had befallen a Roman Catholic and a Greek Orthodox cemetery, the building of the Convent of the Sisters of St. Maria Reparatrix at the corner of the Old City walls near the New Gate, the Syrian Catholic church and monastery near the Damascus Gate, and the southern wing of the monastery of Notre Dame, as well as other buildings. The damage revealed in 1967 served the Arabs and hostile elements in the churches as fuel for their incitement against Israel. They suppressed the fact that the damage had been caused 19 years earlier and that responsibility for it fell equally on both sides.

A few months after the 1967 War, the Government of Israel decided to compensate the churches for all damages, whether caused in 1948 or in 1967 and regardless of which side was responsible. All the churches presented their claims to an Israeli panel of experts, which reached agreements with the churches at the end of 1968. The French Government alone refused to present a claim or receive compensation for the damage caused to the Church of St. Anne. Compensation paid up to 1969 totalled IL 5 million.

The Israeli authorities were keenly aware of the tremendous responsibility they were taking upon themselves with regard to the Christian Holy Places. Even before leaving for the Old City in the afternoon of June 7, the Prime Minister convened the heads of the religious communities in Israel in his office and told them:

Ever since our forces have taken control of the whole city and its vicinity, quiet has been restored. You can be quite certain that no harm of any kind will be permitted to the Holy Places. I have asked the Minister of Religious Affairs to make contact with the religious leaders of the Old City, to ensure regular contact between them and our forces, and to ensure that they can continue their spiritual activity undisturbed. In accordance with my request, the Minister has given the following instructions:

1. Arrangements at the Western Wall shall be made by the Israeli Chief Rabbis.

2. Arrangements in the Muslim Holy Places shall be made by a council of Muslim clergymen.

3. Arrangements in the Christian Holy Places shall be made by a council of Christian clergymen.

With the help of Israel's Rock and Savior, here in Jerusalem, the symbol of peace throughout the ages, the Holy City whose tranquillity has been restored, it is my wish to include you in a call for peace to all the peoples of the region and to the whole world.

Immediately after the occupation, a special force assigned to protecting the Holy Places took up its task, under the command of an officer who had acquired experience in this role in 1956, when he was responsible for the safety of St. Catherine Monastery in Sinai. On the following day, June 8, the Minister of Religious Affairs issued the following proclamation:

Immediately after the entry of the Israel Defense Forces into the Old City and Bethlehem, the Prime Minister announced, in the presence of the leaders of all the country's religious groups, that arrangements for protecting the Holy Places would be made by the religious leaders themselves, each in the places revered by his own religion. I therefore set up a temporary authority and gave detailed instructions on abiding by the principles set down in the Declaration of Independence [with regard to the Holy Places]. A draft of the regulations is now in the process of preparation and in the very near future I will call a meeting of the religious leaders in order to present this legislation.

That same day, General Herzog, Military Governor of the West Bank, met the heads of the Christian churches in East Jerusalem and informed them of the Government's decisions.

It is interesting to compare the declarations of the Israel Government, following the occupation of Jerusalem, with the declarations of the two other states which had captured Jerusalem in the 20th century.

On December 11, 1917, upon officially entering Jerusalem, General Allenby published a proclamation to the public. With regard to the Holy Places, the British Commander-in-Chief said that

... every sacred building, monument, holy spot, shrine, tradi-
tional site ... of whatsoever form of the three religions, will be
maintained and protected according to the existing customs and
beliefs of those to whose faiths they are sacred.

On January 5, 1951, Jordan's King Abdallah published a proclamation dealing with the Holy Places. It stated, among other things, that
law and order will be protected within the framework of the status
quo, *the rights of all religions, mosques and churches will be*
secured so that order, peace and love can reign here, according to
the visions of the great prophets.

These two declarations promise to maintain "the existing customs"
or the *status quo*. The Israeli declaration, on the other hand, is based
on the principles of Israel's Declaration of Independence and,
mainly, on the following phrases appearing in it: "The State of Israel
will ensure freedom of religion, conscience, speech, education and
culture; it will protect the Holy Places of all religions." It is no
accident that the words *status quo* were not mentioned. Israel could
promise protection to the Christian communities, but not by way of
a formal declaration. She could not make a general declaration on
this subject because both in the Mandate itself and in the eyes of the
Mandatory Government the *status quo* affected Jewish Holy Places
as well, and it was in the name of the *status quo* that the Jews were
harassed at the Western Wall. Reaffirmation of the *status quo* by
Israel would have meant guaranteeing to maintain the King's Order in
Council (Western Wall) 1931, with all its degrading and discrim-
inatory regulations. It was utterly unreasonable to expect Israel not
to depart from the *status quo* in this respect. In fact, one of the
Jordanian charges against Israel in a letter to the Security Council,
dated February 23, 1968, was that "the Zionists are changing the
status quo at the Western Wall and in the adjoining area." However,
all this did not affect the Christian Holy Places, where Israel had
every intention of maintaining the *status quo,* although, as will be
explained below, Israel was ready to change it in favor of the Vatican,
in return for a political settlement.

Israeli declarations stressed the principle of administering the Holy
Places independently by members of the different communities. To
anyone who knew the complex history of the Christian Holy Places,
applying this principle was extremely problematical. It was, after all,
the very inability of the Christian communities to solve the problems

263

of internal administration of the Holy Places that led to the *status quo* being instituted, implying a forced agreement imposed by an external force. The Israelis did not have to promise that they would not intervene. On the contrary, it was expected that they would promise intervention to impose the *status quo,* as Jerusalem's previous rulers had done. However, there was one basic difference between the previous rulers and the present ones: the latter were Jews. In the course of 1,300 years, the Christian world had grown accustomed to Muslim rulers. Between 1917 and 1948, there had been a Christian regime; but Jewish rule of the Old City was met with suspicion. Israel wished, as far as she could, to reassure the Christians that she would not interfere in their affairs.

It appears that the Israelis thought that the answer was self-administration. But while the Chief Rabbinate, a recognized body, was appointed to manage the Jewish Holy Places, it was not at all clear who made up the "Council of Christian clergymen" referred to by Prime Minister Eshkol. As to the Muslims, there were Mandatory precedents with regard to the body authorized to make arrangements in their Holy Places; but it was precisely to this group that Israel had good reason to be careful about giving too much independence, as she was to discover within a short time.

While the local Christians received the Israeli declarations quietly, with neither enthusiasm nor forebodings, the Vatican reacted without delay. As early as June 7, 1967, the Pope called for Jerusalem to be internationalized and "turned into a sanctuary for the wounded and helpless, into a symbol of hope and peace for all." On June 9, the Vatican's Press Officer said that "the U.N. resolutions of 1947 and 1948 concerning the internationalization of Jerusalem were in accord with the wishes of the Holy See." With Vatican encouragement, the Italian press, radio, and television initiated an extensive propaganda campaign in favor of the internationalization of the Holy Places. On June 13, the head of the Franciscan Order declared that, in the Pope's opinion, internationalization of the Holy Places was the best solution to the Jerusalem problem.

The heads of other Christian churches were not yet ready to take up positions with regard to internationalization. A survey conducted by the *New York Times,* on June 18, showed that "most churchmen were not opposed in principle to the Pope's idea, but . . . most of them felt that it was not appropriate for religious bodies to fix on a specific plan at this time." The Secretary-General of the World Council of Churches, Eugene Blake, said that the status of Jerusalem was a political issue and that it would only be possible to bring up religious interests after a political agreement was reached. The heads of the Eastern churches refrained from any comment at all. It was not only that they regarded the Vatican's internationalization plans with suspicion; they were also afraid to express any opinion which could cause complications between them and the Arab States.

On June 26, with rumors of annexation increasing, the Pope declared:

> The Holy City, Jerusalem, must remain, for all eternity, that which it represents: a city of God, a free oasis of peace and prayer, a meeting point of inspiration and harmony for all, possessing its own standing and safeguarded by the international community.

Following unification, the focal point of Roman Catholic activity moved to the corridors of the United Nations. The Vatican's U.N. Observer distributed a memorandum stating that only the internationalization of Jerusalem and its vicinity would ensure the protection of the Holy Places.

In the meantime, on June 27, the Knesset had adopted the Law for the Protection of the Holy Places (1967), which stated that "the Holy Places shall be protected from desecration or any other harm, or anything which might affect the access of believers or their feelings for those places." Punishments for transgressors were very severe: anyone found guilty of desecrating a Holy Place could be sentenced to seven years' imprisonment; anyone perpetrating an act that could affect free access might receive five years' imprisonment. The Minister of Religious Affairs was appointed to carry out the law. In his Knesset speech, he explained:

> The policy of the Israel Government . . . is based on the following three principles: complete protection of the feelings of believers from any desecration or harm, free access for the members of all faiths, and internal management of the Holy Places by the authorities of the religion for which the place is sacred.

Eight years after the law's enactment, however, the Minister of Religious Affairs had yet to publish regulations with regard to the Holy Places in Jerusalem. In view of the political situation, there was no hope that such regulations could be enacted with regard to Christian or Muslim Holy Places.

For all the legal complications, the law's enactment permitted Foreign Minister Abba Eban to present the unification of Jerusalem as "an advance toward that situation of peace, reverence, sanctity, and free access, which is the main objective of the world community in relation to the historic and religious interests here involved." However, the law was far from being what Eban termed it: "The first law in modern history enacted for the protection of Holy Places from desecration." With regard to Israeli readiness to hand the Holy Places over to independent management, Eban said:

> Never in human memory has there been any disposition by any government in the region to exclude the Holy Places from its exclusive and unilateral control. This therefore is a statement of great significance, not only in the history of our region, but in the history of mankind.

The enthusiasm of the Israel Foreign Minister, like his far-flung departure into history, was slightly exaggerated. Human history — of the past 50 years especially — did indeed acknowledge such attempts. It was reluctance to exercise "exclusive and unilateral control" that guided the British Government in its efforts to establish a League of Nations' commission of inquiry; its failure stemmed from the rivalries of the Christian communities. There was no indication that Israel had a better chance of achieving an inter-church agreement that would permit internal self-management of the Holy Places.

Israel made a considerable effort to achieve a dialogue with the Vatican. The Holy See did not possess most of the Holy Places in Jerusalem; but its enormous political influence induced Israel to initiate her efforts in this direction.

Ehud Avriel, Israel's Ambassador to Rome, held preparatory talks with the Vatican after the Six Day War. In early June, the Ambassador met with the Pope. During the course of their discussion, Avriel suggested that an agreement be signed between Israel and the Vatican in which Israel would recognize the Pope as coordinator of all Christian interests in Jerusalem and would treat the Catholics as "first among equals" with regard to the other Christian communities in the Holy City. The Pope listened and finally stated that he planned to send a representative to Israel to study the situation.

However, as if to stress the fact that the Pope was not abandoning his regular policy, the Vatican newspaper published an attack on Israel on the day of the meeting, which included the following passage:

There are those who ask why the Vatican was silent for 18 years,
and why only now, that the Israelis are in Jerusalem, has it
awakened to speak of internationalization? . . . Throughout these
years, at every suitable opportunity, the Vatican has repeatedly
demanded the internationalization of Jerusalem. Israel herself was
prepared to accept this in 1950, with respect to that part [of
Jerusalem] not under her control. . . . The Church demands an
international regime based on U.N. principles and on the Declara-
tion of the Rights of Man. . . .

The Vatican Representative, Monseigneur Felici, was sent to Israel
not to negotiate, but to discover the facts, explain the Vatican's
views, and hear what the Israelis had to say. The Israeli press covered
his tour with officially-inspired articles expressing "optimism about
chances of a settlement." According to Christian sources, the Israel
Government proposed that the Holy Places in Jerusalem and Bethlehem be handed over to a commission composed of representatives
of the various Christian communities. Authoritative circles hinted
that extra-territorial status might be granted to the Holy Places.
Israel wanted to issue a joint communiqué at the end of Felici's visit,
since debate was about to be renewed at the U.N. General Assembly;
but the communiqué's wording was vague:

In the meeting between Monseigneur Felici and the Prime Min-
ister, which was held in an atmosphere of friendliness and mutual
understanding, a number of possible formulae were discussed that
could be taken into account towards the aim of achieving a satis-
factory solution to the important issue related to the Holy Places.
The talks will continue.

Israeli sources defined the communiqué as "an historic event," con-
cluding that the Vatican recognized Israel as a partner in a solution
to the problem. The Foreign Minister could make use of it in his
speech at the General Assembly. The other Christian communities,
primarily the Greek Orthodox, began to fear that Israel was about to
make a deal at their expense.

In the official Vatican pronouncement, published after Felici's
return, the internationalization of Jerusalem was not mentioned.
This omission was interpreted by Israel as a change in Vatican policy.
It quickly transpired, however, that the Vatican had begun to use
two alternating formulae: one stressing that there was no change in
its position with regard to internationalization, the other speaking

of "a special, internationally guaranteed status for the Holy Places."

On Christmas 1967, the Pope did not repeat the internationalization formula, and again the Israelis chose to regard this as a change in attitude. However, in May 1968, the Vatican spokesman again repeated the Holy See's support for "the internationalization of Jerusalem and its surroundings in accordance with the decision of the General Assembly of the United Nations in 1947," and added that the Vatican "had not proposed or considered, to this day, any alternatives to this plan." On Christmas 1968, the Pope again spoke of "an agreement protected by international guarantees for . . . Jerusalem and the Holy Places." It was clear, therefore, that there was no real contradiction between the two Catholic formulae, and that they were used solely according to tactical considerations.

During this time, secret negotiations were being held between Israel and the Vatican, led on the Israeli side by Yaacov Herzog, Director of the Prime Minister's Office. The Israeli proposals included changing the *status quo* by giving the Catholics senior status at the expense of the Eastern communities; by recognizing the Pope as the representative of all the Christian groups; and by granting diplomatic status to the Holy Places.

The Vatican would not, however, agree to a bilateral agreement, as this would imply recognition of Israel's sovereignty over unified Jerusalem. It agreed to "accept with its blessing" a unilateral Israeli declaration promising priority status to the Catholic Church. But this seemed to Israel too poor a deal to justify getting involved in a controversial change of the ancient *status quo*.

In early October 1969, the Pope met with Foreign Minister Abba Eban. The actual political value of this meeting was small. The negotiations shifted to the drafting of an agreement between Israel and the Vatican with regard to the status of the Catholic organizations in Israel and problems of property, education and taxes. In formulating the draft the negotiators did not relate the problems of Jerusalem and the Holy Places. The draft agreement was sent to the Vatican. In early 1971, the Vatican rejected it. In a letter to the President of Israel, the Pope explained that the Holy See cannot sign an agreement with Israel, which it does not recognize, because it cannot recognize a country whose borders have not been determined. In addition, the letter said, the Vatican does not see itself as a representative of all the Christian communities.

268

The Vatican's refusal was a hard blow to Israeli politicians who had expended so much effort in an attempt to settle relations between the Jewish State and the Catholic Church. The Vatican, with political wisdom, did not want to antagonize the country in control of the Holy Places and, therefore, was careful to cushion its refusal with various political compliments. The most important of these was an invitation to Prime Minister Golda Meir for an audience with the Pope. The meeting, which took place on January 15, 1973, was described as "historic." It, too, was of little practical political value, but its publicity value was great.

The internationalization of Jerusalem was never mentioned again in official Vatican statements, though, at the same time, Vatican spokesmen were careful to emphasize that "The Holy See has not altered its position with regard to the problems in the Holy Land and its attitude towards Israel."

On Christmas Eve, 1973, the Pope announced to African leaders that the Vatican would see to it that its voice is heard during deliberations over peace settlements in the Middle East. He mentioned not only the rights of every monotheistic religion in Jerusalem, but also the rights of "those sufferers (Palestinians) who have reached a state of despair." An announcement published by the Vatican stated that "Jerusalem must not remain under the exclusive control of one religion" — i.e., Israel.

When U.S. Secretary of State Henry Kissinger visited Rome in early July 1974, the Vatican spokesman spoke of "a special status for the Holy City accompanied by international assurances." Political analysts took this to mean that the Vatican stand, following the Yom Kippur War, is "open and flexible" and that the Vatican does not propose a specific solution for Jerusalem, because it has no such solution.

The Vatican stand can be summarized by stating that its previously unswerving position, which had been interpreted as support for the internationalization of Jerusalem as a *corpus separatum* in accordance wih the U.N. decisions of 1947–50, has been replaced by more flexible formulas. The reason for this change might be in the fact that the make-up of the U.N. has altered so much that at the end of the 20th Century there is no longer a majority of Christian states and therefore no assurance that internationalization would guarantee Catholic interests. The Vatican began talking, instead, about international legal guarantees for Jerusalem's special status. It refrained, apparently on purpose, from expressing a clear and obligatory opinion on the preferred political sovereignty in Jerusalem. The Israelis saw this flexibility as a positive achievement, but there can be no doubt that even this "flexibility" does not mean acceptance of Israel's political status with regard to Jerusalem.

The Vatican continued to view the Jerusalem problem as consisting not only of the Holy Places, and their protection, but of a whole complex of issues connected with Christian presence in Jerusalem. Always, and especially since the 1948 War, the Vatican had been concerned over the reduction in the number of Christians in Jerusalem. It feared that, even if the Holy Places were safeguarded, they would become empty museums, and it was concerned about the perpetuation of educational institutions, religious seminaries, monasteries, and orphanages. The fear that a national state with a profound attachment to Islam would impede the development of Christian life in Jerusalem had proved correct under Jordanian rule. The Vatican had no confidence that the rule of a national state with a deep attachment to Judaism would be better than its predecessor. Even if the Vatican were prepared to consider the Israeli proposals, they would be very difficult — if not impossible — to apply, since their implementation required agreement among all the Christian communities, above all the sanction of the Greek Orthodox community, which held special privileges in the Holy Places. Such an agreement, based on the *status quo,* would have left the Catholics in their position of inferiority. Furthermore, the Holy See could not hold purposeful talks with Israel so long as the political conflict over Jerusalem persisted. Even if an agreed formula had been found, it cannot be assumed that the Vatican, which had not even recognized Israel, would have been able to bring it to a conclusion.

The Greek Orthodox Patriarchate in Jerusalem took a completely different line than that of the Catholics. Since the Middle Ages, the Greek Orthodox had fought for the preservation of their privileged position (*praedominium*) in the Holy Places, and, since the 7th Century, had worked under a regime not of their faith. Fears over a change in the *status quo,* brought about by political pressure from the Vatican and by the Catholic Church's attempts at negotiating with the non-Christian authorities, dictated the Greek Orthodox policy and behavior. They objected to the internationalization of

270

Jerusalem and the Holy Places for the very same reason that the Vatican supported it. They followed with anxiety the negotiations between the Vatican and Israel. In their effort to maintain the *status quo,* which would mean the preservation of their privileged position in the Holy Places, they were ready to reach unprecedented settlements with Israel. At the end of November 1967, the Greek Orthodox Patriarch Benedictos sent a detailed memorandum to the Government in which he proposed signing an official, formal agreement regarding relations between Israel and the Greek Orthodox Church, based on the *status quo.* In his memorandum, Benedictos raised a long list of problems related to jurisdiction, property rights, taxes, and permanent resident visas for monks with foreign citizenship.

Several members of the Israel Government advocated signing the agreement, but those with "Catholic leanings" said that an agreement must first be reached with the Catholics, since they were more influential politically. It has already been noted that the draft agreement suggested by Israel for a settlement with the Catholics had not been signed due to the Vatican's refusal. The agreement with the Greek Orthodox Church was also not signed by the Government, though some partial settlements were made with them on various issues. This situation did not prevent the Greek Orthodox from maintaining excellent relations with the Israeli authorities. They even openly expressed their satisfaction with the situation in Jerusalem and with the Israeli administration at Church conferences all over the world. At the same time, they continued to maintain excellent relations with the Jordanian authorities as well.

The friendly relations between the Patriarch Benedictos and the Israeli authorities annoyed the Catholics. In March 1968, a Catholic prelate asked Benedictos why he was supporting the Israelis and what he expected to receive in return? The Orthodox leader replied that his church did not favor any regime and did not intervene in politics; however, it was opposed to an international regime, since that would lead to increased Vatican influence and would, therefore, certainly not advance the interests of the Eastern churches.

Relations between Israel and the Armenian Church were warm and friendly. This persecuted sect felt that its fate was interwoven with that of the Jewish nation. It saw the Israeli administration as a friendly force, defending it from Arab persecutors. As early as

August 1967, the Armenian Patriarch Yegishé Derderian proposed a formal agreement between his Church and Israel. On most points, his proposal was similar to that of Benedictos, because the Armenians, like the Greeks, were interested in maintaining the *status quo* and in settling the questions of jurisdiction, taxation and property.

The Armenians, however, had a unique problem — the community was being weakened by emigration. They, therefore, asked for permission to allow 50 Armenian families to immigrate to Jerusalem each year from Turkey. Repeated attempts to get government approval for the immigration of these productive and friendly elements to Israel have not, however, been successful.

Protestant clergymen and Western theologians supported the continued unification of Jerusalem under Israeli rule, citing the protection and freedom of access that Israel afforded.

Daily life in the Holy Places followed its regular course. On June 16, 1967, the Government decided to permit every Christian from Israel, or from the occupied territories, to worship at the churches in the Old City. At the same time, non-worshippers were forbidden to visit the churches and army guards maintained their watch on the churches. But when the Military Government was abrogated in the city, tens of thousands of Israeli visitors began to pour into the Christian Holy Places, many of them for the first time in their lives. The continual flow of visitors interfered with the services. People entered in unsuitable dress, spoke loudly, and turned up their transistor radios. Groups squatted near the Church of the Holy Sepulcher, to munch their sandwiches. The heads of the Christian sects met for an emergency discussion and decided to supply the police with instructions concerning behavior during visits to the Holy Places. These rules were also posted on large boards at the entrances to the principal churches.

At first, there was no improvement: the lack of respect for the Holy Places, noisy behavior, names carved on walls, picnics, and the like, were not restricted to Christian sites. Similar complaints were received from those responsible for mosques throughout the West Bank. At the Western Wall, too, some Jews refused to put on hats and defied instructions by eating meals and holding private celebrations there. What had come to light was not so much disrespect for the Holy Places of other religions, as the lack of consideration resulting from poor upbringing.

To complicate matters, during the night of August 3, 1967, a tiara, eight golden hearts, and a pair of golden earrings were stolen from a statue of the Virgin Mary in Golgotha. Admittedly, there had been thefts from the Church of the Holy Sepulcher during the Jordanian period, but the theft, as well as the behavior of visitors, was exploited by Arab propaganda organs to embarrass Israel. The police made extraordinary efforts to trace the thieves and their loot, and both were discovered within a week. The crown and the hearts (less one stone and one golden heart) were restored in a festive ceremony, while the thieves were sentenced to extended periods of imprisonment.

When the volume of Jewish visitors decreased in September 1967, tranquillity returned to the churches of Jerusalem. When they met the personal envoy of the U.N. Secretary-General, Ambassador Thalman, the church leaders could declare spontaneously that:

the Israeli authorities have fulfilled all the principles they laid down, and there is no reason for complaints. The problems that remain are mostly of a practical and physical nature and will find their solution in a spirit of cooperation.

The first test for the Israeli authorities came during the Easter celebrations in 1968, and supreme efforts were made to ensure tranquillity. The police, together with the Ministry of Religious Affairs, prepared a plan of operations that ran to hundreds of pages. Some 400 policemen were mobilized to maintain order and, in cooperation with the different churches, a detailed, almost military, timetable was prepared. At the news conference that preceded the ceremony, the Jerusalem Chief of Police announced that the sects had agreed to one alteration in their arrangements. Unlike previous years, they had agreed that the police should erect mobile barricades within the Church of the Holy Sepulcher, so that the area needed for holding the procession would be kept clear. In previous years, the Jordanians, the British, and the Turks had stationed soldiers who had formed a living barricade. Some 200 Israeli policemen were posted within the Church during the ceremony, to maintain order. Firemen with asbestos gloves were also posted to extinguish the candles.

Few of the Jewish policemen could appreciate the historic moment they were experiencing. Some of the traditional songs sung at the fire festival had, in previous years, insulted the Jews.

All the Easter ceremonies passed quietly and no conflicts occurred among the Christian communities. This time it was the Israeli authorities who supplied the traditional conflict. A few weeks before the beginning of the ceremonies, the Israeli District Commissioner was invited to attend them, according to custom. Throughout the years, the District Commissioner had participated in the processions, with a place of honor being reserved for him on a small balcony between the Catholicon and the Rotunda. The District Commissioner had already taken part in a number of meetings with the police and church representatives, when suddenly the jealousy of Ministry of Religious Affairs officials was aroused. In their opinion, it was they who were deserving of the honor. The heads of the churches sent a letter to the District Commissioner, claiming that his absence or replacement by someone else, especially a representative of the Ministry of Religious Affairs, affected the *status quo*. The Commissioner replied that he could not accept their invitation. The conflict was referred to the Prime Minister, who settled the matter by giving representation to neither, sending his Advisor on Arab Affairs instead. The church leaders were astounded at the internal conflict in the Government, which hardly advanced the prestige of the Israeli authorities, especially when it was explained that, in fact, a District Commissioner in Israel was not a governor, but only a representative of the Interior Ministry. Those who provided the explanation forgot that this same Commissioner had been appointed by the Government to maintain contacts with the foreign consuls and church leaders in Jerusalem.

For a long time, the previous disputes over the use of, or the right of worship in, the Church of the Holy Sepulcher remained suppressed, and cooperation among the principal churches even increased. Reconstruction work in the Church made progress. But at the end of July 1968, a dispute broke out between the Armenians and the Copts over the repair of a hole in a common wall. The Copts' Jewish lawyer applied to the Magistrate's Court and succeeded in getting an injunction against the Armenians. The Armenian priests were astounded and told the clergy of other sects about the injunction. A newspaper report that the matter was to be adjudged in court increased the shock. The attempt to create a change in the *status quo* by means of a court action was a very serious matter, the likes of which had never occurred before. The matter was settled, however, when the Magistrate realized that he had made a mistake. He apologized for forgetting that a 1924 law, still in effect, had withdrawn such matters from the jurisdiction of the courts. After all, no Israeli judge had referred to it for 20 years. The injunction was withdrawn.

Only the Copts and the Ethiopians continued to clash over the possession and ownership of two small chapels, the Chapel of the Four Bodiless Creatures, the St. Michael Chapel (Deir al-Sultan), and the path leading to them. These chapels had been in Copt hands since the 1840s. The Ethiopians alleged that they had been deprived of them due to the hostility of the Ottoman regime. This conflict had gone on for over 100 years, and it was a source of trouble to both the British and the Jordanian authorities. In 1961, the Jordanians appointed a commission of inquiry, which found that possession should be given to the Ethiopians, who then held possession of the chapels for 40 days. After that time, however, owing to Egyptian pressure (the Copts being Egyptian citizens), possession was restored to the Copts. During Easter 1969, there was a serious clash between the two communities. Stones were thrown and the Ethiopian ceremonies were stopped, because of a mass scuffle with the Copts. During Easter 1970, the Ethiopians changed the locks to the disputed passage. When the Copts asked for police aid in restoring the *status quo,* they were refused it. The Copts applied to the Supreme Court, which declared that it was not empowered to intervene in the dispute, but it severely criticized the police for not helping the Copts to restore matters to their previous condition. The High Court made the injunction against the police absolute, ordering them to take the keys from the Ethiopians and restore possession to the Copts, but it gave the Government a year's grace to deal with the conflict. After a year, the Government decided to appoint a special ministerial committee to deal with the dispute, declaring that, in the meantime, "the present *status quo* would remain." The Jordan Government had no interest in quarreling with Egypt over the Ethiopians. The Israel Government, which maintained excellent relations with Ethiopia, had good reason to side with the rights of the Ethiopian priests, especially as a Jordanian committee had recognized the justice of their claim.

Maintaining the *status quo* had never been merely a hard and thankless task; whoever controlled the Holy Places also enjoyed a number of political bonuses.

CHAPTER EIGHTEEN

THE TEMPLE MOUNT AND ISLAM

On the morning of Saturday, June 17, 1967, Israel's Defense Minister Moshe Dayan handed the Temple Mount over to the Muslims. In the long history of the people of Israel, there are few deeds that can compare with the historical significance and profound symbolism of this act. After thousands of years of exile, the Jews had recaptured their holiest place. In fact, it is Judaism's *only* Holy Place, for it is the one place on earth where man stands in the presence of godliness. So sacred is this area that, according to Jewish religious law, no man is fit to enter it, and only the coming of the Messiah — who will purify men — will permit entry.

The Temple Mount possesses more than religious significance. In its time, the Temple in Jerusalem symbolized the national independence of the Jewish people, and its destruction — the loss of that independence. The emotional burden shouldered by every Jew, whether religious or not, when standing at the gates of the Temple Mount is almost unbearable. Yet, in June 1967, an Israeli Jew found himself forced not only to shoulder this enormous emotional burden, but also to decide how to deal with the question of "possession" of this self-same Holy Place, which had been taken over by the believers of another religion.

Dayan did not permit the emotional burden to sway the balance, but, instead, weighed the matter rationally and decided to leave the Muslims in possession. Not sole possession, as will be noted; but neither did he, as a Jew, wish to rob the Muslims of what they considered their own, after having held the area for 1,300 years. Moreover,

Dayan decided swiftly, while it was still within his power to make the decision, before those Israeli bodies and circles motivated by national and religious feeling alone could translate their attachment to the Temple Mount into deeds.

According to the new regulations, Muslims maintained their possession under Jewish rule, and a Jew wishing to visit their mosques must remove his shoes. Furthermore, Jews were forbidden to pray on the Temple Mount and, although Jewish extremist circles tried to put a stop to this *modus vivendi,* the Israel Government firmly maintained the policy that the Defense Minister had initiated.

Even before June 17, Dayan had taken a number of steps that hinted at his intentions concerning the Temple Mount. On his first visit after the conquest, he ordered the removal of the Israeli flag flying over the Dome of the Rock and of the paratroop unit stationed there. On June 11, the whole of the Mount was declared out of bounds to Israeli soldiers, and guards were posted outside its gates. On June 16, the first Muslim service after the War was held. Military Government officers saw to it that all the Muslim religious leaders took part in it. When they made their participation conditional on that of the senior *qadi,* Sheikh Abd al-Hamid al-Sayah, who had left for Jericho during the fighting and remained there, the Military Government saw to it that he was brought back to the city, and Israel Radio broadcast the service.

On June 18, the Government decided to permit all the Muslims and Christians in Israel and the occupied territories to pray at the Holy Places in Jerusalem. The army and the Military Government forecast the arrival of tens of thousands of Muslims who, influenced by extremist elements, would turn the services into a political demonstration, as was the Arab custom during the British Mandate. Approach routes were planned for hundreds of vehicles; large parking areas were laid out; tanks were deployed on the Mount of Olives and at the entrances to Temple Mount.

On Friday, June 23, a mere 5,000 worshippers arrived. The services went off without incident.

On the day the annexation laws were presented to the Knesset, all heads of religious congregations were summoned to the Prime Minister's office. Except for the June 17 meeting with the Defense Minister, it was the first meeting between the heads of the Muslim community and Israel Government leaders. They listened attentively to the Prime Minister's words, especially the last sentences with the operative instructions:

It is our intention to hand over internal administration and arrangements concerning the Holy Places to the heads of the communities to which they belong. The task of implementing all the necessary procedures has been put into the hands of the Minister of Religious Affairs.

The significance of the words, as well as the reason for the meeting, became clear the next day, when the annexation order was issued. The Muslim religious leaders found themselves faced with a complex situation.

By agreement between the Military Government and the Ministry of Religious Affairs, responsibility for the Muslim community was transferred to the civilian authority. The first meeting between the Minister of Religious Affairs and Muslim representatives revealed the political and juridical abyss that divided the Israelis and the East Jerusalem Muslims. The Minister informed the Muslim delegation that with the application of Israeli Law in East Jerusalem, those Israeli laws concerning jurisdiction of the Muslim religious *shari'a* courts, and the affairs of the *waqf,* would automatically be in force.

Sheikh al-Sayah declared that the Arabs did not recognize the annexation of Jerusalem and were not prepared to adjudicate in accordance with the Israeli laws of marriage and divorce, inheritance, women's status and *waqf* affairs. These laws, he said, were not only without force in East Jerusalem, but were also illegal by Muslim religious law. The Muslim establishment was operating on the strength of its appointment by the Kingdom of Jordan and would continue to officiate on the strength of the same appointment and according to Jordanian Law. In accordance with international law, they only recognized the Military Government.

The Minister of Religious Affairs suggested that the Muslim leadership draw the appropriate conclusions. Sheikh al-Sayah answered that they did not intend to resign; if the Israel Government wished to dismiss them, it could do so. When the Minister warned that they would not receive their salaries, the Muslims declared that they would work without pay. It was only at the end of the meeting that tension relaxed, when the Minister suggested that he would like to visit the *shari'a* court. He was given a friendly invitation, and in an official announcement issued that day, a spokesman of the Ministry reported that:

discussions included the preservation of the Muslim Holy Places, the continued operation of the shari'a *courts, and the situation in the managing bodies of the religious endowments in Jerusalem.* . . . *The* qadis *expressed their satisfaction with the arrangements made for the orderly continuation of religious worship.* . . .

In order to understand the roots of this confrontation, it is necessary to elaborate on the political and legal problems involved; not the legal-political considerations which caused the Muslim delegation to question the legalities of Israeli legislative steps in East Jerusalem, but rather with the link between these legislative steps on the one hand, and Muslim law and its religious principles on the other.

Islam does not recognize any separation of religion and state. A Muslim residing in a state not under Muslim rule is required by his faith to maintain an independent juridical system; he cannot recognize an appointment by a non-Muslim head of state, nor take an oath of allegiance to him. Muslim minorities living in Christian states, where there was no communal or religious tension, ignored this rule. In Cyprus and Yugoslavia, for example, the Muslim *qadis* were appointed by Christian governments and they took an oath of allegiance to those governments.

As long as Palestine was under Muslim rule, the problem did not arise. In 1917, however, following the British conquest, Palestine's Muslims found themselves under non-Muslim rule for the first time in modern history. It was necessary to re-organize the Muslim judicial system and the *waqfs,* which were under the jurisdiction of the *shari'a* courts. In Turkish times, all these were subject to the head of the Muslim judiciary of the Empire, Sheikh al-Islam, and to the *Waqf* Ministry in Constantinople. In December 1921, an ordinance was issued establishing a "Supreme Muslim *Shari'a* Council." The first paragraph of that ordinance stated that

A Muslim body shall be constituted for the control and management of the Muslim waqf *and* shari'a *affairs in Palestine, to be known as the Supreme Muslim* Shari'a *Council, having its headquarters in Jerusalem.*

The eighth paragraph of the ordinance listed the main duties of the Council, including the following:

To nominate for the approval of the Government, and, after such

approval, to appoint qadis *of the* Shari'a *Courts, the President and members of the* Shari'a *Court of Appeal, and the Inspectors of* Shari'a *Courts . . . .*

The Council was also given unlimited powers in administering the *ma'dbut waqfs* — that is, all those whose income was allocated to public works, social welfare, the maintenance of mosques and schools — and in the supervision, through the *shari'a* courts, of the *mulhak* (family) *waqfs*. In *waqf* financial matters, too, the Muslim Council was independent of the Mandatory Government. According to the ordinance, it was only required "after approval to transmit the *waqf* budget to the Government for information." Thus, the Council, in the words of the 1937 Peel Commission Report, was "an Arab *imperium in imperio*" (government within a government).

This far-reaching financial and jurisdictional autonomy was given to the Muslim Council not only for religious reasons, or because of the need to transform the Muslims into a religious community like all the other communities, but also in order to appease them politically.

This is not the place to examine the full range of activities of the Muslim Council during the Mandatory period. Suffice it to say that, headed by Haj Amin al-Husayni, it became the force behind all the uprisings and struggles against the British Government and the Jewish community in Palestine, and it used the powerful financial mechanism of the *waqf* to fund these struggles and to suppress opposition within the Arab community. During the 1937 riots, the British Government decided to strip Mufti Haj Amin of all his powers and to abrogate the Muslim Council's jurisdiction over *waqf* affairs. A special ordinance was issued, entitled "Defense Regulations (the Muslim *waqf*) 1937" which appointed a governmental commission to manage the affairs of the Muslim *waqf*. Three Arab Mandatory officials constituted the commission.

The Muslim Council continued its administration of the *shari'a* courts, which functioned throughout the entire Mandatory period, under the King's Order in Council (1922), which defined the internal judicial system with regard to the individual rights of the members of the recognized religions. Paragraph 52 of the King's Order, as amended in 1939, stated, *inter alia,* that

Muslim Religious Courts shall have exclusive jurisdiction in matters of personal status of Muslims who are Palestinian citizens or foreigners who . . . are subject in such matters to the jurisdiction

281

of Muslim Religious Courts, in accordance with the provisions of the Law of Procedure of the Muslim Religious Courts of the 25th of October 1396 A.H., as amended by any Ordinance or Rule . . . .

The British Government was careful not to undermine the *shari'a* and therefore no civil legislation was proposed during the Mandatory period which would have altered any part of the *shari'a* codex.

At the end of the British Mandate, all the heads of the Muslim community left Israel, and their juridical system collapsed. Of the dozens of *qadis* who had officiated during Mandatory times, in the area which became Israel, only one remained. In accordance with the Law of Absentee Property, the Custodian of Absentee Property replaced the administrators of the family *waqfs* — which were defined as absentee property, like any other possession that had been abandoned. The Custodian acted as he saw fit with secular property, while the Holy Places were administered by the Department for Muslim and Druze Affairs of the Ministry of Religious Affairs, which served as the Custodian's agent. In 1965, the Knesset enacted a law permitting certain kinds of *waqf* property to be released by the Custodian of Absentee Property and placed under the administration of Muslim boards of trustees in several cities in the country. However, even after the enactment of this law, the administration of *waqf* property remained in Government hands.

The collapse of the *shari'a* juridical system in Israel obliged the Government to appoint *qadis*. In 1953, the Knesset enacted a law empowering the *shari'a* courts that had officiated before its entry into force. In 1961, the *Qadis'* Law was adopted; it required a *qadi* to be an Israeli citizen, to be appointed by the President of the State at the suggestion of an Appointment's Committee that was presented to the President by the Minister of Religious Affairs. Following his appointment, the *qadi* must make a declaration of allegiance to the State of Israel.

The Muslim community of Israel remained without any central autonomous bodies or powers over its religious and communal affairs, in line with the Israeli policy of preventing any separate Arab organization that might spread anti-Israeli nationalist trends. This state of affairs began in the wake of the complete disintegration of the Muslim community after the 1948 War and the departure of its religious leadership. Those who remained were neither sufficiently numerous nor sufficiently strong to offer any effective resistance to their loss of communal independence and to the policy that subjected them to procedures which contradicted their religious principles.

A number of legislative developments concerning matters of personal status altered the body of *Shari'a* Law in Israel. All of these — affecting women's status, inheritance, marriage and divorce, and the *waqf* — were progressive legislative reforms and were no different from similar legislation in a number of Arab countries. But there is a decisive difference between a Muslim state enacting legislation altering the *shari'a* laws and similar legislation by a non-Muslim state.

Such were the developments in Israel. In Jordan, on the other hand, matters were far simpler, since it was a Muslim state. All the same, the local juridical system was not left untouched. In 1951, the Muslim Council was disbanded and the power to appoint *qadis* was given to the *Qadi-Qudah* (chief *qadi*), the head of the religious juridical system in Jordan. In 1952, the administration of the Palestinian *waqf* was placed under the Ministry for *Waqf* and Islamic Affairs in Amman. Only the department heads for *waqf* affairs remained in the West Bank, at the regional centers in Jerusalem, Nablus, and Hebron. *Waqf* revenues were transferred in their entirety to Amman, where the central Government decided on the amount of aid for welfare institutions, education, worship, and the upkeep of mosques. A trusteeship, under the control of the central Government, was appointed for the reconstruction and maintenance of the al-Aqsa Mosque.

After reunification, the officials of the Israel Ministry of Religious Affairs wanted to impose all the Israeli laws and procedures on the *shari'a* system of East Jerusalem. As long as the Jerusalem *qadis* were not Israeli citizens or had not renounced their Jordanian citizenship and sworn allegiance to the President of Israel, they were not authorized to adjudicate. In addition, they were required to adjudicate not according to the *shari'a* laws in use in Jordan, but as they had been amended in Israel. The Ministry of Religious Affairs also wanted to take over control of *waqf* property, as well as censorship of the sermons delivered on Fridays in the al-Aqsa Mosque. Moreover, on July 18, 1967, the Muslims were ordered to separate the Jerusalem *shari'a* system from that of the West Bank, since Jerusalem had become part of the State of Israel. The West Bank Muslim High

Court of Appeals was required to transfer its seat to Ramallah or Nablus. The Jerusalem Court was ordered to place itself under the Israeli Muslim Court of Appeals, whose seat was in West Jerusalem.

It is easy to imagine the fierce reaction to these demands by the heads of the Muslim community. The head of the Ministry's Muslim Department, a Jew, demanded to see the text of the sermon to be delivered on Friday, July 14. (During the period of the Military Government the sermons were checked verbally.) Upon receiving it, he struck out one verse from the Quran that he considered as anti-Israeli incitement. In response, the Muslim religious leaders boycotted the service at al-Aqsa, and the preacher refused to deliver the sermon. David Farhi, a Military Government official who continued to maintain close ties with the religious leadership, sensed the approaching explosion and tried to prevent it. He arranged with the Ministry officials that sermons would be censored verbally, without erasures from the written text. The visits to *waqf* offices were also terminated.

But it was already too late. The religious and political leadership held a long series of meetings, and on July 24 sent a memorandum to the Military Governor of the West Bank, signed by 22 prominent personalities. Copies of the memorandum were sent to the Prime Minister and the Minister of Religious Affairs. The group of signatories on the memorandum was impressively variegated. In addition to the Arab District Commissioner and the Mayor (who had already been deposed) it included the President of the *Shari'a* Court of Appeals, the *Mufti,* the *Qadi,* three former Ministers, two former Mayors of Jerusalem, the President and Manager of the Chamber of Commerce, two former Members of the Jordanian Senate and a Member of Parliament, two doctors and a secondary-school principal. All streams of political opinion from left to right were represented.

Part of the memorandum read:

We hereby declare that the ordinances annexing Jerusalem issued by the legislative and executive bodies of Israel are null and void, as Jerusalem is an integral part of Jordan and the United Nations General Assembly has decided that annexation is illegal, that the Israeli Knesset does not have the authority to annex the territory of another state, and that the inhabitants of Arab Jerusalem freely exercised their right of self-determination when they voted for unification with the East Bank, in accordance with the unanimous decision of the Jordan Parliament on April 24, 1950.

284

Aside from their non-recognition of annexation, the signatories complained of unlawful interference by the Ministry of Religious Affairs in a manner contradicting Islamic Law on religious matters. As examples, they mentioned the censorship of sermons, the deletion of passages from the Quran, the permission given to Israeli visitors to enter mosques in inappropriate dress, the demolition of the Mugrabi Quarter, the disruption of services in the Tomb of the Patriarchs in Hebron, the interference in *waqf* affairs, and the attempt to interfere in the affairs of the *shari'a* courts, including the Muslim High Court. The "authorized bodies" were requested to abrogate the annexation laws and to cease intervention in matters concerning the personal status of Muslims.

Then came the operative part:

Since the principles of Islamic Law require Muslims to take upon themselves, under conditions such as those now reigning [i.e., non-Muslim rule] all responsibility for matters of their religion, [and since] it is prohibited for non-Muslims to be in charge of Muslim religious affairs,

the signatories were accordingly incorporating themselves as a "Muslim Council responsible for Muslim affairs on the West Bank, including Jerusalem, until the termination of the occupation." Having established itself, this body appointed Sheikh al-Sayah as Chief *Qadi* of the West Bank, transferred to the Muslim Court of Appeals the powers of the *Waqf* Council and the al-Aqsa Control Committee, and made other appointments.

In this statement, the Muslim religious and political leadership deployed itself for life under the conquest of a non-Muslim state. They did not consider the occupation to be illegal and were not defying it, for they agreed that it conformed to the rules of international law. But they refused to recognize Israeli legislation concerning Jerusalem. As they were only willing to recognize the Israeli presence as an occupation, they were re-establishing ("until the termination of the occupation") the same religious organizational framework that had served them during the previous occupation by a non-Muslim power (Britain). The Muslim Council of 1921 was, therefore, restored to life, and it demanded the same rights that it had held previously: responsibility for the *shari'a* courts and for *waqf* affairs. The decisive difference was not in the form of the organization now established, but in its attitude towards the Government.

Previously, the Council was established by order of the authorities and was part of the ruling system; now it was set up in total opposition to the wishes of the authorities.

The memorandum was sent, but before it reached its destination, its contents were made public by all the Arab radio stations. The Israeli press promptly connected the publication of the memorandum with the letter of rejection sent by the members of the disbanded Arab Municipal Council to the District Commissioner; with circulated leaflets, signed by the Palestinian Popular Struggle Movement and calling on the citizens not to collaborate with the occupying power; and with the abortive attempts of Arab priests to get the heads of the Christian communities to sign a memorandum opposing the unification of Jerusalem. Various experts interpreted all these as the first awakening after the shock of the Six Day War.

The Israeli coordinating bodies, as well as the Government, analyzed the memorandum, separating the political sections from the practical complaints. Most Israelis agreed with the criticism that the Muslims had voiced over the behavior of the Ministry of Religious Affairs, while calling for a forceful policy against signs of political disobedience. In their defense, Ministry officials pointed out that censorship had been imposed on sermons in Husayn's time and that they had acted according to the Israeli law regarding the *waqf*.

The immediate problem was the service in al-Aqsa on Friday, July 28. The sermon was not presented for censorship, and when the service began none of the religious leaders was present (they arrived only after prolonged persuasion by David Farhi). The service began late and ended with a short sermon in which the preacher called on the worshippers to "control their tongues, and be men of good deeds, and not of talk," after which there was a prayer to God to "lead us from darkness to light."

Two days later, the Government adopted two decisions related to the crisis. The first was to exile four of the signatories of the memorandum to different places in Israel. They chose secular personalities, including District Commissioner Anwar al-Khatib. The four were arrested at five o'clock in the morning of Monday, July 31, and sent to Safed, Tiberias, Hadera, and Jericho. The second was to remove contacts with the Muslim establishment from the care of the Ministry of Religious Affairs and restore them to the Military Government. On the same day that the four leaders were exiled, the director of the *waqf* was officially informed that henceforth his contacts with the authorities would be via the Defense Ministry and that the following Friday's sermon would not be censored. On August 1, the Defense Minister reached an agreement with the Muslim guardians of the Tomb of the Patriarchs in Hebron regarding a timetable for visits by Jews that would permit the Muslim services to be held regularly.

The Minister of Religious Affairs did not object to the transfer of responsibility. His experience of the past 21 days had rid him of all desire to tackle problems that his Ministry was unable to understand or solve. Interference in *waqf* affairs was stopped. Instead of censoring the written text of the sermons, officers of the Military Government talked them over with the preachers, offering tactful suggestions for certain changes in their contents if there was a need, which seldom occurred. In the view of the Military Government, expressions of Muslim Arab nationalism did not constitute dangerous incitement. On the contrary, they appeared legitimate and acceptable. The Muslim clergy responded willingly to this liberal control, and cooperated. Policemen stationed at the gates of the Temple Mount, and the introduction of stricter control over the behavior of Jewish visitors, removed another cause of the ferment.

These were only secondary matters, however. The central problem, that of finding an arrangement for the juridical autonomy of the Muslim community, had yet to be solved. Negotiations to find a compromise formula began early in August, but they were halted when renewed tension erupted in the middle of the month. But more problems were on the way. Ever since the conquest of the Old City, the Chief Rabbi of the Israel army, Shlomo Goren, had been engaged in extensive research into Jewish Law concerning the sanctity of various sections of Temple Mount and the permissibility of holding prayers there. For the purposes of his research, Rabbi Goren set up an office on the Temple Mount. On August 12, he presented the results of his research to a special convention of military rabbis, and, at the end of the convention, the rabbis, all dressed in army uniforms, went on an extensive and prolonged tour of the Temple Mount. Rabbi Goren proclaimed that it was his intention to hold a special prayer service on the Sabbath immediately following the Ninth of Av. At the same time, the Israeli press published the plans of the Ministry of Religious Affairs to uncover another 90 yards of the Western Wall, for which purpose it would be necessary to demolish a group of buildings south of the Mugrabi Gate.

Members of the Muslim Council, who followed the Hebrew press, approached their contacts in the Military Government and demanded that implementation of these plans be stopped. They were assured that the Government would not permit Jewish prayers on the Temple Mount. Nevertheless, on the afternoon of the Ninth of Av, Rabbi Goren, accompanied by several of the staff of the Military Rabbinate and a group of students, entered the Temple Mount courtyard by way of the Mugrabi Gate, carrying a *Torah* scroll and a *shofar* (ram's horn). They drove away the Muslim guards, as well as soldiers who tried to interfere, and began the afternoon prayers, ending with Rabbi Goren blowing the *shofar*.

The Defense Minister and the Chief of Staff reacted immediately. On Dayan's orders, the Chief of Staff warned Rabbi Goren not to repeat his deeds, and the Chief of Central Command, General Uzi Narkiss, informed him that he would be removed by the Military Police if he should dare ascend to the Temple Mount. The next day, the Ministerial Committee for the Holy Places, which had been established three days earlier, decided almost unanimously that the prayer service planned by Rabbi Goren for Saturday, August 19, was to be banned. On the orders of the Defense Minister, Rabbi Goren announced that "it is not his intention to hold public prayers on the Temple Mount, and all announcements issued [on the subject] are invalid." Military government officials informed the chief *qadi* that "the Government will prevent, even by force, any attempt by Rabbi Goren, or anyone else, to hold prayers on Temple Mount."

The ferment among the Muslim religious establishment died down slightly, but as if purposely designed to arouse indignation, the day that Rabbi Goren announced that he was abandoning his plan, an interview with the Minister of Religious Affairs, Zerah Wahrhaftig, was published in the press. The interview included the following quotation:

Wahrhaftig: King David not only conquered the Temple Mount, he also purchased it from the Jebusites, for a full price.

Q: Haven't several thousand years passed since? Are you trying to say that even today, the Temple Mount and the Tomb of the Patriarchs are Jewish property?

A: Yes, for they were purchased with 'blood,' in both senses of

288

the word [blood in Hebrew also means money]. Many generations
shed their blood to keep the Land of Israel in our hands; and it
was also paid for in full.
Q: Do you want to take these places away from the Muslims?
A: No, no. I don't deny their rights, but I claim that the Jewish
right has precedence and does not depend on any favor by the
Muslims.
Q: Do you demand similar first precedence over the Temple Mount?
A: There is no doubt that the people of Israel have a right to the
Temple Mount, for it is the Holy of Holies of the Jewish people.
Nevertheless, as I understand it, it is not the intention of the
Jewish people to demand that right in our generation by demolish-
ing [the Muslim Holy Places].
Q: In your opinion, do you have the legal right?
A: We have the legal right, and I'm glad that Jewish religious law
states that the Third Temple should be built by the Almighty. I'm
glad that thereby we will not come into conflict with the Muslim
religion.

The Minister may have thought that his final words would reassure
the Muslims and avoid embroiling him in a conflict with them. But
his words — which were translated into Arabic as soon as they
appeared — strengthened the already existing fears of Muslim religious leaders. There was no more room for doubt: the Jews were
about to dispossess them from the Temple Mount and erect the
Third Temple. They could not understand the internal structure of
the Israel Government, whereby the Minister in charge of all religions
can give public expression to his personal opinions on matters that
concern his field of responsibility, even if these opinions are opposed
to those of the majority of the Cabinet. If what was expressed was
the view of the Minister of Religious Affairs, who had been presented
to them only one month earlier as responsible for the safety of all
the Holy Places, the Muslims were sure that it was an indication of
Israel Government policy. If an Israel General (Rabbi Goren), in
uniform, conducts prayers on the Temple Mount, is it conceivable
that he should do so against the orders of his superiors? As for the
prohibitions imposed on Goren, perhaps they were a deliberate
smokescreen of verbal opposition to hide the true Israeli intentions?

Such thoughts were not simply convenient excuses to attack the
Israelis and arouse opposition to the occupation, as the matter was

289

presented by several Israeli observers. The fears had been sown and cultivated more than 50 years earlier, during the disputes over the Western Wall, and they re-emerged now stronger than ever. From 1921 onward, the danger of the Jews gaining control of the *Haram al-Sharif* was a central theme in Arab propaganda. With such a deep-seated suspicion long established in the Arab mind, it is no wonder that events now appeared as evil omens. The historical fact that the Defense Minister had returned the Temple Mount mosques to Muslim possession was forgotten. Muslim reaction was fierce.

On August 22, 1967, a *fatwa* (religious pronouncement) was published, in the name of "the jurists, the *ulemas* and muftis of Jerusalem and the rest of the West Bank," which declared that

> *in light of Israel's intention to broaden the plaza near the Western Wall; Brigadier Goren's prayer service, and the announcement by the Minister of Religious Affairs that the Temple Mount is Jewish property by virtue of conquest and possession,*

the following principles should be noted: the Mosque of Aqsa is "the original kiblah"* and the third holiest Muslim mosque; the area in question includes the entire Temple Mount, the Mosque building; the walls surrounding the plaza, the gates, the plaza, the Dome of the Rock and all the areas bordering on it; anyone damaging the holiness of this area damages the holiness of the Mosque itself.

> *Rights of ownership of the Holy Rock (and the Tomb of the Patriarchs) have been fixed by tradition and decrees dating back hundreds of years, during which Muslims have exercised these rights, and they are not subject to change. They cannot be repealed in a religious court nor by local or international law.*

As to the Western Wall, it is Muslim property and the Jews have the right to visit it according to the King's Order in Council (1931) which

> *ended the Jewish–Arab debate on the subject of this Holy Place and became an internationally accepted document. This debate should not be re-opened as it has been resolved through judicial means.*

---

* Originally, Muhammad established the direction of all Muslim prayer (the *kiblah*) northward, towards Jerusalem. He hoped in this way to attract the Jewish tribes living in the Arabian Peninsula to Islam. But when he realized that he could not accomplish this purpose he changed the direction of prayer southward, towards Mecca. Jerusalem is, therefore, the "original *kiblah*" of the Muslims.

The *fatwa* ended with the following declaration:

Any harm to the Temple Mount area is an infringement on the sanctity of the Mosque itself. The status of the Western Wall area was settled in 1931 and remains in force; and any change in the status quo *on the Temple Mount or at the Tomb of the Patriarchs is a rude blow to the sanctity of places holy to Muslims and constitutes open aggression, which will have far-reaching effects not only on the Jerusalem Muslim community, but on the whole of the Muslim world.*

The declaration also stated that the Muslims were offering free access to the Muslim Holy Places to Jews and non-Jews on condition that their behavior be in keeping with the sanctity of the Holy Places.

The *fatwa* was signed by 29 clergymen from the West Bank. Although it was written in sharper terms than the July 24 declaration, and its contents were broadcast by the Arab countries, the authorities did not take any steps against its signatories this time. On the contrary, the Israeli liaison officers did their best to reduce tension.

As was noted earlier, Muslim guards had been placed at the gates of the Temple Mount, and visitors, Jews or foreigners, were permitted to visit the Mount and its mosques upon payment of entrance fees. After the war, large numbers of Jews wanted to visit the Temple Mount. Israel's Chief Rabbinate regarded this mass trek with concern, since — unlike the Army Chief Rabbi — it ruled that Jews are forbidden to enter the area. The necessity to pay entry fees to the Temple Mount area irritated many of the Jewish visitors. The Jews, in turn, irritated the Muslims by entering the mosques armed or embracing mini-clad girls. At the beginning of August 1967, a number of supplementary guards, under the command of an Israeli police sergeant, were stationed at the Mount, at the request of the Muslim guardians. Their task was restricted to keeping order and guarding the behavior of the visitors. All management and responsibility, including safeguarding the buildings and the opening and closing of the gates of the courtyard and the mosques, remained in the hands of the Muslim *waqf* employees.

During the first week of September, the Israeli authorities awoke to the possibility that the Muslims might close the gates of the Temple Mount and prevent the entry of visitors. One morning, officials of the Military Rabbinate tried to enter their office next to the

Mugrabi Gate and found the gate locked. Upon the orders of the Defense Minister, the gate's key was confiscated, the gate opened, and a Military Police guard was stationed beside it. Despite the protests of the *waqf,* the key was not returned. A significant change had taken place; the Muslims had ceased to be in sole control of the entrances to the Temple Mount.

Visitors entering through the Mugrabi Gate were not required to pay entrance fees and were free to walk throughout the Temple Mount courtyard. Direct control of the Mugrabi Gate prevented any possibility of blocking entry to the Mount. The Muslim Council faced a severe dilemma: if they moved their ticket inspection points to the mosque entrances, they would be giving up their control of the Temple Mount courtyard. But if they left the inspection points at the gates, everybody would enter by way of the Mugrabi Gate and they would lose an important source of income. Arrangements were eventually made whereby those entering by the western gates would pay their entry fees at the gates, while those entering by way of the Mugrabi Gate, without payment, would pay at the entrances to the mosques.

Except for the change in control of the Mugrabi Gate, no change was made in the arrangements in force on the Temple Mount and its approaches. When the *waqf* management made alterations in entry arrangements, by closing most of the gates and directing visitors to a single entrance, the authorities also did not interfere. But there are two sides to every coin. The Muslims' jealous preservation of total independence, and their refusal to involve the authorities in arrangements to protect the Temple Mount, resulted in the creation of conditions that later permitted the al-Aqsa Mosque to be set on fire.

There was still the element of the Jewish Orthodox and nationalist circles to be dealt with, who maintained their attempts to hold public prayers on the Temple Mount; the theological debate as to the sanctified area of the Mount also continued. The Chief Rabbinate adhered to its view that, due to the sanctity of the area, practising Jews are forbidden entry to the entire Temple Mount, lest they inadvertently enter the place where the original Holy of Holies had stood (today it was no longer possible to pinpoint the spot). This unambiguous ruling was challenged by a different view that did not deny the sanctity of the Temple site, but held that it was possible to pinpoint the Holy of Holies in the center of the Rock of Foundation,

292

on which the Dome of the Rock was built. From this starting point, the different sections of the Temple Mount were measured out, and it was found that extensive sections could be entered after purification rites, while a 109-yard-long section, in the southern part of the Temple Mount courtyard, was outside the Temple Mount area, as laid down by the religious law, and might therefore be entered. Those who adhered to this view also presented historical testimony that, during the 10th and 11th centuries, and possibly at other times, too, there were synagogues in this section of the Temple Mount courtyard. Supporters of both viewpoints agreed that the Temple could not be rebuilt in the present generation nor could sacrifices be offered, since these events could only occur when the Messiah came.

The overwhelming majority of religious Jews accepted the view of the Chief Rabbinate as a binding ruling. But extremist circles, basically nationalist rather than religious, adopted the more permissive view and tried, on a number of occasions, to hold public prayers on the Temple Mount. In their view, prayer services on the Temple Mount were the most practical and clearly stressed defense of Jewish rights and ownership of this spot. The Government did not take any position with regard to the theological dispute. The Minister of Religious Affairs informed the Knesset that "There is nothing in the law which forbids a *minyan* [a gathering of ten Jews] from visiting the Temple Mount and praying there." However, he added that the implementation of this right depended on the maintainance of public order, and this was within the jurisdiction of the Minister of Police. The reply of the Minister of Police stated: "The men in charge of the guardpost on the Temple Mount have been given clear instructions not to permit Jews to pray in the Temple Mount courtyard, in order to prevent clashes and disturbance of public order." This statement was made with the authority of the entire Government.

During 1967 and 1968, a considerable number of attempts were made to hold public prayers on the Temple Mount, especially during the Pilgrimage Festivals (Shavuot, Sukkot and Passover). In each case, the police intervened and expelled the worshippers; at times using force. In April 1969, 13 people applied to the High Court of Justice for an *order nisi* against the Minister of Police

> to give cause why [he] should not insure that suitable protection
> be given by the Israeli police, in order to prevent the applicants'
> prayers from being disturbed . . . and to show reason why instruc-

tions should not be given to Israel Police personnel to refrain from interfering in the applicants' prayers. . . .

Because of its importance, the case was heard by five High Court judges. Answering the petition for the Minister of Police, the Attorney-General stated:

The sanctity of the Temple Mount to the people of Israel, with all its implications, is not under discussion . . . it does not depend on the Government, and its place is beyond all discussion, whether legal or otherwise; the Temple Mount is within the sovereign territory of the State of Israel and there is no one who disagrees with their national and historical right to pray on the Temple Mount . . . but it cannot be ignored that since the emergence of Islam over 1,300 years ago, the Muslims have regarded the Temple Mount, or parts of it, as places which are consecrated for them too . . . the legislature wished to treat all religions equally and to ensure the safekeeping of the Holy Places of each religion . . . each religion has different rules and customs with regard to respectful behavior, as well as conditions of entry and regulations. . . . It is not easy to satisfy all obligations, to ensure freedom of access to the followers of one religion, and to respect and avoid hurting the feelings of the followers of another religion.

Because of these complications, he continued, the Holy Places had always been "a subject for political and governmental settlements that were not enforced by the courts." Appropriate solutions were to be found in political decisions by the executive branch, not by juridical authorities. The Government insisted that the King's Order in Council (1924), concerning the Holy Places, was still valid and, therefore, the problem was not within the bounds of jurisdiction of the courts. Furthermore, "the applicants are trying to impose a course of action on the State in the political and governmental sphere," but the right for which they were demanding justice was only one part of a whole complex of questions facing the executive branch, and the Government's responsibility, which induced it to determine its policy, was preferable to "the particular aspirations of the applicants."

The High Court of Justice rejected the application in October 1970, and cancelled the *order nisi.* The judges gave differing reasons for their decision. The majority accepted the State Attorney's contention that the King's Order in Council (1924) was in force in Israel, and that the matter was not, therefore, within the jurisdiction of the court. Those who denied the validity of the King's Order rejected the application because implementation of the applicants' rights was likely to cause a severe disturbance of public order, or, as the decision stated:

> *It would be foolish not to take into account what it would cost, in manpower, to fulfill the applicants' request, and what would be the implications of such a task.... Such an accounting cannot be made without considering our overall political and defense situation, and it is the Government's business to consider its steps in this light.*

Even after this verdict, there were continued attempts to hold demonstrative prayer meetings, and the police continued to remove demonstrators from the Mount. Members of the Muslim Council would protest these attempts, and the Arab States' propaganda organs used these incidents as a means of incitement against Israel and as "proof of Israeli intentions to rebuild the Temple."

The matter became marginal, arousing no response, until, on the eighth anniversary of the capture of Jerusalem, a small group of Jews held a prayer service on the Temple Mount. They were forcefully evicted by the police. The incident would have ended as had those before it, had it not been for the police decision to bring the worshippers to court, on a charge of disturbing the peace. After a trial in the Magistrate's Court, the judge acquitted the defendants and, in handing down her decision, in 1976, admonished the Ministry of Religious Affairs for not establishing regulations which would allow Jewish prayer on the Temple Mount. The ruling shocked both the Israeli authorities responsible for the Temple Mount, and, of course, the Arab populace. The Attorney General announced that he would appeal the decision and the comments made therein, because they contradicted the High Court decision. It was also explained to the Muslim establishment that there was no intention of changing the *status quo* denying Jewish prayer on the Temple Mount. But that was not enough to calm the Arab public. For weeks there were daily demonstrations and strikes, which reached a peak when the police were forced to besiege hundreds of demonstrators who had assembled in the Dome of the Rock. The Muslim establishment tried to restore calm, but the excuse was too good for Arab extremists not to make use of it.

The decision on the Government's appeal, which was handed down in the summer of 1976, did not end the legal problem. Although the District Court overruled the Magistrate's Court and found the defendants guilty, it also stated that this decision was conditioned on a ruling by the responsible authority (in this case the Minister for Religious Affairs) that the Court did indeed have jurisdiction in the matter. The Court based this statement on the possibility that the 1924 King's Order in Council could also affect this case, thus removing it from the Court's jurisdiction and leaving the matter solely within the jurisdiction of the Government. Thus the legal fight of those who sought to pray on the Temple Mount again ended in failure and the Government remained steadfast in its refusal to allow organized Jewish prayer on the Mount because it feared a "disturbance of public order."

Despite the pressures and provocations, the Defense Minister's decision of June 17, 1967, had been adopted and maintained by the Israel Government. The Temple Mount, except for one gate, remained in Muslim possession. Jewish and Arab police, under the orders of a Jewish Government with deep national and religious links, prohibited Jews from trying to hold prayer meetings on the Mount. The opinions and deeds of extremists did not succeed in igniting a serious inter-religious war. On the contrary, the Government's consistency in upholding its decision on such an emotionally charged matter was an important indication of the possibility of peaceful coexistence between the two peoples.

The Muslim Council, that appointed itself at the end of July 1967, was never officially recognized by Israel, nor did it ask for such recognition. All negotiations with it were unofficial. And because it was not recognized, the *shari'a* courts in East Jerusalem operated without legal status, and their verdicts could not be enforced by Israeli bailiffs. In this respect, they resembled the courts of voluntary associations, whose verdicts can only be executed by agreement between the litigants. The courts' documents were also not recognized by Israel; for example, the Interior Ministry did not recognize marriage certificates issued by the East Jerusalem *qadis*.

In August 1968, there was an interesting court case arising from this situation. An inhabitant of East Jerusalem, who wished to be released from his sister's guardianship, applied to the *shari'a* court in Jaffa for its verdict. The Jaffa court, made up of Israeli *qadis*, and acting under Israeli Law, decided that the application was within its jurisdiction, since Israeli Law placed Jerusalem within its area of jurisdiction, while the religious court in East Jerusalem had no status by Israeli Law. The Israeli bodies in charge of contacts with the Muslim Council did not know of this application, even though the Ministry of Religious Affairs knew of and encouraged it.

The Muslim Council regarded the verdict of the Jaffa court as a deliberate change in Israel's attitude, which had until then ignored the Jerusalem court. It issued a sharp statement to the effect that the intervention of the Jaffa court was unlawful, since it was not in accordance with the laws of the *shari'a*; that the verdict was issued by a judge who was not empowered to try Muslims, as he was enforcing laws which contradicted the Quran and had sworn allegiance to a non-Muslim President. Furthermore, the Jaffa court's jurisdiction was based on unlawful annexation. The reaction of the Israeli authorities was typical: they ignored the memorandum and by-passed the incident.

In the course of time, arranging legal matters by way of unofficial procedure gradually struck root. For example, the Israeli Registrar of Muslim Marriages in Jerusalem would add his seal to marriage documents issued by the *qadi* of East Jerusalem, not because he recognized the *qadi*'s juridical authority according to Israeli Law, but because he recognized his *religious* authority. Other acts of the East Jerusalem *shari'a* court were also confirmed by the Jaffa court, which accepted the religious authority of the Jerusalem *qadi*.

Over the years a few attempts have been made to find a judicial-political solution to the problem of the status of the Muslim Council and particularly to the status of the Muslim judicial system. One suggestion was that legal endorsement in Israeli Law be given to the Muslim Council and the authority which it was exercizing *de facto*. Similarly, it was suggested that official endorsement be given to the Muslim courts and legal decisions. Another proposal was that the religious law practised in Jordan be applied to Muslim residents of Jerusalem. These suggestions seemed to answer the problem, as they guaranteed basic Muslim interests and full religious independence on the one hand, while protecting Israeli sovereignty on the other. But the Israelis couldn't reach a final decision on those matters because of fears that such an arrangement would bring about a strengthened, established Arab leadership which could present a political threat to

297

Israel. The Muslims were also undecided, but finally announced that they could not accept an arrangement, no matter how favorable, which implied recognition of Israel's sovereignty over Jerusalem.

"Mutual non-recognition" extended, of course, to the sphere of the *waqf* and the financial affairs of the Muslim Council. The Israelis did not intervene, but neither did they pay the salaries of the *qadis* and other *waqf* officials. In the middle of 1968, the *waqf* faced a severe financial crisis. Income from entrance fees to the Temple Mount, which had been enormous during the mass visits, now decreased. The many tenants of the *waqf's* extensive property stopped paying rent, claiming that the Israeli occupation had caused their financial state to deteriorate. As the Muslim Council did not want to apply to the Israeli courts, it had no way of forcing its tenants to keep to the rental agreements that they had signed.

At the request of the *waqf,* the Jordanian authorities began to take retaliatory action against the recalcitrant tenants when they visited the East Bank, as a result of which income from rent increased. Complaints began to be heard that the *waqf* was transferring its surplus income to Amman, since the Jordan Government insisted that the sums it had paid in previous years were loans that had to be refunded. The head of the *waqf* was obliged to deny these complaints in a press conference, stressing that the *waqf* was still receiving "thousands of dinars" from the Jordan Government to cover its budget deficits. These would continue to grow because of the extensive development program the *waqf* was planning.

All of the above dealt with Muslim Council activities with regard to *waqf* affairs, the courts, and the Holy Places. But the Council did not restrict its activities to these spheres and engaged in outright political activity. Its intention could be gauged from the memorandum it presented upon its formation. Its members included secular leaders, both moderates and extremists. Some of them were also members of the National Guidance Committee which, in various guises and with a changing membership, lead the disobedience and resistance movement. This intermingling of extremist political activity and leadership in religious affairs was especially prominent while Sheikh Abd al-Hamid al-Sayah was in office. From the time of the city's conquest, Sheikh al-Sayah took an extreme and aggressive position, stemming both from his views and his obstinate and irritable character. Under his leaderhips, the more extremist members of the Council set the tone, and they were behind some of the strikes and acts of disobedience in August and September 1967. On September 24, 1967, Sheikh al-Sayah was deported to Jordan, where he was appointed *Waqf* Minister.

He was replaced as chief *qadi* by Sheikh Hilmi al-Muhtasib. The new Chairman of the Council, with his tranquil nature, did not express extreme views and even moderated the activities of the extremists. The banishment from Jerusalem of four extremist leaders led to a marked decline in the Muslim Council's participation in public acts of disobedience, but it continued to express its views in writing.

The Council's way of reacting to Israeli acts was to send memoranda to the Prime Minister. The memoranda remained unanswered. Although the Muslim Council knew that the failure to respond stemmed from the tacit mutual non-recognition agreement, it took advantage of this fact in its complaints to foreign journalists. By the end of 1971, over 100 memoranda on various subjects had accumulated in the files of the Prime Minister's Office. Council members saw to it that the memoranda were distributed to the foreign consuls in East Jerusalem.

In mid-November 1968, the Council decided that, since its complaints were being ignored, it would hold a general meeting of all the religious and secular leaders to protest against the occupation, the land expropriations, the excavations at the Western Wall, the general climate of immorality, and the desecration of the Holy Places. The extremist members demanded that the convention be called without asking the permission of the authorities, but Sheikh Hilmi insisted on applying for permission. At the end of January 1969, the heads of the Council were warned not to carry out their plan. Similar warnings were issued to the religious leaders of the West Bank, and despite the extremists' demands to hold the convention, Sheikh Hilmi decided to cancel it.

As the acts of terror subsided and political tension lessened, the Council gave up dealing with political matters, and accepted the view of Sheikh Hilmi that its very existence was an achievement, since it served as the religious and national leadership of the West Bank Palestinians. Admittedly, the Israel Government did not recognize it, but neither did it hamper the Council's activities. If the Council were to turn into an openly hostile body, the Government would undoubtedly take reataliatory action and disperse it, which would only be detrimental to the Arabs. The Council, therefore, continued its routine activities, and it appeared that the period of confrontation and friction had passed forever. But in the summer of 1969 one of the most tragic events of the postwar period occurred, and relations were disrupted again.

At about seven in the morning of Thursday, August 21, 1969, a mentally disturbed Australian tourist, named Dennis Michael Rohan, took advantage of the changing of the Mosque guards to enter the al-Aqsa Mosque, which was then deserted. He lit some inflammable material soaked in kerosene and petrol, threw it into the Mosque, and fled from the Temple Mount courtyard. The Mosque guards saw him run away and were subsequently able to describe him. The fire was small at first, but it was not extinguished because the Mosque guards did not know how to operate the fire-extinguishers. When the fire brigade arrived in response to the *waqf* guards' call, the flames had already enveloped the whole of the pulpit and were beginning to spread to the thick wooden beams supporting the southern ceiling.

News of the fire spread swiftly. When the radio announced the incident, hundreds of shocked and weeping Arabs assembled in the Mosque, together with several dozen Jews who had rushed there in the line of their duties. Hysterical men and women began to roll up the magnificent rugs and clear the enormous building of all moveable objects. They hampered the firemen at their work, snatching the hoses out of their hands, climbing the hydraulic ladders, and finally breaking the nearest hydrant in their efforts to bring water. Meanwhile, the fire was eating into the pulpit and the wooden ceiling above. The firemen were performing their duty faithfully and efficiently, but the agitated crowd swore and cursed at them, accusing them of spraying petrol on the fire and of being deliberately slow in extinguishing it. Words soon gave way to acts of violence. The police, who were present in force, tried to calm the crowd and refrained from using force, which, in the atmosphere of mass hysteria, would have led to bloodshed.

Two groups stood on the steps leading into the Mosque: one included the chief *qadi*, the head of the *waqf* and other Muslim personalities; the other consisted of Israelis. When the Muslims were asked to calm their people, one answered: "Why? In any case you're going to burn the whole Mosque. Tell your firemen that they're working too fast! " Boys who had salvaged part of the inscription over the pulpit now raised it and marched off in demonstration, chanting "Nasser, Nasser! " East Jerusalem traders closed their shops.

The Israel Government issued a statement expressing its shock and distress at the fire and announcing the establishment of a commission of inquiry. At the same time, another announcement imposed a curfew on East Jerusalem. Hysteria was at such a high pitch that there was a fear of inter-communal rioting.

By mid-day the fire had been totally extinguished, and by the afternoon the police had traced the culprit with the aid of an "identikit" prepared from the testimonies of the *waqf* guards. Although his identity was known to the police, this fact was not reported to the Government. In their ignorance, a number of Ministers continued to venture guesses as to the causes of the fire, including the possibility of a short-circuit or the spontaneous ignition of chemicals. One of the Ministers went so far as to claim (an hour after the deranged Australian had signed a confession), that "it is not out of the question that the Mosque was [deliberately] set on fire, and this may have been done by an Arab provocateur."

The Government and its agencies were shocked by the incident: Israel's credibility, as well as her ability to safeguard the Holy Places, had been placed in doubt. Their confusion was reflected in ill-considered propaganda statements.

The news caused a sensation all over the world. The Arab States fanned the flames of hatred, their incitement reaching unprecedented dimensions: "The Jews burned the al-Aqsa Mosque so as to fulfil their ambition of building the Third Temple at long last." The Jerusalem Muslim Council called a press conference at which it declared, on the strength of the guards' testimonies, that the fire was not caused by a short-circuit, as the Israeli firemen had originally stated, but by deliberate arson. They also accused the Israeli firemen of being deliberately slow in extinguishing the fire and of cutting off the water supply.

The inhabitants of East Jerusalem continued to stay at home even after the curfew was removed. There were demonstrations and clashes with the police on Friday, August 22, and on the following day. The news of Rohan's arrest and his confession, broadcast on Friday night, did not convince the Arabs of East Jerusalem, who believed that the Jews had burned the Mosque on purpose. No evidence could disabuse them of this belief.

The fire at the al-Aqsa Mosque was a profound misfortune. Not only did it damage the third most important mosque in the Muslim world, but it destroyed one of the most famous objects in Muslim history, a memento of one of the Arabs' most important victories. The pulpit which went up in flames on August 21, 1969, had been placed in the Mosque on October 9, 1187, when the Sultan Salah al-Din (Saladin) offered his prayers on the first Friday after Jerusalem's capture from the Crusaders. On a political level, the consequences were equally grave, for the fire "confirmed" the Arabs' long-held suspicions and fears of Jewish intentions to demolish the mosques and rebuild the Temple in their place. These irrational fears could not be dispelled rationally or by clear evidence. Moreover, feelings of frustration, degradation, hatred, and fear towards Israeli rule, which had been covered up for two years by a thin shell of peaceful coexistence, now burst forth. The Arabs sensed that the al-Aqsa incident was a good excuse for them to express their inner feelings in public, without the Israelis daring to retaliate. The Israelis let the Arabs strike and demonstrate, but they were shocked at the extent of the hatred and suspicion. Most of them had tried to believe that the two years since the city's reunification had altered the Arabs' attitudes and that they now accepted unification. Disappointment and anger among the Jews led to sharply anti-Arab expressions. Once again it had been proved that peaceful coexistence could reign only when conditions were normal and peaceful. A drastic incident of a national or a religious nature was capable of disrupting relations, turning the clock back, and showing both peoples how far they were from normal relationships.

The al-Aqsa fire might have been prevented if the *waqf* officials had agreed to cooperate with the Israeli authorities on protecting the Temple Mount and fire prevention there. But they had rejected every proposal for such cooperation, regarding it as the undesired intervention of an occupying power. Israel did not impose the security arrangements for fear of appearing to intervene in Temple Mount affairs for political reasons. Both sides learned their lesson from the incident. The gates of the Temple Mount were closed to visitors for months, and, when they were reopened, a police force of 40 men was stationed there, under the command of an Arab officer who cooperated fully with the *waqf* guards, whose number had also been increased.

Some time after the fire, collections were begun for a fund to restore the Mosque. The Arab States donated large sums. The restoration work took six years and was done by local artisans. With the completion of the work, the Mosque was even more impressive than it had been before the fire.

When tension caused by the fire died down, the Muslim Council's activities continued as though nothing had happened. The Council went on sending memoranda that remained unanswered, maintaining the religious courts, and supervising the *waqf* department. At the beginning of 1972, the Council sent its hundredth memorandum to the Prime Minister. To their great surprise, there was a reply. The Deputy Prime Minister invited them for a talk, visited the Council's offices, and even sent them a written answer. At first, the Arabs thought that there had been a basic change in the Government's attitude, but they soon discovered that the unusual incident had nothing to do with any change in policy, but stemmed from considerations of prestige, and from an internal Israeli political and personal conflict. Differences of opinion between the Muslim Council and the Israel Government, on matters of principle, remained unchanged.

The relationship between Israeli authorities and the Muslim political establishment is perhaps the most important, and without doubt the most complicated, of the practical problems that arose out of the reunification of Jerusalem. The attempt to dictate procedures, aimed at making the Muslim community disintegrate and lose its independence, failed. Politically farsighted Israeli bodies brought about a change of policy in order to create a reasonable *modus vivendi* on the delicate subjects of religion and the Holy Places. The Muslim community continued to maintain its organizational independence on matters of principle, as well as its undisturbed possession of its Holy Places. On juridical matters with basic political implications, there was no room for compromise, but the line that was adopted, postponed confrontation and kept up a prolonged dialogue, without exercising or imposing legal authority. Israeli fears that this *de facto* communal independence would serve to fan disobedience and terror were proved unfounded, once action had been taken to neutralize extremist elements who wanted to take advantage of this

303

independence for their own purposes. The Muslim community learned that the Israel Government did not intend to deprive them of their Holy Places; nor did it aim to cause their disintegration or degradation. The *modus vivendi* achieved was one of the positive components of coexistence in the city.

CHAPTER NINETEEN

THE WESTERN WALL
AND THE JEWISH QUARTER

If the Temple Mount, as we have seen, is a site sacred to both Jews and Muslims, the Western Wall and the Jewish Quarter of the Old City are of religious and emotional significance to the Jews alone. When the staff of the Israel Army Rabbinate loaded the command-car in which they were to follow the paratroopers to the Western Wall, they took along a Torah scroll, a *shofar,* and a bench. On reaching the Wall area, their first acts were to place the bench, to hold up the Torah, and to blow the *shofar.* The Jews had been forbidden to do any of these things by the King's Order in Council of 1931. Performing them symbolized the return of the Jews to the Wall, after 223 months; but more than that, it was a sign that their dream of worshipping without harassment at their most sacred place would be realized for the first time since the Bar-Kochba revolt was crushed in 135 A.D.

The moment the Wall was captured, the Minister of Defense gave the order to clear a route by which "every Jew in the world can get there," insisting that the Military Government have it ready within 48 hours. The route chosen began at the top of Mount Zion (at the end of the "Pope's Road" which was paved in 1964), crossed no-man's-land on the slopes of the hill and joined with an existing roadway, leading from Dung Gate to the Church of St. Peter. Israel and Jordan had both laid mines along this route and the mines had not been charted, so the Israel Army Engineers' Corps began mine-clearing operations.

The real problem faced by the Military Government, however, was to create a place at the Wall where the tens of thousands of expected pilgrims could congregate. Many people lay claim to having been the first to propose the demolition of the Mugrabi Quarter, adjoining the Wall, and, indeed, the idea seems to have been put forward by several people simultaneously. After all, there was nothing new in the plan. Ever since the end of the 19th century, several attempts had been made to get rid of the Quarter, but without success. Now the scheme received the approval of the Minister of Defense and was conveyed to Mayor Teddy Kollek, who volunteered to plan and execute it. He summoned an archeologist, an architect and a specialist on the preservation of historic sites, and they instantly prepared the clearance plan on a scrap of paper. According to this plan, the houses between the Wall square and the alleyway which bisected the Mugrabi Quarter were to be demolished and removed.

On Saturday night, June 10, the families occupying the houses in the Quarter were informed that they would have to evacuate the buildings within three hours. Only a few managed to take all their possessions with them. Bulldozers, that had assembled at the approaches to the area, began to topple the one- and two-storey houses by floodlight. By morning a space of more than one acre had been cleared in front of the Wall, as compared to the 120 square meters previously open. In the morning, it turned out that the bulldozer operators had also mistakenly demolished some houses not originally scheduled for removal. It was then decided to demolish the entire Mugrabi Quarter. Its inhabitants (108 families, comprising 619 persons) found temporary shelter with relatives, in empty school buildings, or in abandoned ruins in the Old City.

Clouds of dust swirled in the Wall area, which was now growing larger by the hour. On every side, the ruined buildings of the Mugrabi Quarter were visible. A journalist reported: "A bulldozer knocked over the last of the houses. Beds and bedding stuck out of the pile of rubble, as did pieces of furniture, kitchen utensils, food and shoes." People who came to see the Wall were stunned. One visitor reported:

> On the right, the Wall was revealed. Its gigantic stones seemed to have shrunk, their size diminished, and in that first moment it seemed as if they were fusing with the stones of one of the houses to the left ... joy gave place to disappointment. The Wall now appeared bigger, higher, of a primeval majesty; but it no longer

permitted the psychic affinity and the feeling that whoever comes here is, as it were, alone with his Maker.

Later, severe criticism was expressed over the demolition of the Mugrabi houses. Foreigners complained of inhabitants being turned out of their houses, while local critics attacked the "frightening disorder" when "enthusiastic amateurs, army rabbis, publicity-hungry politicians, archeologists, contractors, and army officers continue to engage in the replanning of the Old City." Criticism was so severe that at first no one was prepared to accept responsibility for the deed. It was only considerably later that the argument began to determine whose initiative it had really been.

Despite the justified criticism of the hurried expulsion of the Quarter's inhabitants without providing alternative housing, and of the total and uncontrolled alteration in the Wall's historic dimensions, the act itself was seemingly inevitable. The Wall area, too cramped even to contain thousands of worshippers in Mandatory times, could not hold the hundreds of thousands who wished to come in 1967. Not clearing the area would have meant shutting the Wall off from those who were straining to approach it. Beyond the overwhelming practical considerations, however, an irrational impulse was at work. The move was the settling of an historic account with those who had harassed the Jewish people over the centuries, restricting and humiliating it at its holiest place, as well as with those who had prevented access to the Wall for 19 years. The displaced inhabitants of the Mugrabi Quarter were not personally to blame, but it was their fate to be additional victims of the Arab—Israel conflict.

When the mines had been cleared, the Municipality completed the paving of the new access road, and on Shavuot (the Jewish Pentecost), June 14, 1967, the Wall was declared open. That day Jerusalem witnessed a sight such as the city had not known since the pilgrimages in the days of the Second Temple during the 1st century A.D. By noon, 130,000 people had visited the Wall, and, by nightfall, the number had reached a quarter-of-a-million. By Saturday, June 17, the number of visitors had totalled over 400,000.

Throughout the period of the Military Government, the Military Rabbinate was responsible for arrangements at the Wall. Following the Prime Minister's declaration that arrangements by the Western Wall would be determined by the Israeli Chief Rabbinate, a five-man commission was appointed to assume responsibility for the Wall.

Almost immediately, a sharp public controversy erupted over the procedures to be initiated at the Wall, the planning and use of the space that had been cleared in front of it, and the body to be responsible for it.

One of the first actions of the Ministry of Religious Affairs was the erection of barriers along and across the approaches to the Wall, to divide the secular from the sanctified sections. The fenced-in area was also divided into two, with the southern section being allocated to males, while the northern part, which was smaller, to women (the sections were later changed around). Stewards were placed at the openings to separate men and women and refuse entry to anyone without a head covering.

These procedures provoked indignation and fury among the visitors, most of whom were not religious and asked the following pertinent questions:

Who decided that the Western Wall has a purely religious character? Was it not a national historic relic? Was the Wall solely a place to express religious feelings? If the Chief Rabbinate insisted that worship at the Wall conform to the customs of an Orthodox synagogue, why should not one part of the Wall be set aside for that, while the rest would be open to the public without such restrictions as head covering or the separation of the sexes?

The question as to whether the Wall was an historic site or solely a Holy Place occupied public attention for some time. The reply of the Ministry of Religious Affairs was that "the Wall could not be called an historic site, since it was sanctified as a remnant of the Temple, 2,000 years ago, before it became an historic site." Because it was a Holy Place, it came under the Law for the Protection of Holy Sites, and therefore only the Chief Rabbis were empowered to decide on the procedures in force there. "No one will tell the Rabbinate what arrangements to make at the Western Wall, in the same way that no outside body would tell Christian clergymen what to do in their houses of worship." The procedures introduced were in accordance with *halacha* (Jewish religious law), and they required the separation of men and women during prayers. There was no possibility of setting aside part of the Wall for prayer, since the whole Wall was sacred.

The question of the bounds of the sanctity of the Western Wall was to become the subject of a severe controversy some time later, since several of the heads of the Chief Rabbinate believed that the Wall was sacred not only at the traditional place of worship, but along the whole of its length, from the northwest corner of the Temple Mount wall, near the Via Dolorosa, as far as its southwest corner. Chief Rabbi Nissim held that even the approaches to the Wall were holy, and that there would be no differentiation between "worshippers" and "visitors." He also insisted that all of the Temple Mount walls, including the southern and eastern walls, were of the same degree of sanctity as the Western Wall. While being authorized to decide on arrangements at Jewish Holy Places, the Chief Rabbinate was not empowered by law to decide the bounds of the Holy Place, or even to decide what was a "holy" or a "sanctified" place where the Law of Holy Places applied. Such a decision was in the hands of the Government, but it refrained from a clear-cut resolution of the question.

At the very beginning of the public controversy over the arrangements made by the Ministry of Religious Affairs, the Government was asked to intervene. In a radio interview, Prime Minister Levi Eshkol was asked his opinion on these arrangements. He replied: "I have heard from religious people ... that there is no need for them. It isn't a synagogue. I think there is something offensive about it." He used the expression "artificial" to define the partitions and declared that the matter would be brought before a body empowered to take a decision. Among those "religious persons" who publicly expressed the opinion that it was possible to set aside a specific area where the sexes would be separated, were the Deputy Minister of Religious Affairs and the Director-General of the Ministry. The Prime Minister's comments provoked a storm among religious circles, and the question became a party issue. The heads of the National Religious Party convened and voiced their protest against "the attempt to take guardianship of the Jewish Holy Places out of the hands of religious bodies, and the attempts to bypass the Chief Rabbinate."

From the very first, the question of the arrangements at the Wall was bound up with the practical problem of responsibility for designing the Wall's approaches and for carrying out construction work there. Just before the Military Government in Jerusalem ended, the Minister of Defense delegated the National Parks Authority to take charge of the maintenance and construction of historic sites in the occupied areas, including Jerusalem. In the opinion of the Parks Authority, this gave it control of the Western Wall. When responsibility was officially transferred to the Ministry of Religious Affairs, the latter maintained that it was responsible not only for the enactment of regulations governing visits and worship, in accordance with the instructions of the Chief Rabbinate, but also for designing and planning the area and for carrying out reconstruction and restoration work. The Director of the National Parks Authority, on the other hand, demanded that the Wall be put under his charge, guaranteeing that all work would be carried out according to the instructions of the Chief Rabbinate, either through the Ministry of Religious Affairs or directly.

This demand had the support of a majority of non-religious people and gained force as a result of the Ministry's inability to master the situation at the Wall. In the middle of July, a month-and-a-half after the demolition of the Mugrabi Quarter, all the approaches to the Wall were full of garbage and rubble from demolished buildings. A visitor described the situation on July 26, 1967:

It is hard to feel God's presence pervading the place. The whole place looks like a picnic site. Dust and dirt soil clothes and body. Three small Holy Arks donated by the Military Rabbinate have been placed by the Wall, and they lack any ornamentation or majesty. On a precarious table, which threatens to collapse at any moment, there are prayer shawls, prayer books, and phylacteries piled up in a disorderly manner. The overall picture is wretched and only illustrates the behind-the-scenes struggle between the Ministry of Religious Affairs and the National Parks Authority.

In their defense, Ministry officials claimed — justifiably — that they were not responsible for the unplanned demolition of the Mugrabi Quarter and published an advertisement requesting "the public's forgiveness for the suffering caused by the dust and the obstacles." In fact, the demolition of the Mugrabi Quarter houses, and of the stone-paved alleyways, had left the whole area covered with a fine dust which swirled up at every step. Bulldozers were still clearing ruined buildings, thus adding to the turmoil. The great open space did not have a single shady corner. In the center, there was a sole, shrivelled palm, in whose shade dozens of people sought shelter from the sun.

The National Parks Authority claimed that it could overcome the problems of dust, lack of shade, and absence of water and sanitation within three days, thus forcing the Ministry of Religious Affairs to face its dilemma. It had no operational staff, and could only carry out this sort of work by means of the Public Works Department, which demanded detailed plans in advance. On the other hand, it refused to relinquish its responsibility to the Parks Authority. Criticism of the Ministry, however, gave way to derision when the spokesman announced that the Ministry was about to invest IL 5 million in improvements for the Wall's approaches and issue an international bid for planning the layout of the area.

At the beginning of August, the matter was brought to the Cabinet for decision. By then, several problems had accumulated. The members of the National Religious Party saw the complaints as a plot to deprive them of their influence in matters of the greatest importance to them. The fundamental debate over planning the form of the Wall, and over the way that religious and non-religious people were to express their attachment to the Wall, therefore generated into a political squabble within the coalition Government. The majority of the Cabinet had no desire to provoke a crisis over the Wall, so the Government decided to leave its care in the hands of the Ministry. At the same time, it established a Ministerial Committee for the Holy Places, comprising no less than nine members, and headed by the Minister of Religious Affairs.

The public controversy over who was to be held responsible for developments at the Wall died down without being settled, but the debate over arrangements and procedures and over planning its approaches raged on. At the end of July, the Minister of Religious Affairs, after due consultations with the Chief Rabbinate, had issued regulations in accordance with the Law of Holy Places ("the Wall Regulations"), by means of which the Minister of Religious Affairs hoped to give legal force to the arrangements that had been made at the Wall. The Minister proposed establishing a Wall guard, empowered by the regulations to lay down procedures for worship, including the separation of the sexes. The regulations would forbid desecration of the Sabbath, eating and drinking, meetings, the absence of head covering for men, immodest clothing, placing objects at the foot of the Wall, begging, or the sale of souvenirs. According to the law, the Minister of Religious Affairs needed the agreement of the Justice Minister before publishing the regulations; but the

Justice Minister refused to sign because the regulations were, in his opinion, too far-reaching and there was no definition of the precise area where they were to be in force. The Minister of Religious Affairs did not bring the dispute to the Cabinet. The arrangements that had been made at the Wall were therefore maintained without official sanction. In the Cabinet, it was the Minister of Tourism, Moshe Kol, who campaigned vigorously against the religious regulations; but, in the existing coalition, there was little hope that the arrangements could be changed.

The Ministry of Religious Affairs tried to improve the appearance of the Wall approaches by spreading hygroscopic liquid from the Dead Sea on the dust. When it had soaked up sufficient water, the dust stopped swirling, but the approaches to the Wall turned into gray, muddy, unattractive areas. Gradually a plan for the Wall was worked out. On August 16, 1967, it was decided to dig down to a depth of two-and-a-half meters along a 25-meter strip at the foot of the Wall. The purpose of this excavation was to uncover two more layers of the Wall's stones, and to separate the area set aside for worship from the part open to visitors. This separation would, it was hoped, satisfy everyone, since anyone wanting to look at the Wall from above, could do so without putting on a hat or being separated from his or her partner.

A month passed between the adoption and the implementation of the plan. The Ministry did not consider it necessary to request the approval of the Statutory Planning Committee for the work, and the Committee did not consider it necessary to intervene, even though it knew that work was in progress. It was only when work had ended, on the eve of the Jewish New Year, October 2, that the Committee woke up and decided that the split-level plan did not ensure a sufficient degree of safety, since there was a danger that the pressure of a crowd could cause someone to fall from the upper to the lower level. The Ministry of Religious Affairs hurriedly put up thick red-and-white posts at the edge of the upper level. At the beginning of November, the Planning Committee utterly rejected the split-level plan. It decided by majority vote that it was more desirable to create a gradual slope from west to east. The Committee also urged the Ministry to install sanitary services for the crowds of visitors, but the Ministry declared that it did not intend to withdraw the interim plan. When the crisis was about to erupt,

The border fence dividing the village of Beit Safafa from 1949 to 1967

The single meeting which took place between the Israeli Mayor of Jerusalem, Teddy Kollek (left), the Jordanian Mayor, Rauhi al-Khatib, and the Military Commander of Jerusalem, General Shlomo Lahat, on July 21, 1967 (Photo Ross)

Above: Arabs voting in the 1969 municipal elections (Y. Barzilay)

Left: The aftermath of the Mahaneh Yehudah terrorist explosion (Y. Barzilay)

A protest march of Arab women in 1968

The Palm Sunday procession in 1968 (Zev Radovan)

The Western Wall plaza (above) shortly after the demolition of the Mugrabi Quarter, with the *Mahkamah* building on the left (Hans H. Pinn) and the plaza today (S. Scherf)

An Arab mourning procession on the way to the memorial near the Rockefeller Museum on the first anniversary of the Six Day War (Zev Radovan)

The new Jewish neighborhoods — at left and center are French Hill and Ramat Eshkol; Ramot is in the background, Nebi Samwil is on the horizon, and Shu'afat is on the right (Werner Braun)

French Hill as seen from the Jewish Quarter (Y. Barzilay)

Above: A street in the Old City
Right: The Church of the Holy Sepulcher
(A. Strajmayster)

Following page: Aerial view of the Old
City, with Jaffa Gate and the Citadel in
the foreground, the Temple Mount and
the Western Wall in the center, and the
Mount of Olives in the background
(David Rubinger)

someone suddenly discovered that the decision of the Planning Committee was not legal. Then, after the judicial obstacle had been removed, the Committee was asked not to take any decision before the matter had been discussed by the Ministerial Committee for the Holy Places. It was clear that the coalition mechanism would operate once again. Vigorous efforts were made to find a compromise, which was achieved by the intervention of a number of Ministers. It left the lower level as it was, but reduced the step separating it from the upper level to a height of 60 centimeters, while the upper level would be shaped into a slope as far as this step.

However, the Ministry of Religious Affairs continued to work according to the original plan. Work went on for three months, and only when it was nearing completion did anyone notice that it was not being executed according to plan. The dispute was between the Planning Committee and the Ministry, but now the Chief Rabbinate also intervened. Chief Rabbi Nissim agreed with the Planning Committee, that there was no room for separating the worshippers' level from the visitors' level — not out of considerations of safety or aesthetics but precisely for religious reasons, because he believed that there should be no differentiation between the sacred and the secular. Not only was the whole length of the Wall holy, but so was the clearing before it. Rabbi Nissim sent a letter to the Minister of Religious Affairs, complaining that the Ministry was carrying out work contrary to the decisions of the Chief Rabbinate. There were even threats that the Rabbinate, which was authorized to decide on arrangements at the Wall, would hand over responsibility to the Municipality.

One morning, Rabbi Nissim left his office for the site where work was in progress, and with his own hands removed stones from the terrace. Ministry of Religious Affairs officials alleged that all Rabbi Nissim wanted was to show who was the boss. They described the incident as "a tempest in a tea cup." After a number of arguments, accusations, resignations, discussions, and points of order in the Knesset, a compromise was once again found. Work continued, and, when it was completed, no one cared in the slightest what the height of the terrace was. In the course of the arguments, the Planning Committee's demands for sanitary installations in the Wall area were forgotten. The Ministry did not erect them because of the objections of the Chief Rabbinate, in whose opinion religious precepts forbade

313

the construction of toilets facing the Wall. Because of the opposition of the Religious Laws Committee, no trees were planted in the enormous space, nor were any other arrangements made to provide shade. The Rabbinate contended that according to religious law it had been forbidden to plant trees in the Old City ever since the destruction of the Temple.

Now a new conflict arose. This one concerned archeological excavations at the southwest corner of the Western Wall. Archeologist Benjamin Mazar of the Hebrew University had planned excavations at this corner of the Temple Mount Wall as far back as the summer of 1967, with the intention of uncovering the Wall's foundations, the Herodian layers, and possibly even the remnants of the City of David. At this corner of the Temple Mount Wall, only four of the 19 layers dating from the days of the Second Temple, were visible. In the area where the excavations were planned, surveys had been conducted as far back as the middle of the 19th century. The whole area was empty of buildings. After having obtained the necessary permission, Professor Mazar also asked the Chief Rabbinate for its approval. Here he encountered total opposition. A special Committee for Religious Law decided that "all four walls around the Temple Mount are sanctified and, according to the laws of the Torah, it is forbidden to conduct archeological excavations beside the four Temple Mount Walls." The dispute was taken to the Ministerial Committee for the Holy Places. Rabbi Nissim sent a memorandum to the Committee, detailing his objections:

> The excavations may go on for many years. In addition, should ancient buildings be found, this will preclude worship. We are in charge of protecting the place from desecration. We must make sure that no deed will in any way impair its sanctity, for praying at the Wall is the main thing, and everything else is incidental.

Rabbi Nissim repeated his demand that the whole length of the Western Wall be cleared of all the buildings adjacent to it and that it be made available for worship.

In March 1968, the dispute reached its peak. The matter was about to be discussed in the Ministerial Committee for the Holy Places when, without waiting for its decision and without warning, Professor Mazar began excavations at the Southern Wall. On March 6, the Ministerial Committee convened. During the discussion, it transpired that there were differences of opinion between the two

314

Chief Rabbis. Chief Rabbi Nissim stood firmly by his opinion that all of the Temple Mount Walls were of the same degree of sanctity, while Chief Rabbi Unterman held that only the Western Wall was sacred. At the same time, Rabbi Unterman confirmed Rabbi Nissim's demand that the whole length of the Western Wall be uncovered. Faced with these disagreements, the Ministerial Committee suggested a compromise formula by which excavations would take place only at the Southern Wall and be defined as "uncovering the Wall," not as "archeological excavations." All sides were prepared to accept this proposal; but then the archeologists began to dig at the Western Wall too, starting at the southwest corner and working north as far as the remains of Robinson's Arch.

At first, only a narrow trench was dug, at the foot of the Temple Mount Wall, but gradually the excavated area was extended until it included the entire section from the group of Arab buildings near the Mugrabi Gate, to the Dung Gate. The whole section was enclosed and entry was forbidden except on guided tours. The archeologists wanted to limit visits as far as possible, because they feared the visitors would disturb excavations. Tension still existed between the Chief Rabbinate and the archeologists; but even though the area under excavation extended to the Western Wall section, there were no further clashes. It transpired, however, that Rabbi Nissim's fears were justified. A section of the Wall had been removed from the control of the religious bodies. A new situation had been created. The part facing the traditional place of worship remained in the charge of the Ministry of Religious Affairs and became a Holy Place, maintained in the traditions of an Orthodox Synagogue. The parts south of the Mugrabi Gate remained in the hands of a secular body and became a historic site, where archeological excavations were carried out. To the west of the two sections — the religious and the secular — there was a neutral area, the space created by the demolition of the Mugrabi Quarter. The two sections were divided by a "no-man's-land" of about 20 apartments, which remained in the possession of Arab inhabitants, as well as a rampart of earth leading to the Mugrabi Gate. Within a year of the Western Wall's capture, the debate about whether the Wall was a Holy Place or a historic site had been settled empirically, without a formal decision: it was both. While the dispute would be renewed every now and then, coexistence between the religious and the secular bodies was, on the whole,

315

maintained, since neither was interested in interfering with the other.

As was previously noted, the Chief Rabbinate had unanimously demanded that the whole length of the Western Wall be uncovered. As the southern section was in the possession of the archeological expedition, the Ministry of Religious Affairs went north. Here, attached to the Wall, stood the Muslim School, the *Mahkamah,* built by the Mamaluk Emir Tanqiz in the 14th century. It is a massive Mamaluk building, constructed on the top of earlier vaults. In Turkish times, the *Shari'a* Court was housed here, and in Jordanian times the building served the secretariat of the Muslim Committee for Jerusalem. After the 1967 War, the building was deserted; fearing that the Jews would seize the building, the heads of the *waqf* moved a high school into it.

The southern wall of the building which stands at right angles to the Wall, included three arches. Prior to the war, only the tops of the arches protruded above ground level. But following the lowering of the ground level near the Wall, and the demolition of a low stone wall, the arches were revealed in their full height. When the Ministry of Religious Affairs presented its plan for the Wall courtyard, it included the construction of prayer rooms where Torah scrolls were to be stored. The Planning Committee rejected the plan for prayer rooms, and the problem arose as to where the scrolls would be kept. In April 1968, Ministry officials decided to open up the sealed arches. The plan of the *Mahkamah* basement was known to them, since the area had been mapped and surveyed in the 19th century. At first they only intended to find a place to store the Torah scrolls. But as the basements were progressively cleared of the piles of rubble, the planners discovered an enormous hall extending to the north.

On April 18, 1968, Israel officially expropriated the entire area of the Western Wall. The Government was careful not to expropriate any mosque or school building, and when a Mamaluk *Madrassa* was confiscated by mistake, the Government informed the *waqf* that it would be willing to exclude it from the expropriated area on condition that the Arabs promised to renovate it. The Western Wall itself was not expropriated. The Arabs claimed possession of it, as part of the wall of the Haram al-Sharif. During the time of the Mandate, the Jewish view was that the Wall did not come within the category of property to be entered in the Land Registry, but was, rather, a *Res*

Dei and, therefore, the Arab claim was meaningless. In either case, the Government was careful not to take possession of the Western Wall itself.

After the expropriation, the eviction of the Arab inhabitants who were still living near the Wall was speeded up. As each house was cleared, it was demolished by bulldozers. The demolition of the evacuated houses undermined those still occupied, which was an added incentive for their inhabitants to look for safer homes. Gradually, the rampart between the Wall clearing and the Mugrabi Gate was uncovered. The two bodies sharing control of the Wall area — the archeological expedition to the south and the Ministry of Religious Affairs to the north — cast covetous eyes on the vacated area. The archeologists wished to extend their excavations, while the Ministry wished to extend the prayer area. There was also the problem of access to the Mugrabi Gate if all the houses, and the rampart, were removed.

The archeologists had an answer. Exactly underneath the Mugrabi Gate, a few meters below the level of the prayer area, was one of the original Temple Mount gates, Barclay's Gate. Inside the Barclay Gate, there was a vaulted passage, also dating from Second Temple times, that led to the Temple Mount Courtyard. The archeologists suggested removing the earth rampart, uncovering the gate, breaking through the stone wall which blocked it, and thus opening up a new access route to the Temple Mount. The plan was daring, but it suffered from one major defect. The ancient gateway into Temple Mount had, in the past, served as an underground mosque. Entering by way of Barclay's Gate would require the removal of this mosque. The plan was therefore postponed, along with the further demolition of the buildings next to the Mugrabi Gate. In July 1968, the Foreign Minister asked the Minister of Religious Affairs to halt the demolitions and bring the matter before the Ministerial Committee for the Holy Places. This request followed a complaint by a UNESCO representative, who claimed that the demolitions were in violation of the convention for the preservation of cultural treasures, to which Israel was a signatory. The houses near the Mugrabi Gate were from the Mameluk period, and were protected by the Antiquities' Law. The Minister of Religious Affairs ordered work stopped but had it leaked to the newspapers that the step had been taken following the intervention of the Foreign Minister.

In the meantime, work was continued on cleaning up the cellars of the *Mahkamah* building. In June 1968, the Minister of Religious Affairs announced the opening of a synagogue in the *Mahkamah* basement. He also announced that work would go on to uncover the Western Wall beneath the *Mahkamah,* in a northerly direction. At the same time, Ministry employees carried on cleaning out a complex of underground vaults extending to the west. Everything cleaned up by the Ministry automatically became a Holy Place, and entry was conditional on a head-covering being worn.

This activity did not, of course, escape the scrutiny of Muslim Council officials, who continued to send memoranda and complaints to the Prime Minister that the work endangered the al-Aqsa Mosque. These complaints were not answered, but representatives of the Council were invited to tour the excavations, and were given explanations about the steps taken to ensure the stability of the walls. This convinced them that the Jews were not planning to undermine the foundations of the Temple Mount Wall, for any damage to the Western Wall would be a greater misfortune for the Jews than for the Arabs.

The Muslims also complained about the excavations underneath the *Mahkamah* building. Their complaint stressed that the building had not been expropriated and that the cleaning operations involved, were, therefore, acts of trespass. They submitted certified Land Registry entries, proving their ownership, and demanding that operations be halted immediately. Report that a synagogue was being constructed in the basement made the situation even worse.

The problem of whether to continue cleaning near the Mugrabi Gate, as well as that of cleaning out the *Mahkamah* basements, was brought before the Ministerial Committee for Jerusalem, which decided to demolish all the houses, except two that were adjacent to the gate itself. Regarding the *Mahkamah* building, it was decided to establish a Safety Committee consisting of representatives of the Municipality, the Ministries of Religious Affairs, Defense and Labor, and of the archeological expedition. This Committee, which had been set up to deal with the purely technical aspects of the excavations, turned into a platform for debates between the archeological expedition, the Ministry of Religious Affairs and the Municipality of Jerusalem. Supervision of safety measures was placed in the hands of experts.

With work proceding on excavations under their foundations, the houses remaining beside the Mugrabi Gate showed dangerous cracks. The affair of the Mugrabi Gate houses came to an end in June 1969. The last remaining building, a souvenir shop, was cleared and demolished on June 25.

Two years after the capture of the Old City, the whole of the southern section of the Western Wall, from the *Mahkamah* building to the southwest corner, had been uncovered, and all the adjacent buildings had been removed. The two parties which controlled the Wall cooperated in removing the buildings, but, the moment the work was completed, a fierce conflict broke out between them for control of the new "no-man's-land" which had come into being. The archeologists wished to excavate it, the Ministry of Religious Affairs wanted to make it into a place of worship. Each belligerent tried to create *faits accomplis*: the archeologists began trial digs, while Ministry officials started to construct steps. Two days before the Ninth of Av, July 27, 1969, there was a violent clash, when dozens of worshippers broke through the barbed-wire fence put up by the archeological expedition. The archeologists sent in a bulldozer. The police were called, but declined to intervene. The Deputy Prime Minister was called in, and he declared a compromise arrangement. With a stick he marked out a division of the disputed section, the larger part being set aside for worship, and the smaller section for excavation. Then a special session of the Ministerial Committee decided to freeze the situation, with the disputed section serving neither prayers nor excavation. On the eve of the Ninth of Av, hundreds of worshippers broke into the area, taking advantage of the fact that the Ministry had illuminated the disputed sections with powerful spotlights. Once again, the police refrained from intervening.

The adversaries began to attack each other in public. The Minister of Religious Affairs accused the archeologists of entering a section over which they had no rights and claimed that their excavation licence was illegal. The heads of the archeological expedition demanded vigorous Government intervention in order to permit them to complete their task without disturbance. There were complaints that "This is the first time in history that Jews have stopped other Jews from worshipping at the Wall."

Before long, however, calm was restored. The Minister of Defense declared that he considered access to the Mugrabi Gate vital and would not agree to the rampart leading to it being cleared. Access to the Temple Mount by way of the only gate controlled by the army could not be impeded for a single moment. In view of this, excavations were halted. Committees were called together to plan mobile bridges and prayer platforms, but, in practice, both of the warring sides withdrew from the disputed section. The *status quo* between the religious and the secular bodies at the Wall had been restored.

The Ministry of Religious Affairs now turned its efforts northwards. As tunnels were extended along the Wall, their roofs became progressively thinner and their depth gradually decreased. Those supervising the operation calculated the point at which the tunnels would surface. Up to that time, uncovering the Western Wall could be accomplished, underground, without harming adjacent buildings; from then on, it required demolition. The excavators of the Ministry of Religious Affairs reached the critical point in December 1971 and the Ministry requested approval for the demolition of an ancient, ramshackle building that blocked the extension of the tunnel. The Government decided to reject the request and to renovate the building. At the same time, heavy pressure was exerted on the Government to permit the Wall to be uncovered further.

No other excavation or cleaning projects have been carried out on the northern side of the Wall since 1972. In fact, Government funds have been used to repair a number of Mameluk buildings adjacent to the Wall in this area. The Muslim *waqf* leaders repaired the cotton merchants' market (Suq al-Qatanin) in this area, which dates back to the Middle Ages, and rented it to souvenir dealers.

The continuing excavations in the area of the Wall served as an excuse for the Arab states to condemn Israel in various political forums. This propaganda effort reached a climax in November 1974 when the UNESCO General Conference condemned Israel for these excavations which, it insisted, "constitute a danger to (Jerusalem's) monuments." The condemnation aroused waves of protest throughout the world. Opponents of the politicization of UNESCO cited the organizations' own expert, Prof. Lemaire, who periodically visited the excavations and reported that they

> *are being carried out by a perfectly well qualified team of experts of various kinds, who are extremely attentive to all aspects and to all periods of which remains have been found on the site. The*

same care is expended on the preservation of remains of the Ommayad palaces as on those of the Herodian period.

In the course of the years, many attempts were made to establish a national coordinating body to plan both parts of the Wall area. These attempts failed, however, because the Ministry of Religious Affairs insisted that it had exclusive authority there and only agreed to the establishment of coordinating bodies if they were constituted under its Ministry. The problem was brought before the Cabinet on a number of occasions, but the Ministers avoided overruling their religious colleagues.

Early in 1972, the Company for the Development of the Jewish Quarter, which was responsible for the area bordering the Western Wall, joined with the Jerusalem Municipality in inviting architect Moshe Safdie to draw up plans for the Western Wall area. The invitation was praised by the Minister of Justice, who was Chairman of the Ministerial Committee on Jerusalem. An attempt was made to have the Ministry of Religious Affairs participate in ordering the plan, with the hope that this would guarantee their cooperation in the project. But the Ministry avoided any involvement. The plan was completed and presented to the Prime Minister, the Cabinet and the Chief Rabbis. Its main principles were: excavation of the entire area in front of the Wall down to bedrock level, in order to uncover the entire Herodian Wall and all the layers of stone now buried underground; development of a multi-levelled archeological garden, in which all the structures found in the excavation — from the Herodian to the Arabic periods — would be restored and preserved; creation of an amphitheater extending from the slopes of the Jewish Quarter (the ancient "Upper City") up to the Wall; creation of an arcaded street, in which all commercial enterprises would be centralized; construction of a service center near the Dung Gate; planning of an easy approach to the Mugrabi Gate.

The plan — ambitious and inspired but difficult and expensive to implement — was greatly praised. But various factions objected to the way in which it was ordered. Basically, they objected to the fact that there was no open competition between architects and that they were, therefore, presented with only one plan without any alternatives. The question was not one of aesthetics but, again, of politics. The Ministry of Religious Affairs refused to adopt the plan and in light of the arguments aroused, the Government, too, decided not to decide. A committee of experts was set up to make suggestions as to what should be done with Safdie's plan and, more importantly, what should be done with the area of the Western Wall. The committee debated for a year-and-a-half. In early 1976, they began formalizing their proposals, but the Ministry of Religious Affairs made it clear that it would not accept them.

Under the conditions of the *status quo* existing between secular and religious forces in Israel, there was little hope of finding an acceptable solution in which to embody the Jewish nation's aspirations for its Holy Places.

CHAPTER TWENTY

NAMES AND MEMORIALS

Only a few of the listeners to Israel Radio's Arabic program on August 20, 1967, noticed that the announcer had altered the station's identification. Instead of announcing the broadcast from *Urshalim,* he announced it from *al-Kuds.* The Arabs listening did not attach much importance to the change, but the Jews (who were not listening) regarded it as a matter of principle and of great symbolic importance.

In Israel, Jerusalem's official Arabic title had been *Urshalim,* as decided in 1950 by the Government Names Committee, then engaged in giving Hebrew place names to geographical locations in Israel with Arabic names only. Hundreds of Arabic names for villages, rivers, hills, and other topographical elements were replaced by Hebrew names. The Committee tried, as much as possible, to restore historical Hebrew names, discovering, as it did so, that most of the ancient Hebrew names had been preserved, with slight alterations, by the Arabs. Moreover, after their conquest of the country, the Arabs had reinstituted Hebrew names altered by the Romans and Byzantines: Skythopolis reverted to Beisan (Hebrew: Beit She'an), and Apolonia to Arsuf (Hebrew: Reshef). Speaking a Semitic language closely resembling Hebrew, the common people, in most cases, discarded the foreign Greek names and went back to the old Semitic ones.

Some places, such as Jerusalem and Hebron, were given Arabic names that differed from the Hebrew original but maintained some connection with Hebrew tradition. Hebron, for example, was called *al-Khalil* (The Friend) after the patriarch Abraham, whom the Arabs call "The Friend of God" and who had lived there. Jerusalem became *al-Kuds al-Sharif,* or *al-Kuds* (The Holy) for short.

In 1950, Israel Foreign Minister Moshe Sharett, who was a linguist with a thorough knowledge of Arabic, was asked how Jerusalem should be referred to in Arabic. He settled for the name used in the Arabic translation of the New Testament, *Urshalim*. This name had never come into popular use and was found solely in this translation. As West Jerusalem had virtually no Arab inhabitants, and since there was a practical need to distinguish the Israeli part of Jerusalem from its Jordanian.section (naturally named *al-Kuds*), the suggested name *Urshalim* was accepted and became the official Arabic name for Jerusalem in Israel. But after the Six Day War, those Israeli bodies dealing with the affairs of the Arab population were again faced with the problem of the Arabic name for Jerusalem. The Jews felt that it would be awkward to stick to the 17-year-old name *Urshalim,* used only in official publications and on the radio, while relinquishing *al-Kuds,* the only name the Arabs used for the city.

On August 13, 1967, the Municipality of Jerusalem asked the Government Names Committee to again take up the question of the Arabic name for the city of Jerusalem. The letter of request suggested that the city should be called *al-Kuds,* since the name *Urshalim* had never been mentioned in any Arabic source and "continued reference to the city as *Urshalim* would be interpreted by the Arabs as an attempt to force them to accept alien ways."

At the same time, the matter was being discussed by the staff of the Israel Radio's Arabic programs, as well as by the editorial board of the Israeli Arabic daily, *al-Yaum*. In addition to historical considerations, some stressed the need to emphasize the city's unity, and using the universally accepted name of *al-Kuds* would not necessarily highlight the Arab or Islamic nature of Jerusalem. A further consideration was propaganda: the Iraqi peasant listening to Israel Radio broadcasts from *Urshalim* would not know where it was coming from; but if he heard Israel Radio from *al-Kuds* he would know very well where it was from, and appreciate the significance of the fact. Meanwhile, on the day before Israel Radio first broadcast from *al-Kuds,* the Jerusalem Town Clerk was ordered to have the name *Baladiyat al-Kuds* printed in Arabic on the Municipality's note paper.

When the newspapers reported the change, there was a wave of protests in Israel. The step was regarded as giving in to the Arabs. "The emerging trend," editorialized the paper of the right-wing Gahal opposition, "is to conciliate the Arabs and to appear before the civilized world as good children." Both parties to the debate claimed that they were stressing the city's unity. The Minister of Religious Affairs opposed the use of *al-Kuds* and demanded that the Government decide on the name. The outcome, as usual, was a compromise: the city's Arabic name became *Urshalim al-Kuds,* which is how it has been written and broadcast ever since. "Now we're certain," the Arabs smiled, "that we're talking of two cities: your Jewish one, *Urshalim,* and our Arab one, *al-Kuds.*"

No sooner was the debate over Jerusalem's Arabic name settled than a new one began over street names in the Old City and in the Arab quarters. Names for the Old City streets were first officially given in 1918, when a committee consisting of Jews, Muslims, and Christians gave names to streets that lacked them and translated the names of the historic streets into all three official languages. The British Governor of Jerusalem also ordered that the street names be written in black on ceramic plaques with a white background and a decorative green frame. After the city's partition in 1948, the Arab Municipality altered the names of several streets. Jews' Street became Warriors' Street, named for those who had stormed the Jewish Quarter. St. Stephen's Gate Street became The Street of the Holy Warriors. Beyond the Old City walls, the Street of Sulayman the Magnificent was re-named King Husayn Street. The form of the street plaques was also changed. In 1965, the Arab Municipality finished posting Old City street names in Arabic and English, the names being set on elongated ceramic plaques in black, green and white.

Following the conquest of the Old City in 1967, all street signs put up by the Arabs were left in place, with the exception of the one on the Western Wall, which was removed at the order of David Ben-Gurion on his first visit to the Wall. At the beginning of July, the Municipality was asked to furnish the Survey Department with an official list of Hebrew street names for the Old City so that a new map could be printed. The Municipality Names Committee decided on 22 Hebrew names, all of which had been in use before 1948.

Once the names had been chosen and the Municipality decided to display them on the signs in the Old City streets, it became necessary to deal with the Arabic and English names on the signs. The decision was to leave them as they were and add another row of tiles carrying the Hebrew names. The additional tiles were ordered from the same Armenian ceramics workshop that had made the other plaques. As for Jews' Street, which had been re-named, the Municipality decided to put up the Hebrew name without altering the Arabic one.

As the Names Committee continued working, however, it began to depart from its own decision of principle. At the end of October, it decided that the street named for the Caliph Omar Ibn al-Khatab, who captured Jerusalem in 638, be changed. Part was to be called Citadel Square, another part, Armenians Street, and a third part, Batei Mahseh Street. It also decided to alter the name of the main street running along the Old City's northern wall from Sulayman the Magnificent (who built the Old City wall) to Paratroopers' Street. Other units that took part in the capture of Jerusalem also had streets named after them, producing names like Central Command Square (for the crossroads where the famous Mandelbaum Gate had stood), Jerusalem Brigade Street and Harel Brigade Street. The square named for General Allenby became Zahal (Israel Defense Forces) Square.

These decisions aroused sharp reactions, principally against the eradication of names connected with the chronicles of the city, and the fact that the Arabs would regard such deeds as a severe blow to their feelings. The Mayor intervened in the controversy, urging the Names Committee to alter its decision. As in the debate over the Arabic name for Jerusalem and so many other debates and decisions, this one was a purely inter-Jewish matter, without any Arab protest against the decision. When one Arab was asked privately for his opinion, he said:

I didn't think you would act differently. After all, you plan to erase everything Arab in this city. You've already done worse things: for example, you've changed our school syllabus. Now the time has come to eradicate the names of our heroes. Everything you do is planned.

Faced by a wave of protests, the Names Committee convened to change its decision. Caliph Omar's name was left on the entrance to the Jaffa Gate, which became the Square of Omar Ibn al-Khatab. Sulayman Street got a "musical chairs" type of compromise: the first part of the street was called Paratroopers' Street, while the second part, from the Damascus Gate onwards, continued to be named after the Magnificent Sultan. It was King Husayn who was the loser: the second part of the street had been named after him, but no one protested when his name was removed.

When the controversy died down, it was proposed that two Arab members be added to the Names Committee. When this proved impossible, an Arab municipal employee was coopted, and the Committee continued its work. Streets inhabited by Arabs were given the names of Arab philosophers, poets and historians. When the Arab employee proposed naming a street for Ragheb Bey Nashashibi, Mayor of the United Municipality of Jerusalem for many years, and an opponent of Arab chauvinism, the Committee objected on the grounds that he had been "anti-Jewish."

At the same time, the street leading to Mount Scopus, which was populated solely by Arabs, was named Hadassah Martyrs' Street, in memory of the victims of the Hadassah convoy brutally murdered by the Arabs in 1948. This name was opposed by several City Councillors, one of whom claimed that, while he understood the desire to commemorate the victims, thought must be given to those who would have to use the name for practical purposes, such as printing visiting cards or addressing letters. These people would all be Arabs, since the street was in an Arab quarter. Rather than carry on in such a fashion, he said, it would be better to stop naming Arab streets altogether. Just as the Jews objected to the Arabs commemorating heroes and happenings connected with their wars against the Jews, the Arabs could hardly agree to having their streets named after Jewish personalities and events connected with the wars against them. After a fierce debate, the Municipal Council decided to override the Names Committee decision on Hadassah Martyrs Street.

With the approach of the first anniversary of the occupation of Jerusalem (according to the Hebrew calendar), various bodies began planning festivities to mark the day. The Chief Rabbinate proclaimed it "a day of prayer, thanksgiving, and religiously ordained festivity." The Municipality was asked to organize the events, but Mayor Teddy Kollek refused to take the responsibility, proposing that a Jewish public committee do so instead. The Municipality, he contended, was also responsible for 70,000 Arabs, for whom unification day was not a festivity but a day of mourning. His view found support in the Prime Minister's Office, which was interested, for reasons of foreign policy, in playing down events connected with the unification of Jerusalem.

At the Cabinet meeting held on April 7, 1968, the Minister of Religious Affairs proposed making Jerusalem Unification Day into "an official day of thanksgiving," but his proposal was not adopted. The National Religious Party became the standard-bearer of the campaign for official celebrations. Despite considerable public support, Kollek was in the minority in the Municipal Executive, which decided to celebrate Jerusalem Day and to organize its events.

Plans were prepared for the festivities, and the city was decorated, but the organizers decided not to decorate the Arab neighborhoods. Then, ten days before Jerusalem Day, the Government decided that there was no point in any special festivities that year in view of the Independence Day celebrations and the military parade held in Jerusalem a few weeks earlier. There were political reasons behind the Government's decision. A few days earlier, the U.N. Security Council had passed a severe vote of censure against Israel on the question of Jerusalem. Friendly governments advised Israel to avoid festivities because of the provocative nature that could be attached to them. The Government's decision would have restricted the festivities to lessons in schools and prayers at the Western Wall.

The people of Israel, however, only took notice of the hesitations that stemmed from sensitivity and tolerance, and not of the restraint imposed by political considerations. Over 100,000 journeyed to Jerusalem that day to visit the monuments to the soldiers who had fallen in the war and to pray and sing beside the Wall. As for the Arabs, they did not even know that it was Jerusalem Day. Their "Jerusalem Day" fell on June 5, and they marked it with a commercial shutdown and mourning processions.

The subjects of commemoration and mourning also arose in another context. A few hours after the sounds of battle had died down in Jerusalem, small piles of stones sprung up at different places in the city. These were improvised monuments erected by soldiers of the units that had fought in Jerusalem, in memory of their fallen comrades. The heaps of unhewn stones were crowned with blackened weapons and the helmets of the dead. The stones were daubed with short inscriptions in red and black paint. The soldiers erected the improvised memorials at the scenes of the fighting or at the points where the units had massed before battle. In this manner, 12 improvised monuments were erected, in addition to two inscriptions on the walls of buildings. Following the war the monuments were visited by bereaved families and comrades-in-arms, who replaced any displaced stones, restored the painted inscriptions, and laid wreaths.

With the approach of the first Memorial Day after the war, on the eve of Independence Day, the Jerusalem Municipality, in conjunction with the Defense Ministry and representatives of the units, decided to replace the improvised mounds with permanent monuments. At first, the bereaved families and some of the units opposed this plan since they wished to preserve the spontaneous nature of the memorials. They were also afraid that the memorials would be re-located. When told that permanent memorials would be built out of the original mounds of stones, with only the addition of a uniform marble plaque, their objections vanished.

Because all the monuments had been erected at the scenes of the fighting, they were either on the old border or in the heart of Arab neighborhoods. Some of them stood on plots of land belonging to Arabs; one was in close proximity to a mosque on land belonging to the *waqf*, which first objected to the erection of the monument, but later withdrew its objection. When payment was offered for the use of the spot, it was refused. On Memorial Day, May 1, 1968, the new memorials were consecrated in commemoration services. One hundred and eighty-one Israeli soldiers who fell in the battle for Jerusalem were honored in this way.

The Arab population observed the commemoration services in silence. Parents were careful to warn their children not to touch the wreaths or to play at the monuments, all of which were kept clean. But some of the Arab inhabitants were also prompted to find a way to commemorate their war dead. It is impossible to judge whether they adopted the idea from the Jews or whether it was their independent initiative. The situation being what it was, they could not expect any official body, not even the Muslim Council, to take such action. In consequence, the initiative was taken by individuals.

On the night before June 4, 1968, the Nusaybah family erected a memorial in their garden. On the following morning, passersby in St. George Street noticed an elongated marble monument inscribed with the Quran verse usually found on soldiers' graves: "Do not regard those who were killed for Allah as dead, but as living, receiving a blessing from their Creator." In addition, those approaching the

329

memorial were urged to recite the opening *sura* of the Quran. The monument bore the inscription: "Victim *(Shahid)* of June 5, 1967," and supported a helmet and a wreath of flowers. This was not a monument but an actual grave. On the night of June 6, 1967, an unknown Arab soldier was killed there and buried by the family. Now they had erected a memorial stone on the grave.

It will be remembered that some of the Arab dead were buried where they had fallen. On Ammunition Hill, Israeli soldiers put up a sign to mark the mass grave of Arab soldiers. Several hundred who had not been buried by the Israeli soldiers were interred by the Municipality. After unification, the Muslim *waqf* began the task of transferring the bodies from their temporary graves at the scenes of the fighting, to the Muslim cemetery. The identity of most of the dead was unknown, since their documents and identification tags had disappeared. Between July and September 1967, 214 Arab dead were brought to burial in 16 groups, according to where they were found. Since most of the dead were unidentified, the stone on the mass grave would be inscribed with the name of one of the group who had been identified, in the following manner: "Here lies Husayn al-Kurd and his comrades." The transfer of bodies was carried out without a funeral and without attracting any attention.

Israeli journalists, who noticed the Nusaybah gravestone, asked the Municipality for its views. Mayor Teddy Kollek replied:

If bereaved Arab women go there tomorrow to lay wreaths, I shall respect it. The Arabs had many unknown dead in the latest war, and if we wish to live together in this city for a thousand years, we have to show understanding.

Sure enough, the next day, June 5, bereaved women came to this gravestone, as well as to another on Ammunition Hill, where a number of paratroopers were mourning their dead friends, while on the other side of the fortified hill a group of Arab women in black mourned their dead ones. There was a similar encounter at the Arab and Jewish memorials near the Rockefeller Museum. The Arab mourning processions set out from the Temple Mount courtyard, carrying palm fronds and wreaths. Acting on orders it had received, the police permitted the wreath-bearers to pass, but they were followed by a crowd which burst out of Damascus Gate and began hurling stones at the police. In the skirmish that resulted, several policemen were injured and 19 demonstrators were arrested.

The wreath-bearers went on their way without hindrance, laying their wreaths on the soldiers' graves in the cemetery, while others continued to march in mourning processions on the following day as well. By Sunday, June 10, there were six memorials, and, by the end of the week, another seven had been erected. Put up under cover of darkness, they all consisted of small mounds of stones upon which cloth inscriptions with verses from the Quran were laid. Some of the inscriptions were slogans such as: "Blessings to the fallen, heroes of the homeland, who fell for the homeland." The memorials were covered with wreaths, which were renewed each day.

At first there was no Jewish reaction to the erection of the Arab memorials, and no one demanded their removal, but the large number of memorials, and their daily proliferation, caused concern to the security authorities who feared that, with the memorials spread all over the city, it would be difficult to maintain public order, and hard to keep control of dozens of mourning processions moving in all directions. The matter was discussed at a meeting on June 26, 1968, when it was generally agreed to take steps to reduce the number of memorials. No one suggested removing them all. As a first step, it was decided to make certain that there were no bodies buried underneath the memorials. Improvised memorials put up by pupils could be taken down, but actual gravestones were an entirely different matter. A municipal employee (not representing the Municipality but appointed by the Government) was delegated to negotiate with the Muslim religious leaders, to make sure that there were no bodies underneath the memorials — and if there were, that they be removed to the cemetery. He was also authorized to reach an agreement determining a minimum number of memorials. An Israel Defense Forces representative declared that the army had no objection to the proximity of the Arab memorials to I.D.F. memorials.

In the meeting between the Muslim religious leaders and the Government representative, it transpired that the Arabs did not know of any bodies under the memorials, with the exception of one memorial on Givat Hamivtar, where it was impossible to move the bodies since the area had been covered by three meters of earth during the erection of grandstands for the Independence Day parade. To dispel any doubt, the man who had carried out the burials signed a declaration that: ". . . following numerous inquiries, I am certain that there is no body interred beneath the temporary memorials put up by the Arab inhabitants of Jerusalem."

It now became possible to enter into negotiations over the number and location of the memorials. The heads of the *waqf* demanded four: on Givat Hamivtar, on Ammunition Hill, beside the Rockefeller Museum, and on the old border, not far from Shmuel Hanavi Street. It was then resolved to prolong negotiations as long as possible while checking on the proposed form and plans; the locations would be discussed afterward.

Negotiations over the plans of the memorials and their locations, as well as the inscriptions on them, went on for three months. On October 15, 1968, the heads of the Jerusalem *waqf* presented an official request to erect memorials, to the Municipality's Administrator for East Jerusalem. Attached were a map showing their locations and a detailed plan of two types of monument, as well as the inscriptions they wished to engrave, which were the same as the inscription on the memorial in the Nusaybah garden. The application was discussed on December 17, when it was decided to approve the erection of four memorials but to alter the location of one of them. Negotiations went on, as the Municipality's representative was not certain that it would be desirable to put up a monument on Ammunition Hill, which was to be the site of a large Israel Defense Forces memorial, even though the I.D.F. had no objections to the monument. The *waqf* agreed not to put up that particular monument for the time being. Negotiations came to an end with the dispatch of a memorandum approving the erection of three monuments, including their exact dimensions and the wording of the inscription. The *waqf* also took it upon itself to remove all the temporary memorials erected during the past year. The accompanying letter stated that the approval was not a substitute for the approval of the Local Planning Commission, as required by law.

As soon as it received the letter, the *waqf* began to erect a memorial next to the Muslim cemetery; its location had been agreed to by the security authorities, who could maintain complete control of the situation in case demonstrations were held at this spot. Until that moment, the matter had been kept secret, throughout the six months of negotiations. On December 17, however, the *waqf* officials released the story to the correspondent of a Hebrew newspaper. When the official responsible for negotiations was approached by journalists, he confirmed the existence of an agreement, adding: *Seventy thousand inhabitants wished to erect monuments in memory of their dead, and there is no reason in the world why it should not be allowed. When people die, no political accounts remain, and the memory of the dead should be honored. I hope Jewish public opinion will show understanding.*

Hassan Tahbub, head of the *waqf*, commented: "In the agreement reached, the Municipality has shown understanding for the feelings of Arab families who lost their dear ones."

The agreement with the *waqf* jarred a very sensitive Jewish nerve, and the shock waves were powerful and prolonged. Parties represented in the Municipal Council called on the Mayor to put an immediate halt to the erection of the three monuments. The matter was brought up in the Knesset, and, subsequently, in the Cabinet. There was not a single newspaper that did not devote a leading article to the issue.

Those who opposed the monuments brought up various contentions:

Is this hour to put up monuments to the glory and splendor of the murderers of our people; to those who received orders to exterminate the civilian population, too; to those who were ordered by their king to 'Kill Jews wherever they found them'?

If monuments are put up, they will become a focal point for clashes between Jews and Arabs and centers of Arab incitement.

What if neo-Nazis get up tomorrow and decide to erect a monument to Adolf Eichmann in Jerusalem? He, too, was a soldier, he too was a hero, he too had admirers. It would be hard to conceive even today, 30 years after the blitz raids on Britain, that it would enter the heads of the relatives of Luftwaffe pilots to demand the erection of memorials in Trafalgar Square!

Those in favor of allowing the construction of the monuments argued that the question was not whether the enemy is worthy of having memorials put up in Israeli territory, but whether or not tens of thousands of Arab inhabitants of Jerusalem be permitted to honor their dead even when living under Israeli rule.

(These Arabs) have been destined to accept a regime they did not choose . . . to feel that they are both losers and a minority . . . as

333

they have been so destined, it is our duty to defuse the justified bitterness, even if it was not we who caused it.

They also pointed out that a monument can serve a role by subliminating anti-Israeli feeling. Most important, however, was the right of 70,000 inhabitants of Israel to express their legitimate desires.

In a public opinion poll conducted by one of the newspapers, 67% of the inhabitants of Jerusalem who were questioned opposed the erection of the monuments. Eighteen percent of them believed that losers have no rights; 28% contended that those who intended to exterminate them should not be commemorated; others objected for reasons such as: "My brain says it should be allowed, but my feelings are against it, and in this case my feelings are stronger than my intellect."

The Arabs did not take part in the controversy. One Arab leader confined himself to expressing "astonishment at the resistance to a simple humanitarian gesture." After a prolonged series of discussions and minor crises, with responsibility being transferred from one body to the next, a compromise was worked out. The monument upon which construction had started would be completed, while the others would not be erected. The *waqf,* which was also the scene of internal disputes over the form of the monument, accepted the verdict. It was asked to put forward an application, as required by law, to the Statutory Planning Commission. The application was presented to the Municipality, to be forwarded to the Commission, but before there was time to do so the *waqf* employees had completed the monument. They had hurried, because of the approach of a festival on which Muslims visit their cemeteries. An attempt was made to stop the work, but it was continued at night. The monument bore the inscription engraved on the memorial in the Nusaybah garden, with the addition of the sentence: "In memory of the dead of the war of honor in June 1967."

All the improvised memorials (except the one in the Nusaybah garden) were removed, as had been agreed. Upon its completion, the single monument became the focal point for pilgrimages by bereaved families and school pupils on memorial days. The fears of its opponents that the monument would become a center of clashes and of Arab incitement did not materialize; not a single clash or disturbance has taken place there, since the monument was built.

The "Affair of the Monuments," as the Israelis called it, was not soon forgotten — and its effects were still felt years later. In the 1969 municipal elections, those responsible for the agreement with the *waqf* came under sharp attack. They were called "the builders of monuments to the (Arab) Legion murderers." One of them gained the title of *Sayif al-Islam* ("the Sword of Islam") and was subjected to a campaign of denigration.

The affair also left a marked impression on the attitude of the Jewish population toward the Arabs of East Jerusalem. The Arabs' right to self-expression, as an ethnic group, had been put to the test. Their demand was for self-expression, in the sphere of human sensitivities. They did not try to use the dead as an excuse for harassing the authorities. Had they wanted to embarrass the authorities, they could, for example, have held mass funerals for the dead soldiers. Instead, they transferred the bodies in a quiet and dignified manner. Unlike their custom in other matters, here they did not deny the competence of the Israeli Municipality, and scrupulously fulfilled everything they took upon themselves. In the face of such behavior, it was impossible to avoid a decision on the pretext that the Arabs intended to disrupt public order or to provoke incitement against Israel. The Jewish population was united in its desire to maintain the integrity of Jerusalem, under Israeli rule. Parts of it now grasped, for the first time, that united Jerusalem included tens of thousands of Arabs who were not content with civil rights as individuals, but demanded the right to self-expression as a community. As long as the desire for self-expression took the form of stubborn and total opposition to Israel and its authorities, it was impossible to pay it any heed. But in the "Affair of the Monuments" the situation was different, despite all the attempts to present it otherwise.

There was some justice in one of the contentions of the critics that the *time* was unsuitable. When the agreement concerning the monuments became known, Arab terror in Jerusalem had reached a peak, with an explosion in the Mahaneh Yehuda market place, resulting in a heavy death toll. The battles in the Jordan Valley were at their height. A community in an active state of war finds it difficult to make subtle distinctions. It was very hard for an Israeli soldier, in constant battle against Arab soldiers, to grasp why the dead brethren of those firing at him should be commemorated in the city he considered to be his own. Like many difficult problems, this one arose at the worst possible time; but it was impossible to postpone its solution.

If one is to judge by the survey mentioned above, a majority of the people of Jerusalem were opposed to the official decision. However, all those engaged in the affairs of Jerusalem were united in the opinion that not only were the Arabs fully entitled to put up monuments to their soldiers, but honoring their right to do so would de-escalate the conflict, reduce hatreds, and consolidate coexistence.

The matter still served as a subject for political harassment, but a majority of the public had learned a lesson. There were no objections when the Government sanctioned the holding of the mourning procession after Nasser's death, or when the Jordanian syllabus was permitted in Israel government schools. The Arabs' right to collective self-expression, within the framework of the law, had been comprehended and accepted by a majority of the Jewish population.

CHAPTER TWENTY ONE

A TOWN OF
TWO PEOPLES

Returning to the actual scenes of the historic events that had made the Jews into a nation was an experience so powerful that it had few parallels, even in the chronicles of such an ancient people. It deeply affected the Jewish people as a whole and every one of its members singly. For the devout, it was the beginning of redemption; cynics and atheists suddenly found themselves linked again into the long chain of the generations that had whispered: "Next year in Jerusalem." It was a religious experience in the true sense of the term. It inspired individuals and groups to undertake pilgrimages to the Holy Places, to want to participate and to quarrel over the right to take part in these historic deeds. It blurred political conflicts and united the Israelis more than at any time since 1948, when the State was proclaimed.

There were no doubts as to the future. Moshe Dayan expressed the feeling of the people, when he said, on the day the Old City was captured, that "we have returned to the holiest of our Holy Places . . . and we shall never again be parted from them." This was not a political declaration; he was establishing a fact that no human power could change. Jerusalem, said Abba Eban at the United Nations, is

beyond and above, before and after, all political and secular considerations . . . the eternal link between Israel and Jerusalem [is] a link more ancient, more potent, and more passionate than any other link between any people and any place.

As a sovereign state, Israel was obliged to give concrete expression to this transcendental link. The way chosen was to enact the Unification Law. There might have been another way; but it was the fate of this law that, having been cast in the furnace of such a profound emotional experience, it immediately became an inalienable national treasure. Critics and opponents of Israel's policies did not grasp the symbolical significance of the Jerusalem Unification Law, did not understand that it was the concrete expression of an indescribably profound experience. Seizing on one detail or another, these critics argued whether the move meant occupation, annexation, or liberation, or was merely administrative. But all the quibbling was meaningless. Israel had reunited Jerusalem and was in control of the city. There was no force capable of removing her: that was the decisive fact. The practical form of this control was a secondary matter, so long as her exclusive connection and complete hegemony were assured.

Like any other collective spiritual experience, the experience connected with the reunification of Jerusalem was the exclusive possession of the people who had shared it. It united the Jewish people and simultaneously created a barrier between it and other peoples. It turned the Israelis' attention inwards, making them impervious to everything outside themselves. This self-centered view extended to the outside world, which was organized into a structure in keeping with that view. Without anyone being aware of it, the Israelis' attitude to real facts became selective. Those facts which fitted their subjective viewpoint were absorbed; those which did not fit were rejected as though they did not exist. Such facts as could not be ignored were interpreted in a manner that would not upset the fundamental concept. Outsiders' political views and assessments were taken to extremes: favorable ones were enthusiastically received, while negative ones were defined as hostile acts, betrayal, or, at the very least, tragic misunderstandings.

Songwriter Naomi Shemer, whose ballad "Jerusalem of Gold" expressed the yearnings for Jerusalem the unattainable, for the city "captive in a dream," unwittingly gave poetic expression to the secret feeling of exclusivity that ignores the existence of those who do not share those yearnings. One of the song's verses (altered after the war to fit in with the new state of affairs) relates: "How the cisterns have dried up! The marketplace is empty, and no one visits the Temple Mount in the Old City." In other words, if there are no Jews in the marketplace, it is empty; and if no Jews visit the Temple

Mount, then no one visits it at all. The thousands of Arabs who filled the marketplace and the Temple Mount did not exist. It was as if the songwriter had paraphrased the famous epigram: "I feel, therefore I am," and, in reverse, anyone who does not feel as we do, does not exist.

It was exactly this attitude that moulded the outlook towards the Arab population and the modes of dealing with it. The euphoria accompanying the realization of a distant dream gave rise to the most optimistic hopes concerning the chances of solving the Arab—Israeli conflict. If the age-long dream of Jews returning to the Holy City could come true, why couldn't the dream of peace be realized? At the moment of their triumph, the Israelis felt that the Arabs, too, would of necessity feel that the millennium had come. Perhaps they could not share the emotional experience of a reunited Jerusalem, but they would eventually accept it because the new situation was also to their advantage. They too were tired of war, and they really had no choice. "Tomorrow it shall become clear to all," said a poet, "that most of the Arab citizens of Jerusalem wished to see the city united and the capital of Israel." The shock that had struck the Arabs dumb, contributed to Israeli optimism. In the first days after reunification, nothing had been done or said by the Arabs to shake this hope of reconciliation. Everyone thought that "a shortcut to normalization and peace" had indeed been found.

But bitter reality soon re-emerged. The dream of reunification had come true; but peace and reconciliation were as far off as they had ever been. It would not be long before a few skeptics and cynics would start wondering − in private, of course − whether unification and peace were not mutually incompatible. In the meantime, however, the subjective view continued to sift objective reality. The protest memorandum of the Arab leaders, which was a firm challenge to annexation and expressed the true feelings of the Arabs, was received contemptuously, because "it only expresses a frustrated minority of unemployed leaders." Optimism would not pass away; the dissonance that had jarred the harmony was nothing more than the voice of a minority. "The leaders are mutinous, but the masses don't support them."

No wonder then that when the first general strike broke out, it came as a complete surprise to both Jewish public opinion and the security services. Now, not even the most naïve could continue to indulge in pipedreams. The conflict was still alive, not only beyond the borders but also in the heart of Jerusalem. It became necessary to confront this reality and to respond to it. Reactions were many and various, but all were influenced by the fundamentally subjective viewpoint. The extreme nationalists adhered to the clichés of the past, claiming that the Arab demonstrators were "the incited mob we got to know during the 1929–36 disturbances," members of the Muslim Council were "the Mufti's hirelings and successors." They tried to sharpen the conflicts by depicting the refusal of an Arab trader to add a Hebrew inscription to his shop sign as "a hostile act and incitement against the reunification of the city." Arab houses built beside the Western Wall had been put up "purposely, so as to conceal the Wall, and so that their sewage would defile and desecrate it."

Convinced that Israel's connection to Jerusalem was an exclusive one, the extreme nationalists were forceful in their demands that this tie be given concrete form. They insisted that any compromise or hesitation weakened the credibility of Israel's uncompromising stand over Jerusalem and was, therefore, dangerous. These circles did not suffer doubts stemming from ambivalent feelings. The Law of Unification had set a norm, and they would ensure its full implementation. Not that they wished to persecute the Arabs. Arabs could have their personal rights, as long as they adapted to the new state of affairs. But the Arabs not only had to give up their national aspirations and their communal independence, they also had to concede that the Israeli attachment to Jerusalem had precedence over theirs and that they must not resist when some expression of this attachment came at their expense. In such an event, the Arabs were entitled to appropriate financial compensation.

These extremist circles believed that their approach was liberal and democratic; the proof being the fact that they were prepared to give Israeli citizenship "to every Arab who wants it." What could be more democratic, they contended, than agreeing to give the Arab population equal personal status with Jews? The stress was on the words "who wants it." Heaven forbid that they should be forced to accept citizenship, for that would be undemocratic. They knew perfectly well that only very few of the Arab inhabitants of Jerusalem would apply for citizenship. Faced with this "rejection of our outstretched hand," these circles could have the best of both worlds: they had

340

made a generous, liberal proposal while knowing very well that they would not have to deal with new citizen-voters who might blur the State's Jewish character. Accordingly, there was no room for the consideration of Arab demands or for responding to their declarations, for these were attacks on the State of Israel and did not have to be treated on their merits. The Arabs were objects to be overcome, not negotiated with.

In most cases, the demands of the nationalist circles for total Jewish hegemony rested on the legal and moral superiority of the Jewish national interest. However, there were also many other demands, based on the contention that Jews were denied rights awarded to Arabs. When trying to force the Government to permit Jewish prayers on the Temple Mount, their demand rested on the claim that the Jews were discriminated against, since the Arabs were allowed to conduct prayers while the Jews were not. When the Municipality offered to pay for the installation of an electric grid to serve the Arab quarters, or to impose taxes by stages in East Jerusalem, the representatives of the nationalist and religious parties complained against favoritism towards Arabs, because Jews would not get municipal assistance for their hook-up to the electricity grid and were obliged to pay their taxes in full.

These circles were very noisy and had considerable influence on public opinion, but they lacked any influence on the practical administration of the affairs of the Arab population, because those responsible for such affairs were guided by far more complex concepts and approaches. No one disputed Israel's right to give concrete expression to her hegemony by imposing her jurisdiction and administration, confiscating land, and building new residential quarters in East Jerusalem. All these decisions were adopted unanimously and implemented in a spirit of harmony between all the political factions. At the same time, however, there was a significant difference in the ideological justification for these steps.

The extremists were convinced that Israel's connection to Jerusalem was so far superior, from both a national and a moral point of view, that its implementation was not a subject for discussion, and that there was no need to take any notice of opposing positions or views. The moderates were far more perplexed. Their liberal-socialist philosophy did not permit them to ignore the fact that the Jewish attachment to Jerusalem collided with an opposing Arab attachment

341

and that the Jewish tie was being given practical expression at the expense of the Arab one. Sensitivity to injustice, aversion to oppression, refusal to regard themselves as hated conquerors, and a true desire for peace and reconciliation, kept them from identifying fully with the policies of their own people.

These ambivalent feelings were overcome in a number of ways. First of all, the moderates attempted to discount the symmetry of the two opposing attachments, by playing down the validity of the rival ties: "The Arabs," they claimed, "are not as attached to Jerusalem as we are." They never made it into their capital, even when they could have. In 1948, they chose Amman. For the Jews, Jerusalem is the one and only Holy City, while the Arabs place Jerusalem third in their scale of sanctity, after the two holy cities of the Hijaz. They neglected Jerusalem and allowed the city to deteriorate. They did not look after the treasure that came into their possession in 1948, destroying some Jewish Holy Places and refusing Jews permission to visit the others. Therefore, they had no right to demand that the city be restored to them. The Jordanians invaded Jerusalem and captured it illegally; therefore, they have no rights there. The local Arabs had never consolidated any political force; in any case, a majority of the local population consisted of migrants from Hebron. The Arab demand for self-determination was unjustified, for Arabs had always been a minority in Jerusalem. There can be no talk of the national self-determination of a small minority. The united city has a Jewish majority, which has the right to decide on its future by dint of constituting a democratic majority. What counted was the desire of the *majority* for self-determination. Justification for Jewish hegemony therefore rested on the principles of democracy and self-determination, and on a stronger and more profound tie.

There was yet another line of thinking, that tried to justify the city's unification by the benefits it had brought to the Arabs. Unification had resulted in economic development and a considerable improvement in living conditions, full employment, better education, free access to all, and equal rights and status for Jew and Arab. Progress and an improved economic standard was of greater interest to the masses than hollow political slogans. Within a short time, economic improvements would moderate nationalist aspirations and lead to a recognition of the benefits of unification under Israeli rule. In general, the national problem was not so important to the Arabs;

342

it would be more accurate to define the Arabs according to religious allegiances. The city contained a Muslim community and a Christian community, as well as the dominant Jewish community. It was possible to satisfy the religious requirements of these communities, and that would put an end to the conflict.

The conflict consisted of two layers: one emotional and the other political. Over the years of fighting and military confrontation, fear, vindictiveness and personal hatred had mounted. The emotional conflict could be eliminated by meetings between members of both peoples and by non-political communal activity. Only by removing the barriers of hatred would it be possible to clear the way towards elimination of the political conflict.

The desire to depict the conflict as non-political — whether economic, social or emotional — was very common. Stress was placed on sports activities, bi-national get-togethers, the study of Hebrew and Arabic, encouragement of youth clubs and communal centers. Many of those active in these spheres were Jews from English-speaking countries who tried to apply their experience in dealing with racial conflicts abroad, to the realities of Jerusalem. They thought that social work, in the manner of communal action among the under-privileged classes in New York or Boston, would lead to a reduction of tension between Jews and Arabs in Jerusalem.

Another common approach was the paternalistic and philanthropic one, which insisted that the Arab hatred for Jews was rooted in their inferior culture and their poor economic state. It was thought, therefore, that if they were to acquire Western cultural values, if the men were taught technical professions and the women were instructed in cooking, sewing, and baby care, hatred would diminish. Improved economic conditions, as well as living together on terms of social and cultural equality, would lead to the emergence of a new generation of Arabs who would take over the leadership and work for a peaceful settlement. This was a variation on the theme of "The White Man's Burden," allegedly adapted to the twentieth century and applied to the conditions prevailing in Jerusalem.

All of these approaches shared a common element: the desire to avoid the focal point of the problem, which is a deep-seated national and political conflict and a head-on collision between two legitimate, but conflicting, attachments. All those who adhered to these views wanted to neutralize Arab national aspirations and divert the energies

343

of the Arab community into non-political channels. They were aware of, and sensitive to, Arab feelings of frustration and injustice, but could do nothing to remove them, because the causes of these feelings were the national policies of Israel, with which they themselves identified. Liberal as one's views might be, Israeli hegemony was a basic assumption. Nevertheless, being men of peace and goodwill, they wished to do something to reduce tensions and to achieve fraternal coexistence. The only path open to them was to deal with problems of a neutral character in the hope that their solution would, in some miraculous manner, dissipate the underlying conflict. They were prepared to make any effort, in any sphere, that had no bearing on the principal Israeli effort. But, in their quest for spheres in which compromise and peaceful coexistence were feasible, they slowly began to touch on matters which had traditionally been considered unassailable Israeli basic principles.

A few skeptics and eccentrics began to think aloud as to whether the time had not come to revise these principles, and whether it was not possible to extend Jewish—Arab *entente* to new spheres without harming basic Israeli interests. These thoughts and questions, together with the deeds they engendered, were the basis of the dispute between liberals and nationalists. It was not a clash about Israeli hegemony as such, nor about giving concrete expression to her national attachment to Jerusalem. On this, all were united. The issue in question was: in which spheres precisely did the Israeli national interest have to be totally dominant, and in which was it possible to reach a compromise without harming Israel's national interest?

The desire to seek new ways of coexistence arose despite the lack of external pressures, however strange that may seem. Most of all, it was an expression of inner confusion, of the distress and discomfort that resulted from the unpleasant task of controlling a hostile populace. This change in approach was first expressed in symbolic ways, such as changing street names and celebrating the reunification of Jerusalem. But there were also practical expressions, such as imposition of taxes by stages, concessions on the issue of identity cards, and the use of Arabic in official documents. The campaign waged over these issues was not inspired by Arab complaints. Those Israelis who were engaged in the affairs of the Arab population sensed that justice, coexistence, and tolerance required a change in attitudes and a greater sensitivity to Arab sensibilities.

344

After some time, this process continued as a result of external pressures. The Arabs began to display stubbornness in several matters that were not necessarily connected with the basic conflict, but influenced the manner in which they were to run their lives. At one point the liberal Israelis began to ask themselves why the Arabs should not be left to run their lives as they wished, if such freedom could be reconciled with the requirements of law and public order.

At this point they came into head-on collision with traditional Israeli policy in the Arab sector, which was based on the view that any independent Arab organization must, of necessity, be of an anti-Israeli character. Since the Arab—Israel confrontation was total, it seemed to be out of the question to permit any form of Arab identification, even of a non-political nature. Israel's Arabs were entitled to personal freedom and equal rights, but solely as individuals. This was the approach that had guided the Government in its first steps in Jerusalem. During the early period, not only was no form of *political* organization permitted, but even Arab *social* clubs, such as the Rotary or the Lions, were not allowed to continue their activities. Israeli bodies, which were not accustomed to any expression of opposition by Israeli Arabs, thought that they would be able to apply the same policy in Jerusalem without encountering opposition.

The first signs of opposition were interpreted as sacrilege and punished severely. Gradually, however, it was recognized that the Arabs of East Jerusalem were different from Israeli Arabs. Their national solidarity and their readiness to stand up for themselves presented a dilemma for the authorities. Should they employ all possible force to break the Arabs or should they compromise on matters that did not conflict with direct Israeli interests? No decision was reached in principle, but there evolved a series of *ad hoc* decisions that treated each issue on its merits. A clear trend emerged to abandon the traditional Israeli view of independent Arab organization. The number of issues that had previously been considered vital for the preservation of Israeli national interests was reduced, while those areas in which compromise arrangements were permissible were extended.

This process was, of course, fiercely opposed, at every stage, by Israeli extremists, who regarded it as hesitation, a sign of weakness, or the abandonment of vital interests; but their objections were not strong enough to halt the trend. It is characteristic that, in the debates

345

between liberals and nationalists, the former stressed the quest for compromise not as an aim in itself, but principally as a way of achieving Israeli hegemony. Tolerance and calm in the city were vital, they contended, above all to ensure Israeli control. Tension and violence would discourage potential immigrants, call for outside intervention and renew attempts at imposing a settlement.

Early in 1972 the general feeling was that the "liberal policy with regard to the Arabs of East Jerusalem" (the term used by the Israeli press) had borne fruit. The city was calm; there were no terrorist incidents; the leaders of the Arab community had put aside their expressions of opposition, and the extremist Jewish groups voiced no disagreement with the careful policies of the Government. The analysis of the situation, widely accepted during that period, was as follows: The complex problems – those that were created by unification, those that followed, and those that were anticipated – were neutralized. Quiet reigns in the city. A sensitive policy, flexible and enlightened, dulled the sting of those factors which would have caused tension between the conquerors and the conquered. There is an agreement between the leaders and the responsible parties – Jews and Arabs – that life in one basket demands a *modus vivendi*, not as an enforced value but as a realistic necessity.

Perhaps the reality in Jerusalem, so the Israelis thought, was not a total "success story," but it was, undoubtedly, "an attempt that did not fail." They were sure that the Arabs valued the economic development, the lack of any outward signs of conquest, the attempts to equalize municipal services, and the benefits of the Israeli welfare state.

Into this atmosphere of self-satisfaction suddenly burst the evidence of Arab political discontent and resistance, revealed in mid-1973, scattering the sweet illusions. When several Palestinian leaders, including Kamal Nasser, were killed during an Israel Army raid on Beirut, the Arabs reacted with open and bitter resistance. If these revelations had come in 1968, the Israelis would have reacted calmly. But in mid-1973 their reaction was sharp, not because of the seriousness of the demonstrations, but because they caused a painful awakening.

Yet, it was still hard to shake off the illusions. The quiet which encompassed the city during the Yom Kippur War, in October 1973, seemed like positive proof that the Arabs had accepted the situation as a fact of life. But the reaction of the Arab populace to the 1973

War, the mood of the Arabs in light of the possibility that the occupation would now end, their increased self-esteem brought about by the rising power of the Palestinian organizations, and their joy over Israel's international isolation — all these scattered the last vestiges of any illusions held by even the most naïve Israelis.

The Israeli reactions to the Yom Kippur War also contributed to this feeling of polarization and to the shattering of the illusion that the Arabs had made peace with their lot. The euphoria rampant after the Six Day War ended and was replaced by frustration. The arrogance and self-assurance now gave way to feelings of insecurity and grave doubts about the future. The readiness to achieve limited compromises from a position of strength was replaced by extreme caution and the lack of political direction. The realization that sooner or later they would have to deal with the problem of Jerusalem, as an all-encompassing political problem, stopped the Israelis from continuing their search for a practical, day-to-day *modus vivendi*. The practical settlements which they had achieved up to the Yom Kippur War were preserved, but they were not developed further. The common denominator which had been attained — the lessening of hatreds, the personal and public relationships which had been established — was not affected. But everyone now realized how limited was their relationship, how thin and vulnerable.

Arab attitudes, like the Jewish ones, went through several distinct stages. Military defeat in 1967 and conquest were blows that descended on the Arabs with a force that is hard to over-estimate. Their profound shock underwent several stages of modification. At first, there was a primal fear of physical annihilation. Initially, the Arabs were convinced that everyone, or at least all the males, would simply be executed. They believed their own propaganda, which had depicted the Jews as bloodthirsty vampires who would exterminate the entire Arab nation after they triumphed. Memories of the 1948 battle for Deir Yassin (where hundreds of Arab civilians lost their lives), inflated for the purpose of atrocity propaganda, were still fresh in their minds. The feelings of relief that overcame the population when they discovered that no one was going to harm them were similar to those of a man who had been reprieved at the eleventh hour. It led to an atmosphere of optimism among the Arabs which aroused anticipation about the possibility of a swift political settlement. During the first week of the occupation, Arab leaders proposed

347

calling a convention of Arab notables in Jerusalem to discuss a peace settlement between Palestinians and Israelis. Leaders and officials cooperated readily with the Israeli authorities. This feeling of optimism easily fused with the similar feeling engendered among the Israelis by their victory, thus creating the unique atmosphere of Unification Day.

But the removal of the fear of imminent death did not dissipate the other factors that comprised the Arab feeling of shock. The Arabs were overcome by shame at their defeat and the occupation of their land. The events of June 1967 had struck a severe blow to one of the most basic Arab self-concepts: the image of a triumphant Islam, of the victorious faith spreading throughout the world by virtue of the military superiority of its believers. The Arab downfall was complete because the victorious Jews were, according to Muslim myths, "protected vassals," destined to exist as a tolerated minority under Muslim rule. Most Jerusalem Arabs were not prepared to define their feelings in such a manner. However, they did admit that their feelings about their defeat stemmed not only from wounded pride or from the political setback, but were also bound up with concern about Arab existence as a whole. During the first weeks after the occupation, they did not feel any special concern about their status in Jerusalem or about the city's future. The majority believed that the occupation would be short-lived, and their leaders began to debate what would happen when the Israelis withdrew. Some hoped for Palestinian independence, others for a democratization of the Jordanian regime. All agreed that the situation prevailing up to 1967 should not be reintroduced.

But Israel's decision to annex Jerusalem shattered their optimism, and fears of Israeli expansionism again took over. The deep belief, shared by every Arab, that it was Israel's intention to drive the Arabs into the desert and take control of the whole of the Fertile Crescent, in accordance with a preconceived plan, emerged again. The residents of Jerusalem began to fear the loss of *Arab* Jerusalem. Their fears were expressed in different ways. Copper etchings and wood engravings depicting the Dome of the Rock began to appear in Arab homes in Jerusalem, in the West Bank, and in the Arab countries. Poets began to write laments. A song about Jerusalem and its sufferings "under the boot of the conqueror" was broadcast frequently by radio and television stations and played every night in the movie houses of Cairo and Beirut. Religious conventions were called to save Jerusalem. Politicians swore "not to rest and not to remain silent, until Jerusalem was liberated from Zionist conquest."

The general Arab and Muslim ferment over Jerusalem encouraged the leaders of the local population; but they alone were obliged to take steps against what they regarded as the danger of a Zionist takeover. They could not, in any manner or circumstance, accept the annexation of Jerusalem. Their deep emotional attachment to, and their desire to preserve the Arab nature of, the Holy City, totally ruled out such a possiblity. It has been noted earlier that Israelis tried to diminish Jerusalem's importance to the Muslims, claiming that the city was third in the scale of sanctity for Islam. But this was self-delusion. The strength of the Arabs' love for their city did not rest on the assessments of others. The inhabitants of Jerusalem, like all Palestinians, have more of an emotional and religious attachment to Jerusalem than to any other place. As one Jewish scholar put it —

Their emotional attachment to Jerusalem is, by the nature of things, more powerful than their attachment to Mecca. There are special religious customs here, tied to the Holy Places . . . and to longstanding local customs. The peculiar history of this country has resulted in the places that are dear to us being sanctified and loved by the country's Arabs.

For the Arabs, Jerusalem was simply home, the city where they had been born, like their ancestors for 1,300 years.

The Arabs did not express their love for Jerusalem in great works of poetry or by developing a cultural treasure centered around it. But, when the Jews pointed out this lack of expression of feeling for Jerusalem to prove that the Arabs' love was weaker than their own, the reply was: A man who lives with his beloved feels no need to give poetic expression to his feelings, for she is tangible. Only he who has lost his beloved, or is far away from her, is forced to give poetic expression to his longings. We are attached to the stone fence father built, or to the fig-tree great-grandfather planted. No one writes poems about that kind of attachment, but it is no less deep than that you display in your poems. Would you deny the love of a Greek or a Polish peasant for his land, just because he does not pour it out in verse filled with longings? If, heaven forbid, we are fated to undergo 2,000 years of exile, we too will write poems full of yearnings for Jerusalem no less profound than yours.

Political factors were also a part of the Arab attachment to Jerusalem. As noted previously, the Arabs of Jerusalem strove to enhance the status of their city under Jordanian rule, and even when they failed they did not lose their sense of pride in Jerusalem and their hopes for better days. They were not prepared to concede to the Israelis what they had refused to concede to the Jordanians. On the contrary, their indignation over the city's neglect by the Hashemites only increased after the Israeli conquest. In their pain, they contended that if Jordan had invested half as much in Jerusalem as she put into Amman, there would be at least 200,000 Arabs living in Jerusalem, and then Israel would not have dared to annex the city. Jordan and Israel, they felt, had conspired together against the Arabs of Jerusalem and deprived them of their city.

Furthermore, the annexation of Jerusalem meant that the Arab inhabitants would have to agree to become a minority. But they could not accept being absorbed by a majority with a different cultural, national, and social background. They described that as "being turned into strangers in their own town." To concede, would be tantamount to murdering the Arab character of Jerusalem with their own hands. When one of them was asked to define this character, he answered:

> The Arab character [of Jerusalem] consists of architecture, customs, religion, language, and inhabitants. . . . The city will lose its Arab character when the Arabs cease to be a majority in its streets.

While discriminated against as Palestinians by the Jordanian regime, Jerusalem's Arabs had nevertheless achieved a *modus vivendi* with the Hashemites, who rewarded them with positions of seniority. What was their hope, they asked, of achieving a similar status in Israel? As one East Jerusalemite put it:

> Let us suppose, for a moment, that I agree to become an Israeli citizen. What can you offer me? What can I hope for? To become the Knesset member of some small Arab slate tied to a Jewish party? To become a Deputy Minister of Communications?

As we have seen, the Arabs distinguished between conquest and annexation. They recognized the legality of Israeli occupation, and were prepared for far-reaching cooperation, if the Israelis were ready to revoke the imposition of their administration in East Jerusalem. But they could not accept the steps resulting from annexation. Theoretically, their choices were: armed insurrection, active civil dis-

350

obedience, passive non-cooperation, or pretended acceptance of the situation while taking advantage of "the rules of the game" imposed on them to further their aims. These were the theoretical options, but before deciding which path to take, they had to examine the forces available to them. The first question was: who would make decisions and provide the leadership? There were wise and experienced men among the Arab population, but there was no united leadership accepted by the masses. The absence of such a leadership, which resulted from strong — traditional, tribal, regional, and family — loyalties, had always been the principal malaise of the Palestinian people. The patriarchal and hierarchical structure of Arab society, created a barrier between the wealthy and educated classes and the masses. Even during the 1948 War, when the Arabs were fighting a life-or-death battle, they only succeeded in producing one charismatic leader, Abd al-Kadr al-Husayni. When he was killed in battle, no one could be found to replace him. After 1948, the Hashemite regime followed a consistent policy of eliminating any independent Palestinian leadership, both by repression and by enticing them to take up posts in the service of the Government. The Israeli conquest found the leadership divided and remote from the masses. It included all hues of Arab politics, from the Marxist left and the Ba'ath to the Hashemite monarchists.

In the course of trying to decide on a plan of action, the Arab leaders divided into three camps: extremists, moderates, and the undecided. Only rarely did they succeed in agreeing unanimously on a certain line of action, and only in a few cases did they implement it. Their attempts to choose a leader failed. Even when, at long last, they agreed on someone, gossip about him would start to spread the moment he was elected.

The extremist leaders usually held the upper hand, taking control of all the executive bodies, insofar as they existed, by threatening to denounce the moderates as traitors, and by taking advantage of the front organizations that they controlled.

It would be inaccurate to say that the Arab population is not interested in politics. The average Arab shows great interest in political affairs, and expresses his opinions about them with considerable enthusiasm. But one of the Arab's characteristics is his ability to make a psychological distinction between the two planes of reality: the political and the practical. He is quite capable of following a way

351

of life in conflict with his political views, without seeing it as a contradiction or hypocrisy. He is capable of giving very warm support to a certain political line and even expressing his support in deeds. But he sees no contradiction in maintaining close commercial contacts with the Jews, immediately after having participated in a demonstration against "the Zionist conquest." Neither do his brethren consider this as hypocrisy or treason; rather, they consider it in the spirit of "Render unto Caeser that which is Caesar's, and unto God, that which is God's." This dichotomy finds its symbolic expression in the fact that the Arab as a politician speaks literary Arabic, while, for every-day purposes, he uses spoken Arabic.

Politically, the masses supported the anti-Israeli line, but, as practical people, they were prepared for economic integration with the Jewish sector. In these circumstances, the leadership's ability to mobilize the masses for practical acts of disobedience, such as boycotting Jewish employers or Israeli institutions, was extremely limited. The average Arab would be prepared, in the extreme case, to participate in a commercial shutdown, and then only after he had complained sufficiently about his feckless leaders. But, the next day, he would return to his non-political occupations, which were becoming more and more bound up with Jews. Another outcome of this dichotomy was the Arab unwillingness to face the personal risk or economic suffering involved in a political struggle.

The Arab leadership had to take all these characteristics into account, in addition to another potent factor — the Israeli reaction. As educated men with experience in different professional fields, they were well able to assess Israeli ability. During the Jordanian period, they had tended to believe Arab propaganda, which depicted Israel as a country on the verge of starvation and economic crisis, consumed by fraternal strife. Their meeting with the real Israel confounded them. Astonishment was followed by the recognition that their adversary was stronger and better developed, while they were weak because of their lag in all fields of modern technology. They developed respect for Israel's power and were envious of her achievements, and this feeling inspired them with fear of Israeli reactions and doubts about their ability to get the better of her. Such fear and respect did not deter them from the contest, but they wanted to be prepared. The encounter with modern Israel was one of the causes of the tremendous urge to study and acquire knowledge, that overtook all strata of Arab Jerusalem society. The number of high school graduates, students, pupils of vocational schools, and of various Hebrew courses, grew enormously.

The Arabs tried each of the four methods of struggle against Israel. They carried out terrorist acts, organized violent demonstrations and strikes, boycotted institutions, and refrained from collaborating on political matters. There was no unanimity among their leaders over the adoption of one line or another, and action was taken by various factions. An extremist minority supported terrorist acts; a large number supported strikes and demonstrations; but only a few actions were taken with the approval of all the leaders, such as the reaction to the al-Aqsa fire. Israeli success in the uncovering of sabotage networks, the dispersing of demonstrations, the preventing of shutdowns, and the expelling of extremist leaders, as well as the policy of responding with deterrent and punitive actions — such as the demolition of houses — made the responsible leaders reconsider their ideas. They soon concluded that, alone, they lacked the strength to force a change in the situation.

Once again, the slogan *Sumud* ("Hold out") came into use after being drowned by the slogans of "armed struggle" and "active resistance." From the outset, the moderates had directed their efforts to ensuring that the Arab population would "hold out." A consensus grew that the most important political trump the Arabs possessed, for the time being, in their struggle against the Israelis was the fact that almost one hundred thousand of them lived in Jerusalem — and hundreds of thousands more in the vicinity — and they must, therefore, make every effort to prevent the population from emigrating.

So great was the importance of remaining in Jerusalem that the leadership believed it necessary to preserve law and order to rob the Israelis of any pretext for repression or intimidation. The Arabs decided to exploit every opportunity to better their economic situation, accumulate economic power, build homes and maintain religious institutions. As one of their leaders put it:

We shall continue to live in Jerusalem; we shall beget children and take your National Insurance grants for them; we shall educate them at your expense; we shall do business with you and make money; we shall take advantage of your freedom of speech to call to our people to hold out; we'll make use of your democracy and your moral sensitivity to improve our living conditions. We won't

353

give you any excuse to throw us out. By the mere fact of being here, we shall remind you every day that the problem of Jerusalem has yet to be solved.

There was no great difficulty in applying this policy. The masses had been following it since the 1967 War, without even sensing that, in maintaining a livelihood and making the most of the economic boom, they were fulfilling a national duty. Neither did they wait for the political approval of their leaders: they just sought bread for their children.

The feeling of suffocation and despair over any possibility of change, increased with the years. Some of the Arabs began to think that they must prepare for a long period of occupation and learn to live as a minority, locked into their own neighborhoods. The Jewish housing projects increased this choking feeling. In June 1970, the reality of Jerusalem was described by an Arab writer in these terms:

The image of the [Arab] city has not essentially changed . . . while, at the same time, the housing projects in the Jewish quarters have reached the walls. [These quarters were built] in order to form a wide dividing strip which will encircle the Arab quarters. . . . I see before me the picture of the Arab quarters in Jaffa, Haifa or Acre, which have become old quarters in which the Arab residents close themselves in as if afraid that if they don't stick together they will disappear completely. . . . I see this picture before me, as it quietly and fearfully moves from Jaffa to Haifa to Arab Jerusalem.

The frustration increased, not only because of their inability to fight the stronger and more numerous Jews, but also because of the pervading feeling that the Arab world had abandoned the Arabs of Jerusalem. But, despite everything, the hope for change remained. The Arab sense of time, so different from that of any Westerner, allowed them to preserve their hopes throughout the long days. Every rumor of a new settlement possibility was exaggerated into a definite peace plan which, according to "those in the know" would be put into effect "in exactly two weeks."

The 1973 Yom Kippur War broke suddenly into this complex of feelings and, just as suddenly, changed everything. The Egyptian crossing of the Suez Canal raised Arab spirits. The image of a victorious Islam, which had been shredded in 1967, was revitalized. The Egyptian and Syrian failures in the last stages of the war and the Israeli victory which brought about the cease-fire, did not dull their

354

feelings of victory. The declaration by King Faisal of Saudi Arabia that the purpose of the war was "the liberation of Jerusalem," raised hopes for an end to the occupation. Now, the Jerusalem Arabs thought, the strongest of Arab leaders has adopted the task of liberation. Their fate was no longer in the hands of the weak Hashemite leader, or in the hands of the Palestinian organizations. There was no doubt in their minds that the day of liberation was close upon them. The debate over the political identity and the nature of the government which would replace that of Israel, was reopened with renewed fervor.

The Jerusalem Arabs had vacillated, during all these years, debating the choice between Hashemite rule. and the Palestinian movements. The split between the Palestinians and the Jordanians, which seemed irreparable after the "Black September" of 1970, was surprisingly short-lived. When Talal, the father of King Husayn, died in July 1972, the East Jerusalem newspapers were filled with notices of mourning and delegations of notables travelled to the King's palace in Amman to express their condolences.

Then, in mid-1973, when it seemed that the King enjoyed general support, the Israel Defense Forces' attack on Beirut, resulting in the death of several Palestinian leaders, reawakened strong pro-Palestine Liberation Organization feelings. The Algiers Conference (at the end of 1973) and the Rabat Conference (at the end of 1974), which proclaimed the "sole right" of the P.L.O. to represent the Palestinians, and Yassir Arafat's invitation to speak before the U.N. General Assembly in the autumn of 1974, almost completely nullified the influence of the Hashemites. But the pendulum swung back again and by the end of 1974 Husayn's influence had risen again.

At the end of 1975, the Arab mood changed once more. Following a lengthy period of strikes and demonstrations in Jerusalem and on the West Bank, local elections were held throughout the West Bank, in the spring of 1976, in which the supporters of the P.L.O. and leftist candidates won a decisive victory. All the Hashemite supporters, mostly members of the "old guard," were defeated. This radical mood apparently also reflected that of the Arabs of Jerusalem who, as residents of the annexed area, could not, of course, participate in the elections.

The Arabs of East Jerusalem disagreed among themselves as to who should rule the city after the Israelis leave, but they agreed that the subject need only be discussed after the occupation is ended. In the meantime, they tended to support whoever seemed more capable of bringing about their liberation.

The expressions of national awakening, which came in the wake of the Yom Kippur War, were widespread. Terrorist acts increased, articles in the Arabic press became more critical, and political strikes and violent demonstrations became more frequent. In clashes with the security forces, Arab demonstrators were killed, for the first time since 1967, by warning shots fired by soldiers of the Israel Defense Forces. Nevertheless, surprisingly, daily life continued on a relatively calm basis. Jews and Arabs strove for opposing goals, but life proved stronger than ideology.

Perhaps most important of all, is the fact that both sides became fully aware of the existence of the other, an existence which one had tried to ignore and the other had seen merely as something to be overcome. They progressed a bit on the road to peace, though they were still very far from any point of no return. It was clear, however, that the two nations living in Jerusalem had no desire to return to the point at which they had started.

CHAPTER TWENTY TWO

THE SEARCH FOR A POLITICAL SOLUTION

Israel's policy on the political future of Jerusalem was determined in the middle of June 1967, when the Government decided upon the unification and the borders of the city. This policy was phrased in differing ways, but there was unanimous agreement that the unified city − at least within those borders fixed in June 1967 − would remain under the exclusive sovereignty of Israel, and that no compromise would be considered which would give political-sovereign status to any other state. This policy has remained unchanged over the years and has been accepted by all of Israel's leaders, including those who, in return for peace with the Arabs, were originally in favor of an almost total retreat from the 1967 cease-fire lines. When questioned as to how this uncompromising position conforms to Israel's willingness to conduct negotiations "without prior conditions," officials reply that Jerusalem's future will also be discussed in direct negotiations, and that there is no contradiction between the absence of prior conditions and "claims made by either side."

Despite this resolute position, Israel's leaders have had difficulties in deciding what to offer the Arabs, if and when negotiations do take place. One school of thought maintains that the Jerusalem problem is so difficult that it had best be left to the final stage of negotiations. A second school of thought maintains the opposite − in other words, precisely because the problem is so difficult, it is best to solve it at the beginning of negotiations, because otherwise no progress will be made on any issue. Contacts between King Husayn and Israeli ministers, as well as between high-ranking Israeli and Jordanian officials, have proved, as expected, that the Jerusalem problem is the main stumbling block to an agreement between the two countries. Contingency-planning groups of Israeli experts were asked, on a number of occasions, to suggest a plan whose objective, in the terms of reference established for one of the groups, was "to ensure the unity of the city under our sovereignty and, at the same time, to satisfy non-Israeli (especially Jordanian) interests." The room for maneuver, within this framework, was extremely limited. As a first step, an attempt was made to satisfy Muslim religious interests, in the hope that this would also satisfy Arab political claims.

Israel was not prepared to recognize the national claims of the Arabs, whether local or Jordanian, but was prepared to recognize the religious interests of the Muslims and Christians in the Holy City. In order to do so, Israel proposed the autonomous administration of the Holy Places. During the extended dialogue with the Vatican, the Government suggested that extra-territorial status be granted to the Christian Holy Places. A similar approach was proposed for the Muslim Holy Places, and it was suggested that the mosques on the Temple Mount be given extra-territorial status and be administered by Jordan, "which would represent the Muslim world." This proposal was suggested in the summer of 1967 by the Minister of Defense, Moshe Dayan. When the experts started to consider the details of the proposal, various ideas were raised, among them, allowing the Jordanians to hoist their flag over the mosques on the Temple Mount, and to place a special guard — like the Swiss Guard in the Vatican — on the Mount. In order to ensure Muslims from Arab countries free access to the mosques, and in order that King Faisal of Saudi Arabia "would not have to step on Israeli soil and receive an Israeli visa on his way to the al-Aqsa mosque," it was suggested that a special road be paved which would be "under the sovereignty" or "under the control" of the Jordanians. At a later date, it was suggested that, instead of paving a road, a tunnel should be constructed. None of these proposals was ever fully crystallized.

All the proposals referred to "the Temple Mount," but when experts pointed out that the Muslims do not distinguish between the mosques on the Temple Mount and the other sections of the Mount, opinions were divided as to whether extra-territoriality should apply to the whole area or just to the two mosques. There was no doubt that Israel could not give up her sovereignty on the Temple Mount, but the exact meaning of "extra-territoriality" was not clear. Nor was it clear whether Jordan would be given "symbolic" or "real" authority over the road.

Proposals were also put forward in other spheres, such as allowing Jerusalem's Arabs to keep Jordanian citizenship, and the establishment of municipal autonomy for the Arabs of East Jerusalem. In the latter instance, several possibilities were suggested. One was to divide the Old City into three sub-units, according to ethnic groups, while another was to create "a single municipal district with dual sovereignty."

This last proposal called for the creation of a new municipal district — "Greater Jerusalem" — which would include united Jerusalem, under Israeli sovereignty, as well as Bethlehem, Beit Jallah and a number of other villages which are not under Israeli sovereignty since they were not annexed by Israel. The administration of this district with dual sovereignty would be similar to that of the Greater London Council, that is, there would be a division into boroughs or sub-municipalities with an overall, federal or "roof"-municipality, each of which would have defined areas of responsibility and authority. The author of this proposal claimed that in this manner it would be possible to ensure a united Jerusalem under Israeli sovereignty while, at the same time, satisfying non-Israeli interests; through the non-annexed sub-municipalities or boroughs, the Arabs could influence the actions of the federal or roof-municipality. But nothing ever came of these proposals, either.

During the contacts with the Jordanians, these ideas concerning the Temple Mount, the road (or tunnel) and municipal autonomy were raised as general proposals, without going into details. They were never fully crystallized for two reasons: firstly, the contacts never developed into a meaningful dialogue; the distance between the two sides was too great for them to attain a common denominator, without which it made no sense to formulate practical suggestions. Secondly, the leaking of these ideas to the Israeli public led to a public outcry so strong that statesmen were forced to deny their existence, let alone the fact that they were seriously suggested. As early as July 1968, an official of the Ministry for Foreign Affairs complained that the suggestion to allow Jordan to hoist its flag over the mosques on the Temple Mount, which had been made earlier by the Minister of Defense without arousing any protest, now encountered strong opposition. He was convinced, "after checking the situation, that there is a hardening of the Israeli position," and in his opinion "a hard fight will have to be waged in order to persuade people on the flag issue."

In April 1971 the proposal to create a "single municipal district with dual sovereignty" was leaked. A campaign of villification, which included telephoned threats of murder, and slogans smeared on the walls of Jerusalem calling for his trial as a "traitor," was organized against the author, who formulated this suggestion in July 1968 as a member of one of the contingency-planning groups. In a Knesset debate, called as a result of the public controversy, the Foreign Minister, who was under attack not only from the opposition but also from members of his own party, was forced to deny that he had ever heard of the proposal before it was leaked, and to state that it had never been adopted by his Ministry.

*   *   *

King Husayn's position on Jerusalem has undergone several permutations. In the period immediately after the war, his enemies — mainly Palestinian radicals — blamed him for refusing to defend Jerusalem. "As soon as the first shots were fired, Jordanian troops retreated from Jerusalem," they insisted, and only after a great deal of effort did Husayn manage to free himself of these accusations. During this period, the King demanded that total control of East Jerusalem be returned to him, and he left no room for compromise. When it became apparent that this position would not advance his cause and did not elicit support even from the Western powers, he tried to retreat into the past and proposed internationalization of the whole city, including West Jerusalem. When he realized that this position, too, would not succeed, he began to hint that he would be satisfied with sovereignty over only part of the eastern sector. At the end of 1971 he suggested that "the Jewish Quarter of the Old City be left under Israeli sovereignty" and that Israel be granted free access to it. At the beginning of 1972 he made this change in his position public and told an Israeli journalist that he claims "sovereignty over the city, or part of it." Explaining this statement, Husayn made it clear that he was "prepared to give up the Armenian Quarter, as well as the Jewish Quarter with the Western Wall plaza."

In other words, he was ready to accept a new border which would pass through Jaffa Gate, along David Street and the Street of the Chain, with the southern half of the Old City thus coming under Israeli sovereignty. In his statements of 1972, he spoke in terms of "an open city," of "a city of peace and cooperation" and of "a place where our two peoples meet." These statements met with the fierce opposition of radical Palestinians and several Arab leaders.

Despite the fact that Husayn's position on a territorial arrangement in Jerusalem has changed and has become more flexible on the practical matter of administering the city, no change has occurred with regard to his basic claim, that sovereign status in the city be restored to him. In their political thinking and actions, between 1948 and 1967, the Hashemites proved that for them Jerusalem was not a focal point; but, at the same time, Husayn saw himself as destined to protect the Arab character of Jerusalem, as the trustee for all Muslims. In view of the refusal of all the Arabs and Muslims to surrender the Arab character of Jerusalem, the Jordanian King cannot adopt a position which will make him responsible for "the loss of the Holy City." At the end of 1972, after he had declared that he was ready to relinquish parts of the Old City, Husayn told an American reporter: "We cannot sign any document in which we would give up sovereignty of the Holy City, simply because future generations would cry out against such a signature." An Israeli expert reached the conclusion that although Husayn

can live with the military fact that Jerusalem has been conquered ... he doesn't see himself being able, and perhaps not even entitled, to give legal approval to the existing situation, even though he is powerless to change it.

In his Jordanian—Palestinian Federation plan, which was published in March 1972, Husayn designated Jerusalem as the capital of the Palestinian region in the federal "United Arab Kingdom." To the Israeli proposals for extra-territorial status for the Temple Mount, Husayn could not agree, both because they did not return sovereignty in the city to him and because, in the words of an Israeli expert,

the Muslim religion ... nurtured the idea of territorial expansion as a result of religious expansion. From this stems the difficulty for Arabs to relate to the concept of 'extra-territorial rights,' as accepted in Christianity, or to the concept of 'free access.'

After the Yom Kippur War, King Husayn's statements hardened. In July 1974 he said:

There can, in fact, be no compromise. The return of Arab sovereignty over the Arab city of Jerusalem, over the Arab section of Jerusalem which was conquered in 1967, is a basic requirement. There can be no peace so long as the Israelis are in control of the whole of Jerusalem.

Yet, Israeli sources reported in 1975 that "Jordanian sources agreed to see Jerusalem as a united city, under two sovereignties and with minor border changes." And, in March 1976, Husayn stated:

In the framework of peace, if sovereignty over the Arab part of the city is returned, I see no reason why it should be a divided city; Jerusalem must be a city of all believers.

These fluctuating positions of King Husayn were, however, much less rigid than those of other Arabs. The position of the Saudi Arabians was particularly uncompromising and that of the leaders of the P.L.O., naturally, made no contribution towards a political settlement.

Reviewing the positions of the two sides since 1967, it becomes clear that the crucial question is one of sovereignty. Israel is not prepared to grant the Arabs sovereign status in Jerusalem and Jordan is not prepared to relinquish such sovereign status. Despite this, however, Israel and Jordan agree on the principle of safeguarding the physical unity of the city.

This blind alley, and the feeling that without a political solution to the problem of Jerusalem a solution to the Arab–Israel conflict is unattainable, has impelled governments, various bodies, and research institutions to formulate ideas for the future of the city.

The official position of the United States has not changed since it was stated by Secretary of State William P. Rogers on December 9, 1969:

. . . we believe Jerusalem should be a unified city within which there would no longer be restrictions on the movement of persons and goods. There should be open access to the unified city for persons of all faiths and nationalities. Arrangements for the administration of the unified city should take into account the interests of all its inhabitants and of the Jewish, Islamic and Christian communities. And there should be roles for both Israel and Jordan in the civic, economic and religious life of the city.

The United States has never officially clarified which practical arrangements are to be made, in its opinion, in order to fulfill these principles. At the end of 1974 it was reported that the Americans support "a unified city with two separate administrations and the transfer of the Jewish Quarter to Israeli rule." In the spring of 1976, the U.S. representative to the United Nations, William Scranton, stated the American position in the following manner:

> That part of Jerusalem that came under the control of Israel in the June War, like other areas occupied by Israel, is occupied territory and hence subject to the provisions of international law governing the rights and obligations of an occupying power. Ambassador Goldberg said, in 1968, to this Council: 'The United States does not accept or recognize unilateral actions by any states in the area as altering the status of Jerusalem.' I emphasize, as did Mr. Goldberg, that, as far as the United States is concerned, such unilateral measures, including expropriations of land or other administrative action taken by the Government of Israel, cannot be considered other than interim and provisional and cannot affect the present international status, nor prejudge the final and permanent status of Jerusalem. The United States' position could not be clearer. Since 1967 we have restated here, in other forums, and to the Government of Israel, that the future of Jerusalem will be determined only through the instruments and processes of negotiation, agreement and accommodation. Unilateral attempts to predetermine that future have no standing.

This formulation, more critical than any which preceded it as far as Israel's actions were concerned, was met with a storm of anger by Israeli Jerusalem.

The American State Department has encouraged a number of groups, including the Brookings Institution in Washington, and the Aspen Institute, to study the Jerusalem problem and suggest solutions. And, in fact, suggestions for a solution have streamed in from various sources. Not many of those making the suggestions were aware of the fact that between the years 1917—1967 no less than three dozen proposals for the solution of the Jerusalem problem had been advanced. A few of these earlier proposals are outlined below.

*   *   *

The "Jerusalem Problem," as a subject demanding a political solution, secured in international agreements, was created in 1917 when the city was conquered by the British, after hundreds of years of Turkish rule.

The European powers, including the Vatican, decided to settle the various contradictory Christian claims to control of the Holy Places, to ensure orderly administration of these sites, as well as of the city in which they existed, and to ensure free access to them. More than a century earlier these claims had become international problems, rather than purely religious ones. The European powers became involved in the trivial conflicts between the various Christian communities because they saw these conflicts as a means towards expanding their political influence, both within their own countries and on the international plane.

In the period before the British conquest, and immediately after it, the European powers decided to solve the problem by placing Jerusalem under international rule. The Sykes—Picot Agreement of 1916 stated that, following the partition of the Ottoman Empire, the area between the Sea of Galilee in the north and Beersheba in the south would come under "an international administration, the structure of which will be decided upon in the future." However, the agreement was never implemented. National interests persuaded the signatories to agree to British rule over Palestine and Jerusalem, subject to a treaty (Mandate) between Great Britain and the League of Nations.

In the wake of this solution to the problem of sovereignty, attempts were made to solve the problem of the Holy Places within the framework of British sovereignty, by an international treaty which would, to a certain extent, limit this sovereignty. None of the proposals, however, was acceptable, and, at the end of 1924, it was decided that the British Administration would also be responsible for the supervision of the Holy Places. In this manner, the Jerusalem Problem was removed from the sphere of international relations, for the time being, and the city became the capital of Mandatory Palestine and the seat of its government.

But, of course, the Jerusalem Problem was not so easily solved. It now became an inter-ethnic bone of contention. The Jewish and Arab residents of the city began a long and on-going struggle for control of the Municipality. The Arabs, relying on precedent, claimed the mayorship and a decisive voice in the Municipality. They argued that, ever since the establishment of a municipality in Jerusalem in 1877, the mayor had always been an Arab, and that the Jewish residents in Jerusalem had to accept this state of affairs, based on precedent and tradition, and agree to the appointment of an Arab mayor. The Jews, on the other hand, argued that thay constituted a majority in the city and claimed the right of a majority to choose its own mayor, in democratic elections. The British attempted to reach a compromise, the practical significance of which was a continuation of the *status quo,* in other words, preferred status for the Arabs. During the 1930s and '40s, Jerusalem always had an Arab mayor, a Jewish deputy mayor with special status, and a Christian deputy mayor. The membership of the City Council was fixed at six Jews, four Muslims and two Christians. In order to reach this balance, prior to the municipal elections the British manipulated the geographical constituencies, as well as the ethnic voting register. They also excluded Jewish neighborhoods from the municipal borders, or included them only together with areas populated by Arabs. The Jewish majority was dissatisfied with the privileged position of the Arabs and as early as 1932, Haim Arlosoroff, Director of the Political Department of the Jewish Agency, suggested that Jerusalem be split into two boroughs. Under his proposal the two Borough Councils would be subordinate to the Council of the united Municipality. The British immediately rejected this suggestion.

The Jewish—Arab conflict over control of the Municipality of Jerusalem was, however, only one part of the overall conflict between the two ethnic groups for hegemony in Palestine. Thus, when the Arab revolt broke out, in 1936, the local problem was absorbed by the general one.

In 1937, the Jerusalem Problem again became an issue which could only be solved on the international plane. The Palestine Royal Commission, appointed by the British and headed by Lord Peel, proposed the partition of Palestine and a permanent British Mandate for Jerusalem with extensive borders and a corridor to the Mediterranean Sea. As for the municipal government, Peel suggested leaving the situation as it was, with elections organized by geographical districts and an ethnic register.

The following year, the Palestine Partition Commission, headed by Sir John Woodhead, was appointed to recommend details of partition. The Jews suggested to the Commission (at the end of 1938) that Jerusalem be divided in two. Part of Jerusalem (the New City and Mount Scopus) would be attached to the Jewish State, and the Old City and the Arab quarters would be within the area of the British Mandate of Jerusalem. The city was to be divided into two boroughs, with integrated services and a single customs zone. The British rejected this proposal outright. In their opinion, the city was an integral unit and it was impossible to divide it. Furthermore, they said that administrative partition demanded close cooperation and good will. It was precisely because of the lack of good will between the Jews and the Arabs that the problem had arisen in the first place; thus, there was no question of dividing the city, given the existing tension between the two groups.

As a result of the total disagreement between Jews and Arabs on every proposal — which was clearly expressed by the failure of the St. James' Conference (winter 1939) — the British published the MacDonald White Paper, in May 1939, which declared the partition proposals "impracticable" and announced their intention of establishing an independent Palestinian state, with an Arab majority, within ten years. The capital of this state was, of course, to be Jerusalem, with no special status, apart from an undertaking that free access be ensured to the Holy Places. The White Paper was not approved by the League of Nations and met with bitter opposition from the Jews, but meanwhile, the Second World War broke out and the solution of the Palestine problem, including that of Jerusalem, was postponed.

However, the inter-ethnic conflict for control of the municipality continued. This conflict reached a climax in August 1944 when the Arab mayor died and the British appointed his Jewish Deputy, Daniel Auster, as his successor. The Arabs protested and the British suggested a rotation every two years, the first mayor being Jewish and the third, British (appointed). The Arabs boycotted the meetings of the City Council and the British dissolved it, appointing in its stead a Municipal Commission, composed of six British officials.

The British also appointed the Chief Justice of Palestine, Sir William Fitzgerald, "to enquire into and report on the local administration of Jerusalem and to make recommendations thereto." Fitzgerald's report was published in August 1945. He did not concern himself at all with the question of sovereignty, which was, of course, to remain British. He viewed Jerusalem not as a municipality but as a county, similar to London. The upper body which would administer the whole area, according to his proposal, would be an Administrative Council. Within the area managed by the Administrative Council would be two boroughs, one Jewish and one Arab, and an area that would be administered directly by the Council. Each borough would have a council and a mayor. The boroughs would have the authority to impose taxes and to fulfill the duties imposed on a municipality by the Municipal Ordinance. City planning would be delegated to each borough, but only after an outline scheme had been approved by the Administrative Council. Each borough would send four representatives to the Council, whose chairman would be appointed by the British High Commissioner. In addition, two representatives would be appointed who were neither Jews nor Arabs. The main job of the Administrative Council would be to co-ordinate the activities of the two boroughs, with a minimum of interference in their internal affairs. The Administrative Council would also deal with the Holy Places, under the direct responsibility of the High Commissioner.

When the Fitzgerald Report was submitted, after the end of the Second World War, the problem of municipal rule in Jerusalem had again been absorbed by the general conflict.

At the beginning of 1946, the Morrison–Grady Committee suggested that Palestine be transformed into a cantonal state consisting of an autonomous Jewish province, an autonomous Arab province, and two areas under the direct control of the central government, with a High Commissioner. One of these areas was to be the Jerusalem enclave and Bethlehem. The municipal administration proposal for Jerusalem was a regular city council, to which would be added several members appointed by the High Commissioner. Both the Jews and the Arabs, as well as the United States, rejected the plan.

The rejection of this last attempt to solve the Jerusalem Problem was among the factors which prompted the British Government to refer the entire problem of Palestine to the General Assembly of the United Nations. The United Nations Special Committee on Palestine (UNSCOP), presented its majority and minority reports in May 1947. The debates at the United Nations which followed and municipal history since 1948 have been dealt with earlier in this volume.

Sixty years after it was first raised as an international political problem, and after thirty-six plans for its solution, the Jerusalem Problem still awaits a settlement. It is not enough that the elusive

367

solution be a brilliant intellectual exercise, full of good will and objectivity. Jerusalem has experienced many of these. The real test of a solution is its accord with the changing reality and its practicability, but most important is the readiness of the two parties to compromise and cooperate. Without a readiness to compromise, no plan, however balanced and inspired, will succeed.

ELEMENTS OF
A SETTLEMENT

The intention of this chapter is not to propose a formula for the solution of Jerusalem's political and ethnic problems. Such a formula does not now exist, nor will it be found within the near future. Instead, the following is an attempt to compile a list — with brief annotations — of the main topics which must be dealt with when discussing the components of a settlement, elements from which various settlements can be constructed, according to the evolving needs and situations.

Most of the topics dealt with below, in condensed form, have already been referred to in previous chapters, which detailed the background of these issues.

As has already been noted, the elements of the Jerusalem Problem are three-fold — sovereignty, municipal government, and the Holy Places — and they will be discussed in this order. In addition, a special section of this chapter is devoted to "partial" or "interim settlements," that is, those elements of a solution which can be carried out step-by-step, in the absence of a willingness to negotiate an overall settlement.

The analysis which follows is based on the general agreement that Jerusalem will remain a physically unified city. The definition of this term was best expressed by the U.S. Secretary of State William P. Rogers, on December 9, 1969:

> . . . *Jerusalem should be a unified city within which there would no longer be restrictions on the movement of persons and goods.*

369

There should be open access to the unified city for persons of all faiths and nationalities. . . .

Both Israelis and Jordanians agree with this definition, though, of course, each of the adversaries adds to it its own elements of sovereignty. The Israeli definition is that "unified Jerusalem is the Capital of Israel," in other words, entirely under her sovereignty. Jordan's definition is that of "an open city, but with the Arab sector returned to Jordanian rule."

The dispute, therefore, is not over the city's unity but, rather, over its sovereignty.

SOVEREIGNTY

It is assumed that regardless of the form of sovereignty — whether it be undivided, divided, limited or joint — the following items will be guaranteed (by law or by treaty): that the city be free of tax borders; unrestricted movement for people, goods, capital and labor; arrangements for a system of justice, police, extradition, municipal services, utilities, transportation, currency, and banking, and for similar matters which do not negate the accepted principles of sovereignty — as, for example, the arrangements between the Benelux countries and between the Scandinavian countries. It is also important to stress that any proposal for a reasonable compromise on the issue of sovereignty in Jerusalem can only be implemented if the border between Israeli and Arab sovereignty (Jordanian or otherwise) passes through the metropolitan region or along its borders. Any solution based on an enclave of sovereignty for one country, within that of another, without a territorial link (or even a corridor) is neither practical nor applicable.

1. ISRAELI SOVEREIGNTY WITHIN THE ANNEXATION BORDERS
Accepted by the Jews, but does not satisfy their demands in the metropolitan region. Not acceptable to the Arabs. Proposals to restrict Israeli sovereignty in certain spheres (such as municipal government and the Holy Places) are acceptable to most Jews, but even if these were to be implemented, it is doubtful if they would satisfy Arab nationalist demands.

370

2. *JORDANIAN SOVEREIGNTY IN THE AREA WHICH HAD*
   BEEN UNDER THEIR RULE BEFORE THE 1967 WAR

Ultimate answer to the Arab demands. Could never be accepted by the Jews.

3. *RESTORING ARAB SOVEREIGNTY TO THE TEMPLE MOUNT*
   AND TO THE ARAB NEIGHBORHOODS, WITH THE EXCEPTION
   OF THE JEWISH NEIGHBORHOODS EAST OF THE ARMISTICE
   LINE, THE JEWISH QUARTER, THE WESTERN WALL
   AND THE MOUNT OF OLIVES

Some Arab circles agreed to this compromise. But the majority would object to it. Most Jews would see it as a "redivision of Jerusalem." Extremely difficult to implement because it would create islands of Jewish and Arab sovereignty.

4. *ISRAELI SOVEREIGNTY WITHIN THE ANNEXATION BORDERS,*
   WITH A SOVEREIGN ARAB CORRIDOR TO THE TEMPLE
   MOUNT, ALSO UNDER ARAB SOVEREIGNTY

Proposed by Israel at one time, even though it is in direct opposition to the principle of "a unified Jerusalem under Israeli rule." The Arabs did not agree to it because it does not meet the nationalist demands of Jerusalem's Arab residents who would remain under the rule of the "Israeli conquerors."

5. *ADDING AREAS OUTSIDE THE ANNEXATION BORDERS TO*
   ISRAEL'S SOVEREIGNTY IN RETURN FOR AREAS WITHIN
   THE BORDERS

Israel is interested in opening axes to the northwest and southwest. Sections which are not annexed within these areas would be ceded to Israel and, in return, Israel would give up Arab neighborhoods within the annexed borders. The Arabs would not agree, because they do not consider it a fair trade, since they believe that all these areas are by right theirs anyway. The Jews see the annexed areas as part of a unified Jerusalem and therefore are not willing to give up any part of them.

371

6. ISRAELI–ARAB CONDOMINIUM
Hard to implement and does not meet the demands of either side.

7. INTERNATIONALIZATION OF JERUSALEM
Impractical and clearly opposed by both sides. (See also p. 385)

8. BLURRING THE SOVEREIGNTY ISSUE
This is achieved by creating a super-municipal unit, secured in the law of both countries, with special powers, and administered on a basis of equality between communities or boroughs (see City Government, Situation C). Can be implemented on the municipal level but very difficult to implement on a governmental level.

CITY GOVERNMENT

Ignoring the problem of sovereignty, suppose that a city government for Jerusalem is to be organized, in the optimum manner. The city's main problems result from the rapid urban rate of growth (about 4% per year) and from its religious and ethnic heterogeneity. Special emphasis must be given in Jerusalem to the preservation of the quality of life and its special urban quality. What should be its municipal boundaries and what municipal governing bodies should it have? The main alternative answers are listed below, as well as the pros and cons of each.

SITUATION A: PRE-1967 BORDERS
Unified municipal boundaries of pre-1967 Jewish and Arab Jerusalem.

1. The Municipal Boundaries

Cons: Too small an area. Even in 1967 there were development pressures and many small suburbs were built outside this boundary. These pressures increased after the 1967 War. In 1975 all the city's reserve land was outside the old boundaries and contained over 1/3 of the population, both Jewish and Arab.

Pros: None.

Cons (Arabs): A lack of opportunity for development; leaves more than half of the Arab population outside the city; guarantees a large Jewish majority.

Pros (Arabs): None.

Cons (Jews): Leaves tens of thousands of Jewish families outside the municipal borders; lack of any opportunities for development.

Pros (Jews): None.

2. Municipal Government

A.   A centralized municipality, with elections by majority vote, without constituencies or the allocation of seats to ethnic groups.

Cons: Does not meet the need for ethnic expression and therefore constitutes a basis for disputes.

Pros: Easy to administer.

Cons (Arabs): A decisive Jewish majority in the City Council and the administration.

Pros (Arabs): None.

Cons (Jews): None.

Pros (Jews): Absolute control of the City Council and the administration.

B.   A centralized municipality, with constituency elections and proportional representation on the Council and in the administration.

Cons: Difficult to implement; guarantees ethnic representation but because of the overwhelming Jewish majority would not guarantee the minority anything; irrelevant in the field of administration.

Pros: Guarantees a centralized administration, thus making the administration of the city uncomplicated.

Cons (Arabs): As in (*A*) above.

Pros (Arabs): None.

Cons (Jews): None.

Pros (Jews): As in (*A*) above.

C. *Decentralized municipality; the creation of two boroughs along ethnic lines, with jurisdictional division.*

Cons: Difficult to implement because of the small size of the Arab borough; does not guarantee representation to the minority because the Arab population and area are small; creates many administrative problems.

Pros: Promises autonomy to the minorities within their neighborhoods and therefore lessens friction.

Pros (Arabs): Ensures limited autonomy.

Cons (Jews): Divides the city; gives the Arabs political expression which could become a platform for agitation.

Pros (Jews): As in (*A*) above.

SITUATION B: POST-1967 ANNEXATION BORDERS

1. The Municipal Boundaries

Cons: The boundaries were fixed by Israeli political and military considerations and are, therefore, unsuitable from an urban point of view. Part of the population (mainly Arab) lives outside the boundary, does not pay taxes and does not receive municipal services. There is a lack of reserves of land for various purposes, such as industrial and business areas, a green belt, areas for the absorption of the growing population, and services for the evacuees of slum areas.

Pros: None.

Cons (Arabs): The boundaries were fixed specifically in order to achieve an artificial demographic balance, with a decisive Jewish majority. The Municipalities of Beit Jallah and al-Birah do not accept the present boundaries since land was transferred from their jurisdiction to Jerusalem.

374

Pros (Arabs): None.

Cons (Jews): Boundaries seen as too small, both from a political and an urban point of view and have been bypassed for the purpose of Jewish settlement, the establishment of an industrial area and roads.

Pros (Jews): The majority sees the boundaries as those of "the complete Jerusalem."

2. Municipal Government

A.   *A centralized municipality, with elections by majority vote, without constituencies or representation for ethnic groups.*

Cons: Does not meet the need for ethnic expression. Even if the Arabs vote for a unified Arab list, which would ensure them more than a quarter of the seats of the City Council, they would still be in the minority; perpetuates a Jewish majority in the administration and gives the Arabs only minority influence in city affairs.

Pros: Easy to administer.

Cons (Arabs): A decisive Jewish majority in the City Council and in the administration.

Pros (Arabs): None.

Cons (Jews): None.

Pros (Jews): Absolute control of the City Council and the administration.

B.   *A centralized municipality, constituency elections, and proportionate ethnic representation on the Council and in the administration.*

Pros and *cons* as in Situation A (2B) above, although there is some improvement in the status of the minority because of the larger number of its voters; hard to apply administratively.

C.   *A decentralized municipality, creation of two or more boroughs, along ethnic lines, with jurisdictional division.*

Cons: Difficult to implement; creates administrative problems, as well

375

as coordination problems and friction against background of nationalist demands; limited possibility of achieving agreement on jurisdiction and on the composition of the higher governing body; need for special legislation.

Pros: Ensures autonomy for the minority in its neighborhoods and therefore lessens friction.

Cons (Arabs): Subordinates them to a higher coordinating body controlled by Jews.

Pros (Arabs): Ensures limited autonomy.

Cons (Jews): Divides the city; gives the Arabs political expression on a territorial basis; can serve as a platform for agitation; decreases their absolute control.

Pros (Jews): Alleviates problem of dealing with Arab population, alleviates pressure for an overall political agreement.

SITUATION C: "THE METROPOLITAN AREA" BORDERS
As defined by urban experts and including the city's immediate hinterland.

1. The Municipal Boundaries

Cons: A very large area; hard to administer by a centralized municipality; contains a very heterogeneous population from the point of view of its type of settlement (villagers, Bedouin, urban dwellers), its standard of services, and its religious-demographic constitution; necessitates establishment of decentralized municipal government, with the possibility of lack of coordination and a cumbersome administration; extends the Jerusalem Problem to additional areas.

Pros: Puts the whole area directly influenced by the city and connected with it, on a daily basis, into one municipal framework; prevents unplanned suburban sprawl; ensures balanced growth, reserves of land for all purposes, optimal urban development from economic, ecological and aesthetic points of view; prevents development of satellite "bedroom suburbs;" ensures optimal municipal organization, without a lack of coordination between independent municipalities, characteristic of a "megalopolis" with a continuous built-up area but divided into numerous administrative units.

Cons (Arabs): Increases the fear of the penetration of a dynamic Jewish initiative into purely Arab areas; eliminates the independence of Arab municipalities in the area (al-Birah, Ramallah, Bethlehem, Beit Sahur, Beit Jallah) and of Arab village councils (more than ten).

Pros (Arabs): Changes the demographic balance in Jerusalem to an almost equal one (about 45% Arabs and 55% Jews), with the hope of an Arab majority through natural increase.

Cons (Jews): Disadvantageously changes the demographic balance and makes the Arabs almost equal to their number, with the additional danger that the Jews will become the minority due to their lower birthrate.

Pros (Jews): Makes possible the development of new areas and increases their influence on the hinterland.

2. Municipal Government.

A. *A centralized municipality, elections by majority vote, without constituencies and without representation for ethnic groups.*
Cannot be implemented.

B. *A centralized municipality, constituency elections and proportional ethnic representation on the City Council and in the administration.*
Cannot be implemented.

C. *A decentralized municipality, with the creation of a number of boroughs, along ethnic and urban lines, with jurisdictional division and internal elections.*

Cons: The characteristics of the area complicate administration; the need to create a large number of sub-units (at least twelve) will make coordination difficult; disagreements over the jurisdiction of sub-units in relation to central roof body; inter-religious Christian—Moslem disagreements (because of the existence of three Christian municipalities in the area); need for special legislation; friction, mainly against a nationalist background, over Jewish initiatives in development areas.

Pros: Tight municipal coordination; a demographic balance between Jews and Arabs; proper urban planning of the whole metropolitan area ensured; allows political manipulations which might "blur" or "solve" problems of sovereignty in Jerusalem ("making the cake bigger and dividing it anew").

Cons (Arabs): Loss of independence of existing municipalities; danger of Jewish penetration into new areas and influence on purely Arab settlements.

Pros (Arabs): Equality with Jews in administration of central roof body resulting from numerical equality.

Cons (Jews): Equality with Arabs in administration of central roof body resulting from numerical equality.

Pros (Jews): Influence over a wider area and the possibility of development in it; blurring of the Jerusalem Problem, in its more limited aspects.

THE PRINCIPAL HOLY PLACES

1. THE TEMPLE MOUNT
Holy to Jews and Muslims.

The Existing Situation:
Free access for Jews, except on Fridays and Muslim holidays; the mosques and courtyards are, in fact, under the sole control of a Muslim body which maintains and adminsters them without interference from the Israel Government and which receives instructions from Jordan; an Israeli police post (normally manned by Arab policemen); limited physical Israeli control, by supervision of one gate (Mugrabi Gate) and an observation post on the roof of the *Mahkamah;* Jews are prohibited (by the Chief Rabbinate) from entering in order to pray, at least "until the Messiah comes;" praying by Jews is prohibited by the authorities "in order to prevent clashes and disturbances of the peace;" the existing arrangement is not based on any binding agreement.

Inter-religious conflict: None exist in the more limited sense; however, from a national Arab—Jewish standpoint, a very bitter conflict exists.

The Jewish position: Satisfied with the existing situation, except for extremist elements.

The Arab position: Relatively satisfied with the existing situation, apart from their demand for the return of control over the Mugrabi Gate and the *Mahkamah*; deep-seated fears of unilateral cancellation of the *status quo* by Israel.

Demands for changes in sovereignty, or special arrangements:

Jews: None, but would not agree to annulment of Israeli sovereignty because of its supreme national and religious importance; will agree to special arrangements.

Muslims: Do not recognize Israeli sovereignty in any shape or form, for religious and national reasons, and do not agree to anything less than return of the whole area (making no distinction between the mosques, the courtyards, and the buildings in them) to Muslim-Arab sovereignty. In Muslim eyes, sovereignty is symbolized by stating the name of the Muslim ruler in their Friday prayers and by the use of Muslim currency as legal tender; since 1967, a Muslim ruler's name has not been mentioned and the legal tender has been the Israeli pound.

Christians: Indifferent.

Proposals for an Agreement

1. Continuation of the existing situation: Reasonable for a short time, but cannot continue in the long run without being institutionalized. An agreed-upon arrangement on the Temple Mount is the key to the solution of one of the main problems associated with the Jerusalem Problem.

2. Cancellation of present status quo *by subordination of Muslim institutions to Israeli supervision:* Will not solve any of the problems and will lead to unnecessary and dangerous tension.

3. Cession of the Temple Mount, either by itself or together with East Jerusalem, with a corridor to an Arab state: This subject has been dealt with above (see Sovereignty, 4).

4. Removal of the Temple Mount from the sovereignty of any state: Vaticanization, in fact, of the Temple Mount, by an international agreement which would establish the responsibilities of the Muslim institution governing the Mount, legal immunity, tax exemptions, and police arrangements on the Mount; the agreement to be signed between the Government of Israel and an Arab-Muslim state. In other matters (customs, duties, boundaries and related subjects) Israeli Law would apply. For Israelis, such an agreement could be accommodated within the principle of undivided sovereignty; however it reduces their control and grants total immunity to a Muslim body. Such an agreement could be accommodated within Muslim Law but does not satisfy nationalist demands.

5. Symbolic Arab sovereignty: Expressed in the right to fly a flag, a uniformed guard, mention of Muslim ruler in sermons, and Muslim currency as legal tender within the confines of the Mount; in all other matters Israeli sovereignty will apply. Symbolic solution, likely to dissatisfy Israelis more than arrangement in section *4* above, and will not satisfy Muslims.

6. Institutionalization of existing status quo *by Israeli legislation:* Might be a short-term solution, but is not a long-term political solution.

2.   THE WESTERN WALL
Holy to Jews.

Existing situation:
One of the most holy places of worship for the Jews, the area has been expropriated by, and is in the hands of, the Government of Israel.

Conflict with another religion: None, apart from the continuation of archeological excavations northwards, which may undermine ancient Muslim buildings.

The Jewish position: Satisfied with the existing situation, apart from the demand of extremist elements to continue excavations northwards.

The Arab position: A formal claim for "the return of the Mugrabi Quarter;" fear of continued excavations "which will endanger the foundations of the al-Aqsa Mosque;" but, in fact, reconciled to the existing situation.

Demands to limit sovereignty or for special arrangements:

Jews: Will not agree to annulment or limitation of Israeli sovereignty in the area.

Muslims: None (apart from the basic demand for a return to the *status quo ante bellum*).

Christians: None.

Proposals for a Solution
Continuation of the existing situation, payment of compensation for expropriated land, coordination with Muslim institutions on the architectural and safety aspects of archeological excavations.

3. CEMETERY ON THE MOUNT OF OLIVES
Holy to Jews.

Existing situation:
The Jews' most holy and ancient cemetery; only a small number of empty plots remain; renovation and reconstruction work underway on tens of thousands of tombstones destroyed under Jordanian rule.

Conflict with another religion: None.

The Jewish position: Satisfied with the existing situation.

The Arab position: No position, apart from the complaint that during restoration work, roads leading to Arab neighborhoods were dug up.

Demands for limitation of sovereignty or special arrangements:

Jews: None. Will not agree to annulment or limitation of Israeli sovereignty in area.

Muslims: None (apart from the basic demand for a return to the *status quo ante bellum*).

Christians: None.

Proposals for a solution
Continuation of the existing situation.

3.   *SYNAGOGUES IN THE JEWISH QUARTER:*
Holy to Jews.

Existing situation:
An integral part of the restored Jewish Quarter.

Conflict with another religion: None.

The Jewish position: Satisfied with the existing situation.

The Arab position: No position, apart from complaint that Arab residents were expelled and property expropriated.

Demands for limitation of sovereignty or special arrangements:

Jews: Will not agree to annulment or limitation of sovereignty in the area.

Muslims: None (apart from the basic demand for a return to *status quo ante bellum*)

Christians: None.

Proposals for a Solution
Continuation of the existing situation.

4.   *DAVID'S TOMB AND MOUNT ZION*
Holy to Jews, Muslims and Christians.

Existing situation:
Holy to Muslims and in Muslim hands until 1948; a Jewish place of pilgrimage, after 1948. During the division of the city it was the

closest point to the Western Wall and was regarded as the most important Holy Place in Israeli hands, but its importance decreased after the Six Day War.

Inter-religious conflict: 1. Conflict between Jews and the Muslims, who controlled the tomb for hundreds of years, until 1948; however, since 1967, there has been no Muslim demand to return the Tomb. 2. Conflict between Muslims and Christians over the Coenaculum, which is the second storey of the structure of David's Tomb. The Jews have no interest in this area.

The Jewish position: Satisfied with the existing situation.

The Arab position: Not known.

Demands for changes in sovereignty or special arrangements.

Jews: Will not agree to annulment or limitation of Israeli sovereignty in the area.

Muslims: None, apart from a possible demand for free access and for the right to pray there.

Christians: The Catholics are interested in making some arrangement regarding prayer rights and maintenance in the Coenaculum hall; these have been withheld from them since the 16th century.

Proposals for a solution
Continuation of the existing situation, with a satisfactory arrangement for the Christians.

5. *CHRISTIAN HOLY PLACES ("THE STATUS QUO"):*
CHURCH OF THE HOLY SEPULCHER, DEIR AL-SULTAN,
CHURCH OF THE ASCENSION, TOMB OF THE VIRGIN.

The Existing Situation:
The *status quo* of 1852 is still in effect; self-administration of Christian communities, almost without any need for outside interference to preserve the *status quo* (the only case, since 1967, was a dispute between Ethiopians and Copts over Deir al-Sultan); Israeli authorities are responsible for law and order; the renovation of the Church of the Holy Sepulcher is continuing.

Inter-religious conflict: Does not exist.

The Jewish position: Satisfied with the existing situation; willing to use control over the Holy Places to obtain a settlement with the churches, which would improve Israel's diplomatic position in Jerusalem.

The Arab position: Indifferent, apart from the basic Arab demand for a return to the *status quo ante bellum.*

The Christian position: Satisfied with the existing situation but concerned over the lack of a binding political settlement. The Catholics are not pressing for a change in the *status quo* as they did in the past, and cannot reach an agreement with Israel for their own internal political reasons. The Greek Orthodox and the Armenians are ready to reach an agreement which will preserve the *status quo* (and their preferential status).

Demands for changes in sovereignty or special arrangements:

Jews: None.

Muslims: None, apart from the basic demand for a return to the *status quo ante bellum*

Christians:
Catholics: No immediate demands, except for an overall solution which will influence sovereignty in the long run.
Greek Orthodox: Claims for special arrangements, but not for changes in sovereignty.
Armenians: Claims for special arrangements, but not for changes in sovereignty.
Other Christian communities: Different opinions, but most will agree to any satisfactory arrangement made with the large communities.

Proposals for a solution

1. Continuation of the existing situation: Reasonable in the short term but does not accord Israel the formal recognition of its control, in which it is interested; creates fear among Christians that Israel will take unilateral action against all the communities, or against one of them, to the disadvantage of another; convenient for Christians since it allows them to evade formal recognition of Israel; guarantees the Arabs continued Christian non-recognition of Israeli rule in Jerusalem; leaves unsolved one of the main problems associated with the Jerusalem Problem.

2. *Transfer of Holy Places to Arab sovereignty:* Will not, under any condition, be accepted by the Israelis; the Christians, also, will not gain any advantage by the return of the Holy Places to Arab-Muslim authority; the Greek Orthodox and the Armenians would suffer in particular, but so would the Catholics who can expect to obtain a more advantageous position from Israel than from the Arabs.

3. *Territorial internationalization of the Old City and the surrounding area:* Not a solution to the web of legal, economic, administrative and political problems; danger of interference by anti-religious elements (Communist bloc) and the non-Christian bloc; inability of United Nations institutions to administer populated territory; both Israelis and Arabs object, as well as the eastern and Christian communities.

4. *Internationalization of the Holy Places only:* All the disadvantages of proposal no. *3,* above, plus added problem of United Nations' administration of the Holy Places; problem of safeguarding law and order.

5. *Transfer of Holy Places (with extra-territorial status) to an international committee to be chosen by the United Nations:* Less disadvantages than in proposals nos. *3* and *4,* but the presence of the United Nations will still be a stumbling block; the problem of safeguarding law and order will arise.

6. *Transfer of the Holy Places to a Christian Council, which will include all the communities represented in Jerusalem, with extra-territorial status for the buildings:* Difficult to implement because of mutual distrust between the leaders of the communities; gives too great an influence to communities which have no religious congregation in the city; complicated administrative structure.

7. *Institutionalization of the existing* status quo *by Israel, with the tacit assent of the Christians:* Special legislation will be passed to safeguard the *status quo,* extra-territoriality, immunity for churchmen, non-interference by the courts in internal quarrels, safeguards for the status of church courts, tax exemptions, continued existence of

schools, and financial support. Decreases Israel's freedom of action, does not ensure her great political benefits, but safeguards the Christians' practical interests and, therefore, will reduce pressure to "reach an overall settlement." If the agreement is given international status, by the signing of a treaty with those countries which are "interested parties," this would be a partial answer to the Vatican's demand for "international guarantees." The Arabs will vigorously object to such a process since it would put an end to their demands for a return to the *status quo ante bellum* and would give Israel great political advantages.

PARTIAL SETTLEMENTS

In the absence of the possibility of reaching an overall political settlement in regard to Jerusalem, the solution of the political, inter-ethnic and religious problems in Jerusalem can be advanced by means of unilateral Israeli action. This action must be taken in consultation with, and with the agreement of, foreign powers (mainly the United States), and by means of negotiations with local elements, who have the support of an Arab state. Using the step-by-step technique, Israel will claim political compensation for every step or number of steps that it makes. All the "partial" or "interim settlements" suggested below are in accord with the principle of Israeli sovereignty.

A.   THE HOLY PLACES

1. The Temple Mount:
Institutionalization of the existing *status quo* by means of a government declaration in the Knesset. Stage two — the drafting of special legislation.

2. Christian Holy Places:
Institutionalization of the existing *status quo* by means of a government declaration in the Knesset; discussions with the Christian communities, followed by special legislation.

386

B. INSTITUTIONS

1. Recognition of the "Muslim Council"

Granting of legal recognition, by means of legislation, to the existing Council, and recognition of the *de facto* jurisdiction which it exercises; official approval of existing *shari'a* courts, by means of a law stating that the Council will appoint the *qadis* and pass their names on to the Government, without any need for Government approval; and determining that the religious law in force in Jordan is applicable to Muslim Jordanian citizens living in Jerusalem.

2. Establishment of an Arab Education Board

This committee will be responsible for the administration of Arab education, with full autonomy.

3. Municipal Affairs

Transfer of municipal-administrative functions in the Arab neighborhoods to an Arab committee with its own budget.

4. Planning Committee

Establishment of a "Planning and Building Subcommittee," whose members will be Arabs, and which will authorize building plans in Arab neighborhoods, on the condition that they are in accord with the Jerusalem Outline Scheme.

5. The Arab Chamber of Commerce

Formal recognition of the Chamber and guaranteeing its *de facto* authority over all matters it deals with today.

C. MISCELLANEOUS

1. Banks

The Arab banks will be reopened according to the formula adopted in 1972.

2. Land Expropriation

A formal declaration will be made stating that the Government will not expropriate additional lands for Jewish housing projects in Jerusalem.

3. Christian Communities

A binding agreement will be signed with those Christian communities which wish to sign such an agreement, guaranteeing the continued *status quo* with regard to school, religious institutions, and taxes and other economic matters.

4. Neighboring Municipalities

Agreements will be signed with neighboring municipalities for the common development of infrastructure, industrial areas and services.

5. Jordanian Citizenship

A binding government declaration will be made to the effect that all citizens who wish to do so, may keep their Jordanian citizenship, and that this status will not lead to discrimination in relation to Israeli citizens.

REFERENCES

I. WHOSE JERUSALEM?

p. 1   Discussions on the seat of the Government in **Sharef, Z.**, *Three Days*, New York, 1962. pp. 158-162

p. 2   Quotations from the Peel Commission in **Palestine Royal Commission,** *Report,* Cmd.5479, London, 1937. Chpt. XXII, Paras. 10, 12 UNSCOP recommendations in **United Nations Special Committee on Palestine,** *Report to the General Assembly,* U.N. Doc. A/364, 1947.

pp. 3-4   Quotation from Sharett in **Sharett, M.,** *Besha'ar Haumot* (Heb.), Tel Aviv, 1958. p. 91
1947 United Nations partition resolution in **United Nations General Assembly,** *Resolution No. 181 (II),* November 29, 1947.

pp. 4-5   Quotations from Ben-Gurion in **Ben-Gurion, D.,** *Bimdinat Israel Hamitkhadeshet* (Heb.), Tel Aviv, 1969. pp. 191, 195
Draft Trusteeship Council statue for the city of Jerusalem in **United Nations Trusteeship Council,** *Official Records of the Second Session, Second Part,* U.N. Doc. T/118, January 26, 1948.
Count Bernadotte's plans in **United Nations,** *Text of Suggestions Presented by the U.N. Mediator on Palestine to the Two Parties on June 18, 1948,* U.N. Doc. S/863, July 3, 1948 and **United Nations General Assembly,** *Official Records of the Third Session; Supplement No. 11: Progress Report of the U.N. Mediator on Palestine,* U.N. Doc. A/648, September 1948.

p. 6   Proclamations on Jerusalem in **State of Israel,** *Official Gazette,* No. 12, Tel Aviv, 1948. p. 66f

p. 7   Quotation from Rabbi Berlin in *Hatsofe* (Heb. newspaper), April 4, 1968.
Israel Government debates and votes in **Ben-Gurion,** *op. cit.,* p. 288 and **Nakdimon, S.,** *Ma'ariv* (Heb. newspaper), October 4, 1970.

p. 8   Quotation from Sharett in **Sharett**, *op. cit.* p. 308f
        Quotation from Pope Pius XII in **Encyclical** *Acta Apostolica Sedis*,
        XL, Rome, 1948. pp. 433-436

p. 9   Arab States new position on internationalization in **United Nations
        General Assembly**, *Official Records of the Fourth Session*, 58th
        Meeting, 1949

p. 10   Israeli—Jordanian negotiations in **al-Tal, A.**, *Memoirs* (Heb. trans.),
        Tel Aviv, 1960; **Sassoon, E.**, *Ma'ariv*, September 3, 1971; **Israel—
        Jordan Mixed Armistice Commission**, *Memoranda, Letters and
        Minutes*, (unpublished archives).

p. 11   Palestine Conciliation Commission plan for Jerusalem in **United
        Nations General Assembly Ad Hoc Political Committee**, *Official
        Records of the Fourth Session*, U.N. Doc. A/973, September 1949.
        United States position on internationalization in **United Nations**,
        Official Records, op. cit., 60th Meeting, 1949.

pp. 12-13   January 2, 1950 Knesset debate in **State of Israel**, *Divrey Haknes-
            set* (Heb.), Vol. 4, Jerusalem—Tel Aviv, 1949-1950.

pp. 13-14   United Nations debates and resolutions on internationalization in
            Bovis, H.E., *The Jerusalem Question, 1917-1968*, Stanford, Calif.,
            1971. pp. 70-91
            Plans for Jerusalem by Trusteeship Council, and its President
            Garreau, and Israel in **United Nations General Assembly**, *Official
            Records of the Fifth Session; Supplement No. 9: Question of an
            International Regime for the Jerusalem Area and Protection of the
            Holy Places; Special Report of the Trusteeship Council*, U.N.
            Doc. A/1286, 1950. Annex I and II
            1949 Israeli plan for the functional internationalization of Jerusa-
            lem in **United Nations General Assembly Ad Hoc Political Com-
            mittee**, *Official Records*, U.N. Doc. A/AC.31/L.42, 1949.
            The Swedish proposal for Jerusalem in *ibid.*, U.N. Doc.
            A/AC.31/L.53, 1950.

II.   PALACES IN AMMAN

p. 17   Jordanian intervention in **Glubb, J.B.**, *A Soldier With The Arabs*,
        London, 1962. p. 109ff; **al-Tal**, *ibid.*

pp. 18-27   Events in East Jerusalem under Jordanian control in *Hamizrakh
            Hakhadash* (Heb. quarterly), Jerusalem, 1949-1966; **Abidi, A.H.H.**,
            Jordan: A Political Study, 1948-57, London, 1965.

p. 21   Quotations from the Jordanian Law of Unification in **Whiteman,
        M.M.** (ed.), *Digest of International Law*, Vol. I, U.S. Department of
        State 7403, Washington, 1963. pp. 1164-1168

p. 23   Quotations from Anwar Nusaybah and 'Aref al-'Aref in **State of
        Israel Archives**, *Archives of the Jordanian Security Police*.

390

p. 24   Jordanian discrimination against Jerusalem in **Abidi,** *op. cit.*; **Municipality of Jerusalem Archives,** *Arab Documents*; Shye, S., *Progress Report on the Preparation of a Development Program for the Administered Areas,* Israel Institute of Applied Social Research, Jerusalem, 1971. pp. 19-21, 48-55

III.   THE DIVIDED CITY — THE ISRAELI SIDE

Statistical data in **State of Israel, Central Bureau of Statistics,** *Statistical Abstract of Israel,* Jerusalem, annually.

p. 32   The composition and character of Jerusalem's neighborhoods in **Municipality of Jerusalem,** *Master Plan Working Papers,* Jerusalem, 1968.

p. 38   Quotation on Israeli curriculum in **Eisenstadt, S.M. and Y. Peres,** *Some Problems of Educating a National Minority,* U.S. Department of Health, Education and Welfare, Contract No. 0E 621013, Washington, 1968

pp. 39-40   Physical planning of Jerusalem in **Shachar, A.,** "The Urban Geography of Unified Jerusalem," *Yerushalayim Ledorotehha* (Heb.), Jerusalem, 1968; **Gosenfeld, N.,** *Spatial Division of Jerusalem, 1948-1969* (Doctoral Thesis), Los Angeles, 1969.

IV.   THE DIVIDED CITY — THE JORDANIAN SIDE

Statistical data in **Hashemite Kingdom of Jordan, Department of Statistics,** *First Census of Population,* Vol. I (1961), Amman, 1963, and *Population Census and Internal Migration,* Amman, 1967; **State of Israel, Central Bureau of Statistics,** *Census of Population and Housing (East Jerusalem), 1967,* Jerusalem, 1968; **Brown Engineers International,** *Jerusalem General Plan,* Jerusalem—Amman, 1964.

pp. 46-47   Physical planning of Jerusalem in **Brown Engineers,** *op. cit.*; **Gosenfeld,** *op. cit.*

p. 51   Jordanian school curriculum in **Eisenstadt,** *op. cit.*

p. 52   Quotations from Jordanian textbooks in **Handawi, Z.,** *Textbook in Arab Civics for the Twelfth Grade* (Arab.), Amman, 1966.

p. 53   Quotation from Rauhi al-Khatib in **Municipality of Jerusalem Archives,** *op. cit.*

Statistics on Christian population in **Hashemite Kingdom of Jordan,** *First Census, op. cit.* p. 72

pp. 54-57   Development of Christian communities in East Jerusalem in **Zimhoni, D.,** *Tmurot Bemivne Haedot Hanotsriyot Ubema'amadan*

391

Birushalayim (Heb.), Unpublished research project, Jerusalem, 1971.

pp. 60-61   Comparative statistics on standard of living in **Roman, M.**, *Seker Kalkali-Khevrati al Yerushalayim Hashlema, 1967* (Heb.), Jerusalem, 1968.

V.   THE HOLY PLACES

pp. 64-68   The Western Wall see **Great Britain,** *Report of the Commission to Determine the Rights and Claims of Moslems and Jews in Connection with the Western or Wailing Wall at Jerusalem,* London, 1931; **Lurie, B.,** *The Western Wall,* Jerusalem, 1969.
            1931 Order in Council in **Government of Palestine,** *Official Gazette,* Jerusalem, June 8, 1931.

pp. 70-71   Jewish access to the Wall in **Israel—Jordan Mixed Armistice Commission,** *op. cit.*

pp. 72-73   On the *status quo* see **Cust, L.G.A.,** *The Status Quo in the Holy Places,* Jerusalem, 1929.

p. 74   Text of Turkish *firman* of 1852 in **Zander, W.,** *Israel and the Holy Places of Christendom,* London, 1971. p. 178ff

p. 76   King Abdallah's order quoted in *ibid.* p. 87f

p. 80   Jordan Radio broadcasts in **Dishon, D.** (ed.), *Middle East Record,* Vol. 3 (1967), Jerusalem, 1971.
            Prime Minister Eshkol's message, in **United Nations General Assembly,** *Official Records of the Fifth Emergency Special Session,* U.N. Doc. A/PV 1526, 1967 (Abba Eban's speech).
            King Husayn's reaction in *Der Spiegel* (German magazine), September 4, 1967.

p. 81   Arab casualty figures in **Author's Archives,** *Lists of Dead Soldiers and Civilians Buried by the Jerusalem Municipality and the Muslim Waqf,* July-October, 1967.

p. 87   Text of proclamation in **Israel Defense Forces,** *Proclamations, Decrees and Appointments* (Heb.), Jerusalem, August 1967.

p. 89   Defense Minister Dayan's directive in **Tevet, S.,** *The Cursed Blessing,* London, 1970. p. 32

PART II.   JERUSALEM UNITED

In the second section of this book, which deals with the period following the Six Day War, it is difficult to cite sources which are available to the general public. Almost all of the facts, statistics and quotations which appear in this section are based on documents, records and correspondence to be found nearly exclusively in the author's archives. Quotations of public statements, for which no source is cited, have been taken, largely, from the local press (Hebrew, Arabic and English) whose reports are based on local sources and international news agencies, as well as newspapers from all over the world.

For those readers interested in additional details concerning facts cited in this section, an excellent source is the daily *Press Digest*, issued by the Spokesman of the Municipality of Jerusalem and which can be found in the Archives of the Municipality. The Archives also contain translations of articles from the Arab press and transcripts of Arab radio broadcasts which concern Jerusalem.

The only book which deals with the period from 1967 to 1973 is **Benziman, U.**, *Yerushalayim, Ir Lelo Khoma* (Heb.), Tel Aviv, 1973. For the period up to 1968 see also **Bovis**, *op. cit.*

VIII. UNIFICATION

p. 109   The three "Unification Laws" (Law and Administration Ordinance, Municipal Corporation Ordinance and Protection of Holy Places Law) in **State of Israel**, *Sefer Hakhukim*, No. 499, Jerusalem, June 28, 1967. p. 74f
           The Jerusalem (Enlargement of Municipal Area) Proclamation in **State of Israel**, *Kovets Hatakanot*, No. 2065, Jerusalem, June 28, 1967. p. 2694f

pp. 109-110 The legal debate on unification in **Lauterpacht, E.**, *Jerusalem and the Holy Places*, London, 1968; **Blum, A.**, "The Missing Reversioner," *Israel Law Review*, 1968; **Dienstein, Y.**, "Zion Bemishpat Habinleumi," *Hapraklit* (Heb.), Vol 27, No. 1, 1971; **Gerson, A.**, "Trustee—Occupant: The Legal Status of Israel's Presence in the West Bank," *Harvard International Law Journal*, Vol. 14, No. 1, 1973.

p. 112   The Law of Legal and Administrative Arrangements in **State of Israel**, *Sefer Hakhukim*, Jerusalem, 1968. p. 247

p. 118   President Johnson's statement in **U.S. Department of State**, *United States Policy in the Near East Crisis*, Publication 8269, Washington, 1967. p. 16ff

pp. 118-120 The United Nations debate on unification in **United Nations General Assembly**, *Official Records of the Fifth Emergency Special Session, op. cit.*

p. 122   Israel's reply to U.N. Secretary-General U Thant in **United Nations General Assembly**, *Official Records*, U.N. Doc. A/6753 and **United Nations Security Council**, *Official Records*, S/8052, 1967.

p. 156   The compensation bill (Law of Absentee Property (Compensations)) in **State of Israel**, *Sefer Hakhukim*, No. 701, Jerusalem, 1973. p. 184

394

British Mandate in **Great Britain,** *Mandate for Palestine,* Cmd. 1785, London, 1922.

Arlozoroff's partition plan in **Zionist Archives,** *File S25–9953,* Jerusalem.

Peel Commission recommendation in **Palestine Royal Commision,** *op. cit.*

The Woodhead Commission proposals in **Palestine Partition Commission,** *Report,* Cmd. 5854, London, 1938.

The Jewish Agency's 1938 proposal for the partition of Jerusalem in **Jewish Agency,** *Memorandum on Jerusalem Under Partition,* Jerusalem, 1938.

The MacDonald White Paper in **Great Britain,** *Palestine, Statement of Policy,* Cmd. 6019, London, 1939.

The Fitzgerald Report in **Government of Palestine,** *Report by Sir William Fitzgerald on the Local Administration of Jerusalem,* Jerusalem, 1946.

The Morrison–Grady plan in **Great Britain,** *Proposals for the Future of Palestine,* Cmd. 704, London, 1947.

UNSCOP majority and minority plans in **United Nations Special Committee on Palestine,** *op. cit.* Chpts. 3-7

See also Chapter One, above; **Bovis,** *op. cit.*; **Meyuhas, A.,** *Plans for the Political Solution of the Jerusalem Problem,* (unpublished), Jerusalem, 1975.

Material relating to the Municipality of Jerusalem during the Mandatory period, including Jewish and Arab claims, electoral wards, composition of the Council, powers of the Mayor and Deputy Mayor in **State of Israel Archives,** *File G/5/34,* Docs. 73A, 80, 93A; **Municipality of Jerusalem Archives,** *A/1,* Files 1-20, 1-22, 1-40, 1-41; **Central Zionist Archives,** *Auster Papers,* A/1297/27, A/297, Files 21, 24.

INDEX

Galilee 5
Gaza 18, 85
General Israel Workers' Union
    See Histadrut
Gilo 250
Givat Hamivtar 79, 331
Gloria Hotel 104
Glubb, John B. 17, 26, 195
Goren, Rabbi Shlomo 82ff, 287ff
Greek Orthodox 57, 72f, 258, 270
"Green Line"
    See Cease-Fire Line
Gur, Motta (Colonel Mordechai) 82

Habash, George 222
Haram al-Sharif
    See Temple Mount; Aqsa, Mosque al-;
    Mosque of Omar
Handawi, Zuqan al- 51
Hashemite Family 2, 27, 48
Hashemite Regime 23, 48, 52, 223,
    351
Hebrew University 35, 40, 82, 220,
    225, 233, 241, 244, 260
Hebron, Hebronites 20, 22, 44f, 48
    50, 66, 219, 323
Herut Political Party 12, 34, 147
Herzog, Chaim 85, 91, 262, 268
Higher Muslim Council 24
Hillel, Shlomo 214
Hilmi, Ahmad 18
Histadrut 171ff
Holland 14
Holy Places
    Christian 54, 63, 71-77, 91f,
    257-275, 358
    Jewish 63-71, 277, 287-297,
    305-321, 337, 342
    Mulsim 63, 74, 83, 91, 277-304,
    349, 358
    Free Access to 11, 45, 71, 120,
    122, 266, 361
    Ministerial Committee for 313ff
    Protection of 2, 5, 9, 11, 13, 84,
    86, 90ff, 118ff, 262, 265, 364

Hospitals
    Augusta Victoria 81
    East Jerusalem 25
    Hadassah, Ein Karem 81
    Hadassah, Mt. Scopus 233
    St. Joseph's 81
Hurva Synagogue 69, 83
Husayn, King (Jordan) 25ff, 56f,
    79ff, 222f, 286, 355, 357, 360f
Husayni, Abd al-Kadr al- 351
Husayni, Haj Amin al- 18f, 24, 45,
    64ff, 281
Husayni Family 22, 24

Iraq 18
    See also Arab States
Islam
    See Muslims
Israel, Government of
    Arab Education 195ff
    Arab Resistance 212ff, 336
    East Jerusalem Economic Affairs
    175, 182, 189f, 192, 254
    Holy Places 69, 91, 160, 260ff,
    265, 278f, 289, 293, 301ff, 309,
    341, 358
    Internationalization of Jerusalem
    5, 7f, 11ff, 76
    Jerusalem Municipality 34, 145
    Land Expropriation 153ff,
    235ff, 260
    Muslim Establishment 92, 282
    Partition of Jerusalem 4ff, 10
    Restoration of the Old City
    233ff, 325
    Six Day War 79ff, 107
    Talks with Jordan 8
    Unification of Jerusalem 84ff,
    101, 104, 107ff, 149ff, 182, 223,
    233ff, 238, 248, 252f
    Vatican 271f, 358
    West Bank 10, 86
    West Jerusalem 25, 42
    Western Wall 70, 83ff
Israel, President of 14, 283

401

406